Principles and Procedures in the Administration of Justice

Administration of Justice Series

INTRODUCTION TO THE ADMINISTRATION OF JUSTICE
Robert Blanchard, Volume Coordinator
Riverside City College and the American Justice Institute

PRINCIPLES AND PROCEDURES IN THE ADMINISTRATION OF JUSTICE
Harry W. More, Volume Coordinator
State University, San Jose

LAW AND THE ADMINISTRATION OF JUSTICE
Vernon Rich, Volume Coordinator
Southern Illinois University, Carbondale

EVIDENCE AND PROCEDURE IN THE ADMINISTRATION OF JUSTICE
Kenneth Katsaris, Volume Coordinator
Tallahassee Community College, Tallahassee

COMMUNITY RELATIONS AND THE ADMINISTRATION OF JUSTICE
David P. Geary, Volume Coordinator
University of Wisconsin, Milwaukee

Principles and Procedures in the Administration of Justice

HARRY W. MORE

Volume Coordinator

Chairman, Department of Administration of Justice

San Jose State University

San Jose, California

John Wiley & Sons, Inc.

New York London Sydney Toronto

Credits for Photographs

The South Carolina Department of Corrections, Columbia, South Carolina, Ken Sturgeon, Special Projects Officer: Figures 9-1, 9-2, 9-3, and 16-2.

The Federal Bureau of Prisons, Washington, D.C., Courtesy Leo M. Dehnel: Figure 17-3.

New York City Police Department, Bureau of Public Information: Figure 5-4.

The Rio Hondo Police Academy, Rio Hondo, California, Richard Wright, Photographer: Figures 5-1 and 5-2.

Fred McDarrah: Figures 14-1 and 17-1.

Mark Quieto: Figure 7-1

Brooks—Monkmeyer: Figure 17-2

Sybil Shelton—Monkmeyer: Figure 12-1

Hella Hammid—Rapho-Guillumette: Figure 16-1

United Press International: Figure 2-1

Library of Congress Cataloging in Publication Data:

More, Harry W.
Principles and procedures of the justice system.

(Administration of justice series)
Includes bibliographies.
1. Criminal justice, Administration of—United States. I. Title. II. Series
KF9223.M643   345'.73'05   74-7062
ISBN 0-471-61508-0
Printed in the United States of America

10 9 8 7 6 5 4 3 2

Contributors

Dr. Harry W. More:
Volume Coordinator
Jim George: Rewriter

Charles E. Anderson
Gavilan College

Kenneth Braunstein
University of Nevada, Reno

Jeffrey T. Burton
San Jose State University

Donald G. Clark
Modesto Junior College

Richard Cook
San Jose City College

Donald Lee Dahlstrom
*University of Maine at Portland—
Gorham*

Joseph P. Davey
Hartnell College

Frank Dell'Apa
WICHE
Boulder, Colorado

Vern L. Folley
Harrisburg Area Community College

Dr. Tom Gitchoff
San Diego State University

Jack Kuykendall
San Jose State University

Dr. V. A. Leonard
Washington State University

Don Mathews
San Jose State University

Barbara Millett
*Kentucky State Department
of Child Welfare
Pineville, Kentucky*

James A. Palmer
Indiana University, Bloomington

Scott Phelps
Cabrillo College, California

David J. Spisak
San Diego State University

Bill Tafoya
Pacifica, California

Peter Unsinger
San Jose State University

Walter D. Weaver
University of Nebraska, Omaha

Fred Wegener
Indiana University of Pennsylvania

Introduction to the Series

Wiley has undertaken a significantly different approach to the development of five textbooks. The "Administration of Justice" series responds to the belief that teachers should be given an opportunity to state their textbook needs and to define how the organization and contents of a textbook can best serve these needs. Although teachers are generally asked to react to a book after it is published, we sought advice before final decisions were made.

Traditional textbook publishing has assumed that an author is all-knowing about the content of his book and how the content should be organized. The results often have been disappointing for the following reasons.

1. Some books are very long because they attempt to ensure that there will be something for everyone in the text.
2. Some books are written with one type of student or one section of the United States in mind.
3. Other books reflect an author's strengths and weaknesses; they are sound in some areas (where the author is strong) and superficial in other areas.

We began by working with five tentative outlines that were sent to hundreds of educators and professionals within the criminal justice system. Feedback on the outlines—on how they could be strengthened and improved—was excellent and encouraged us to sponsor a series of meetings throughout the United States. Many participants helped us to synthesize the comments received on the outlines, and each participant prepared revised outlines based on the responses evoked by the questionnaires. We especially thank the participants. The books could not have been produced without the help and enthusiasm of Bernard Barry, Scott Bennett, Bob Blanchard, John Boyd, Wordie Burrow, Tom Cochee, Bill Cusack, Stan Everett, Matt Fitzgerald, Ed Flint, Jack Foster, George Gaudette, Dave Geary, Henry Guttenplan, Karl Hutchinson, Keith Jackson, Ken Katsaris, Art Kingsbury, Roger Kirvan, Martha Kornstein, Harry More, and Vern Rich.

Several sets of new outlines resulted from the regional meetings, and these outlines were further expanded and refined at a final meeting. Responsibility for the final outlines was placed with the following educators, who managed the process of evolving the outlines into books with great care, professionalism, and perseverance.

Robert Blanchard, Riverside City College and the American Justice Institute, *Introduction to the Administration of Justice.*

Harry W. More, San Jose State University, *Principles and Procedures in the Administration of Justice.*

Vernon Rich, Southern Illinois University, *Law and the Administration of Justice.*

Kenneth Katsaris, Tallahassee Community College, *Evidence and Procedure in the Administration of Justice.*

David P. Geary, University of Wisconsin, Milwaukee, *Community Relations and the Administration of Justice.*

Volume coordinators identified leading national figures whose area of particular competence is represented by a chapter in each volume. Specialists throughout the United States brought their insight and experience to bear on the writing of individual chapters, which met the goals and requirements of our advisory groups. The chapter authors are listed on page v. Thus, five highly authoritative, highly current, exceptionally interesting textbooks have resulted.

Individual chapters were examined by the volume coordinator and then were assigned to professional writers. Joseph Schott, Jim George, Charlotte Shelby, and Betty Bosarge worked hard and well on homogenizing the volumes. In addition to the responsibility of rewriting two volumes, Charlotte Shelby devoted considerable effort, imagination, and skill to enhancing the clarity and excitement of the other volumes.

Our approach to the development of this series, I believe, has resulted in five important textbooks. It will be for the students and instructors to determine how well we have done. Write to me and tell me how the books might be made even more useful to you.

Alan B. Lesure, Editor
John Wiley & Sons, Inc.

Preface

The American justice system functions as the primary social mechanism by which we maintain ordered liberty in our society. It is a complex system that has been established to deal with crime either through its prevention or by the arrest of an offender.

The foundation for our justice system is a highly structured and formalized legal philosophy. As our society has changed from being predominately rural to a highly industralized nation, there has been a similar alteration of our justice system. Formal legal institutions and procedures have assumed a commanding position in the preservation of our social order. The basic principle that is the foundation for the justice system is that every citizen has the inalienable right to demand equal protection under the law.

The means by which a citizen achieves this right is provided for by the complex procedures of the justice system. The system is a legal construct of man; consequently it is not a perfect system but, with all of its weaknesses and frailties, it has proved to be an effective vehicle for balancing the rights of the individual with the collective needs of society.

The ideal mission of America's criminal justice system is justice and it must be a positively mandated goal. In each conflict with the law, justice must be tempered in terms of equity. Each human action or reaction resulting in an infraction of the law must be adjudicated in the interests of justice.

When an infraction of the law occurs, a policeman finds, if he can, the probable offender, arrests him and brings him promptly before a magistrate. If the offense is minor, the magistrate disposes of it forthwith; if it is serious, he holds the defendant for further action and admits him to bail. The case then is turned over to a prosecuting attorney who charges the defendant with a specific statutory crime. This charge is subject to review by a judge at a preliminary hearing of the evidence and in many places—if the offense charged is a felony—by a grand jury that can dismiss the charge or affirm it by delivering it to a judge in the form of an indictment. If the defendant pleads not guilty to the charge, he comes to trial; the facts of his case are marshaled by prosecuting and defense attorneys and presented, under the supervision of a judge, through witnesses, to a jury. If the jury finds the defendant guilty, he is sentenced by the judge to a term of probation, under which he is permitted to live in the community as long as he behaves himself or to a term in prison, where a systematic attempt is made to convert him into a law-abiding citizen.[1]

[1] Advisory Commission on Intergovernmental Relations, *State-Local Relations in the Criminal Justice System* (Washington, D.C.: U.S. Govt. Printing Office, August 1971), p. 67.

The process described above is clearly brief in nature and simplistic in interpretation. Although it does consider each phase of the process, the actual procedures are complex and almost labyrinthic in nature.

The primary purpose of this textbook is to provide a comprehensive analysis of the principles and procedures of the justice system. It is a current, concise, and unified treatment of the subject. It is written for preservice and in-service personnel and provides the reader with an understanding of the foundations of the justice system.

Traditionally, texts about procedures have been written for attorneys, but this book is written for the criminal justice student. Its uniqueness is that it provides not only a detailed treatment of substantive legal procedures, which all students should become acquainted with, but it includes an in-depth consideration of the application of other bodies of knowledge to the justice system. The behavioral sciences have given increasing attention to the system in recent years and this knowledge is applied throughout the text, but with particular emphasis to the chapters on diversion, discretion, juvenile justice, overcriminalization, and the justice system.

Three of the chapters deal with the major components of the system— law enforcement, the judiciary, and corrections. Historical and developmental aspects are considered, and each component is discussed in terms of its relationship to the criminal process.

The remainder of the chapters focus on the traditional elements of the criminal process by highlighting each of the major phases or justice-actors. Included are chapters on the justice process, legal foundations, the prosecutorial process, bail, the judicial process, prosecuting attorneys, and defense attorneys.

The breadth and depth provided here was accomplished by utilizing the talents and knowledge of twenty criminal justice specialists. Authors were selected from throughout the nation to ensure that the best wisdom and expertise would be applied to the pervasive aspects of the criminal process. The technique of multiple authorship provides an inclusive coverage of this vital area of concern to every individual who is concerned with justice.

Harry W. More

Contents

Part One

Foundations of Justice

The study of this chapter will enable you to:

1. Differentiate between the concepts of normative control and legal control.
2. Write a short essay that delineates the basic characteristics of criminal law.
3. Identify the index crimes as set forth in the Uniform Crime Reports.
4. List the elements that perpetuate a nonsystem approach to achieving justice.
5. Identify the objectives proposed in the *Challenge of Crime in a Free Society*.
6. List the eight functions performed by the police.
7. Identify the major function performed by the courts.
8. List the three processes of corrections.

1
Society and Justice

An obvious characteristic of our social environment is its propensity for very rapid social change. From the rough, early American frontier to our aerospace technocracy, a new life-style has emerged in America—that of a mass society. The United States is a pluralistic, multigroup collective of more than 210 million men, women, and children who live in physical and social proximity and who interact within a common cultural context. Although segmented and subculturized, our society exerts a massive influence on each individual. It molds the personality, it arbitrates or accentuates interpersonal conflict, and even though it generates freedom in some areas, society, at the same time, restricts certain types of personal activity and some forms of individual liberty. Life in modern American society is further complicated by an obvious disparity in real as well as perceived power, and there is a tremendous stress on majority-minority distinctions. America is a unique social system composed of castes and classes, and there is an emphasis on racial, religious, ethnic, and social status differences.

Society and the Law

The tumultous social environment of the 1970s—in which we are currently experiencing a youth revolution, a racial revolution, a sexual revolution, an ethical revolution, and the most far-reaching technological revolution in history—is indicative of anything but group cohesion or social solidarity. Political disenchantment, antiwar sentiment, the generation gap, racism, and criminality have combined to create an atmosphere of alienation, depersonalization, human exploitation, and personal

3

apathy. The cultural conflicts created by these social and technological revolutions aggravate the feelings of helplessness and frustration that characterize many of our citizens. The situation is worsened by highly emotional debate, an insensitivity to the rights of others, and a call for aggressive—at times violent—revisionism.

Among certain groups there is a rejection of current norms and a vociferous attack on established social institutions. There are demands from all quarters for a share in the riches of contemporary life, for the right to partake of the American Dream, and for the right to engage in the processes of participatory democracy. Criminal justice, an integral component of mass society as well as a byproduct of the various complex social relationships taking place within society, has not been spared by these upheavals.

With the emergence of mass social living, and its acute population problems, its mobility and sense of rootlessness, and its tendency to promote feelings of personal isolation, there has been a general lessening of internal normative restraints based on group shared expectations. As a result, there has been an increasing reliance on the use of written law as the primary vehicle for social control. Criminologists Korn and McCorkle have assessed the complexities of modern social interaction and related them to the lawmaking process:

> There are two general ways in which the social order maintains conformity and copes with the problems arising when individuals deviate in ways that injure or offend others. One way relies largely on the individual's enforcing social rules on himself. The person is, in effect, his own policeman, and if he violates, he becomes his own punisher (normative control). The second way, which appears to have arisen in response to a breakdown of the first, relies on the threat of punishment to prevent violations, and on the application of suffering or restraint to incapacitate the offender or to deter him in the future (legal control).[1]

Law, then, appears to have emerged from custom-in-decay. Criminal law relates specifically to behavior that is presumed to jeopardize public safety or to threaten the integrity of the state. Crime is behavior—whether an act or an omission—that is in violation of the criminal law. Criminal law, in turn, is defined as:

---

[1] Richard Korn and Lloyd McCorkle, *Criminology and Penology* (New York: Holt, Rinehart & Winston, 1965), p. 81.

A body of specific rules regarding human conduct which has been promulgated by political authority, which apply uniformly to all members of the classes to which the rules refer, and which are enforced by punishments administered by the state.[2]

According to this definition, the basic characteristics of criminal law are politicality, specificity, uniformity, and penal sanction.

Central to the democratic tradition that has developed in the United States is the concept that all groups should have access to some political power as well as a meaningful input into the lawmaking process. The criminal law, which includes legislative enactments, judicial interpretations, and certain administrative decisions, is formulated by the political representatives of those segments of society with the power to shape public policy. Instead of being a moral directive from God, the criminal law is a cultural product. It results from man's interaction with other men within a sociopolitical environment. Criminal law represents a compromise of conflicting interests or the shifting supremacy of one special interest over another. The criminal law, then, represents a synthesis of values, special interests, and power. As values, special interests, and power shift from one group to another, so does the focus of the criminal law. Hence, criminal law is both a sociopolitical product and a temporary accommodation. The emphasis of law is always relative to the conditions existing within a particular culture or subculture at a given point in time. When cross-cultural comparisons are made, it is not difficult to find cases where the criminal law commands a certain type of behavior in one situation and prohibits the same behavior, by statute, under similar circumstances in another.

The emergence of modern mass society has also brought with it a rational and contractual orientation. As a result, the criminal law is viewed as a binding agreement between the state and the individual. We rely on legalism to regulate our relationships with others, and we base this approach on a contractual model. Hence, the criminal law is required to state specifically that behavior which is designated as acceptable and that behavior which is outlawed. The law must be stated in clear and explicit language. As a society, we require forewarning—through publication—prior to the application and enforcement of any law. When the criminal law is applied and enforced, we demand to know the specific

[2] Edwin Sutherland and Donald Cressey, *Criminology*, 8th ed. (New York: J. B. Lippincott, 1970), p. 4.

methods to be used, the legal procedures to be followed, and the rules of evidence that will be employed by the government. If these expectations are not fulfilled, each person has the right to initiate certain kinds of constitutionally prescribed corrective measures. Vague laws and questionable procedures are subject to judicial review through the appellate process up to and including a hearing by the U.S. Supreme Court.

A basic premise of our contemporary sociolegal philosophy is that the law, while it must be just, must also be applied in a uniform manner. Equality before the law is one of our most cherished ideals. And yet, many of the legal processes associated with the administration of criminal justice contain elements that are inherently nonuniform. Police discretion, plea negotiation, judicial license, and traditional executive prerogative and influence, coupled with a myriad of political considerations, precludes absolute adherence to the concept of uniformity. The Supreme Court's recent capital punishment ruling was based on the fact that the death penalty had, in the past, been applied in a discriminatory, haphazard, and nonuniform manner and that the application of the death sentence had been subjected to social, political, and other nonjudicial considerations. The Supreme Court's decision was a landmark attempt to achieve more uniformity in the dispensing of criminal justice.

The deterrent value of criminal law is primarily associated with the certainty of the application of negative sanctions. There is also a threat of retaliation by the social group coupled with the implied right of the state, in the name of the people, to force the offender to undergo punishment or treatment on an involuntary basis. This increases society's influence over the individual and tends to promote a certain amount of conformity to legal expectations.

Criminal law, as the primary vehicle for social control, however, even when combined with normative self-regulation, cannot succeed in deterring all criminally deviant behavior. Nor has it been able to prevent the development of criminal career patterns. As a result, crime and delinquency, organized crime, and white-collar crime have become a national concern and a dominant topic of debate. The President's Commission on Law Enforcement and the Administration of Justice, initiated by the late Lyndon B. Johnson in response to the apparent paralysis of criminal justice, the impact of certain heinous crimes on the nation, and the sometimes overzealous demands from some quarters for a return to "law and order" at any cost, made the following assessment of the crime problem and the crisis in criminal justice:

There is much crime in America, more than is ever reported, far more than ever solved, far too much for the health of the nation.[3]

The report of the Commission, *The Challenge of Crime in a Free Society*, called for a massive, multilevel assault on crime and a reordering of social and political priorities in an effort to insure maximum freedom, with justice and security, within a democratic framework.

Crime and Society

An analysis of the national crime statistics compiled by the Federal Bureau of Investigation in the Uniform Crime Reports (UCR) succinctly illustrates the magnitude of the crime problem in this country (Table 1-1). Nearly seven years after the publication of *Challenge*, there were approximately 6 million major crimes reported to the police. This represented an all-time high. The designation "major crime," which includes criminal homicide, forcible rape, aggravated assault, robbery, burglary, larceny, and auto theft, refers to Class One Offenses or Index Crimes. It should be noted that the designation major crime is used as a unit of measurement based on standardized definitions of particular offenses promulgated by the FBI for purposes of uniformity in reporting, ease of statistical tabulation, and comparison.

A review of this statistical data reflects not only an increase in the total volume of criminal activity reported to the police, but it also indicates that some of our most basic assumptions concerning the nature of crime may, in fact, be incorrect. For example, most Americans are conditioned to fear violent crime, and yet the overwhelming majority of reported major crimes are offenses against property; a minority of all reported crimes are crimes against the person.

For purposes of clarity as well as comparison, the UCR data in Table 1-2 reflects the trends in the rate of reported crime since 1960. Major crime has increased by an almost incomprehensible 151.2 percent. Add to these startling figures the millions of lesser crimes (including misdemeanors and summary offenses) reported to the police each year, and

[3] President's Commission on Law Enforcement and the Administration of Justice, *The Challenge of Crime in a Free Society* (Washington, D.C.: U.S. Govt. Printing Office, 1967), p. 1.

TABLE 1-1.   Index of Crime, United States, 1972

Area	Population[1]	Total Crime Index	Violent[2] Crime	Property[3] Crime	Murder and Non-negligent Man-slaughter	Forcible Rape	Robbery	Aggra-vated Assault	Burglary	Larceny $50 and Over	Auto Theft
United States total	208,232,000	5,891,924	828,151	5,063,773	18,515	46,431	374,555	388,650	2,344,991	1,837,799	880,983
Rate per 100,000 inhabitants		2,829.5	397.7	2,431.8	8.9	22.3	179.9	186.6	1,126.1	882.6	423.1
Standard metropolitan statistical area	147,640,000										
Area actually reporting[3]	97.7%	4,980,123	720,626	4,259,497	14,391	39,237	358,018	308,980	1,955,027	1,496,620	807,850
Estimated total	100.0%	5,038,715	726,587	4,312,128	14,596	39,718	359,493	312,780	1,979,377	1,517,216	815,535
Rate per 100,000 inhabitants		3,412.8	492.1	2,920.7	9.9	26.9	243.5	211.9	1,340.7	1,027.6	522.4
Other cities	23,547,000										
Area actually reporting	91.0%	412,345	43,212	369,133	1,041	2,353	8,309	31,509	161,931	170,927	36,725
Estimated total	100.0%	451,470	48,357	403,113	1,195	2,581	9,104	35,477	177,618	185,873	39,622
Rate per 100,000 inhabitants		1,917.3	205.4	1,711.9	5.1	11.0	38.7	150.7	754.3	789.4	168.3
Rural	37,047,000										
Area actually reporting	75.5%	320,530	36,732	283,798	1,826	3,136	4,426	27,344	154,034	109,131	20,633
Estimated total	100.0%	401,739	53,207	348,532	2,724	4,152	5,958	40,393	187,996	134,710	25,826
Rate per 100,000 inhabitants		1,084.4	145.6	940.8	7.4	11.2	16.1	109.0	507.5	363.6	69.7

[1] Population is Bureau of the Census provisional estimate as of July 1, 1972.
[2] Violent crime is offenses of murder, forcible rape, robbery and aggravated assault; property crime is offenses of burglary, larceny $50 and over, and auto theft.
[3] The percentage representing area actually reporting will not coincide with the ratio between reported and estimated crime totals since these data represent the sum of the calculations for individual states which have varying populations, portions reporting, and crime rates.

Source: Federal Bureau of Investigation, *Uniform Crime Reports* (Washington, D.C.: U.S. Govt. Printing Office, 1973), p. 61.

principles and procedures of the justice system

TABLE 1-2. Index of Crime, United States, 1960-1972

Population[1]	Total Crime Index	Violent[2] Crime	Property[2] Crime	Murder and Non-negligent Manslaughter	Forcible Rape	Robbery	Aggravated Assault	Burglary	Larceny $50 and Over	Auto Theft
Number of offenses:										
1960—179,323,175	2,019,600	285,980	1,733,600	9,030	17,050	107,340	152,580	900,400	507,300	325,900
1961—182,953,000	2,087,500	286,880	1,800,600	8,660	17,060	106,170	154,990	937,300	529,600	333,700
1962—185,822,000	2,219,000	298,900	1,920,100	8,460	17,390	110,340	162,710	981,500	574,300	364,300
1963—188,531,000	2,441,900	314,230	2,127,700	8,560	17,490	115,930	172,250	1,072,400	649,900	405,400
1964—191,334,000	2,761,700	361,030	2,400,600	9,280	21,250	129,780	200,760	1,197,600	733,500	469,500
1965—193,818,000	2,937,400	384,020	2,553,400	9,880	23,200	138,040	212,900	1,266,000	794,000	493,400
1966—195,867,000	3,272,200	426,470	2,845,700	10,950	25,590	157,250	232,680	1,391,900	896,500	557,300
1967—197,864,000	3,811,300	495,470	3,315,600	12,130	27,380	201,970	254,260	1,611,100	1,049,300	655,200
1968—199,861,000	4,477,200	590,160	3,887,000	13,690	31,380	261,620	283,470	1,835,000	1,273,800	778,200
1969—201,921,000	5,013,100	656,520	4,356,600	14,640	36,840	297,460	307,580	1,956,400	1,527,800	872,400
1970—203,184,772	5,581,200	732,940	4,848,300	15,860	37,650	348,240	331,190	2,176,600	1,749,800	921,900
1971—206,256,000	5,995,200	810,020	5,185,200	17,630	41,890	385,910	364,600	2,368,400	1,875,200	941,600
1972—208,232,000	5,891,900	828,150	5,063,800	18,520	46,450	374,560	388,650	2,345,000	1,837,800	881,000
Percent change 1960-1972[3]:	+191.7	+189.6	+192.1	+105.2	+172.6	+248.9	+154.7	+160.4	+262.3	+170.3
Rate per 100,000 inhabitants:[3]										
1960	1,126.2	159.5	966.7	5.0	9.5	59.9	85.1	502.1	282.9	181.7
1961	1,141.0	156.8	984.2	4.7	9.3	58.0	84.7	512.3	289.5	182.4
1962	1,194.2	160.9	1,033.3	4.6	9.4	59.4	87.6	528.2	309.1	196.0
1963	1,295.2	166.7	1,128.6	4.5	9.3	61.5	91.4	568.8	344.7	215.0
1964	1,443.4	188.7	1,254.7	4.9	11.1	67.8	104.9	625.9	383.4	254.6
1965	1,515.5	198.1	1,317.4	5.1	12.0	71.2	109.8	653.2	409.7	245.4
1966	1,670.7	217.7	1,452.9	5.6	13.1	80.3	118.8	710.7	457.7	284.5
1967	1,926.2	250.5	1,675.7	6.1	13.8	102.1	128.5	814.2	530.3	331.1
1968	2,240.2	295.3	1,944.9	6.8	15.7	130.9	141.8	918.1	637.3	389.4
1969	2,482.7	325.1	2,157.6	7.3	18.2	147.3	152.3	968.9	756.6	432.1
1970	2,746.9	360.7	2,386.1	7.8	18.5	171.4	163.0	1,071.2	861.2	453.7
1971	2,906.7	392.7	2,514.0	8.5	20.3	187.1	176.8	1,148.3	909.2	456.5
1972	2,829.5	397.7	2,431.8	8.9	22.3	179.9	186.6	1,126.1	882.6	423.1
Percent change 1960-1972[3]:	+151.2	+149.3	+151.6	+78.0	+134.7	+200.3	+119.3	+124.3	+212.0	+132.9

[1] Population is Bureau of the Census provisional estimates as of July 1, except Apr. 1, 1960 and 1970, census.
[2] Violent crime is offenses of murder, forcible rape, robbery and aggravated assault. Property crime is offenses of burglary, larceny $50 and over, and auto theft.
[3] Percent change and crime rates calculated prior to rounding number of offenses. Revised estimates and rates based on changes in reporting practices.
Source: Federal Bureau of Investigation, *Uniform Crime Reports* (Washington, D.C.: U.S. Govt. Printing Office. 1973). p. 61.

it becomes possible to begin formulating parameters with which to comprehend the magnitude of the "official" crime problem. And yet, there is still another dimension that must be accounted for; that is, "official" crime statistics cannot reflect the total crime picture because not all crimes are reported to the police.

Crimes go undetected, unreported, and underreported. Leading criminologists, government statisticians, and law enforcement officials are convinced that "official" crime is only the visible portion of the total crime problem. It has been estimated that only one major crime in five is reported to the police. Considering that the clearance by arrest rate for major crime is very low, this multidimensional view of crime tends to perpetuate dissatisfaction with the agencies of government that are responsible for crime prevention and control. As a result, the crisis in criminal justice represents one of the most significant social problems facing this nation.

The Nonsystem

Prior to the publication of *Challenge* in 1967 and the tremendous modifications that were subsequently made in the delivery of justice services, criminal justice as a system existed only in theory. The concept of justice, with its presumed impartial administration, had been "sold" to the American public as a practical reality and a functional approach to the preservation of the liberty and "due process" guaranteed by the Constitution. Flow charts depicted the schematic movement of the accused offender through a system of distinct, yet interrelated agencies—each with some check or balance on the others and each committed to the same goals—justice, equal treatment, rehabilitation of the offender, and the protection of society. The obvious flaw in this simplistic conceptualization, however, was in the idea of a "system." In reality, those agencies charged with dispensing criminal justice and the safeguarding of personal liberty had become isolated, autonomous, and largely uncoordinated units of government. They had a multiplicity of legitimate and quasi-legitimate functions, and they were afflicted by disorganization, duplication of service, inefficiency, and lack of communication. Using Webster's definition of a system—a regularly interacting or interdependent group of items forming a unified whole—it would have been more appropriate to describe the delivery of criminal justice services prior to *Challenge* as occurring within a "nonsystem."

The unique American nonsystem approach to the dispensation of criminal justice developed in response to, and mirrored the dynamics involved in, the growth of the United States. It reflected the transition from a fairly simple social order to a complex mass society. The sociopolitical and legal orientations of the founders were predicated on Anglo-Saxon tradition. There was an earnest attempt to transplant what they considered to be a proven philosophy of justice and an acceptable method of its administration. The American experience, however, altered the course of events, and it left an indelible imprint on the political and legal institutions that finally emerged. As American culture diversified, and as the society became more and more stratified, the original emphasis on equality and justice for all seemed to dissipate. Americans were far too busy with the challenges of survival, adversity, and the need-to-succeed syndrome to pay attention to such an abstract philosophical notion as justice.

As a consequence, a lag developed between our stated sociolegal philosophy and our behavioral manifestations. Hence, the accused and the confirmed criminal were both considered to be social liabilities, inferior, and, in many cases, degenerate. As a result, accusation and conviction became synonymous in the minds of many people. Criminals were stigmatized, deprived of their constitutional rights, and subjected to dehumanization. Criminal justice agencies reacted to the tenor of a changing society. They became politically oriented bureaucracies dedicated to the maintenance of social order through repression and to the preservation of the status quo.

The criminal justice agencies—police, prosecution, courts, and corrections—depended on tax revenues and the good will of politicians for survival. As a result, their commitment to idealism became secondary to practical considerations. This capitulation, however, did not produce the desired effects. Criminal justice agencies received little additional revenue and even less political support. In an era of greed and the aggrandizement of power, criminal justice, although exploited politically, remained grossly underfunded and neglected. Personnel in these agencies were often substandard and nonprofessional; many of the employees engaged in the administration of criminal justice had received their positions as patronage for supporting the "right" political candidates. Partly because of these political ties, the criminal justice agencies were seldom subjected to public scrutiny and, as a consequence, they continued to stagnate and deteriorate. Since the politicians and their proteges—many of them engaged in the administration of justice—changed with a high degree of regularity, long-range planning was virtually nonexistent, and very few proponents of reform emerged from within the system.

To the detriment of society; injustice, the nonsystem, and politics became intertwined in a vicious cycle of mutual mystification and deceit. As a result, criminal justice agencies became even more isolated from the public, more detached from each other, and more removed from their original commitment to the ideals of justice. The agencies, since they were seldom held accountable, became virtual fiefdoms; they developed into bastions of conservatism, symbols of the corruption of justice. American history is filled with horrid examples of the miscarriages of justice and the denigration of the rights of certain classes of people. This untenable conflict of values destroyed citizen confidence in the agencies of justice and led to increased feelings of impotence, disinterest, and apathy. Thus, despite the fact that some progress had been made in correcting the ills that plagued the administration of justice, basic philosophical as well as structural flaws remained. The Constitution was continuously short-circuited or entirely circumvented. As a result, the agencies charged with the delivery of criminal justice services were unable to cope with the massive social and crime problems that culminated in the late 1950s and early 1960s. The still insufficient nonsystem of justice, outmoded and unstable, failed to meet the challenge of crime in our society. The obvious failures of criminal justice—widely publicized by the mass media— caused widespread consternation among the people, generated a great deal of introspection, and created powerful demands for revision and reform within the administration of justice services.

The Commission on Law Enforcement and the Administration of Justice
Basic dissatisfaction with the nonsystem approach to the administration of criminal justice, together with a nagging awareness of government's inability to operate efficiently or effectively to prevent or control crime and criminal behavior and the public's growing comprehension that much was wrong with the various segments of the criminal justice system, prompted the President to establish the Commission on Law Enforcement and the Administration of Justice.

The Challenge of Crime in a Free Society (1967), with a renewed emphasis on the concept of system and a call for a revitalized commitment to fair and impartial justice for all, laid down the gauntlet. The Commission challenged the American people as well as the myriad of governmental units comprising the federal system (local, state, and national) to reorder their ethical and sociolegal priorities in a concentrated effort to streamline the delivery of justice services. *Challenge* urged the people and the government to fulfill the justice-for-all ideal through citizen involvement and governmental activism. The Commission made the following recommendations.

Preventing Crime. Prevention of crime covers a wide range of activities: eliminating social conditions closely associated with crime; improving the ability of the criminal justice system to detect, apprehend, judge, and reintegrate into the community those who commit crimes; and reducing the situations in which crimes are most likely to be committed.

New Ways of Dealing with Offenders. The Commission's second objective—the development of a broader range of alternatives for dealing with offenders—is based on the belief that, while there are some offenders who must be completely segregated from society, there are many instances in which segregation does more harm than good. Furthermore, by concentrating the resources of the police, the courts, and correctional agencies on the smaller number of offenders who really need them, it should be possible to give all offenders more effective treatment.

Eliminating Unfairness. The third objective is to eliminate injustices so that the system of criminal justice can win the respect and cooperation of all citizens. Our society must give the police, the courts, and correctional agencies the resources and the mandate to provide fair and dignified treatment for all.

Personnel. The fourth objective is that higher levels of knowledge, expertise, initiative, and integrity be achieved by police, judges, prosecutors, defense attorneys, and correctional authorities so that the system of criminal justice can improve its ability to control crime.

Money. The police, the courts, and correctional agencies will require substantially more money if they are to control crime more efficiently.

Responsibility for Change. Individual citizens, social-service agencies, universities, religious institutions, civic and business groups, and all kinds of governmental agencies at all levels must become involved in planning and executing changes in the criminal justice system.[4]

The basic function of the administration of justice in America is that of a sequential crime-control process with built-in inalienable safeguards for the protection of both the rights of society and the constitutional rights of the accused. According to Weston and Wells, the primary function of the system is:

> The prevention, detection, discovery, and suppression of crime; the identification, apprehension, and prosecution of persons accused as criminals; and the incarceration, supervision, and reform and rehabilitation of convicted offenders. These are accomplished primarily through six major functional areas of government: police, prosecution, criminal courts, probation, prisons and other institutions for the care and treatment of offenders, and parole.[5]

Schematically then, the criminal justice system is composed of multiple, interacting subsystems. The system is concerned with the enforcement of legal norms (laws) and the imposition of legal sanctions (treatment and punishment) in order to prevent crime or social disorder and to preserve the peace of the community. Similarly, the system is designed to protect life, property, and personal liberty.

The Police

The police and closely allied law enforcement agencies at all levels of government are charged with the enforcement of the criminal laws enacted by the legislative branch of government. The police are, in addition, the first line of defense against social disorder and criminality. As such, their primary mission, as currently defined, involves the following:

1. Crime prevention activities
2. Crime repression

[4] President's Commission on Law Enforcement and the Administration of Justice, *The Challenge of Crime in a Free Society* (Washington, D.C.: U.S. Govt. Printing Office, 1967), pp. vi-xi.
[5] Paul Weston and Kenneth Wells, *The Administration of Justice*, 2nd ed. (Englewood Cliffs, N.J.: Prentice-Hall, 1973), p. 1.

3. Apprehension of offenders
4. Recovery of property
5. Identification, collection, preservation, and presentation of evidence
6. Regulation of noncriminal behavior
7. Provision of services
8. The protection of personal liberty

The police function is a component of the executive branch of government. Police authority and conduct, however, rest on foundations and regulations in accordance with the Constitution (specifically the Bill of Rights), the Congress of the United States, the Supreme Court, state legislation, local enactments, and legal precedent. There are more than 500,000 persons involved in the delivery of police services in over 40,000 separate police agencies. The police represent the largest, most fragmented, and most criticized component of criminal justice, primarily because they are highly visible and have the most frequent contact with the people.

The Prosecution

The office of prosecutor (or district attorney, as he is often called) is generally an elective position within the hierarchy of county government. There are more than 3000 elected prosecutors in the United States, each having a staff and, at least in theory, capable of fulfilling the prosecutorial role: that is, the successful prosecution of offenders and the protection of the innocent. The district attorney occupies a pivotal position in the delivery of criminal justice services.

The prosecutor is expected to act as a liaison between the various components of the criminal justice system as well as an effective check on the police. Based on an evaluation of the data presented to him, the prosecutor is charged with deciding whether there is sufficient evidence to warrant prosecution, a strong enough case to sustain a conviction, whether he should accept a plea, or reduce the charge against the defendant. The prosecutor has wide latitude in applying the prosecutorial process. This discretion is firmly established in American legal tradition. At the same time, the prosecutor acts as the legal advisor to certain departments within the executive branch of government, presents criminal

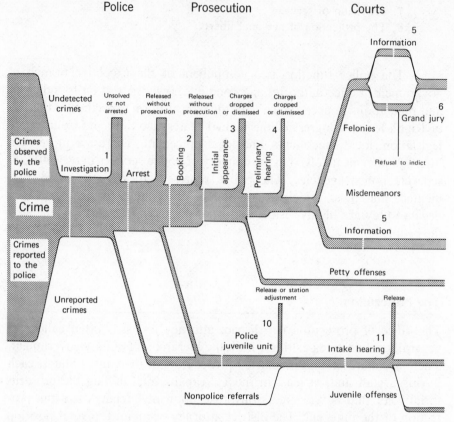

Figure 1-1. A general view of the criminal justice system. This is a simple, yet comprehensive view of the movement of cases through the system. Procedures in individual jurisdictions may vary from the patterns shown here. The differing weights of line indicate the relative volumes of cases disposed of at various points

1 May continue until trial.

2 Administrative record of arrest. First step at which temporary release on bail may be available.

3 Before magistrate, commissioner, or justice of peace. Formal notice of charge, advice of rights. Bail set. Summary trials for petty offenses usually conducted here without further processing.

4 Preliminary testing of evidence against defendant. Charge may be reduced. No separate preliminary hearing for misdemeanors in some systems.

5 Charge filed by prosecutor on basis of information submitted by police or citizens. Alternative to grand jury indictment; often used in felonies, almost always in misdemeanors.

6 Reviews whether government evidence sufficient to justify trial. Some states have no grand jury system; others seldom use it.

in the system, but this is only suggestive since no nationwide data of this sort exists.
Source: President's Commission on Law Enforcement and the Administration of
Justice. *The Challenge of Crime in a Free Society* (Washington, D.C.: U.S. Govt.
Printing Office, 1967), pp. 8, 9.

Corrections

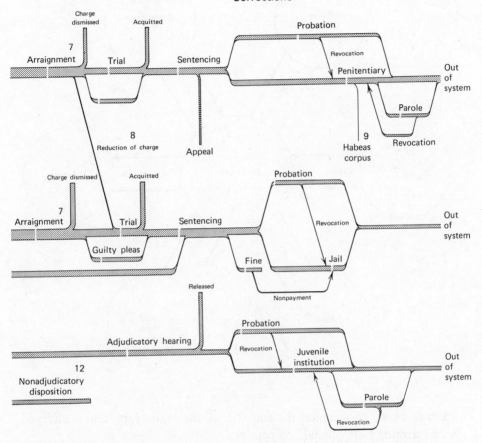

7 Appearance for plea; defendant elects trial by judge or jury (if available); counsel for indigent usually appointed here in felonies. Often not at all in other cases.

8 Charge may be reduced at any time prior to trial in return for plea of guilty or for other reasons.

9 Challenge on constitutional grounds to legality of detention. May be sought at any point in process.

10 Police often hold informal hearings, dismiss or adjust many cases without further processing.

11 Probation officer decides desirability of further court action.

12 Welfare agency, social services, counselling, medical care, etc., for cases where adjudicatory handing not needed.

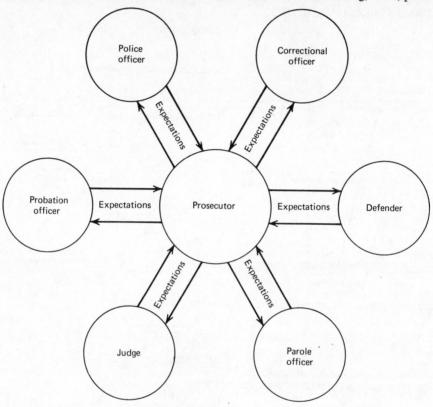

Figure 1-2. *The role of the prosecutor.* Source: The American Justice Institute, *Survey of Role Perceptions for Operational Criminal Justice Personnel Preliminary Research Design.* Commission on Peace Officer Standard and Training, 1971, p. 55.

cases in court, coordinates the activities of the grand jury, and is charged with ferreting out "official" corruption.

The counterpart of the prosecutor is the defense attorney or the public defender. Based on the Sixth Amendment, it is the legal counsel's function to present an adequate defense for all charges brought by the state and, at the same time, it is his responsibility to counsel an accused as to the most beneficial and appropriate course of action to be taken. Those citizens who can afford private counsel have, by and large, been adequately represented. The poor have not always been as fortunate. Unrepresented or underrepresented, the poor and other minority groups have often endured a discriminatory application of criminal justice and the deprivation of their constitutional rights. In response to this basic inequity, the Supreme Court, in *Gideon* v. *Wainwright*, reaffirmed the right of the accused to have an adequate defense—regardless of his race, religion, or social status. The Court held that indigent defendants were entitled to adequate legal services and that the costs of such defense be assumed by the state. As a result, the concept of the public defender emerged. The state, through the public defender, acts as a champion and an advocate. Hence, the state plays multiple roles; it acts as prosecutor and defender. The courts act as the arbiter.

The Courts

The function of the judiciary is responsible supervision. The judiciary has a high duty and a solemn responsibility to overview the work of the police, the prosecutor, opposing counsel, and jurors; to preserve the due process of law throughout the arrest-to-release procedure in the administration of justice; and to translate into living law the sanctions which may be imposed upon the offender after a fair trial.[6]

Courts are charged with monitoring procedures and with coordinating the activities of those criminal justice practitioners engaged in the prosecutorial and trial processes to insure that justice is carried out in a fair and impartial manner within a constitutional framework, in order to sustain innocence or prove the guilt of the accused. The court is also responsible for the sentencing, based on the protection of society and the rehabilitation of the offender, of the convicted criminal.

Each state, as well as the federal government, has a unique approach to the organization and administration of the judiciary. There are a myriad of titles, types of jurisdiction, and procedures employed. However, as a general rule, courts—from the justice-of-the-peace level to the U.S. Supreme Court—can be categorized as trial courts and appellate courts.

[6] Paul Weston and Kenneth Wells, *The Administration of Justice*, 2nd ed. (Englewood Cliffs, N.J.: Prentice-Hall, 1973), p. 105.

Trial Courts

These are courts of original jurisdiction. They empanel a jury, hear evidence as well as the arguments of opposing counsel, instruct the jury as to the law, and sentence the accused if and when he is found guilty of a crime.

Appellate Courts

These courts review, both for substance and procedure, cases that were originally tried in the lower (trial courts). They either affirm the lower court's action or precipitate corrective measures to rectify errors.

Corrections

The correctional process is charged with carrying out two fundamental responsibilities of government: (1) protection of society, and (2) the rehabilitation of the convicted offender. The correctional function is apportioned primarily among three distinct processes: probation, institutionalization, and parole.

Probation

Probation is a sentencing alternative. It permits the convicted offender (if the circumstances warrant) to serve his sentence within the community without going to prison, under the supervision of the probation service. Probation is a judicial act based on the right of the judiciary to suspend the imposition or execution of sentence. The probationer agrees to adhere to certain conditions established by the court. Failure to observe the conditions of probation or the commission of a new offense can result in a revocation of probation. While on probation, the probationer receives treatment, guidance, assistance, and varying degrees of supervision.

Institutionalization

When it is determined that the convicted offender is not a suitable candidate for probation, that he needs to be segregated from the community or that involuntary treatment is required, he will be sent to a correctional institution.

There are numerous types of institutions, ranging from minimum to maximum security, which specialize in specific kinds of treatment and the custody of certain types of offender. Prisons and other types of correctional institutions historically have been the most isolated component of the criminal justice system. Traditionally understaffed, underfunded, and seriously neglected, they became a warehousing operation with an overriding commitment to custodial responsibilities. Recidivism was invariably high and, according to many authorities, imprisonment did more harm than good. Although great strides have been made in correctional technology and the development of correctional strategies, there is still a long way to go before correctional institutions can become truly correctional. Few people are aware of this need more than those who administer our prisons.

Parole

Parole (French for "word of honor") refers to the release of the prisoner from imprisonment, but not from legal custody. Thus, the parolee is given treatment, guidance, assistance, and supervision outside the prison and within the community.

Parole is a function of the executive branch of government. It is based on the chief executive's right to commute or suspend sentences imposed by the courts. The authority to release offenders—for cause and good conduct—is usually delegated to a parole board. Release on parole is generally based on inmate readiness, past conduct, and a prognosis for success. The prisoner signs a parole agreement (the equivalent of the conditions of probation). If the agreement is violated or a new crime committed, the parolee may be returned to prison following a revocation hearing.

The Law Enforcement Assistance Administration

In response to the publication of *Challenge* and as a result of some national soul searching, Congress passed the Omnibus Crime Control and Safe Streets Act of 1968. This legislation created the Law Enforcement Assistance Administration (LEAA) and allocated millions of dollars for the rehabilitation of the criminal justice system and the restoration of the American commitment to justice. The primary responsibility of LEAA is, through revenue sharing and technical assistance, to expedite the implementation of the Presidential Commission's recommendations regarding the prevention of crime, the development of new correctional methods, the achievement of equity in the administration of criminal justice, the promotion of research activity, the infusion of money, and the development of total involvement by all segments of the community.

The major thrust of *Challenge of Crime in a Free Society* and the Law Enforcement Assistance Administration, while recognizing that significant renovations within the justice system might be necessary, places a high priority on the revitalization and strengthening of the present system. Each of the components of the system must be as structurally sound and as efficient as the other components in order for the theoretical checks-and-balances to become operative. Interagency conflict must be minimized and competition for scarce resources must be strictly regulated; coordination of services and the elimination of duplication must be a paramount consideration. Similarly, it should be noted that the functional utility of a systems approach to the administration of justice services is predicated on the quality of the personnel selected to perform the various criminal justice roles.

Professional personnel with a commitment to "equality and justice for all" are the key to the equitable dispensation of justice. They are ultimately responsible for the ethical orientation of the system, and they will determine the modifications that will eventually take place within the system. As previously noted, the recruitment, selection, and training of criminal justice personnel have been adversely affected by political considerations and public apathy. Certain segments of the system have traditionally required high levels of educational proficiency and a demonstrable ability to perform successfully. But until recently, other components of the system have not had the impetus to exploit educational opportunities or develop professionalism.

Justice-Actor Conflict

As a result of these gaps, standardized role expectations evolved. There is an imbalance, then, in prestige, power, and potential, known as justice-actor conflict. Stereotypically, justice-actor conflict pits the undereducated, untrained, unskilled, overworked law enforcement officer against the more perceptive, articulate, educated, and manipulative legal mind. The conflict accentuates the estrangement or mismatch of the expectations of the professional parole agent and his counterpart in the institution, the correctional officer. In other words, education, training, and a healthy self-concept lead to power, and when the power within the system is unequal, conflict develops and resentment sets in, and justice suffers.

Challenge, the LEAA, the International Association of Chiefs of Police (IACP), and others have called for a resolution of justice-actor conflict in order to maximize the efficiency of the system in achieving its goals. The Law Enforcement Assistance Administration has committed itself, not only to the purchase of hardware, but also to the upgrading of personnel at both the inservice and preservice levels. Millions of dollars have gone into the recruitment, screening, and selection of competent personnel for all of the components of the system: police, prosecution, courts, and corrections. There has been a concerted effort by the state planning agencies to provide inservice professional training and to subsidize education through the Law Enforcement Education Program (LEEP). Additional millions have been spent to identify the various roles played by criminal justice personnel, to ascertain whether or not these roles are appropriate in free society, and to provide the training necessary to perform those roles more effectively. Coupled with the other modifications required to streamline the delivery of criminal justice services, the elimination of justice-actor conflict is essential for the successful administration of justice in a democratic society.

Conclusions

By now it should be apparent that if the criminal justice system functions properly, its goals—the protection of society, the rehabilitation of the offender, and the preservation of individual liberty—will be attained. If, on the other hand, the system fails to function, as has been the case during much of our history, the crisis in criminal justice will continue to generate hostility, more and more intense resentment, and additional efforts by some to destroy the very foundations of American government. Therefore, it is imperative that we coordinate the components of the system in a superhuman effort to achieve the ideals of justice that have been hailed as the cornerstone of our form of government. A proliferation of agencies and a duplication of essential services must not be allowed to camouflage gross ineffectiveness and inefficiency in the administration of justice. Unless the challenges contained in the report of the President's Commission on Law Enforcement and the Administration of Justice are met head-on, American justice will be a myth, and professionalism in criminal justice will not occur.

Student Checklist

1. Can you distinguish between the concepts of normative and legal control?
2. Are you able to identify the basic characteristics of criminal law?
3. Can you list the Uniform Crime Reports index crimes?
4. Can you list the elements that perpetuate a nonsystem approach to achieving justice?
5. Are you able to identify the major objectives proposed in the *Challenge of Crime in a Free Society?*
6. Can you list the eight functions performed by the police?
7. Can you identify the major function performed by the courts?
8. Are you able to list the three processes of corrections?

Topics for Discussion

1. Discuss the concept of justice-actor conflict.
2. Discuss the liaison function performed by the prosecutor's office.
3. Discuss the consequences of justice system conflict among the major components: law enforcement, courts, and corrections.
4. Discuss the basic characteristics of American criminal law.
5. Discuss the impact of the report entitled, *Challenge of Crime in a Free Society.*

ANNOTATED BIBLIOGRAPHY

Adams, Thomas F. *Law Enforcement*, 2nd ed., Englewood Cliffs, N.J.: Prentice-Hall, 1973. A detailed and descriptive analysis of the roles and responsibilities of the contemporary police officer; the text reviews theory, the impact of the U.S. Supreme Court, and the recommendations of the President's Commission on Law Enforcement and the Administration of Justice.

Bopp, William J., and Donald O. Schultz. *Principles of American Law Enforcement and Criminal Justice.* Springfield, Ill.: Charles C. Thomas, 1972. An analysis of criminal justice in American society; along with the historical perspective, each of the components of the criminal justice system is reviewed in detail. The text takes a functional approach and deals with the philosophical foundations of the criminal justice system.

Clark, Ramsey. *Crime in America.* New York: Simon and Schuster, 1970. Clark develops a unique and controversial perspective of crime and justice in America. Coupled with a review of the structure and function of justice, the author adds a philosophical dimension based on his experience as a lawyer and an attorney general.

Kerper, Hazel B. *Introduction to Criminal Justice System.* St. Paul: West Publishing, 1972. A legally oriented analysis of the criminal justice system coupled with a detailed structural and functional view of the various components of justice administration in the United States.

President's Commission on Law Enforcement and the Administration of Justice. *The Challenge of Crime in a Free Society.* Washington, D.C.: U.S. Govt. Printing Office, 1967. A detailed analysis of the criminal justice system with an emphasis on the concept of "system." The text also lists recommendations as to solutions for the crime problem in American society. *Challenge* is a classic and provided the impetus for major modifications within the system of criminal justice.

Weston, Paul B., and Kenneth M. Wells. *The Administration of Justice,* 2nd ed., Englewood Cliffs, N.J.: Prentice-Hall, 1973. A review of criminal law enforcement from the initial arrest to the final disposition. The text also contains an analysis of recent court decisions and elaborates on changes taking place within the system of criminal justice.

The study of this chapter will enable you to:

1. Differentiate between the rule of law and the rule of man.
2. Identify the purpose of law in a democracy.
3. Identify the three means of changing the law.
4. List the guarantees that certain rights would not be abridged as set forth in the Bill of Rights.
5. Identify the landmark decisions that have refined the interpretation of the Fourth Amendment.
6. Write an essay on the interpretation of the Fifth Amendment's self-incrimination clause and its application to the states.
7. Trace the legal history that provides for the accused's right to counsel.

2
Legal Foundations

The American system of criminal justice is a vast, complex enigma. Based on some of the most noble and praiseworthy ideals to which any society has ever given recognition, it is regularly marred by incidences of overwhelming injustice. The gap between the ideals at the foundation of our system and the inequities that occur in its daily workings is a gap that should be closed. If equal justice for all is to become a reality, it can only be through the rule of law.

The Rule of Law

At the outset it is important to distinguish between two separate concepts: the rule of law and the rule of man. If a parent disciplines a child whenever he finds the child's behavior distasteful, then the child is governed by the rule of an individual, not the rule of law. The parent who disciplines his child only after the child has broken a previously stated "rule of the house" has a child whose behavior is governed by the rule of law.

The rule of law makes governmental response to citizen behavior predictable, and the predictability of those responses makes them palatable. When citizens know in advance what types of behavior will result in arrest, prosecution, and punishment, they are safeguarded against the "kind of discretion that results from broad penal statutes, as in Nazi Germany, Fascist Italy, or Soviet Russia, where social offenses of the widest definition unloose the uncontrolled power of officialdom."[1] A

[1] Harry W. More, *Critical Issues in Law Enforcement* (Cincinnati: W. H. Anderson, 1972), p. 154.

27

criminal justice system based on the rule of law—instead of on the whim of an individual—is a system that is far more likely to win acceptance and support from the citizenry. And without that support, no system can survive indefinitely.

Social Control Through Law

Human relations is a subject as complicated as the nature of humanity itself. Wherever two or more human beings encounter one another, countless potential conflicts exist. In a wolf pack, a family of primates, or a pride of lions, most potential conflicts are avoided by educating the young in the customs of the species. Actual conflicts are resolved by the rule of violence—the fittest will prevail.

"Primitive man contrived methods of regulating the behavior of humans, particularly when it became apparent that doing so was necessary for survival."[2] In human societies today the young are socialized by their elders in a complex educational process wherein children are taught the customs and mores of their society. As the child grows he learns a more sophisticated version of the rules of society, and most of the potential conflicts inherent in encounters with other humans are effectively neutralized. The rules of the game of living with others are designed to promote harmony in society. When the rules are unclear and actual conflicts occur, they are ideally resolved, not by violence, but by reason.

It is this unique gift of man—his ability to reason—that has enabled him to formulate laws that serve as guidelines for human relations. The purpose of law is to regulate human behavior so that the individual may reasonably expect other members of society to respect his rights. All laws—criminal law, housing regulations, or the Internal Revenue Code—are justified only if they are designed to ·assure the orderly flow of social relations.

Plato said that justice can be simple only if man is simple. The complexity of human relations gives rise to the complexity of laws that govern those relations. There may be oppressive and unfair laws that do not promote social order, but one thing is clear: without law, there can be no order.

[2] Coffey, Eldefonso, and Hartinger, *Human Relations: Law Enforcement in a Changing Community* (Englewood Cliffs, N.J.: Prentice-Hall, 1971), p. 52.

Balancing the Rights of Society and the Individual

Once it has accepted the idea that law is a tool designed to be used for control of society, that society must determine which kind of control it wants. If the purpose of law is simply to bring about social order, then certainly the criminal justice system of totalitarian regimes would seem to be the most effective. In George Orwell's classic look at the political regime of the future, *1984*, the reader is repelled by the misery and the barrenness of life when the government exercises virtually absolute control over every aspect of the individual's existence. But no one could criticize the rate of crime in the world of *1984*. Orwell's government eliminated crime by severely limiting freedom.[3]

It is apparent that a delicate balance must be struck between freedom and order. The right of the individual to choose freely his modes of behavior is a principle held dear by Americans. The right of society to protect itself by punishing certain kinds of antisocial behavior is a right recognized by even the most avid civil libertarian. So-called liberal jurists tend to put emphasis on the former principle; so-called conservative jurists emphasize the latter.

During the 1960s, decisions made by the Supreme Court brought about substantial changes in criminal proceedings. The Warren Court was comprised of a liberal majority that rather consistently emphasized the individual rights of citizens charged with crimes. Since 1968 four justices have retired. Justices Warren, Black, and Fortas were generally considered liberal. Justice Harlan most often sided with the conservatives. All of them have been replaced on the court by justices who stress the need for "law and order," that is, the right of society to protect itself even at the cost of individual freedoms. The four Nixon appointees, Burger, Blackmun, Rehnquist, and Powell, were selected on the basis of their "conservative" views. How far the pendulum may swing back is a matter of conjecture. What is important to note is that both liberal and conservative justices—while observing society from different viewpoints—are nonetheless equally concerned about balancing, in their own way, the rights of society and the individual.

[3] George Orwell, *1984* (New York: Harcourt, Brace, 1949).

Figure 2-1. The Justices of the U.S. Supreme Court. Front row: *Associate Justices Potter Stewart; William O. Douglas; Chief Justice Warren E. Burger; Associate Justices William J. Brennan, Jr.; and Byron R. White.* Back row: *Associate Justices Lewis F. Powell, Jr.; Thurgood Marshall; Harry A. Blackmun; and William H. Rehnquist.*

Change and Law

In the three decades following World War II our social system has undergone dramatic changes unprecedented in American history. But our legal system is still in the process of catching up to these changes. Modern technology has forced our legislatures and courts to consider problems as diverse as air pollution control, electronic eavesdropping, and even regulation of heart transplants. Changing social attitudes toward divorce, nontherapeutic abortion, and the personal use of marijuana have forced legislators and judges to reevaluate and revise outmoded laws.

Change in the law takes three forms: legislative, judicial, and constitutional. Legislative change is the most common. Candidates for public office on the state or federal level try to determine public attitudes on various issues, and, to the extent that they are free from control of special interest, cast their votes for legislation reflecting the attitudes of the majority of their constituencies. Many state legislatures, for example, ar presently modifying abortion laws in response to increasing demand from women voters and a general change in societal attitudes toward abortion.

The judicial approach to changing the law is less common than the legislative and has frequently been criticized by those opposed to what they call "judicial legislation." A court may be asked to evaluate the constitutionality of a law and declare it void. The U.S. Supreme Court, for instance, recently held that state laws that prohibited abortions in the first three months of pregnancy were unconstitutional and therefore unenforceable. This was a change in the law that reflected both new medical knowledge on the subject of abortion and new social attitudes toward individual rights.

The third method of changing law is through constitutional amendment. Let us suppose that a majority of Americans favored reform of abortion laws and that the legislature responded to their demands by legalizing abortion at any time during pregnancy. Let us further assume that the Supreme Court takes the view that the unborn fetus is a "person" within the meaning of the Fourteenth Amendment and, as such, is entitled to due process of law before being executed. Abortion of an innocent fetus would therefore be an unconstitutional deprivation of its rights, causing the new laws to be considered invalid.

Are the people then powerless to resolve the impasse that results from this rather unlikely situation? The answer is no. Through the process of constitutional amendment the term "person" could be defined to exclude unborn fetuses and the high court could no longer raise constitutional objections to abortion. The potential for abusing this process and establishing a dictatorship of the majority was clearly in the minds of the framers of the Constitution, and it is for that reason that the amendment process was deliberately made complex. The hope of the framers was that people would have the opportunity to reflect soberly on constitutional amendments before they made hasty decisions.

The Structure of Law

After having considered the rule of law and briefly analyzed its importance in the criminal justice system, it is important that the student understand something of the legal foundations of the criminal justice system and the structure on which American law is built, including the Constitution, the amendments, and state law.

U.S. Constitution

The U.S. Constitution is the supreme law of the land. It is the oldest constitution in the world today and has been the model for innumerable other constitutions drafted over the past two centuries. Throughout all of American history the Constitution has served as a symbol of national unity and has enjoyed both emotional and rational support from nine generations of Americans. It is the framework by which the American legal system withstands the pressures of changing times.

The Constitution may be divided into three parts: the original seven Articles, the Bill of Rights (or first ten amendments), and the Amendments Eleven to Twenty-Six.

The Seven Articles. The original seven articles provide the basic structure of the American political system. They provide for a federal system wherein the individual states retain their sovereignty while granting certain powers to an umbrella government. The Constitution creates a government of enumerated powers, a government limited to those powers specifically granted to it by the Constitution. Governmental power is separated into three branches with the idea that such separation will create a system of checks-and-balances calculated to avert tyrannical exercise of power by any one branch. Articles I, II, and III provide for Congress, the Presidency, and the Judiciary, respectively.

Article I provides for a bicameral legislature composed of the Senate and the House of Representatives. In the Senate each state is given equal representation regardless of size or population. The House of Representatives is more democratically structured, with each state being represented in proportion to its population. All members of the House face reelection every two years, whereas Senators are elected for a six-year term. Every two years, one third of the Senate seats are filled by an election.

In Section 8 of Article I the powers of Congress are set forth. Congress has no power to pass any law that is not authorized in this section. How could the framers of the Constitution have anticipated the needs of future generations and grant the congressional power necessary to deal with those needs without granting almost absolute dictatorial power? The answer lies in the fact that the wording of the provisions in Section 8 are sufficiently general to be adapted to the changing needs of future generations through congressional interpretation of the "elastic clause."

The "elastic clause" provides that Congress will have the power "to make all laws which shall be necessary and proper for carrying into execution the forgoing powers. . . ." Congress is thereby authorized to pass any legislation necessary to implement any of the powers itemized in Section 8.

For example, one of the powers granted to Congress in Section 8 is "to regulate commerce among the several states." Reading the commerce and elastic clauses together, Congress has claimed the right to regulate all forms of commercial intercourse, transportation, and communication, and more recently, to prohibit racial discrimination in business enterprises which affect interstate commerce. The framers of Article I could not have anticipated a future need to regulate television advertising. But by providing an "elastic clause," their foresight allows the Congress to stretch the meaning of the commerce clause to accommodate such needs.

Article II provides for a President to be elected every four years. He is made the Commander-in-Chief of the Armed Forces and is empowered to make treaties, appoint ambassadors and Supreme Court judges, and to "take care that the laws be faithfully executed. . . ."

Article III authorizes a federal judiciary and vests ultimate judicial power in the U.S. Supreme Court. Through judicial interpretation[4] this article has been read to provide for "judicial review," or the power of the courts to interpret the Constitution and refuse to enforce those measures that they determine to be in conflict with the Constitution.

In Article IV the framers offer some basic guidelines for interstate relations. Article VI includes the "supremacy clause" wherein the Constitution is made the supreme law of the land, and Article VII sets forth the procedures for ratification of the Constitution by the states. The framers realized that future needs of the American political system would necessitate changes in the Constitution, and in Article VI they provide for an amendment procedure.

The Amendments. The amendment process of any constitution is designed

---

[4] Marbury v. Madison, 1 Cranch 137, 2 L.Ed. 60 (1803).

to assure both stability and flexibility. A constitution is the fundamental law guiding the relationship of the members, and that guidance should be consistent, not subject to change with every whim of the majority. The framers of the U.S. Constitution were successful, to an extraordinary degree, in providing a procedure designed to assure orderly change in our fundamental law.

There are presently 26 amendments to the Constitution. The first ten are commonly called the Bill of Rights and will be discussed in the next section. The Amendments Eleven to Twenty-Six were ratified over a period of 160 years and were generally designed to rectify some specific problem with which Congress did not have the authority to deal. The Sixteenth Amendment, for instance, provides for an income tax, which had been thought to be unconstitutional. The Eighteenth Amendment extends suffrage to women, a gesture that could not have been accomplished through legislation. With the exception of the Fourteenth Amendment, very few court decisions involve interpretation of any of these 15 amendments. They are perhaps of more interest to the student of American history than to the student of constitutional law.

State Law

The vast majority of American criminal law is made not in Washington, D.C., but in the 50 state capitals. The states are entitled, within the limits of due process requirements, to establish their own criminal justice systems.

At the foundation of these systems lie the state constitutions. State constitutions, in general, resemble the U.S. Constitution in calling for an executive, a bicameral legislature, and a court system. (The Constitution of the state of Nebraska, however, provides for a one-house legislature.) Most contain many of the provisions found in the Bill of Rights, and all contain provisions acknowledging the supremacy of the U.S. Constitution within the boundaries of the state. State constitutional provisions that violate the U.S. Constitution will be nullified by federal courts. The legislatures of the several states are empowered to pass all state law. Characteristically, state legal systems will contain penal codes, evidence codes, and codes of criminal procedure.

Penal codes catalogue all state crimes, dividing them into felonies, misdemeanors, and infractions, and specify the appropriate punishment for each. Evidence codes set forth in statutory form the rules for admitting and evaluating evidence during a criminal trial. Most evidence statutes originated in court decisions and after many years were codified for the purpose of simplifying the rules of evidence. Codes of criminal procedure provide the guidelines for prosecuting criminal suspects. The codes vary from one state to the next, setting forth procedures designed to accord to all defendants the fundamental fairness required by the Bill of Rights as interpreted through the due process clause of the Fourteenth Amendment.

Civil Liberties:
Interpreting the Bill of Rights Through the Due Process Clause

When the Constitution was presented to the American people for ratification, it was viewed with much skepticism in many quarters. One of the complaints frequently voiced by the colonists was the absence of a bill of rights. The memory of the oppressive governmental policies in which the British had engaged was still vivid in the colonial mind. The prospect of a new government—a federal government engaging in policies similar to those of the British—prompted the colonists to demand a catalogue of specific restrictions on the new government's power. That catalogue of restrictions—ratified by the states in 1791—is called the Bill of Rights.

The Bill of Rights
The student of constitutional law should remember that the Bill of Rights was designed and written as a protection for the citizen against the *federal* government. State governments were familiar to the colonist who believed, to some extent, that his state would not engage in unfair practices against him. But that trust did not extend to the "new government" and it was from that government that he wanted a guarantee that certain rights would not be abridged.

The Bill of Rights is that guarantee. It assures Americans that their rights to free speech, press, assembly, and religion will not be abridged; that they will be free from unreasonable searches, coercive interrogations, or double jeopardy. It guarantees a fair trial and prohibits cruel and unusual punishment. The federal government's power to employ fundamentally unfair procedures against citizens is thereby restricted.

But what of state governments? The overwhelming majority of criminal cases are handled on the state level, and the average citizen has far more contact with state law enforcement agencies than he has with the federal government. Is there nothing in the U.S. Constitution that would prohibit the state from engaging in those practices prohibited by the Bill of Rights? In light of the history of the Bill of Rights it is clear that the framers of the first ten amendments did not intend to apply their provisions to the states. What, then, protects the American people against state encroachment of civil liberties? The answer is found in the due process clause of the Fourteenth Amendment.

Due Process

Nothing in the U.S. Constitution has been the subject of greater controversial interpretation than the term "due process of law." There never has been—and perhaps cannot be—a precise definition of due process, and its meaning today retains what jurists call a convenient vagueness. Behind this vagueness, courts have justified a wide range of decisions, arguing that the conclusions they had reached were mandated by due process considerations.

For the student encountering the concept of due process for the first time, a useful method for grasping its real meaning is to think of it as a restriction on the government's right to treat citizens in a "fundamentally unfair" way. If a law that requires only fundamental fairness strikes the student as being particularly susceptible to interpretations varying directly with the political philosophy of the members of the Supreme Court, it is an indication that he is beginning to understand the due process clause.

Procedures that may appear fundamentally unfair to a liberal Supreme Court justice may strike a conservative as necessary for the protection of society. For example, is it unfair to deny a criminal suspect an attorney at a lineup? Five Supreme Court justices said it was not. The remaining four believed it was.[5] The requirements of due process change

---

[5] Kirby v. Illinois 92 S.Ct. 1877, 121 Ill. App. 2d 323,257N.E.2d589 (1972).

from one generation to the next as courts continue to evaluate and refine the procedures used in American criminal prosecutions.

Adding to the confusion surrounding the due process concept is the fact that the term itself appears not once but twice in the Constitution. In the Fifth Amendment the federal government is enjoined from denying a citizen ". . . life, liberty, or property, without due process of law." In the Fourteenth Amendment the state governments are subjected to an identical prohibition. The question that arises from this duplication is whether or not the authors of these two amendments—separated as they were by four generations—intended to place identical restrictions on both federal and state governments. A brief examination of the history of civil liberties and of the cases in which the courts have used the due process clause to evaluate the criminal procedures of the various states will help to answer this question.

Civil Liberties

If the history of American civil liberties were divided into two equal parts it would probably not be an exaggeration to make the first half encompass the years between the passage of the Bill of Rights in 1791 and the Supreme Court case of *Mapp* v. *Ohio* in 1961. The second half would begin with *Mapp* and continue through today. What has happened in such a short period of time that would warrant so much attention being given the development of civil liberties in recent years?

"From the 1960–1961 term through the 1968–1969 term—with the Fourteenth Amendment as a lever—nearly all the guarantees of the Fourth, Fifth, and Sixth Amendments have been made binding on the states. At the same time, numerous U.S. Supreme Court decisions have strengthened these guarantees. The Court's extension of the mantle of federal protection to persons accused in state criminal proceedings, and its bolstering of these protections, have brought about dramatic changes in the criminal law."[6] Perhaps the most dramatic of these changes came in the Fourth Amendment.

Searches and Seizures. The Fourth Amendment prohibits federal officers from conducting unreasonable searches—searches not based on probable

---

[6] Editors of the *Criminal Law Reporter*, "The Criminal Law Revolution" (Washington, D.C.: Bureau of National Affairs, 1969).

cause. In 1948 the Supreme Court heard the case of *Wolf* v. *Colorado*[7] and refused to exclude illegally seized evidence from state courts. Then came *Mapp* v. *Ohio*.[8]

In 1961 Doll Ree Mapp was suspected of harboring a fugitive in her apartment. Cleveland police searched her apartment without a warrant, seized obscene material, and sought to introduce it against her in court. Her attorney argued that the Fourth Amendment protected Mrs. Mapp against unreasonable searches by state officers, and that the court should exclude all evidence illegally seized, as was done in federal courts.[9] The U.S. Supreme Court overruled *Wolf* and said that the due process clause of the Fourteenth Amendment required that the provisions of the Fourth Amendment be applied to the states. Since the court had previously held that illegally seized evidence must be excluded from trial, the obscene material could not be used against Mrs. Mapp. That is, the court held that to allow the state to use evidence that had been illegally seized was fundamentally unfair.

During the decade following *Mapp*, numerous other Supreme Court decisions refined the interpretation of the Fourth Amendment. Evidence seized through wiretapping was held to fall within the protection of the Fourth Amendment, and strict standards for obtaining a warrant to wiretap were enunciated by the court.[10]

The right of police to search an impounded vehicle without a warrant was scrutinized by the court.[11] The right of privacy guaranteed by the Fourth Amendment was used to strike down state laws concerning both birth control[12] and abortion.[13] The area that may be searched during a search incident to an arrest was limited by the court in the case of *Chimel* v. *California*.[14] In that case the court reasoned that since the justification for allowing a warrantless search during an arrest stemmed from the need of law enforcement to prevent the suspect from destroying

---

[7] Wolf v. Colorado 338 U.S.25, 93L.Ed.1782,69S.Ct.1359 (1949).
[8] Mapp v. Ohio, 367 U.S. 643, 81 S.Ct. 1684, 6L.Ed. 2d. 1081 (1961).
[9] Weeks v. U.S., 232 U.S. 383, 34S. Ct. 341, 58 L. Ed. 652 (1914).
[10] Katz v. U.S., 389 U.S. 347, 88 S.Ct. 507, 16 L.Ed. 2d. 576 (1967).
[11] Chambers v. Moroney, 399 U.S. 42, 26 L.Ed. (2d) 419, 20 S.Ct. 1975 (1970).
[12] Griswold v. Connecticut, 381 U.S.479, 85 S.Ct. 1678, 14 L.Ed. 2d. 510 (1965).
[13] Roe v. Wade 93 S.Ct. 705 (1973).
[14] Chimel v. California, 395 U.S. 752, 23 L.Ed. (2d) 685, 89 S.Ct. 2034 (1969).

evidence or securing a weapon, the police should be limited in their search to that area into which the suspect could possibly lunge.

The Fourth Amendment was also used during the 1960s to challenge the constitutionality of a common police practice known as stop-and-frisk. The question asked was, "Does a police officer have the right to stop anyone, anytime, and question him in the absence of enough information to justify his arrest?" Put another way, the question is, "Does an American citizen have the right to ignore a police officer's questions and walk away?" If he does not have the right to walk away, will the courts assume that an illegal arrest has been made? If the arrest is illegal, of course, evidence found in an incidental search will be excluded from the trial. Commenting on the stop-and-frisk "field interview" the American Bar Foundation said: "Such detentions are authorized by the Uniform Arrest Act . . . but there is no agreement on the desirability or constitutionality of such an enactment."[15]

In 1967 most police officers assumed they had the right to stop and frisk suspicious persons even if they lacked probable cause for arrest. Most civil libertarians assumed that in such situations they had the right to either be arrested or walk away. The argument reached the Supreme Court in the case of *Terry* v. *Ohio*.[16]

Writing for the majority, Chief Justice Warren sustained the right of police to stop and frisk suspects. "Where a police officer," he states, "observes unusual conduct which leads him reasonably to conclude in light of his experience that criminal activity may be afoot and that the persons with whom he is dealing may be armed and presently dangerous,"[17] he is justified in stopping and patting down the outer clothing for weapons.

While allowing the stop-and-frisk procedure the court made it clear that the purpose of the frisk was for the police officer's protection and not the pursuit of evidence of a crime. A search that goes beyond a protective pat-down is still a violation of the Fourth Amendment, and evidence found during the search will be excluded from the trial.

Self-Incrimination. The history of the Supreme Court's application of the

---

[15] Wayne LaFave, *Arrest: The Decision to Take a Suspect into Custody* (Chicago: Little, Brown, 1965).
[16] Terry v. Ohio, 392 U.S. 1, 20 L.Ed. 2d 889 88 S.Ct. 1868 (1968).
[17] Ibid.

Fifth Amendment's self-incrimination clause to the states starts with the 1936 case of *Brown* v. *Mississippi*.[18] In that case a black defendant was beaten by sheriff's deputies until he confessed. In reviewing the case the Supreme Court held that the due process clause required that a confession coerced in such a manner be excluded from trial. The justification for this exclusion was that coerced confessions were frequently untrue, having been prompted by fear instead of remorse. If a confession can be said to be given freely and voluntarily, then it will be admissible. The difficult question, of course, is deciding the issue of voluntariness. In 1958 the court found a confession involuntary where a 19-year-old murder suspect was held incommunicado for three days and told there was a mob outside who wanted to "get him."[19] The following year the court rejected another confession given by a suspect after he had been refused an attorney, questioned in relays for eight hours, and told that his friend would be fired from the New York City police department if he did not confess.[20]

In *Culombe* v. *Connecticut*[21] the state sought to introduce a confession signed by the defendant after four days of lengthy interrogation. Culombe had not been arraigned, had been refused an attorney, and had been confronted by his wife and sick child during the custodial interrogation. In rejecting the Culombe confession the Supreme Court underlined the fact that the mere absence of physical coercion is not enough to render a confession voluntary. The court discussed the "psychological coercion" present in this case and concluded that at the time of signing the confession "it is clear that this man's will was broken. . . ." It was the court's search for such subtle coercion that brought it to what was unquestionably the most controversial decision during the 1960s, *Miranda* v. *Arizona*.[22]

Ernesto Miranda was arrested by Phoenix police on March 13, 1963 and charged with kidnapping and rape. He was questioned for two hours, after which he signed a written confession. The police used neither force nor threats of bodily harm. The confession was used at the jury trial over Miranda's objection. After conviction on both counts, Miranda

[18] Brown v. Mississippi, 297 U.S. 278, 80 L.Ed. 682 (1936).
[19] Payne v. State, 365 U.S. 560, 2L.Ed. (2d) 975, 78 S.Ct. 844 (1958).
[20] Spano v. New York, 360 U.S. 315 (1959).
[21] Culombe v. Connecticut, 367 U.S. 568, 6L.Ed. (2d) 1037, 81 S.Ct. 1860 (1961).
[22] Miranda v. Arizona, 384 U.S. 436, 86 S.Ct. 1602, 16 L. Ed. 2d 694 (1966).

appealed to the Arizona Supreme Court, which affirmed. The U.S. Supreme Court granted *certiorari* (a writ calling for the record of the lower court for review) and heard the case along with three other similar cases in the spring term of 1966. The court held that the admission of Miranda's confession violated both the self-incrimination clause of the Fifth Amendment and the right to counsel guaranteed by the Sixth Amendment. The essence of the *Miranda* rationale is that the Fifth and Sixth Amendments reach into the station house and that all suspects must be advised of their rights under the Constitution. Even where no active steps are taken to coerce a confession, a defendant who does not know his rights may feel compelled to answer incriminating questions. Steps must be taken by the police to guarantee that the defendant's confession is not a product of this compulsion. The court itemized what it considered "adequate protective devices" and introduced what have come to be called the Miranda Warnings—that the defendant be informed before interrogation that he has a right to remain silent, that anything he says can be used against him, that he has a right to an attorney, and that if he cannot afford an attorney one will be appointed for him.

The public response to the *Miranda* decision was overwhelming, in contrast to the usual public apathy toward Supreme Court decisions. The Omnibus Crime Control and Safe Streets Act was working its way through the Congress at the time and "by the time the bill was passed several controversial amendments were added embodying the increasing concern with law and order."[23] One of these amendments dealt with the Miranda Warnings and can be viewed as a legislative attempt to overrule a Supreme Court decision.

Section 3501 of the Omnibus Crime Control Act provides that even if the Miranda Warnings have not been given, a judge may decide that the confession was freely and voluntarily given and admit it over the defendant's objection. The constitutionality of this statute has not been tested. Even though it is a federal statute it is clear that if this procedure is constitutional in a federal court then it is constituional in state courts.

Ultimately, the Supreme Court will rule on this provision and the future application of the *Miranda* decision will be made clear. In the

[23] Richard Quinney, *The Social Reality of Crime* (Boston: Little, Brown, 1970), p. 311.

interim, the best policy for police on federal and state levels is to continue giving the warnings and to avoid the possibility of having a confession excluded.

The Right to Counsel. The Sixth Amendment guarantees the right to a speedy and public trial, compulsory process for the defendant, jury trials, confrontation by witnesses, and the assistance of counsel. The last of these rights—the right to assistance of counsel—has had the most far-reaching effect on the criminal justice system. In interpreting the right to assistance of counsel, the first question asked by American jurists is whether counsel was "required" or simply "permitted." If an indigent could not afford an attorney, did the Sixth Amendment require that the government provide him with one or did it simply guarantee his right to hire an attorney—a somewhat empty right under the circumstances.

In 1932 the Supreme Court ruled that in state criminal cases involving the possibility of capital punishment, an indigent must be represented by court-appointed counsel.[24] Six years later the Court ruled that in federal courts an attorney must be appointed to assist any defendant charged with a felony.[25] The question of court-appointed counsel in noncapital state cases was temporarily resolved in 1942 when the Court ruled that the Sixth Amendment did not require counsel in such cases and that the Fourteenth Amendment's due process clause was not offended by the absence of an attorney.[26]

Twenty-one years later the Court considered the case of *Gideon* v. *Wainwright*[27] and reversed its earlier decision regarding noncapital state cases. Gideon was an indigent charged with breaking and entering, a felony under Florida law. His request for counsel was refused and he was convicted. In reversing his conviction the Supreme Court stated, "The right of one charged with crime to counsel may not be deemed fundamental and essential to fair trial in some countries, but it is in ours."[28] Anyone charged with a felony anywhere in the country was thereby guaranteed the assistance of counsel. In interpreting the due process clause of the Fourteenth Amendment and the Sixth Amendment's guarantees of

---

[24] Powell v. Alabama, 287 U.S. 45, 77 L.Ed. 158, 53 S.Ct. 55 (1932).
[25] Johnson v. Zerbot, 304 U.S. 458, 58S.Ct. 1019, 82 L.Ed. 1461 (1938).
[26] Betts v. Brady, 316 U.S. 455, 86 L.Ed. 1595, 62 S.Ct. 1252 (1942).
[27] Gideon v. Wainwright, 372 U.S. 335, 83 S.Ct. 792, 9 L.Ed. 2d. 799 (1963).
[28] Gideon v. Wainwright, 372 U.S. 335, 83 S.Ct. 792, 9 L.Ed. 2d. 799 (1963).

counsel, the court concluded that it would be fundamentally unfair to convict someone for a felony without offering him the assistance of counsel.

But what of misdemeanors? Every day hundreds of indigents are sentenced to county jail after conviction of a misdemeanor. Are they not entitled to court-appointed counsel? In 1972 the court considered the case of *Argersinger* v. *Hamlin* and ruled that "absent a knowing and intelligent waiver, no person may be imprisoned for any offense, whether classified as petty, misdemeanor, or felony, unless he was represented by counsel at his trial."[29] The circumstances under which a defendant is entitled to be represented by counsel are clear: if a conviction could result in a jail sentence and the indigent has not waived his constitutional rights, he must be given a court-appointed attorney.

A more difficult problem for the Court has been the question of deciding when, in the criminal prosecution process, the right to an attorney attaches. In the landmark case of *Escobedo* v. *Illinois*, the Court held that counsel should be made available to a criminal suspect at the earliest possible point in the prosecution. "Where . . . the investigation is no longer a general inquiry into an unsolved crime," wrote Justice Goldberg for the majority, "but has begun to focus on a particular suspect," that suspect has the right to an attorney.[30] Lawyers and judges may spend hours debating at what point the investigation began to focus on the suspect. Police officers do not often have hours to spend in debate, and must frequently make crucial judicial decisions in a matter of seconds. The *Escobedo* ruling may well have resulted in widespread uncertainty among police officers making arrests had it not been for the *Miranda* decision, which more clearly spelled out the ground rules. Today, the distinction between investigatory interviews and custodial interrogations is more apparent than at the time of the *Escobedo* case, and so long as the Miranda Warnings are given prior to interrogation, the Sixth Amendment is complied with.

Cruel and Unusual Punishment. The Eighth Amendment prohibits cruel and unusual punishment. This guarantee—like the guarantee of due process—retains a certain vagueness that allows a wide range of interpretation. Punishment that one court may feel is cruel and unusual may

---

[29] Argersinger v. Hamlin, 92 S.Ct. 2006 (1972).
[30] Escobedo v. Illinois, 378 U.S. 478, 12 L.Ed. (2d.) 977, 84 S.Ct. 1758 (1964).

be accepted as necessary in another court. Writing for the majority in *Robinson* v. *California*, Justice Stewart argued that laws prohibiting drug addiction were unconstitutional because "in the light of contemporary human knowledge, a law which made a criminal offense of a disease would doubtless be universally thought to be an infliction of cruel and unusual punishment·"[31] Seven years later the court spoke again on cruel and unusual punishment and held, in *Powell* v. *Texas*, that chronic alcoholics can be sent to jail for being drunk in public.[32] The distinction between the *Robinson* and *Powell* cases is that in *Robinson* the statute sought to punish "status" and in *Powell* the statute punished "behavior," that is, being drunk in public. It is believed that alcoholism is a disease that renders its victims incapable of making responsible decisions. And yet a law that makes it a criminal offense to manifest the symptoms of this disease in public was not considered cruel and unusual punishment. The vagueness of the whole concept is readily apparent.

In the 1972 spring term the Supreme Court considered one of the most dramatic cases in history. Over 600 men throughout the country were awaiting execution for capital offenses. But all executions had been stopped in 1967 pending the outcome of the constitutional challenge being made on the death penalty itself. The argument of the petitioner in *Furman* v. *Georgia* was that capital punishment violated the Eighth Amendment, which is applicable to the state through the due process clause of the Fourteenth Amendment.[33] The Supreme Court agreed that the due process clause does incorporate the prohibition against cruel and unusual punishment and in a 5-4 decision—with nine separate opinions written—the court declared the *present* system of capital punishment (as practiced by the states) unconstitutional.

This decision does not mean that the death penalty will never again be used in our criminal justice system. Only three justices (Douglas, Brennan, and Marshall) argued that the death penalty is cruel and unusual per se. Justices Rehnquist, Powell, Blackmun, and Burger held the opposite view. The two remaining justices, White and Stewart, joined with the first three in opposing the death penalty, but only because of the unfair manner in which the death penalty was being administered by

[31] Robinson v. California, 370 U.S. 660, 82 S.Ct. 1417, 5 LEd. 2d. 758 (1962).
[32] Powell v. Texas, 392 U.S. 514, 20L.Ed. 2d 1254, 88 S.Ct. 2145 (1968).
[33] Furman v. Georgia, 92 S.Ct. 2726, 225Ga.253, 171S.E.2d501 (1972).

the states. If a state can devise a method of revising the inequities present in the imposition of the death penalty, there is no doubt that at least one of the swing voters would join the conservative wing of the Court and uphold its constitutionality. The method most commonly suggested is mandatory sentences of death on conviction of certain crimes. If all those convicted of capital crimes—rich and poor, black and white—are given the *same* sentence, then a majority of the Court will no doubt find the death penalty neither cruel nor unusual. Many state legislatures have already rewritten their capital offense statutes, and an early test of the revised rules of administering the death penalty is anticipated.

Civil Rights: An Example of Social Change Through Law

The controversy that accompanied the revolution in civil liberties during the 1960s has been overshadowed by (and often confused with) the revolutionary push for civil rights. Civil rights refers to the demands of minority groups for equal protection of the law through the elimination of racial, ethnic, and, more recently, sexist discrimination. An understanding of the historical development of civil rights legislation will better enable the student to understand the state of civil rights laws today and at the same time offer a good example of social change through law.

History of Civil Rights Laws

At the time of the Civil War, enslaved American blacks possessed virtually no legal rights. The rights that white Americans accepted as fundamental were denied to black Americans, who were denied the right to marry, to own property, to enter into contracts, or even to bring suit in a court of law. Since the law viewed them as the property of their white masters, there seemed no reason to extend to them the rights to which other Americans were entitled.

In the post-Civil War period, Americans ratified the Thirteenth, Fourteenth, and Fifteenth Amendments to the U.S. Constitution. The Thirteenth Amendment abolished slavery. The Fifteenth Amendment guaranteed suffrage to former slaves. In the Fourteenth Amendment all citizens were guaranteed equal protection of the law regardless of race, creed, or color, and states were prohibited from denying anyone life, liberty, or property without due process of law.

It was the federal guarantee of equal protection of the law, combined with the sociopolitical realities of the era, that gave rise to the odious doctrine of "separate but equal"—a legal principle on which racial discrimination would be justified for three generations. In the Supreme Court case of *Plessy* v. *Ferguson*[34] eight of the nine justices agreed that racially segregated schools did not violate the equal protection clause of the Fourteenth Amendment so long as both races were given equal facilities. The fact that, in reality, segregated facilities were never even close to being equal was ignored by the Court, and the quality of the public facilities available to a citizen often was determined by the color of his skin. "The great difference in quality of service for the two groups in transportation and education was merely the most obvious example of how segregation was an excuse for discrimination."[35] The Jim Crow laws that regulated the quasi-plantation world of black Americans throughout most of this century was undergirded by the separate-but-equal doctrine.

Brown versus the Separate-but-Equal Doctrine

In 1954 Leroy Brown was refused admission to a white school in Topeka, Kansas because he was black. The case was appealed to the Supreme Court. Brown's attorneys argued that separate schools for blacks were inherently unequal because of the implication of racial inferiority upon which such separation was based.[36] The court unanimously overruled the separate-but-equal doctrine and the civil rights revolution burst into full bloom.

Within a few years of the *Brown* case, numerous state segregation statutes were challenged in the courts and held to be unconstitutional. Segregation was outlawed in public parks, libraries, transportation facilities, hospitals, golf courses, beaches, and government-operated facilities. But the equal protection clause of the Fourteenth Amendment prohibited

---

[34] Plessy v. Ferguson, 163 U.S. 537 (1896).
[35] Gunnar Myrdal, *An American Dilemma* (New York: Harper & Row, 1944), p. 581.
[36] Brown v. Board of Education, 347 U.S. 483, 98 L.Ed. 873, 74 S.Ct. 686 (1954).

segregation by state law only. Segregation of races in privately owned businesses was still both constitutional and commonplace.

Once the civil rights movement had achieved all that it could in the courts, the need for new legislation became apparent. The Supreme Court had guaranteed black Americans the right to equal access to state facilities, but it could go no further in principle; it was now operating in full accord with the constitutional provisions for full equality. The Court found nothing in the Constitution that was violated by the widespread racial discrimination with which blacks lived from day to day.

Congress soon responded to the demand for equal treatment for blacks in the private sector. In 1964, the most important of all civil rights laws was passed by the Congress and signed into law by the President. Title II of the 1964 Civil Rights Act provides for equal access to certain public accommodations for all citizens. Title II makes it a federal crime for anyone to deny, on the basis of race, equal use of hotels, motels, restaurants, gas stations, theaters, sports stadiums, or any other privately owned facility that "affects interstate commerce." States rights politicians immediately argued that the federal government had no constitutional right to legislate against private discrimination. The courts, however, have held repeatedly that the commerce clause of Article I gives Congress the right to regulate any business that affects interstate commerce, and the constitutionality of Title II is no longer seriously questioned.

During the early days of the civil rights movement, many observers of American society argued that the problems of American blacks could not be resolved through changes in law. It is probably true that law alone is not enough to resolve complex social problems, but it is apparent today that the skeptics of a generation ago clearly underestimated the role that the law could play in dealing with racial problems. Through numerous court cases and favorable legislation, American blacks have taken substantial steps toward making equal opportunity a reality.

Student Checklist

1. Can you differentiate between the rule of law and the rule of man?
2. Are you able to identify the primary purpose of law in a democracy?

3. Can you list three means of changing the law?
4. Can you list the guarantees that certain rights cannot be abridged as set forth in the Bill of Rights?
5. Are you able to identify the landmark legal decisions that have refined the interpretation of the Fourth Amendment?
6. Can you identify the major cases that have applied to the states in the Fifth Amendment's self-incrimination clause?
7. Can you trace the legal history that provides for the accused's right to counsel?

Topics for Discussion

1. Discuss the problems in balancing the rights of society and the rights of the individual.
2. Discuss the difficulties in developing a precise definition of due process.
3. Discuss social change through law with special reference to civil rights.
4. Discuss the advantage of rule by law.
5. Discuss the Bill of Rights.

ANNOTATED BIBLIOGRAPHY

Coffey, Eldefonse, and Hartinger. *Human Relations: Law Enforcement in a Changing Community* (Englewood Cliffs, N.J.: Prentice-Hall, 1971). The traditional relationship of law enforcement personnel and the community they serve is analyzed. The problems of social transition, crime prevention programs, and racial tensions with police are explored.

Editors of the Criminal Law Reporter. *The Criminal Law Revolution* (Washington, D.C.: Bureau of National Affairs, 1969). A short, concise presentation of the S.C. cases dealing with criminal procedures that were handed down during the turbulent decade of the 1960s.

Lamb, Karl. *The People Maybe: Seeking Democracy in America* (Belmont, Calif.: Wadsworth Publishing, 1971). The author confronts the events of contemporary American politics and concludes that there is reason to hope. He examines the more ignoble features of the American tradition in the hope that such examination may help us avoid the repetition of yesterday's mistakes.

LeFave, Wayne. *Arrest: The Decision To Take A Suspect Into Custody* (Chicago: Little, Brown, 1965). One of a series of works published by the American Bar Foundation, this book examines in detail the numerous factors which go into—or should go into a police officer's decision to make an arrest.

Myrdal, Gunnar. *An American Dilemma* (New York: Harper & Row, 1944). This classic work on the American black presents an in-depth analysis of the racial problems that have faced the United States from its inception. The author approaches his subject from the standpoint of a sociologist and with the detached objectivity of a foreigner.

More, Harry W. *Critical Issues in Law Enforcement* (Cincinnati: W. H. Anderson, 1972). The author examines the perennial problems facing police and objectively suggests some solutions. Civil disobedience, police professionalization, ethnic tensions, and the delicate role of police in a democratic society are all perceptively discussed.

Quinney, Richard. *The Social Reality of Crime* (Boston: Little, Brown, 1970). The author takes a fresh look at the delicate balance between the ideals of justice and individual freedom. His "new" orientation to criminology includes discussion of how criminal definitions are formulated and applied, how behavior patterns develop in relation to criminal definitions, and how criminal conceptions are constructed.

The study of this chapter will enable you to:

1. Compare the views of justice as perceived by the various practitioners of the legal system.
2. Define the term "crime."
3. Identify the ultimate goal of police investigations.
4. List the events that occur at a booking.
5. Identify the contents of an information.
6. Identify the responsibilities of a magistrate at the initial presentment.
7. List the elements of a Miranda Warning.
8. Identify the plea options available to the accused at an arraignment.
9. List the types of pretrial motions available to a defense attorney.

3

The Justice Process

Justice: A Confusing Concept

Justice is a concept that has defied a uniform definition. This may be an unintended benefit, because if justice meant the same thing to everyone, the concept would be static. Because justice is so essential to the American way of life, it must be in a constant state of change if it is to keep pace with society's everchanging value system.

Theoretically, American justice implies a system for insuring that the laws governing our land are applied and upheld in a fair and impartial manner for all, regardless of age, sex, religion, wealth, or national origin. It is the ultimate, Utopian goal for those who administer the American legal system. Similarly, the average citizen must view justice as the hub of our nation's legal process. Mankind must be concerned with the fact that if the legal system does not function with a sense of dignity, equality, and consistency, if it does not reflect the expectations of society, then all hope of receiving justice through the law is lost.

The Fourteenth Amendment to the Constitution holds that, ". . . nor shall any state deprive any person of life, liberty, or property, without due process of law; nor deny to any person within its jurisdiction the equal protection of the laws." Although the Constitution is regarded primarily as a legal document, the social goals of its authors are reflected in its content. The document would appear to suggest ideals for future social control or what "should be," instead of "what was" at the time it was written. It is doubtful that the framers of the Constitution expected automatic equality under the law simply because the document proposed it. As a matter of fact, some of them would not sign the document until the first ten amendments were included. Just as we attempt to constantly interpret the meaning of equality as stated in the Constitution, so will future generations of Americans interpret, modify, and change the understanding of the concept. There will always be attempts to reach a state of total equality, or "pure" justice.

Equality under the law for all is still an unfulfilled dream for many Americans. In reality, what we have in this country might be likened to George Orwell's comment in *Animal Farm* that "all animals are equal but some animals are more equal than others."

No one can deny that many injustices exist in our scheme of justice. Stuart Nagel has stated that:

> *Justice . . . may have a blindfold, but it may also have a price, a complexion, a location, and even age and sex; and those with enough money, the right complexion, in the right court, and even sometimes of the right age and the right sex, can often get better treatment. The "least equal" in America are generally those the Fourteenth Amendment was apparently designed specifically to protect—the Negro, the poor, and the ignorant.*[1]

The Supreme Court in 1956, after reviewing the case of *Griffin* v. *Illinois*, stated that "There can be no equal justice where the kind of trial a man gets depends on the amount of money he has."[2] A 1963 report vividly pointed out how "ability to pay" may affect the quality of justice received from time of arrest through postconviction appeals.[3]

Justice: The Citizen's Viewpoint

Justice is really what each of us thinks it is or should be. Our personal definitions largely depend on our knowledge of the legal system and whether we are law-abiding citizens or criminal offenders.

To the victim of a crime, justice can probably best be equated with the phrase "law and order." His point of view would invariably suggest that—since crime is a violation of law—if justice exists in reality,

[1] Stuart S. Nagel, "The Tipped Scales of American Justice," in *The Scales of Justice*, Abraham S. Blumberg, ed. (Chicago: Aldine, 1970), p. 32.
[2] Griffin v. Illinois, 351 U.S. 12, 76 S.Ct. 585, 100 L.Ed. 891 (1956).
[3] Attorney General's Committee on Poverty and the Administration of Federal Criminal Justice, *Poverty and the Administration of Federal Criminal Justice* (Washington, D.C.: U.S. Govt. Printing Office, 1963), pp. 1-11.

the offender should be convicted and punished. In short, the victim seeks some type of punishment because it is symbolic of justice.

The perpetrator of the crime quite likely holds a different view of justice. Only if he is treated fairly and impartially (but, above all, is acquitted or receives some type of nonpunitive disposition), is justice a reality to the accused.

To practitioners of the legal system involved in a criminal case, justice has a meaning that can differ with their respective roles. The arresting police officer insures justice to the public by placing the offender in custody. Because the prosecuting attorney represents the public and, therefore, the victim, he is most interested in receiving a conviction should the case go to trial. If no trial results, justice might best be served by securing a guilty plea to a reduced charge. The defense attorney would be most pleased with getting the case dismissed, the charge reduced, or with a finding of not guilty. Even if he is successful only in getting a reduced charge, he feels that some form of justice has been insured for his client.

Role-playing and societal expectations have all served as important factors in shaping the various perspectives of justice; each participant is totally committed to his respective role. Perhaps the only person who can be objective in the matter is the magistrate or judge assigned to hear the controversy. But, as expressed by Jerome Frank:

> The influences operating on a particular trial judge when he is listening to and observing witnesses cannot be neatly caged within the categories of his fairly obvious social, economic, and political views. . . . When it comes to "finding" the "facts" in lawsuits where the oral testimony is in conflict, these obscure idiosyncrasies (psychological) in the trial judge are bafflingly at work. The judge's sympathies and antipathies are likely to be active with respect to the witnesses. His own past may have created plus or minus reactions to women, or blond women, or men with beards, or Southerners, or Italians, or Englishmen, or plumbers, or ministers, or college graduates, or Democrats. A certain facial twitch, a cough, or a gesture may start up memories, painful or pleasant. . . .[4]

Although personal definitions of justice differ, most laymen seem to have confidence that equality and fairness, in varying degrees, can be

[4] Jerome Frank, *Courts on Trial* (Princeton: Princeton University Press, 1950), p. 151.

found in the legal system. Those with the strongest reservations about the quality of justice meted out are usually those who actively work in the system or those who have violated a law, been apprehended and, as a result, have personally witnessed the judicial machinery at work.

The average person has scant familiarity with the functions of the many agencies that comprise the American criminal justice system. To have faith in something, even something as important as justice, does not necessarily require understanding. Our minds are "programmed" to believe that cases are disposed of only through trial by jury and, since jurors are selected on the basis of their supposed impartiality toward the crime and the defendant, the accused will theoretically receive that which is due him according to established law.

Probably few citizens are deeply concerned with, or interested in, what does or does not constitute justice. De Tocqueville said that man has the habit of considering himself as standing alone, as being an individualist. He tends to separate from others—feeling that his destiny is in his own hands. It is usually difficult to interest such a person in the affairs of his country because he is often reluctant to find out what effect the state can have on his and others' fates. Unfortunately, such public apathy—as described by De Tocqueville over 100 years ago—is still quite prevalent, although to a lesser degree.

Only when we feel threatened, or when a particular legal issue shocks our concept of right and wrong, do we express alarm. Capital punishment is a case in point. Even though the death penalty had not been used during the five years preceding the 1972 U.S. Supreme Court ruling, most people felt secure just knowing that the death penalty was "in the books." When the Court ruled that executions, as previously used, constituted "cruel and unusual punishment" according to the provisions of the Eighth Amendment, a majority of Americans expressed disbelief. In order to bring back this "most important" facet of justice so abruptly taken away, letters were written to representatives in government, polls were taken, elections held, and new laws were written to revitalize the death penalty.

Thus far we have discussed justice in theory and in reality. We have attempted to focus on justice and injustice both from individual and group perspectives. Now, what can be done to rebuild this legal system that many noted authorities say is on the verge of collapse?

In 1967, the President's Commission on Law Enforcement and

the Administration of Justice, after concluding detailed studies into all aspects of the criminal justice system in America, stated:

> One of our objectives is to eliminate injustices so that the system of criminal justice can win the respect and cooperation of all citizens. Our society must give the police, the courts, and correctional agencies the resources and the mandate to provide fair and dignified treatment for all.[5]

Ignorance and complacency will not alleviate the injustices within the legal system that so many have witnessed or read about. Many significant steps have been taken and are being taken to insure that every individual will receive fair treatment. John Hannah stated that equal justice under the law remains an ideal, not a reality and, for this, we should not apologize. He said that our concern should be directed to the size of the gap between the ideal and reality and the progress being made to close this gap.[6]

Entering the System

Through a complex maze of federal and state statutes and local ordinances, the American legal system seeks to prohibit certain forms of conduct that are detrimental to society as a whole. These laws not only define those acts that violate the statutes; they also prescribe the penalties to be imposed upon conviction. Adult violations of laws are called crimes or criminal acts. If juveniles are involved, the terms delinquency or delinquent acts are applied even though the same offenses, if committed by adults, would be termed crimes.

A crime is an *act or omission forbidden by law and made punishable upon conviction*. The type of punishment prescribed varies according to the seriousness and the circumstances of the offense. Normally,

---

[5] President's Commission on Law Enforcement and Administration of Justice, *The Challenge of Crime in a Free Society* (Washington, D.C.: U.S. Govt. Printing Office, 1967), p. viii.
[6] John A. Hannah, "Equal Protection Under Law—Fact or Fiction" in *Police and Community Relations: A Sourcebook*, A. F. Brandstatter and Louis A. Radelet, eds. (Beverly Hills: Glencoe Press, 1968), p. 16.

a felony conviction will result in imprisonment and/or a fine, while misdemeanors are punishable by fines and/or terms of up to one year in jail.

By definition, a crime can be committed. Arson, theft, and murder are examples of criminal acts. In addition, failure to act to prevent such crimes, when it is humanly possible to do so, may constitute a crime. Failure to file an income tax return or failure to register for the draft, when required by law, are acts of omission. Failure to provide food, clothing, shelter, and medical care for dependents is an act of omission that may be punishable. In such cases, the law states that there is an obligation to act. Failure to act may result in the filing of criminal charges, conviction, and punishment, even though no crime was "committed."

Investigation and Arrest

Once a crime is committed or alleged, law enforcement agencies conduct an investigation. The ultimate goal of any police investigation is the apprehension and arrest of the offender. Through arrest, the offender is ushered into the criminal justice system so that he may be held to answer the charges against him.

There are various methods by which police investigation of a criminal offense may be initiated. In a majority of all crimes committed, however, detailed investigations are not required because many violations are witnessed by a police officer. These offenses are generally misdemeanors, not felonies and, instead of being arrested, offenders are usually issued a *citation*.

A citation is often used instead of formal arrest for less serious offenses although, in some states, a citation may be issued by a police officer for more serious crimes. A citation notifies the offender of the time and place at which he is to appear to answer the charges against him. In misdemeanor cases, he will generally appear in a police or municipal court. After signing the citation, the offender is free to leave the presence of the police officer. It is this latter characteristic that distinguishes arrests from citations: an arrest results in the offender being taken into custody; a citation does not.

If the violator refuses to obey the conditions set forth in the citation, the magistrate of the court in which he was to appear may issue a misdemeanor warrant. Figure 3-1 is a sample warrant for arrest—for

Figure 3-1. Warrant for arrest—for misdemeanor. Courtesy of the Miami, Okla-homa Police Department.

NO._____

WARRANT FOR ARREST — FOR MISDEMEANOR

MUNICIPAL COURT — CITY OF

VS.

DEFENDANT: ADDRESS   CITY, STATE

_____

ISSUED _____ MONTH _____ DAY, 19____ FILED _____ MONTH _____ DAY, 19____

_____
Clerk of the Municipal Court

ANY SHERIFF, CONSTABLE, CHIEF OF POLICE, MARSHAL, OR POLICEMAN IN THE STATE OF

COMPLAINT UPON OATH HAVING BEEN THIS DAY MADE BEFORE THE MUNICIPAL COURT OF THE CITY

OF   IN   COUNTY, STATE OF   BY_____

_____ THAT THE OFFENSE OF SECTION_____, PARAGRAPH_____,

(DESCRIPTION _____) OF THE MUNICIPAL ORDINANCE OF THE CITY

OF   HAS BEEN COMMITTED AND ACCUSING THE ABOVE NAMED THEREOF.   YOU ARE THEREFORE

COMMANDED FORTHWITH TO ARREST THE DEFENDANT AND BRING HIM BEFORE SAID COURT FORTHWITH.

☐ A.M.
WITNESS MY HAND AT   THIS _____ MONTH _____ DAY, A.D., 19____ AT ____ ☐ P.M.

_____
Judge of the Municipal Court of the City of

SUPPLEMENTAL INFORMATION

Race	Sex	D. O. B.	Ht.	Wt.	D/L No.	State	Veh. Make	Yr.	Style	Color
Tag No.	Yr.	State	Employer		City			Employer Address		

OFFICER'S RETURN

STATE OF   COUNTY OF   CITY OF

I RECEIVED THIS WARRANT ON THE _____ DAY OF _____, 19____,
AND EXECUTED SAME BY ARRESTING THE ABOVE NAMED DEFENDANT, AND NOW HAVE HIS BODY IN
THE COURT BEFORE THE NAMED MUNICIPAL COURT OF THE CITY OF   AS HEREIN COMMANDED.

_____

_____
CHIEF OF POLICE

GOSNEY PTG. CO., INC.   BY _____ OFFICER

misdemeanor. This warrant authorizes any police officer in the state to arrest the offender and bring him into court. The magistrate may also mail a *bench warrant notice* to the violator. This notice informs the offender that a misdemeanor warrant has been issued and, in order to prevent the warrant from being served, he should contact the court at once. See Figure 3-2 for a sample bench warrant.

Any person who commits a felony in the presence of a police officer is generally placed under arrest. After informing the subject of his intention to make the arrest, the officer may use whatever force is reasonable under the circumstances to effect custody. There are no specific words an officer must use in making an arrest. He may say, "You're under arrest," or the arrest may be effected by the offender's submission to the apparent authority of the officer. There are instances when the

Figure 3-2. Bench warrant—misdemeanor or bailable felony. Courtesy of the Ottawa County, Oklahoma, District Attorney.

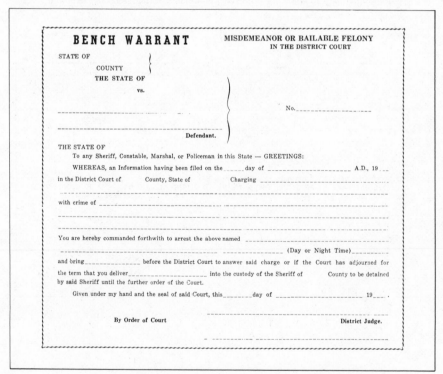

officer's intention to arrest cannot be communicated to the offender. For example, drunks, addicts, and those suffering from severe mental defects may not understand or be aware of their impending custody.

Complaints are frequently used in misdemeanor offenses not witnessed by a police officer. It has long been held that a policeman cannot make arrests for misdemeanors not committed in his presence.[7] For example, those apprehended for shoplifting can be taken into custody only if store personnel are willing to sign a complaint. The victim of assault and battery (a misdemeanor in most states) must sign a complaint if the perpetrator is to be taken into police custody. Even though an officer may see the actual results of the battery, he is powerless to act unless a complaint is signed and an arrest warrant is issued.

The *presence* requirement is not as restrictive as it might appear. A policeman can use any of the five senses to make warrantless felony or misdemeanor arrests. He may smell the distinct odor of marijuana or taste the bitterness of heroin. Counterfeit currency or coin may be detected through touch, or he may hear gambling information being transmitted on the telephone. In each instance, a crime is deemed as having been committed in his presence.

All police arrests must be based on *probable cause*. A specific definition of probable cause cannot be given, since it varies according to each crime. Generally, it is defined as a "set of circumstances or events which would cause the reasonable person to believe that a crime has been, is presently, or will be committed." Therefore, in order to make an arrest, the policeman need not possess evidence sufficient to convict the offender, but he must have more than mere suspicion. He cannot "think" that a person is engaged in some form of criminal activity. He must have reason to "know" that, in all likelihood, a particular person (as opposed to a number of individuals) is responsible. Particularly in cases of property crimes, and sometimes in regard to crimes against persons, probable cause is not easily established. For instance, police investigations initiated by an informant's tip may be conducted for weeks or months before sufficient evidence is available to make an arrest. Similar problems are often encountered when undercover officers are assigned to investigate such vice offenses as illegal abortion, gambling, narcotics, and liquor law violations. In fact, one of the most frustrating

---

[7] Garske v. United States, 1 F.2d 620 (8th Cir. 1924).

aspects of police work is to know that a particular person committed a crime, yet not be able to establish probable cause for his arrest.

Booking
The arrested offender is generally taken to a police department or precinct station for booking. Booking involves making a formal entry of the name of the violator; the date, time, and location of the offense; and the nature of the charges. The seriousness and type of crime committed will determine what, if any, other procedures are to accompany booking. Booking policy in some police departments requires that all felony offenders be fingerprinted and photographed. In specific cases such as embezzlement, forgery, and bookmaking, handwriting samples may be requested. A police *lineup* or *showup* may also be a part of booking. Mug shots, handwriting samples, and fingerprints are types of non-testimonial evidence. Therefore, the police are not violating the subject's Fifth Amendment rights regarding self-incrimination when they request his cooperation in securing these types of identification.[8]

There are times when the arrested person will be taken to the police department but not booked. Instead, certain types of *stationhouse adjustment* may be used. A commanding officer, upon reviewing the circumstances of an arrest, may decide that probable cause was questionable or that the evidence, while justifying the arrest, is too weak to present to the prosecuting attorney. In other instances, the police may determine, upon interrogation of the subject, that he did not, or could not, have committed the offense. There may be other times when the police feel that a verbal reprimand will correct a problem and that further legal proceedings are not required. In each of these instances, the subject is released from custody.

The Prosecution Decision
After booking, the arresting police officer will generally meet with the district attorney or his representative to review all evidence obtained in the case. The decision as to whether or not further legal action against

[8] "Compelling Nontestimonial Evidence by Court Order," *FBI Law Enforcement Bulletin, 40,* No. 2 (February 1971), pp. 21-31.

the accused is to be taken rests with the prosecuting attorney. If the police investigation has been lengthy or has involved complicated legal questions, the district attorney is probably already familiar with the case and knows what action is required. At other times, he must rely totally on the officer's investigation and arrest reports before making a decision.

It has been estimated that, in major cities, 30 to 50 percent of all offenders arrested for felonies and misdemeanors are not prosecuted. How many case dismissals are made by the police and how many are made by the prosecutor is difficult to determine. Surprisingly, the total dismissal rate for felonies is only slightly lower than for misdemeanors.[9] In smaller cities, lower caseloads and greater accessibility to the prosecutor's office promote more dialogue between police and the district attorney in the decision-making process. This is particularly true with the more serious felony charges.

There are many reasons why all cases brought to the attention of the district attorney are not prosecuted. Just as the police may release an offender after arrest, so might the prosecutor, in some instances, best carry out his function by not pressing charges. Offenses perpetrated by offenders suffering from mental disorders might best be disposed of by referral to a social agency. Addicts and alcoholics may be permitted to undergo treatment instead of prosecution. The President's Commission stated that:

> Among the types of cases in which thoughtful prosecutors commonly appear disinclined to seek criminal penalties are domestic disturbances; assaults and petty thefts in which victim and offender are in a family or social relationship; statutory rape when both boy and girl are young; first offense car thefts that involve teenagers taking a car for a short joyride; checks that are drawn upon insufficient funds; shoplifting by first offenders, particularly when restitution is made; and criminal acts that involve offenders suffering from emotional disorders short of legal insanity.[10]

Most district attorneys realize that more harm than good may result from invoking legal action in these, and other cases. An uncon-

[9] Livingston Hall, et al., *Modern Criminal Procedure* (St. Paul: West Publishing Company, 1969), p. 9.
[10] President's Commission on Law Enforcement and Administration of Justice, *Task Force Report: The Courts* (Washington, D.C.: U.S. Govt. Printing Office, 1967), p. 5.

trollable chain of events might be triggered by labeling someone a criminal—be he juvenile or adult. No one knows for certain how many inmates are in our nation's correctional institutions today as a result of having been convicted of some minor offense and, once having been subjected to imprisonment and exposed to other criminals, became repeat offenders.

Another reason for nonprosecution is that the district attorney may not have sufficient evidence to continue the case. Or, in cases involving lesser felonies, he may drop charges in exchange for information about other, more serious crimes. In addition, it is not at all unusual that witnesses to a crime suddenly become reluctant to reveal their knowledge of the case. At other times, the district attorney's major caseload is so time consuming that he often has to forego action on less serious matters.

These and other reasons help to explain why not all police arrests result in prosecutions. Although nontrial dispositions may be beneficial in certain cases, problems may occur when the offender is dropped out of the system. Invariably, because of the lack of community agencies available to deal with specific problems, the behavioral tendencies that led the offender to commit a crime will go untreated. The legal system is so involved with offenders remaining to be heard and tried that it neglects to care about or follow up on those whose cases were dismissed. Statistics indicate that those dismissed without treatment will probably be arrested for similar or more serious crimes at a later time.

In cases requiring prosecution, the district attorney prepares an *information* that cites the name of the offender and the charge, and is then signed by the complainant. If a police officer witnessed the crime or otherwise has established probable cause, he becomes the complaining witness. If a private citizen witnesses a crime, he may go directly to the district attorney, who will then prepare the information. As with misdemeanor complaints, the information must be sworn to by the complainant. A sample information is shown in Figure 3-3.

Once the information is signed, the prosecutor appears before a proper judicial officer for issuance of an arrest warrant. In some states, a judge can issue this warrant without the consent of the district attorney. Once the judge signs the warrant, any law enforcement officer in the state can arrest the offender and take him into custody. If the offender is already in custody, the warrant serves to authorize his continued detention pending further court proceedings.

Figure 3-3. An information. Courtesy of the Ottawa County, Oklahoma, District Attorney.

IN THE DISTRICT COURT IN AND FOR   COUNTY, STATE OF

THE STATE OF   Plaintiff

vs.   **INFORMATION**

.... Defendant   No.........................

IN THE NAME AND BY THE AUTHORITY OF THE STATE OF OKLAHOMA:

Now comes .... the duly qualified and acting District Attorney in and for .... County, State of .... and gives the District Court of said County and State to know and be informed that

did in said County and State, on or about the............day of .... in the year of our Lord, One Thousand Nine Hundred and.......................... and anterior to the presentment hereof, commit the crime of

in the matter and form as follows, to-wit:

contrary to the form of the statutes in such case made and provided, and against the peace and dignity of the State of Oklahoma.

STATE OF
County of

I,.......................... being first duly sworn, on oath state that I have read and know the contents of the foregoing information and the statements therein are true.

....
(Complaining Witness)

Subscribed and sworn to before me this .... day of .... 19......

.... District Judge

ENDORSEMENTS

.... **District Attorney**

By..........................
                Assistant District Attorney

the justice process   **63**

Initial Appearance

After booking, the accused is taken before a magistrate for the *initial appearance*. This step is sometimes referred to as the *initial presentment* or as the *arraignment on a warrant*. Technically speaking, it is not an arraignment because, in felony cases, no plea is entered to the charges at this point in the proceedings.

Guilty pleas are generally entered to misdemeanor charges, but if the subject wishes to plead not guilty, the magistrate may proceed with case disposition at this time if the arresting police officer is present. This allows a determination of guilt or innocence to be established at the time of the initial appearance. In other instances, the accused may request a delay in the misdemeanor case or even request a trial. The magistrate may allow or refuse the request for a continuance, depending on the reasons offered by the accused. When requested, the magistrate will set a trial date for the case.

In *McNabb* v. *United States*, the U.S. Supreme Court stated that it is the duty of the police to take any arrested person charged with a crime before the nearest available U.S. Commissioner (for federal crimes).[11] Later, in *Mallory* v. *United States*, the Court again said that arresting officers must conform to the Federal Rules of Criminal Procedure and individual state statutes by taking the arrested subject before the proper magistrate "without unnecessary delay."[12]

Although the Court seemed to imply that without unnecessary delay meant immediately, there are instances where short delays cannot be avoided. In larger cities, where substantial numbers of felony arrests are made daily, it may require some time to process all offenders through the booking procedure. Also, magistrates may not be available at all times, especially when arrests are made late at night or on weekends. In other instances, the accused may consent to undergo police questioning. This, too, will delay his initial appearance. The Court has agreed that certain police procedures are essential and that certain delays may be necessary. The Court's concern is that the police may delay the accused's appearance in court simply to extract a confession through coercion or duress.

Initial police reaction to the Court's decision to require more

[11] McNabb v. United States, 318 U.S. 332, 63 S.Ct. 608,87 L.Ed. 819 (1943).
[12] Mallory v. United States, 354 U.S. 449, 77 S.Ct. 1356, 1 L.Ed.2d 1479 (1957).

prompt appearances was generally negative. Officers skilled in eliciting information from various types of offenders felt that they had been stripped of a fundamental police tool.

At the initial presentment, the magistrate has the responsibility of establishing the identity of the accused, informing the accused of his constitutional rights, stating the charges, and fixing bail, if necessary.

The Miranda Warning requires that the accused be informed that he has the right to remain silent. If he does not remain silent, anything he says can be used against him in a court of law. He also has the right to be represented by counsel of his choice, and, if he cannot afford to hire a lawyer, one will be appointed to represent him at state expense. If the magistrate finds that the accused is indigent, he may appoint a lawyer at this time to handle the case.[13]

Probably the most important function of the magistrate at the initial appearance is to set bail when a *bailable offense* has been committed. Generally, all offenses are bailable, including (as a result of recent court decisions) capital crimes. Presently, no guidelines exist for determining how much money should be required to secure release on bail. In fact, there is some dispute as to whether money bail should be required at all. The Eighth Amendment states, in part, that excessive bail shall not be required. Court decisions have not clarified what excessive bail is, but it is generally considered to be an amount of money greater than that needed to insure that the accused will appear for trial. Most judges have bail schedules that cite minimum and maximum amounts required for each statutory crime. Such schedules are adhered to unless unusual circumstances accompany the crime.

In deciding whether or not to set bail, the judge must resolve several questions. Is the offender likely to flee (jump bail)? Is he a first offender or a recidivist and, if so, what types of crimes has he committed in the past? Is there any chance that he will attempt to interfere with witnesses against him? Is he a threat to the community?

The bail system was conceived as a method for preventing flight of the accused pending further criminal action. The rationale is that the offender, after posting a specified amount of bail money, will not risk forfeiting his bail by not appearing in court. The bail system has long been attacked because of the emphasis on money to secure release. The

---

[13] Miranda v. Arizona, 384 U.S. 436, 86 S.Ct. 1602, 16 L.Ed.2d 694 (1966).

offender who has no means for posting bail may seek a bondsman to obtain his release. If, for example, the bail was set at $2000, a bondsman would advance this amount for the accused. For this service, he would charge a commission of from 10 to 20 percent. When the defendant appears for trial, the bondsman's investment is returned by the court. The accused would still be indebted to him for $100 to 200, depending on the fee charged for the temporary use of the bondsman's money. This system, like bail, works a financial hardship on the indigent defendant. Even if eventually found innocent, he "pays the price" for his participation in the criminal justice system.[14] (See also Chapter 11 for a fuller discussion of the bail system.)

Preliminary Hearing

During the initial presentment, the magistrate will inform the defendant of his right to have a preliminary hearing. After meeting with appointed or retained counsel, the defendant and his attorney will discuss the case and decide whether or not to request this optional hearing. The accused may also waive his right to the hearing and be scheduled for arraignment where he will plead to the charges against him.

The purpose of the preliminary hearing is to determine if probable cause exists to hold the accused for trial. Courtroom participants at the hearing are the judge, defendant and counsel, the district attorney, and prosecution witnesses. The prosecutor has the *burden of proof* at the preliminary hearing. He must prove that a crime has been committed and that the accused probably committed the offense. To establish probable cause, the district attorney will call witnesses to the stand to testify. He will elicit information from them by direct examination. After direct examination, the defense attorney may cross-examine each witness.

From the defendant's viewpoint, the preliminary hearing is a pretrial glimpse of the prosecutor's case. His own attorney is at liberty to question any state witness, but is not required to reveal any of his witnesses, evidence, or defense tactics. This permits the defense to learn more about the strengths and weaknesses of the plaintiff's case in the event a trial ensues. Nor will the prosecutor enter all available evidence

[14] Suggestions for bail reform may be found in: American Bar Association, "Standards Relating to Pretrial Release," Institute of Judicial Administration, New York, Approved Draft, 1968.

or produce each witness at the preliminary hearing. He does not want to reveal his entire case to the opposition. Generally, those called to testify are the arresting police officer, several witnesses if needed, and perhaps the victim. The prosecutor may also wish to introduce fingerprints, lab reports, or other types of evidence that will assist in associating the offender with the crime. When reasonably certain that probable cause has been established, he will rest his case.

If the magistrate finds that probable cause is sufficient, he will have the accused *bound over* for trial in a court of competent jurisdiction. Failure to show probable cause will require that the case be dismissed and the accused freed. This does not mean that he can never be tried for the dismissed crime; he can be rearrested if additional evidence is secured.

Indictment and Presentment

The Fifth Amendment provides that, "no person shall be held to answer for a capital or otherwise infamous crime, unless on a presentment or indictment of a grand jury." Thus, by federal law and the laws of slightly more than one half of all states, probable cause to hold a person for trial must result from grand jury action. Infamous crimes requiring grand jury indictments include all offenses punishable by "imprisonment at hard labor in a state prison or penitentiary or other similar institution."[15]

A grand jury is an investigative body that has authority to return indictments or presentments upon a finding of probable cause. The number of persons serving on a grand jury is fixed by state statute. Some states require as few as 6 while others may require as many as 23.

Various methods exist for initiating a grand jury investigation into alleged criminal activity. A judge will order a grand jury to convene upon receiving a petition signed by a cetrain percentage of registered voters. Or, upon his own motion or the motion of the district attorney, a judge can order a grand jury to meet. Where grand juries are permanently established, they have the power to initiate their own investigations.

Upon meeting, the grand jury has responsibility for determining if probable cause exists to charge a person with a crime. The grand jury

---

[15] Ex parte Wilson, 114 U.S. 417, 5 S.Ct. 935, 29 L.Ed. 89 (1885).

may call witnesses—including the accused—to testify. When probable cause is established in actions ordered by a judge, the grand jury will return an *indictment* against the accused. In grand jury-initiated investigations, a *presentment* results from a finding of probable cause. With both indictments and presentments, there is no requirement that there be a unanimous finding of probable cause. As a general rule, approximately three-fourths of the quorum must find probable cause before an accused is charged. (Chapter 12 presents an in-depth discussion of the grand jury.)

An indictment or presentment states the name of the offender and the time, place, and nature of the crime. Subsequently, a warrant is issued for the arrest of the accused. When arrested, he is entitled to each of the procedural steps discussed thus far. However, for federal crimes, no preliminary hearing is held. Federal grand juries determine probable cause just as a judge would in state preliminary hearings.

Arraignment

Having been bound over for trial as a result of the preliminary hearing (or after waiving the preliminary), the accused appears in court for arraignment. At arraignment the offender enters a plea to the charges against him. Plea options that might be available to the accused are (1) guilty, (2) not guilty, (3) *nolo contendere* ("no contest"), and (4) not guilty by reason of insanity.

Plea of Guilty. A guilty plea will be accepted only when the judge has reason to believe that the defendant understands the charge he is pleading to, knows what acts constitute the particular offense, and has been made aware of the consequences of the plea. In short, the guilty plea must be made "knowingly" and "understandingly."

The guilty plea acknowledges complete responsibility for every material element (the *corpus delicti*) of the crime charged. Only when the judge senses that the plea is made as a result of force, coercion, or duress will it be refused. Also, judges in some states cannot accept a guilty plea in crimes where the potential punishment, upon conviction, is life imprisonment without possibility of parole. These cases must be presented at a jury trial.

Plea of Not Guilty. By pleading not guilty, the accused is denying responsibility for each material element of the crime charged in the indictment or information. This plea requires that a trial date be set to determine guilt or innocence.

Plea of Nolo Contendere. Nolo contendere, where allowed, is a plea of no contest to the criminal charges, but should a civil suit ever be filed as a result of the criminal act, the issue of guilt or innocence must be proven as though no plea had ever been made.

Plea of Insanity. The plea of insanity may require that one or two trials result, depending on the individual states. In some states the plea of not guilty is joined with "not guilty by reason of insanity." This plea requires two trials, the first to decide the issue of insanity and the second to decide the issue of guilt. If the defendant is found insane, he will be committed for treatment and no trial is necessary to decide guilt. However, if found sane at the first trial, a second trial is held to determine guilt. Only if found both sane and guilty may he be punished for the crime.

In other states, the question of insanity is determined at a single trial where the jury decides both the question of guilt and insanity. Disposition of the offender is the same as mentioned under the dual (bifurcated) trial system discussed above.

Plea Bargaining

Very few defendants ever go to trial. In most jurisdictions, a majority of felony cases are resolved through *plea bargaining* (see Chapter 7). Plea bargaining, or the "negotiated plea," is a cooperative venture between the defense and district attorney. Generally, the prosecuting attorney agrees to reduce the charges against the accused in exchange for a guilty plea. In other cases he will agree to recommend a more lenient sentence if the defendant pleads guilty. The prosecutor may also agree to drop all charges if, in return, the accused will agree to become a witness for the plaintiff against codefendants or in some other pending case. Plea bargaining is viewed as an indispensable method for clearing crowded court dockets. It is, however, not without its faults.

Pretrial Motions

Prior to entering a plea at arraignment, the defense attorney may file a *motion to quash* the indictment or information. The *motion to dismiss* is used in federal proceedings. The motion to quash is used when the indictment or information is not filed as outlined in the statutes; when the grand jury was improperly selected; if the crime charged is not punishable in the state; or when the charge is filed in a court that does not have proper jurisdiction.

When additional time is needed to prepare the case, the defense attorney may request a *continuance*. A continuance is sought when key witnesses will not be available; when pretrial publicity may have temporarily caused prejudice toward the defendant; or when the defendant is unable to stand trial because of some physical or mental defect. Where good cause is shown, the judge may reschedule the proceedings at a later date.

A motion for a *change of venue* is requested when the defense feels that pretrial publicity and the nature of the crime would make it impossible to select a fair and impartial jury in the location where the trial is to be held. Through this motion he is asking the court to move the trial to a site where a fair trial can be conducted.

The *demurrer* is filed to challenge either the indictment, the information, or the evidence presented against the accused. This motion will be sustained when the indictment or information is defective; if more than one offense is charged; or if the facts as stated do not constitute a public offense. In cases where the evidence against the accused is true, but does not constitute a crime, the demurrer is filed with the court.

Trial

The defendant may be tried by the court or by jury. In some states, court trials are prohibited in capital cases: the accused must be tried by a jury of his peers. Waiving a jury trial might be advantageous when the defense feels that a jury of peers cannot be selected, or when the evidence and motions to be presented are so complicated that only the judge would be able to understand the proceedings.

A jury trial begins with the selection of jurists. As required, names of prospective jurors are selected at random from lists of those who have paid personal property taxes or those registered to vote. One may be called to jury service if he meets certain age and residency requirements, if he has not been convicted of a felony, and if his occupation is not so crucial that it would prevent him from serving.

The number of jurors to be selected to hear a case varies from state to state. Six- and twelve-member panels are most common. In *Williams* v. *Florida* the U.S. Supreme Court held that the twelve-man panel is not a necessary ingredient of trial by jury."[16]

Because prospective jurists may be disqualified by various attorney *challenges*, more are asked to appear in court than actually will be needed once the first evidence is presented. Upon appearance in court, a specified number of jurists will be called to take their seats in the jury box. Names of those initially called are selected at random from a tumbler containing names of all prospective jurors. After taking an oath, the first six or twelve jurists called undergo *voir dire* ("to speak or tell the truth") examination. Jurists are asked to tell the truth about their possible knowledge of the crime, or whether they know either counsel, the defendant, any witness, or the arresting police officer. Questions may be directed toward discovery of prejudices toward the defendant or the type of crime committed.

If either attorney suspects bias or prejudice within a prospective juror, or that a juror may have knowledge of the crime or its participants, he may ask the court to excuse the juror for cause. These *challenges for cause* are unlimited. So long as the attorney can show the court reasons why a particular juror could not be fair and impartial, the judge may excuse that person from serving on the panel. When excused, the jury seat vacated will be filled by the random selection of another name from among those remaining. After all jurors have been questioned and approved by opposing counsel, they are *passed for cause*.

Even though jurists are passed for cause, they can still be removed from hearing the case. Both defense and prosecution have an equal number of *peremptory challenges*. The number is specified by state statute and varies according to whether the crime charged is a misdemeanor, felony, or capital crime. Peremptory challenges require no showing of cause. A juror can be excused for no more reason than that counsel does not like his attitude, the way he parts his hair, the clothes he is wearing, or the shade of lipstick worn by a certain woman! The purpose of the challenges is to secure a fair and impartial jury that represents the defendant's peers. Theoretically, the panel that is eventually sworn to hear the case is balanced; half are favorable to the defendant and half to the prosecution.

---

[16] Williams v. Florida, 399 U.S. 78, 90 S.Ct. 1893, 26 L.Ed.2d 446 (1970).

After the jury is sworn, presentation of evidence begins. First, the district attorney is afforded the opportunity to make a brief opening statement to the jury. He will outline the plaintiff's case and reveal what proof of guilt will be presented. Next, the defense may give his opening statement. Usually, however, he will delay this statement until that point in the trial when his evidence and testimony is presented. In some jurisdictions, the defense must wait until the prosecution has rested its case before an opening statement can be made.

The plaintiff presents evidence first. Each witness called to the stand to testify will undergo *direct examination* after which the defense will *cross-examine*. The purpose of direct examination is to elicit testimony that will probably be favorable to the plaintiff. In a criminal case, this is an attempt to show the defendant's guilt beyond a reasonable doubt, not by a mere preponderance of evidence. Cross-examination is used to discredit the witnesses' testimony. Counsel will try to weaken or discredit evidence that is damaging to his side of the litigation. *Redirect examination* is used to rebuild testimony discredited by cross-examination. *Recross-examination* may follow the redirect.

The district attorney will rest his case after each of his witnesses has testified. Then the defense attorney may make his opening statement, but, as a rule, this is preceded by a *motion for judgment of acquittal* or a *demurrer to the evidence*. The motion or the demurrer may have some foundation, but they are generally strategy moves by the defense. They are used to cast doubt on the prosecution's case. In effect, the defense counsel is saying, "To this point the district attorney has not proven my client guilty beyond a reasonable doubt. If this is all the evidence he has, the court has no recourse but to dismiss the charges."

Normally, the motion for acquittal and the demurrer are overruled. If so, the defense will proceed with his opening statement and presentation of evidence. Defense witnesses undergo direct and redirect examination by the defense attorney and cross- and recross-examination by the district attorney.

At the conclusion of defense evidence and testimony, the judge will *charge the jury*. The statute defining the crime as charged will be read, and instructions will be given as to how a verdict is to be reached based on the evidence presented. In those states where juries have responsibility for recommending a sentence upon reaching a guilty verdict, they will be briefed on the punishment for the crime.

After the jury has been instructed, or charged, the prosecutor will present his *summation* (closing argument). When finished, the defense will make his final statement. A brief closing remark may then be made by the district attorney. Closing arguments are refresher courses for the jury. Each side explains which testimony or evidence has proven guilt or innocence. Attempts are also made to show the shortcomings of certain evidence or inconsistencies in testimony offered by opposition witnesses. Once all instructions have been given and the closing arguments presented, the jury retires to the jury deliberation room.

Laws of most states still require that a unanimous verdict be reached before a defendant can be convicted or acquitted. However, in *Apodaca* v. *Oregon*, the U.S. Supreme Court ruled that the Sixth Amendment, made applicable to the states by the Fourteenth, does not require jury unanimity. In his concurring opinion, Associate Justice White commented that, "Requiring unanimity would obviously produce hung juries in some situations where nonunanimous juries will convict or acquit."[17] If a verdict agreement cannot be reached after all sincere efforts to break the deadlock have been exhausted, the result is a *hung jury*. A hung jury necessitates a new trial with a different jury and judge. Testimony and evidence must be presented again in their entirety.

A jury vote of not guilty means that the accused will be released from custody and can never be tried again for the same crime. If found guilty or convicted, the accused will be held in custody or, in some instances, released on bail pending sentencing.

Sentencing
After pleading guilty to the charges at arraignment or upon being found guilty by verdict of the judge or jury, the defendant appears in court for sentencing. This is one of the most critical points in the proceedings. This is where the offender learns what punishment is to be assessed for his criminal act.

A presentence investigation is normally conducted in those states where the sentencing function rests entirely with the judge. The purpose

[17] Apodaca v. Oregon 406 U.S. 404, 92 S.Ct. 1628, 32 L.Ed.2d 184 (1972). Also Johnson v. Louisiana, 406 U.S. 356, 92 S.Ct. 1620, 32 L.Ed.2d. 152 (1972).

of this investigation is to obtain information about the offender that is not already known by the judge, and that will be beneficial to him as he considers a proper sentence. Information concerning the defendant's education, employment, prior criminal record, and mental and physical history are part of this report. Narrative accounts of the crime by the defendant might also be included, as well as statements by friends, relatives, and former employers who know the defendant and who may provide insight into his past life and prospects for the future. Information in this report is collected by a probation officer assigned to the court. In rural areas, a member of the district attorney's staff may conduct the investigation.

After considering the nature of the crime, the defendant, and the presentence investigation report, the judge makes the sentencing decision. Such decisions are not easily made. The judge must consider what is best for the defendant and what is best for society. The goal, not always reached, is that both sides will be served satisfactorily by the judge's decision. In the majority of states, the jury is permitted to recommend or fix punishment at life imprisonment in capital cases, and, in about one-fourth of the states, the jury determines the type and length of punishment in some or all crimes. In those states, the only responsibility of the judge is to insure that the recommended punishment conforms to the statutes, or that excessive, but legal, punishments are modified to become consistent with the nature of the crime. The primary obligation of the judge, when exclusive sentencing authority rests with him, is to make certain that he is familiar with all types of dispositions for the particular crime. The most common dispositions upon conviction for felonies are (1) probation, (2) fixed (definite) sentences, (3) indeterminate sentences, (4) concurrent (consecutive) sentences, or (5) sentencing under various habitual criminal statutes.

Probation does not involve incarceration. Instead, the offender is released to the community to serve his sentence. He will not be imprisoned unless he violates a rule of probation that his probation officer believes is serious enough to warrant his return to court for enforcement of the original sentence.

The fixed, or definite, sentence means that a specific number of years are to be served in prison. The judge informs the defendant that he is to serve, for example, ten years in the state penitentiary. This sentence is different from the indeterminate sentence, which does not require that a definite number of years be served in prison. For example, the judge tells the defendant that he is to serve "no less than one nor more than five years in the state penitentiary." Release from prison with the indeterminate sentence can be at any time between the minimum and maximum sentence, depending on the efforts made by the defendant toward rehabilitation, and by decision of the parole board.

A concurrent (overlapping) sentence may be prescribed when the defendant has committed multiple crimes or several counts of one crime. For example, the defendant might be found guilty of committing three counts of burglary and sentenced to "three years for each count, the sentences to run concurrently." For three counts of burglary under the concurrent sentence, he would serve a maximum of three years; however, if the judge used the consecutive, or "stacked," sentence in the same case, a total of nine years would be assessed.

Habitual criminal statutes serve to increase the punishment for those who are continually committing crimes. The application of these statutes varies among jurisdictions. In some, the punishment can only be increased if the defendant has previously been convicted for a similar offense. In other jurisdictions, the punishment can be increased upon conviction for a certain number of felonies, regardless of the type.

Appeals

Upon pronouncement of sentence, the defendant may be released to the custody of the sheriff or, if convicted of a federal crime, to the U.S. Marshal for transportation to a designated correctional institution. Before sentencing, however, or within a specified time period after sentencing, the defendant may wish to make certain posttrial motions to the court. A *motion in arrest of judgment* is used when the defendant feels that the indictment or information failed to charge an offense or when the court lacked jurisdiction to hear the case. A *motion for a new trial* may be based on juror misconduct, prejudice of the judge, negligence of counsel, perjury, or other trial errors. The prosecution's evidence may be challenged at the conclusion of his case, at the close of evidence, or after the return of a guilty verdict, through the *motion for judgment of acquittal or directed verdict*.

If motions proposed by the defense are overruled by the court, appeals may be filed before the proper appellate court. There is no constitutional right to appeal a case, but all states provide for review of cases by appellate courts. Normally, appeals must be filed within ten days following judgment. Most states do allow extension of this time period when good cause is shown.

In an appeal, the defendant notes legal errors committed during his trial or constitutional rights that were violated. An appellate court will only review errors in law and constitutional violations. It does not review conflicts in the evidence presented, nor will it reverse the decision of the lower court because of minor errors. Appeals may be *affirmed, reversed,* or *reversed and remanded* by the appellate court. When an appeal is affirmed, the conviction of the lower court is upheld. Reversal means that the accused will be released because of irreversible error committed during or preceding the trial. Reverse and remand means that there has been an error committed, but the error will be corrected at a new trial. Here the accused is provided another trial or is remanded, or sent back, for further proceedings.

If the appellate court affirms the decision of the lower court, the defendant has other remedies in law. He may appeal his case to the highest court in the state, or, if the appeal focuses on a violation of a constitutional right, he may appeal to the U.S. Supreme Court.

Postconviction Remedies

In all jurisdictions there is a desire to bring each case to a close—to reach finality. As expressed by the President's Commission:

> *The function and scope given the* writ of habeas corpus *is the result of a balance between our desire to assure a sense of finality in criminal judgments and our concern for the fairness of the criminal process. Finality of judgment, a feeling that a case is over and decided, is an all-important value for the defendant and for society. In all jurisdictions the desire for finality yields initially to the right of a defendant to appeal his conviction. A defendant convicted in a state court may have the record of his trial reviewed for error by at least one appellate court, normally the highest court of the state. When he has exhausted his state appeals, he may petition the Supreme Court for review of claimed violations of federal rights in the process leading to his conviction. . . . When these direct appeals are exhausted, or when the time for taking an appeal has passed, the defendant who has not obtained a reversal of his conviction and a new trial must begin to serve his sentence.*[18]

---

[18] *Task Force Reports: The Courts,* p. 45.

Even though all appeals have been made, another remedy must be available to those defendants sentenced to prison who can show cause for unjust detention. *Habeas corpus* (literally, "you have the body") is generally the final remedy. The *writ of habeas corpus* is used to free a person from unlawful detention or illegal custody. The right to apply for this writ is protected both by federal and state constitutions. The person being unlawfully confined or anyone acting in his behalf may make application for a *writ of habeas corpus*. This application cites the name of the person being held and identifies those holding him in custody. Next, the application is presented to the court where, upon receipt, the judge will order those having custody of the person to present him in court and to show cause for his continued detention. Upon presentation in court, a hearing is held to determine if there is any merit to the claims proposed by the person who has been confined. Only claims concerning denial of fundamental rights during the trial process may be raised on *habeas corpus*. In turn, those having custody of the person must show cause for his continued detention. If cause is shown by the writ applicant, he is released from detention pending further proceedings; however, if cause for continued detention is substantiated, he is returned to custody.

Student Checklist

1. Can you distinguish between the views of justice as perceived by the various practitioners in the legal system?
2. Can you define the term "crime"?
3. Are you able to identify the ultimate goal of a police investigation?
4. Can you list the events that occur at a booking?
5. Are you able to identify the contents of an information?
6. Can you identify the responsibilities of a magistrate at the initial presentment?
7. Can you recite the elements of a Miranda Warning?
8. Can you list the plea options available to the accused at an arraignment?

9. Are you able to identify the types of pretrial motions available to a defense attorney?

Topics for Discussion

1. Discuss the impact of the Miranda Warning on the investigative process.
2. Discuss the concept of justice and its application to the American justice system.
3. Discuss the proceedings that occur in a typical trial.
4. Discuss the problems in defining what is a crime.

ANNOTATED BIBLIOGRAPHY

American Bar Association. *Standards Relating to Pretrial Release.* Approved Draft. New York: Institute of Judicial Administration, 1968. Contains suggestions for modifying the bail system in the United States to make it more equitable for all.

Attorney General's Committee on Poverty and the Administration of Federal Criminal Justice. *Poverty and the Administration of Federal Criminal Justice.* Washington, D.C.: U.S. Govt. Printing Office, 1963. Comprehensive study of poverty and problems for those in the criminal justice system with limited means.

Blumberg, Abraham S., ed. *Law and Order: The Scales of Justice.* Chicago: Aldine, 1970. Series of essays by various authors whose articles have appeared in *Trans-action* magazine. Each author relates some facet of American justice and his personal analysis of the problem.

Gould, James A., ed. *Classic Philosophical Questions.* Columbus, Ohio: Charles E. Merrill, 1971. Edited book of readings designed to introduce the student to philosophy through exposure to problems with which he is familiar.

Hall, Livingston; Yale Kamisar; Wayne R. LaFave; and Jerold H. Israel. *Modern Criminal Procedure,* St. Paul: West Publishing, 1969. Cases, comments, and questions are posed concerning all aspects of criminal procedure including constitutional rights, arrest, search and seizure, the trial, and appeals.

Lineberry, William P., ed. *Justice in America: Law, Order, and the Courts.* New York: H. W. Wilson, 1972. The basic premise is that the breakdown in the American system of justice is now complete. Selected articles and book excerpts are used to illustrate problem areas as well as showing potential solutions or "what has to be done" to prevent a collapse of the system.

President's Commission on Law Enforcement and Administration of Justice. *The Challenge of Crime in a Free Society.* Washington, D.C.: U.S. Govt. Printing Office, 1967. A general report that includes all major findings resulting from detailed studies into every facet of crime and law enforcement in the United States.

Tocqueville, Alexis De. *Democracy in America.* Henry Steele Commager, ed., London: Oxford University Press, 1965. A Frenchman's observations of the fundamentals of democracy and its people.

Wasserstein, Bruce, and Mark J. Green, eds. *With Justice for Some: An Indictment of the Law by Young Advocates.* Boston: Beacon Press, 1970. Essays that point out the fact that in America, the ignorant, the accused, and the inconsequential defendant do not receive justice. This book probes the failures of contemporary law and its effects on a wide range of victims.

The study of this chapter will enable you to:

1. Define discretion as it applies to the administration of justice.
2. Write a short essay that identifies the nature and significance of discretion in the justice system.
3. Identify the importance of civilian discretion to the criminal justice system.
4. Identify the factors that influence the prosecutor's discretion.
5. List the four factors that effect correctional discretion.
6. Write a short essay that identifies the major discretionary points in the justice system.
7. Identify the need for controlling discretion within the justice system.

4
Discretion

Previous studies or analyses of discretion in the administration of justice have either been conspicuous by their absence or have given only passing review of a superficial nature.

Discretion should be a major consideration in the study of the justice system. Unfortunately, there is little in-depth literature and research in the area of discretion. It may be that the whole concept and application of discretion in the justice system is so complex and controversial that few scholars or researchers have even attempted to understand the area.

Discretion is generally defined as being discreet; having the freedom or authority to make decisions and choices; and having the power to judge or act. This is readily seen in the police officer's use of discretion to determine whether or not to arrest, or in the parole officer's decision whether or not to revoke parole.

Kenneth Culp Davis, one of the few scholars who has studied the area of discretion, defines the term in the following manner: "A public officer has discretion whenever the effective limits on his power leave him free to make a choice among possible courses of action or inaction."[1] In Davis' definition, it is important to stress the proposition that discretion is not limited to what is authorized or what is legal but includes all that is within the "effective limits" of the officer's power.

"This phraseology is necessary," Davis states, "because a good deal of discretion is illegal or of questionable legality. Another facet of the

---

[1] Kenneth C. Davis, *Discretionary Justice* (Chicago: University of Illinois Press, 1971), p. 4.

definition is that a choice to do nothing—or to do nothing now—is definitely included; perhaps inaction decisions are 10 to 20 times as frequent as action decisions. Discretion is exercised not merely in final dispositions of cases or problems but in each interim step. . . ."

When a police, judicial, or correctional officer exercises discretion, three principal ingredients are considered in rendering his decision. They are (1) facts, (2) values, and (3) influences. An officer, in exercising discretion, seldom separates these three elements; most discretionary decisions are intuitive. Responses to influences often ignore values, according to Davis. An example of this can be seen when a youthful, long-haired minority student fails "to pass the attitude test" by arguing with the police officer, justifiably or unjustifiably. This applies not only at the entry level of arrest, but throughout the criminal justice process if the arrestee is hostile and exhibits "rebelliousness or disrespect for the law." Here, emotions guide the officer's actions instead of facts or values.

Nature and Significance of Discretion

It appears that the most frequent abuse of discretionary power occurs where rules and principles provide no adequate direction; where emotions negatively affect the officer's judgment; and where political or other favors may influence decisions (i.e., the Watergate scandal and the Ellsberg trial).

The nature and significance of discretion are simultaneously good and bad, depending on which side of the bar of justice one is located and the influences brought to bear. The literature is replete with the notion of a double standard of justice: one for the rich and powerful, one for the poor and powerless. But discretion, per se, is not evil, nor unworkable. The efforts made by scholars and decision-makers should stress the application of equitable discretion for all, regardless of social or political status. As governments come to realize their dependency on discretion in their justice systems, the informal discretionary sanctions will become more formalized, coordinated, and positively applied.

Davis states:

Discretion is a tool, indispensable for individualization of justice. All governments in history have been governments of laws and of men. Rules alone, untempered by discretion, cannot cope with the com-

plexities of modern government and of modern justice. Discretion is our principal source of creativeness in government and in law. . . . Let us not overemphasize either the need for discretion or its dangers, let us emphasize both the need and its dangers. Let us not oppose discretionary power; let us oppose unnecessary discretionary power. . . . Let us not oppose discretionary justice that is properly confined, structured, and checked; let us oppose discretionary justice that is improperly unconfined, unstructured, and unchecked.[2]

Without "discretionary justice" the entire criminal justice system would undoubtedly collapse under the weight of congested jails, courts, and prisons. By the same token, plea bargaining (prosecutorial and judicial discretion), with both its positive and negative aspects, could not be eliminated without producing a chaotic breakdown of the judicial system. We must dissect, study, and understand the complex nature of discretion so that those delegated to apply the law will not abuse the exercise of discretion in any sector of the justice system.

Civilian Discretion

Most discussions of judicial discretion in the criminal justice system begin with the examination of the discretionary role of the police. But little attention is paid to a facet of the system that, in most cases, precedes police decision to invoke or not invoke the criminal process. The citizen, rarely mentioned as an integral part of the process, often makes the first decision—the decision to call the police. It is also the private citizen who defines the matter as criminal in a high percentage of cases. Consider, for example, a simple assault that takes place between Citizen A (victim) and Citizen B (suspect). Citizen A calls the police and reports that he has been assaulted. When the police arrive at the scene, the crime has, of course, already occurred. There is no physical evidence of this assault. Citizen A must present the evidence of the crime verbally. If between the time of the call to the police and the time of their arrival Citizen A has been mollified in some fashion, he may have less desire to invoke the criminal sanction. The police officer may feel strongly that a crime has taken place, but without the verbal evidence of the victim, he is legally

[2] Davis, *Discretionary Justice,* pp. 25-26.

constrained from defining the behavior as criminal and from taking any action. In this case it is within the discretion of the private citizen to define the criminality of the act—not the police. And the police must have reasonable cause, which requires, at the very least, that Citizen A admit that he is the victim of a crime. Generally speaking, a misdemeanor must occur within the presence of the officer for him to legally take unilateral action. In the more serious category, he must have reasonable cause to believe that a felony has occurred before unilateral action may be taken. In the vast majority of cases the officer must rely on the citizen's definition of the crime. The citizen must make the arrest or agree to swear out or sign a complaint before the police may act. Often in assault cases the criminal sanction is not invoked by the citizen because the suspect is a relative or friend.

Another way to view this phenomenon is to consider clearance rates by police. The majority of crimes cleared, or solved by police, are by arrest, where the suspect is taken into custody; or by exception, which means that the suspect is known to the police but that the victim is unwilling to prosecute. Reiss reports that the clearance rate by the Chicago Police Department during one month of 1966 for rape and aggravated assault was 28 percent by arrest and 32 percent by exception.[3] Citizens do exercise discretion in defining criminal action and in determining how many people will enter the criminal justice system.

Conventional wisdom asserts that police arrest many people for improper charges, and cite as evidence the high percentage of those arrested who are released uncharged; usually a 30 percent figure is given. Officials in Washington, D.C. were concerned with this phenomenon and "tracked" their arrested persons. In November 1972 they found that 41 percent of those arrested for assault with a dangerous weapon or simple assault did not have charges filed by the U.S. Attorney's office. A review of these cases revealed that many of them were intrafamily assaults that occurred during the heat of an argument, and the family members did not wish to charge criminally.[4]

In these cases the private citizen used his discretion to invoke

[3] Albert J. Reiss, Jr., *The Police and the Public* (New Haven: Yale University Press, 1971).

[4] Geoffrey M. Alprin, "D.C.'s Case Review Section Studies the 'No-paper' Phenomenon," *Police Chief, 40,* No. 4 (April 1973), p. 40.

initially the criminal sanction—suspect arrested by the police—and at a later time withdrew that decision. Considering the earlier example of a simple assault, but viewing Citizen A as victim-wife and Citizen B as suspect-husband, Citizen A's decision to withdraw her complaint now becomes clear. Like many people in the Washington, D.C. study, she has now had opportunity to assess the full implications of the loss of the family breadwinner. By invoking the criminal sanction at the time of the arrest, she solved the immediate crisis. By withdrawing the criminal sanction at a later time she confines the impact of punishment. "The citizen's . . . decisions to mobilize the police are a principle source of input into the system, and these decisions profoundly affect the discretion exercised by the police."[5]

Police Discretion

As suggested earlier in the chapter, it is a euphemism that this country operates solely on the principle of rule of law. In practical terms, where does the police administrator start in determining the level and extent to which a law should be enforced? Many police administrators claim that their agency adheres to a policy of full enforcement of the law. Although the nation's jails and prisons are clearly overcrowded, it would be difficult to imagine the conditions in those institutions were "full enforcement" a reality. The fact is that few departments could even begin to fully enforce all of the laws available to them. Discretion is clearly an administrative reality. Some scale of values or ranking of priorities must be established to balance available resources against community expectations and needs of enforcement. The law, uninterpreted and fully enforced, would be a heavy burden for police and citizen alike.

Assuming that the police administrator has arrived at a level of enforcement that he determines is reasonable and appropriate for his community, these policies are transmitted through his organization to the patrolman. The issue of police discretion, far from being resolved, now emerges as a daily situational problem. On the one hand, if the patrolman is not suspicious enough in a given situation to justify intervention, the opportunity to prevent a crime or apprehend a criminal may be lost. On

---

[5] Reiss, *The Police and the Public*, p. 114.

the other hand, if he is overzealous in intervention he may touch off a riot, or unnecessarily harm or kill someone. Administrative policy to guide the patrolman is transmitted through academies and in-service training programs. While these programs attempt to limit discretion by setting down policy guidelines, they are noticeably ambiguous and often rely on phrases such as, "use your own good judgment" or "common sense will dictate. . . ." "Patrolmen are thus left to make decisions on the basis of their own opinions, the observations of more experienced officers, and some informal, and often divergent advice from precinct personnel who review those arrests which are made."[6]

The policeman will tend to use discretion more often in minor or less serious crimes. Whether or not to arrest in a shoplifting case when the value of the loss is a few dollars can be a difficult decision without clear organizational guidelines. For serious crimes, such as armed robbery or murder, an arrest will always be made if the suspect is available. Rarely will an officer use his discretionary powers not to arrest in a serious crime.

Prosecutional Discretion

Interestingly enough, this order of discretionary utilization is reversed with prosecutors. The prosecutor will, in most cases, decide to issue a complaint on a variety of factors largely independent of the seriousness of the crime. For example, he takes into consideration the strength of the case, the workload of his office, and the community attitude toward the crime and the defendant before he finally makes a determination to proceed. These factors are weighted differently in various communities. The prosecutor has greater discretion than the police in felony matters, largely because the public, who expects the apprehension of a suspected felon, rarely follows a case through the judicial process. This occurs because there is a long time lag, in most instances, between apprehension and trial. During this period the prosecutor has ample opportunity to exercise discretion.[7]

[6] Wayne R. LaFave, *Arrest* (Boston: Little, Brown, 1965), p. 158.
[7] George D. Eastman, ed., *Municipal Police Administration* (Washington, D.C.: International City Managers Assoc., 1969), p. 321.

Political factors often affect the decisions in the prosecutor's office. If the head of the agency is an elected official, there will be a tendency to desire high conviction rates as a sign to the electorate that the incumbent is doing a good job. This would be emphasized during election campaigns when he advertises his high conviction rate. A high rate is maintained largely through plea bargaining and issuing complaints on only the strongest police cases where guilty pleas can be expected. When the chief prosecutor is an appointed official and serves at the will of a political person, the appointing authority's influence is usually evident. This would tend to take the form of specific types of cases being encouraged and others discouraged. Encouragement is accomplished by issuing complaints on certain crimes (reinforcing police expectations), and refusing to prosecute in those areas where enforcement is not desired (punishment of police by not charging). "The prosecutor wields almost undisputed sway over the pretrial progress of most cases. He decides whether to press a case or drop it. He determines the specific charge against a defendant. When the charge is reduced, as it is in as many as two-thirds of all cases in some cities, the prosecutor is usually the official who reduces it."[8]

Plea bargaining is widely held to be an improper use of discretionary power by the prosecutor. Some recommendations call for the elimination of all plea bargaining by 1977. Aside from the physical improbability of this happening, the argument fails on one point: there are cases where a lesser charge serves the best interests of justice. To the extent that this belief is sincerely held by the prosecutor, plea bargaining should continue. Plea bargaining should not, however, be based on a factor of crowded court calendars. One important injustice inherent in plea bargaining is that, for the most part, it is an invisible procedure not open to public scrutiny or review. It is also, in some jurisdictions, theoretically illegal. "In order to satisfy the court record, a defendant, his attorney, and the prosecutor will at the time of sentencing often ritually state to a judge that no bargain has been made."[9]

[8] President's Commission on Law Enforcement and Administration of Justice, *The Challenge of Crime in a Free Society* (Washington, D.C.: U.S. Govt. Printing Office, 1967), p. 11.
[9] Ibid.

Court Discretion

The magistrate uses less discretion than the law allows him when the suspect first appears. He is entitled to question whether a crime has been committed and if there are grounds for holding the suspect. Congested court calendars too frequently do not allow the time to be thus spent. Bail is usually set by the magistrate, and in some districts he also appoints counsel to represent the defendant. Generally speaking, this magistrate exercises less discretion than the law allows.

Because the law recognizes the necessity of matching sentences to individual defendants, trial judges have wide discretionary powers in sentencing convicted persons. The greatest difficulty in passing sentences for a judge is not time or inadequate information; rather it is a lack of correctional alternatives from which to choose. "Few states have a sufficient variety of correctional institutions or treatment programs to inspire judges with the confidence that sentences will lead to rehabilitation."[10]

Correctional Discretion

Correctional discretion suffers generally for four reasons. First, correctional personnel do not, as a rule, have a working relationship with others in the system. (Police and prosecutors, for example, interact daily; prosecutors and police both interact with judges.) Second, correctional facilities are frequently physically isolated from the larger society. Third, the legislative charge given to correctional administrators is contained in very broadly reviewed statutes and its decisions are rarely reviewed by the appellate courts. Fourth, ". . . (and) perhaps most importantly (they suffer) by the fact that the correctional apparatus is often used—or misused—by both the criminal justice system and the public as a rug under which disturbing problems and people can be swept."[11]

The parole decision, next to sentencing, has the greatest impact on the offender. This invisible administrative decision is rarely reviewed and is seldom open to attack, but it is of critical importance in determining

[10] Ibid.
[11] Ibid., p. 12.

how much of the maximum sentence the offender will serve. The decision to parole or not to parole has historically been given without a statement of reasons or justification for the decision. This wide discretionary power, coupled with little or no controlling policy, allows arbitrary and discriminatory decisions to pass unchecked. Revised criminal justice standards recently proposed by the American Bar Association, the National Commission for Criminal Justice Standards and Goals, and in the Congress, would make it standard practice for parole boards to inform inmates of reasons for refusing parole.

Discretion Points in the Justice System

One usually thinks of the justice system as being comprised of three components: police, courts, and corrections. While this is generally correct, a further refinement is necessary to analyze the discretionary points or steps. Figure 4-1 is a generalized depiction of this discretionary flow. Observe that some of the discretion points fall in overlapping areas of responsibility. For example, discretion point B, defining the act, is within the ability of both the private citizen and the police to invoke. Point H, to reduce, is within the authority of both the prosecutor and the judge to invoke. The discretion points on the chart, in basic form, are

Figure 4-1. Model discretion points.

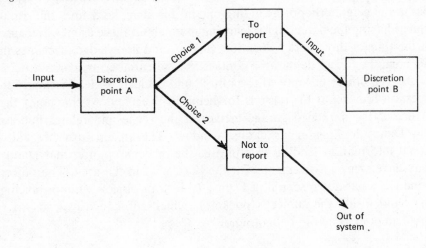

nothing more than the selection of a course of action from two or more available choices. Figure 4-2 depicts such a discretion point in more detail. The individual at point A has the choice of two alternative courses of action. If he selects choice 1, that choice becomes input for discretion point B. Graphic representation of all choices available at each discretion point has not been attempted.

The best way to illustrate the process and its function is by example—a crime and a suspect traced through the system (Figure 4-2). Danny, a 24-year-old white male living with his parents, has used heroin for six months. He supports his habit by selling heroin to a select group of clients and by burglarizing homes. A neighbor has been suspicious of Danny for several months. One evening she observes Danny loitering in the alley near another neighbor's garage. The neighbor telephones the police (anonymously) to report a suspicious person lurking in the alley. This citizen was acting within her discretionary rights in notifying the authorities of activity that she labeled criminal.

The police dispatcher receiving the call had to evaluate the incomplete information that had been furnished by the anonymous caller. His decision to dispatch may have been based on knowledge that there had been crimes in that neighborhood, that there was a patrol unit in the area available, or simply on a departmental policy to dispatch on all calls regardless of complete information. The opposite could have been equally true and no dispatch would have been made.

The patrol officer responded to the radio call and arrived in the alley just as Danny was about to enter his own backyard (discretion point B in Figure 4-2). Since the officer knows of several recent burglaries in the neighborhood, including one in this alley, he defines the situation as having the potential for learning more about those crimes. Because of the time of day (dark), location (alley), and knowledge of crimes in the area, the officer defines the contact as a potential crime contact.

The officer has moved to point C and decided to detain Danny to question him about his reasons for being in the alley. At this point the owner of the darkened garage arrives at the scene and relates that he saw Danny looking in his garage window. The citizen furnishes additional information tending to reinforce the officer's opinion that Danny may have some involvement with the burglaries in the area. The officer conducts a pat-down search of Danny (a feel for objects without placing the hand inside the subject's pockets), which subsequently leads to a small amount of heroin being found.

Figure 4-2. The discretion process.

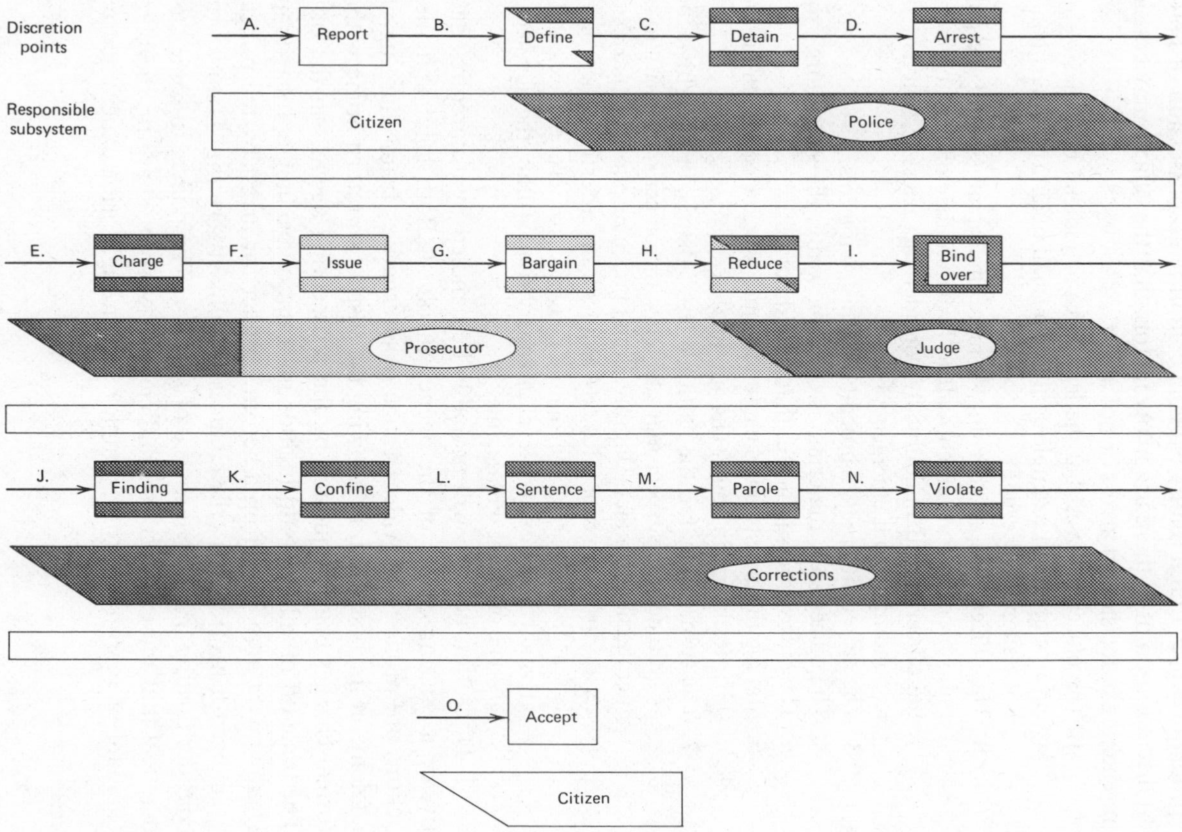

Discretion points	A.	Report	B.	Define	C.	Detain	D.	Arrest	
	E.	Charge	F.	Issue	G.	Bargain	H.	Reduce	I.	Bind over
	J.	Finding	K.	Confine	L.	Sentence	M.	Parole	N.	Violate
	O.	Accept							

Responsible subsystem: Citizen, Police, Prosecutor, Judge, Corrections, Citizen

Danny is placed under arrest for possession of a controlled substance—heroin (discretion point D). At this point the officer does not know for a fact that the material is heroin. His decision is based on "probable cause" that a felony is being committed—possession of heroin. At discretion point D there are many factors that the officer may consider in reaching a decision to arrest or not arrest.

1. The officer believes that the legislative or judicial body desires non-enforcement (an example could be a small quantity of marijuana or a 50¢ shoplifting crime).
2. The officer feels another duty is more important (should the police radio broadcast an urgent call to assist another officer in the area, the officer would undoubtedly consider the arrest less urgent than responding to that emergency).
3. The officer interprets a broad law in his own terms.
4. The officer feels the crime is common within the subculture group.
5. The only witness indicates that he will not testify.
6. Making the arrest would cause too much work (too late in his work shift, testifying in court, and the like).
7. The suspect may fail the "attitude test," that is, through his actions or attitudes the suspect may challenge the officer's authority to conduct the field contact. Unprofessional police response is to arrest the person to "teach him a lesson" although the arresting officer knows that a charge cannot be maintained in court. To the extent that internal control exists (level of supervision) within the department, this type of arrest will decline.[12]

Discretion point E will probably be handled by a narcotics detective or a ranking officer of the agency involved. Both legal and illegal actions are prone to provide a range of alternatives from charging with a felony on the one hand, to allowing the suspect to return home without formal charges being requested by the prosecuting agency on the other. The trade-off of values could include information exchange; for example, Danny might agree to set up a heroin supplier for arrest by the police in exchange for his freedom (the chances are almost zero that Danny would consider turning in his own source of supply). The police, in some cases, may feel that the evidence is insufficient to warrant charging the person (amount of marijuana, for example), or through prior experience with

[12] For a more comprehensive list of factors, see Davis, *Discretionary Justice*, pp. 82-83.

the prosecutor they may know that he will not issue a complaint in a particular crime.

While the list of factors involved in this discretion point is long, the issues raised are of concern for every police administrator. With the exception of new evidence coming to light during the follow-up investigation showing the innocence of the suspect, arrests made by the police should be presented to the prosecuting agency for review. Clear policy guidelines on arrest procedures, effective training, and good communications between prosecutor and line officers would minimize all other situations with the exception of outright criminal actions on the part of some police officers. During this phase of the follow-up investigation, for example, the material that led to Danny's arrest could be found to be talcum, not heroin, and a complaint would not be sought.

In the hypothetical case, the narcotics officer handling Danny's case found the material to be heroin and decided to take the case to the prosecutor. At discretion point F, the prosecutor would examine the police case for legal (technical) weaknesses, and in the light of the most recent case law. At discretion point G the prosecutor would, in all likelihood, attempt to extract a guilty plea from Danny or his attorney. The offer, if made, would possibly include offers of recommending probation or other inducements favorable to Danny. Ninety percent of criminal cases are dealt with in this or similar fashion. (See earlier discussion for more complete treatment of discretion points F and G.)

Danny has moved into the subsystem of the judiciary as he arrives at discretion point H. This point is shared by both the prosecutor and the judge, since both have the power to reduce the charge. The prosecutor may reduce the charge as part of the plea bargaining transaction. The judge may reduce the charge to a lesser offense after inquiring into the facts surrounding the arrest and crime. Reduction may be based on social values attached to various subcultures, by prosecutors and judges who typically come from middle-class backgrounds.

Generally, the magistrate has three choices: he can reduce the charge, dismiss the complaint (discretion point H), or bind over for trial, that is, set a trial date for Danny (discretion point I). Discretion point J deals with the trial findings of guilt or innocence by a judge or jury. The discretion of the trial judge extends from directing a jury to find not guilty to overruling a jury's guilty finding. In a well-publicized trial in Los Angeles, Daniel Ellsberg and Anthony J. Russo were charged with theft, espionage, and conspiracy against the U.S. government. Following four and a half months of trial, Judge William Matthew Byrne, Jr. declared a mistrial and granted the motion to dismiss. The case was dismissed because the judge found that "the conduct of the government precludes the fair, dispassionate resolution of these issues by a jury. The totality of the circumstances of this case offends a 'sense of justice.' "[13] Of special interest here is the range of alternatives available to the judge, one of which would have been to allow the case to go to jury and, if they found the defendants guilty, overrule the jury and find the defendants not guilty. This considerable judicial discretion is infrequently abused for two reasons. First, the trial takes place in the view of the public; second, the results are subject to close review by the appellate subsystem.

Earlier in this chapter we discussed discretion to confine (point K) with the problem centering less on abuse of discretion by the judge than on lack of alternatives available to the judge. In inferior courts there is a marked lack of information available to the judge (frequently lack of probation support for misdemeanants), which sometimes results in arbitrary sentencing terms (discretion point L). The same can be said for superior courts, where lack of sentencing standards results in a wide variety of sentences for similar offenses by similar offenders (e.g., recent 10,000-year sentences in Texas). Assistance to the judge in deciding whether to confine and how to sentence effectively appears to be moving in the direction of more input for judges. In California, greater use of a section of the penal code is allowing behavioral and social scientists to advise the court on mitigating circumstances and recommend programs for offender rehabilitation.

In some, if not most, cases of serious nature the parole authority is also involved in the sentencing decision. In California, for example, under indeterminate sentencing, the judge sets broad limits of incarceration. The adult authority determines how much of the time is spent inside correctional facilities. For example, the judge could sentence Danny from two to ten years. The parole authority has almost unlimited discretion in determining if he is placed outside in less than two years or serves the entire ten years in prison (discretion point M). The principal danger in the use of discretion focuses on the lack of review of parole decisions and the lack of objective guidelines to assist parole personnel in reaching meaningful conclusions.[14]

[13] *Time* (May 21, 1973), p. 28.
[14] Davis, *Discretionary Justice*, p. 11.

When Danny is placed on parole, he faces daily the prospect of being "violated" (his parole revoked) and returned to prison. Discretion point N is jointly in the hands of Danny's parole agent and the parole board. One of the parole agent's major concerns is to keep Danny "clean," that is, not using heroin. If he discovers that Danny is using marijuana, for example, he may well view that violation as a positive means of avoiding heroin addiction. He uses his discretion at this point by not returning Danny to prison for use of marijuana; however, he would probably "violate" Danny if he returned to regular heroin usage. The decision not to violate is invisible. The decision to violate is subjected to little, if any, review by the courts.

In the example, Danny successfully completed his parole period and is fully on his own. Returning now to Figure 4-1, to the place where Danny's criminal behavior was first defined—in interaction with other citizens of his community—what are the chances of the cycle being repeated? Unfortunately, quite high. It could easily be argued that one of the reasons for this probability is the frequent abuse or lack of control or review of discretion that can occur at each step in the criminal justice process. In addition to this, problems that originally faced Danny have probably not been dealt with effectively and he carries the stigma of the ex-con label for life. Independent of the system's treatment of Danny, the discretion used by these same citizens can assist him in successfully reentering the community. In the final analysis, the citizen's ability to define discretion is all-important to the successful functioning of the criminal justice system, both objectively and subjectively.

Control of Discretion

Our discussion, which focused on the 5 subsystems of the criminal justice system and the 15 identifiable discretion points, has raised specific questions about the use of discretion by these subsystems. Clearly, there is room for improvement in the use of discretion within the system, but what controls or checks-and-balances on discretion are presently available in the system? Are there specific ways to improve use and control of discretion?

The powers of the government have been divided into three major branches to avoid consolidation of power in the hands of any single branch of government. Thus, the legislative, judicial, and executive bodies are each involved in reviewing and monitoring the work product of the other two. This can provide a strong check on abuses by any one body. Within the criminal justice system, the relationship has certain built-in reviews. For example, the legislature passes a law in the form of a relatively broad mandate. The executive is responsible for implementing and enforcing this law. Through the executive bureaucracy the broad law is refined in policy and procedure decisions and ultimately enforced by the police. Following an arrest for this law, the courts are in a position, on appeal, to rule on the validity of the executive process whereby the individual was arrested, and on the original law as passed by the legislature.

The relationship of the three branches of government is shown in Figure 4-3. There are areas of exclusive discretion and jurisdiction, areas of overlap between two branches, and areas where interests of all three branches overlap. The flow of input in the overlap of two branches sets the stage for discretion by the branch receiving the input. Thus, the legislature provides input to the executive by passing laws. The executive provides input to the judiciary by arresting offenders. The judiciary provides input to the legislature by refining the laws.

Figure 4-3. Relationship of the branches of government: checks and balances.

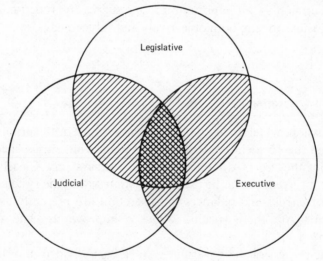

Each branch is capable of checking the discretion of the other two branches. The legislative branch, by passing restrictive laws, narrows executive discretion. By rewriting laws found unconstitutional by the courts, it can supersede judicial discretion by rewording and passing a similar law. The judicial branch, for its part, can rule the rewritten law unconstitutional when a new case reaches them. The judicial branch has the power to limit the discretionary power of the executive, as Warren Court rulings have shown. The executive, for its part, can effectively check the legislature by failing to implement legislation or, more frequently, by modifying the legislation through administrative bureaucratic procedures.[15] The executive can control judicial discretion by withholding input to that branch in the form of failing to prosecute, as noted earlier in the chapter.

Carefully constructed and clearly stated enforcement policies would aid and limit law enforcement discretion. Similarly constructed and stated charge policies would help prosecutors. Sentencing policies would aid judges, and specific parole policies would assist and limit parole discretion.

Police administrators must develop such policies to limit the wide use of unnecessary discretion by field officers in the areas of questioning citizens, arrest procedures, and the use of firearms. They must strengthen their internal investigations capability to maintain unit integrity. External controls of the police must be broadened by providing community input at policy-making levels. The prosecuting agency should actively provide input to police agencies through daily review of all arrest cases and by providing input for enforcement policy based on case law and legislative changes. In all of these areas the involvement of citizens in understanding and assisting the development of enforcement policy is most crucial to the successful and fair limitations of police discretionary powers.[16]

The discretionary power of prosecutors to charge or not charge a

[15] For an example of the "administration" process see Robert S. Lorch, "Toward Administrative Judges," *Public Administration Review 30*, No. 1 (January/February 1970), pp. 50-56.

[16] Hazel B. Kerper, *Introduction to the Criminal Justice System* (St. Paul: West Publishing, 1972) Chapter 5. See also Reiss, *The Police and the Public,* Chapter 4; and *Task Force Report: The Police* (Washington, D.C.: U.S. Govt. Printing Office, 1967) Chapters 2, 3, 5, 7, and 9.

defendant should be retained. Specific policy guidelines for charging must be developed and publicized. This would not only limit the discretion of the prosecutor; public awareness of the charge policies would effectively limit unwise police field practices. Plea bargaining should be limited and closely reviewed by the courts to help eliminate the abuses of this discretionary power. The cloak of secrecy and shadow of illegality must be removed from this process.

The judges must be provided with better information in the form of workable alternatives to confinement at the time of sentencing in both superior and inferior court levels. Revised sentencing provisions of the penal codes would limit the wide discrepancies now present in this area. Judges, not juries, should do all sentencing, and standard sentencing procedures should be implemented in the interest of fairness.[17]

The need for corrections to move out of the relative physical and procedural obscurity in which it now finds itself is a primary factor for reform in this area. Review of parole decisions is a basic requirement, as is increased control and responsibility by the courts for the people they sentence to the institutions. Parole board members must be selected on merit to avoid political interference. Generally, the courts should have greater control of the discretionary powers of corrections.

Future efforts to control or standardize discretion will probably occur when review of decisions by an agency outside the subsystem is made; or when specific internal policies to limit discretion within the subsystem are formulated; and when openness and sharing of discretion with the public—to the widest possible manner by all subsystems—becomes a reality. Ideal control of discretionary abuse will occur only when education, enlightened administrators, and practitioners jointly agree on guidelines that are considered equitable and just—in the eyes of the recipient.

[17] Wallace Mendelson, "Hugo Black and Judicial Discretion," *Political Science Quarterly, 85* (March 1970), pp. 17-39, for a valuable discussion of the judicial practice of "balancing." Mendelson states (p. 38) that ". . . the 'realist' view (is) that the law is anything a judge may boldly assert and plausibly maintain."

Student Checklist

1. Can you define discretion as it applies to the administration of justice?
2. Are you able to identify the nature and significance of discretion?
3. Can you list the factors that influence a prosecutor's discretion?
4. Can you identify the major discretionary points in the justice system?
5. Are you able to list the four factors that effect correctional discretion?
6. Do you know what is important about civilian discretion?
7. Can you identify what is needed to control discretion?

Topics for Discussion

1. Discuss the relationship of the three branches of government with particular emphasis on the areas of exclusive discretion.
2. Discuss the relationship of discretion to the professionalization of the justice system.
3. Discuss the disadvantages of controlling the discretion of a law enforcement officer.
4. Discuss the impact of civilian discretion on the justice system.

ANNOTATED BIBLIOGRAPHY

Ahern, James F. *Police in Trouble*. New York: Hawthorn Books, 1972. A fast-reading, authoritative look inside the police establishment illustrating by example the police discretion at work. This volume is of great value in understanding the pressures on individual as well as organizational policemen, and suggests thoughtful methods to limit unnecessary and illegal police discretion from the policy level to the beat level.

Becker, Theodore L., and Vernon G. Murray, eds. *Government Lawlessness in America*. New York: Oxford University Press, 1971. This reader is especially valuable to introduce the inexperienced student to the wide range of discretional abuse present in our justice institutions. The editors have collected pertinent, timely, and thought-provoking selections that range from outright lawlessness to white-collar, administratively shrouded abuses of discretion. Section VII, "In Pursuit of a Remedy," is of special value in focusing on solutions to the dilemma of discretion.

Davis, Kenneth C. *Discretionary Justice*. Chicago: University of Illinois Press, 1971. Thoroughly discusses all aspects of discretion. A definitive work, necessary to understanding the total ramifications of discretion in modern government. Many excellent examples of abuse of discretion in the governmental system. Especially detailed in the areas of confining and structuring discretion.

Goldstein, Abraham S., and Joseph Goldstein. *Crime, Law and Society*. New York: The Free Press, 1971. Part 2, "Process," is of particular value to the study of discretion. The selections discuss the reality versus the ideal of the criminal justice process. This anthology provides legal themes necessary for the balanced appreciation of discretion.

Kaplan, John. *Criminal Justice*. New York: Foundation Press, 1973. Merges the interdisciplinary areas of law and social science in a casebook style. Format considers typical law school case material with expansion into the criminal justice agencies' operations and structures. Good compilation of articles dealing with the discretionary power of the police, legal rules versus discretion, discretion in three styles of policing, and politics and police discretion.

La Fave, Wayne R. *Arrest*. Boston: Little, Brown, 1965. Examines and analyzes problems relating to the decision to arrest or not arrest a suspect. Detailed discussion of a variety of decision points, including when to arrest, whether or not to invoke further criminal processing, custody, prosecution, and extralegal tactics. Contains an excellent discussion of police discretion and its control.

Packer, Herbert L. *The Limits of the Criminal Sanction*. Stanford: Stanford University Press, 1968. Analyzes the rationale process and limits of the criminal sanction. Parts II and III are of particular interest, describing the characteristics of the justice process and defining the effective limits of the criminal sanction. Thorough bibliographical notes and index make this volume useful as a reference source.

Part Two

Components of Justice

The study of this chapter will enable you to:

1. Identify the two primary areas of modern police power and authority.
2. Define arrest and search and seizure.
3. Identify the two major categories of crime.
4. Recite the Fourth Amendment to the Constitution.
5. List the three elements of penal code guidelines for arrests by a peace officer.
6. Define the term reasonable cause.
7. Identify the "no knock" principle.
8. List the sources of expectations for identification of the police role.
9. Identify Hopkins's police war theory of crime control.
10. List the six methods that a law enforcement agency uses to police a community.

5

Law Enforcement

Most Americans tend to view law enforcement through the image that has been created by the mass media. On any given night, one has only to turn on the television to find that law enforcement is an exciting, dangerous occupation involving the pursuit of clever criminals—a pursuit that ultimately ends with justice triumphant. This highly misleading portrayal omits what is essentially the primary contribution of law enforcement to the justice process. The popular image conceals the careful planning, the application of legally correct arrest and custody techniques, and the detailed written preparation that is necessary for the justice process to function. Law enforcement assumes the responsibility of identifying those individuals who have violated the criminal laws, and of introducing these violators to the justice system in a manner that meets the requirements established by the Constitution. If this responsibility is not properly met, the justice process cannot begin.

Police Power and Authority

Modern police power and authority can be defined as existing in two primary areas: arrest and search and seizure.

Arrest consists of custody, or simply removing the freedom of movement from an individual because of the suspected violation of a criminal statute. The search for and seizure of evidence consists of the careful collection of related material that may assist in a conviction or acquittal, even though it may consist, under extraordinary circumstances, of violating what would normally be a right to privacy.

Police power and authority can be traced to early English history and the application of common law. The private citizen was given the primary responsibility of the protection of society. The only designated peace officers during this period were the shire-reeve, or sheriff, and the constable. The powers of arrest did not differ between the private citizen and the peace officers, and initially it was expected that common law arrests would be made under the authority of a warrant issued by a magistrate. Eventually, a distinction was made based on the seriousness of the offense, and two categories of crimes were established. A violation of the king's peace—such as murder or robbery—was referred to as a felony. A simple breach of the peace was referred to as a misdemeanor. To arrest for a misdemeanor, the peace officer and the citizen could only arrest under the authority of a warrant, or if they observed the misdemeanor being committed. Greater power and authority was extended to the peace officer and the citizen to arrest for a felony without a warrant. In this case, an arrest could be made based on reasonable grounds to believe that the person to be arrested committed the felony.

> *Many of the arrest practices developed in England prior to the adoption of the U.S. Constitution were brought to America by the colonists and became a part of the American legal tradition. Due to necessity and changing conditions most states, by statute, have modified and deleted some of the more technical requirements of the common law of arrest.*[1]

If the police power and authority to arrest stem from early English common law and our own Constitution, it is equally true that the power and authority to search and seize also originated from this source. As the Constitution was being written and readied for ratification, it was argued that there was no provision for individual protection from the new federal government. As a result, the Bill of Rights, the first ten amendments to the Constitution, were included. A specific consideration was given to arrest, search, and seizure. The Fourth Amendment to the Constitution states:

> *The right of the people to be secure in their persons, houses, papers, and effects, against unreasonable searches and seizures, shall not be violated, and no warrants shall issue, but upon probable cause, supported by oath or affirmation, and particularly describing the place to be searched and the persons or things to be seized.*

[1] John C. Klotter and Jacqueline R. Kanovitz, *Constitutional Law for Police*, 2nd ed. (Cincinnati: Anderson, 1971).

The application of these legal concepts to contemporary police have grown much more complex than may be readily apparent. Originally, it was intended that these concepts applied only to agents of the federal government, with state and local police being governed by the more loosely constructed Fourteenth Amendment. In 1962, in *Ker* v. *California* (374 U.S. 23) the U.S. Supreme Court ruled that arrests by state officers are subject to the same constitutional provisions governing arrests by federal officers. Additionally, police powers of arrest and search and seizure, as provided in the state and federal constitutions, are under continuous scrutiny. What may be an acceptable and legal arrest technique in one generation may turn out to be unacceptable and illegal in another. As an example, prior to 1964, a suspected offender could be freely questioned about his suspected involvement in a criminal offense. But since the 1964 *Miranda* v. *Arizona* Supreme Court decision (384 U.S. 436), care must be given to ensure that an individual is aware of his constitutional guarantees prior to questioning, either immediately before or following an arrest.

Arrest: Requirements and Execution

Laws governing the authority to arrest vary in detail from state to state. However, they are basically the same, and all distinguish between felonies and misdemeanors. In one state, for example, a section of the penal code outlines the following guidelines for arrests by peace officers.

A peace officer may make an arrest in obedience to a warrant, or may, without a warrant, arrest a person:

1. Whenever he has reasonable cause to believe that the person to be arrested has committed a public offense in his presence.
2. When the person arrested has committed a felony, although not in the officer's presence.
3. Whenever the officer has reasonable cause to believe that the person to be arrested has committed a felony, whether or not a felony has in fact been committed.

The first subsection dealing with public offenses, or misdemeanors, states that the peace officer must have *reasonable cause to believe* that a public offense has been committed in his presence; or that the actions he witnessed amounted to the violation of a misdemeanor offense. For example, a policeman observed a vehicle being driven erratically, with the driver exhibiting all of the classic signs of intoxication. This appears to be a misdemeanor being committed in the presence of the officer and would usually end in an arrest. However, had the defendant been ill with diabetes or other similar illness—a fact unknown to the officer—a misdemeanor would not have been committed, although the officer would have been justified in making the arrest.

As opposed to arresting for misdemeanor violations, a peace officer does not necessarily have to observe a felony being committed in his presence to make an arrest. For example, an officer is told by a citizen that a man wearing a red coat has broken the front window of a jewelry store, taken several wristwatches, cut his right hand in the process, and run down the street. If the officer observes such a man with a wristwatch in his hand, he could arrest him even though he had not observed the crime being committed. But suppose again that, unknown to either the witness or the officer, the suspect had accidently broken the window by leaning against it with his right arm, broken his watchband, and cut his hand reaching in to retrieve it. In the confusion, realizing how his actions may appear to others, he fled from the scene in fear. In both situations, the officer would have cause to make an arrest, even though the latter situation would result in a release from custody when the truth became known.

The basis for the arrests in the above examples centers on a concept referred to as *reasonable cause*. This term is sometimes used interchangeably with *probable cause*. Reasonable cause is based on a normative standard, or what an average individual would have done under like circumstances. "In dealing with probable cause, as the very name implies, we deal with probabilities. These are not technical; they are factual and practical considerations of everyday life on which reasonable and prudent men, not legal technicians, act. Probable cause exists where the facts and circumstances within the arresting officer's knowledge, and of which he has reasonable trustworthy information, are sufficient in themselves to warrant a man of reasonable caution in the belief that an offense has been or is being committed." [*Carroll* v. *United States*, 267 U.S. 132 (1925).][2]

[2] Livingston Hall, et al., *Modern Criminal Procedure* (St. Paul: West Publishing, 1969).

The type of arrest encouraged by the courts in the United States is an arrest pursuant to the authority of a warrant. Such an arrest includes an inspection of reasonable cause prior to the arrest from the less partial eye of a magistrate, and is the only form of arrest specifically sanctioned by the Constitution. An officer who makes an arrest pursuant to the conditions specified by an arrest warrant cannot be held responsible for false arrest.

The content of a warrant is generally standardized from state to state. A typical state penal code requires that the name of the defendant, the charge, and the bail be stated on the actual warrant. If the name of the defendant is not known, a "John Doe" warrant may be issued if it particularly describes the person to be arrested. In addition, felony warrants can normally be served anytime during the day or night. Misdemeanor arrest warrants can only be served during daylight hours unless it is specifically stated that they may be served during nighttime.

The right or power of a peace officer to arrest, with or without warrant, is generally limited to his particular area of jurisdiction. For example, a peace officer may not normally enter the county or state jurisdiction of another to make an arrest. He must allow the agency in whose jurisdiction the suspect is found to make the arrest, and then await the proper legal process that would return the defendant to the original jurisdiction. An exception to this rule is an arrest based on the concept of *fresh pursuit*. Most neighboring jurisdictions, whether county or state, have established reciprocal agreements with other agencies based on the Uniform Fresh Pursuit Act. This legislation provides for the arrest of felony suspects when they have crossed jurisdictional boundaries and peace officers are in immediate pursuit. A requirement of fresh pursuit is that it must be immediate pursuit without an extraordinary lapse of time, although the suspect need not be kept in constant view.

> *As regards pursuit of a suspect, it should be noted that it must be reasonably prompt. The same officer need not be in constant pursuit. In fact the suspect need not be in continuous view. Thus a suspect may be chased by several officers who may even be from different agencies. If the suspect vehicle is lost from sight and then relocated, the suspect is still being pursued. The test therefore requires that police be in reasonably fresh pursuit of the suspect from the crime scene.*[3]

[3] C. A. Pantaleoni and James C. Begler, *California Criminal Law* (Englewood Cliffs, N.J.: Prentice-Hall, 1971).

There is normally no provision for fresh pursuit arrests in misdemeanor cases. A peace officer must stop pursuit at a jurisdictional boundary when pursuing the suspected violator in such a case. Only one or two states allow fresh pursuit entry across their boundaries for minor offenses. In any other case, a peace officer visiting another jurisdiction may arrest under authority of a private citizen.

Authority to Detain

Suppose that a peace officer observes an individual, known to him as a burglar, leave the rear of a building in a commercial area at an unusual time of the night. If there is no obvious violation of the law present, by what authority does the peace officer stop and question him? If the suspect wishes to leave at the moment the officer approaches him, and the officer does not have probable cause for an arrest, by what authority does the officer continue to detain him? These are more difficult questions than they first appear. There has been much confusion in legal minds as

Figure 5-2. After discovering the weapon used in the robbery (as a result of the "pat" search), reasonable cause is established and a felony arrest is made.

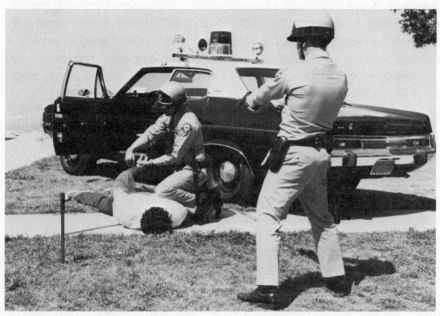

to where this authority originates. *Terry* v. *Ohio* [392 U.S. 1 (1968)] approached this problem from two directions. First, a peace officer has a right to detain under conditions in which he may believe a criminal act has occurred or is about to occur, even though probable cause to arrest does not exist. His cause must go beyond mere suspicion and be articulated to the satisfaction of a court. "A police officer may, in appropriate circumstances and in an appropriate manner, approach for purposes of investigating possible criminal behavior even though there is no probable cause to make an arrest."[4]

Second, during such a detention, a peace officer may take reasonable precautions to protect himself and others. This consists of patting down the outside of a suspect's clothing only for those objects that could reasonably be a weapon. He may enter the clothing only to retrieve a weapon. This 1968 case, along with a New York legislative act providing for similar safeguards, has become known as stop-and-frisk.

[4] Klotter and Kanovitz, *Constitutional Law for Police.*

"No Knock" Principle

Although a great amount of controversy has centered around the "no knock" law, few people actually understand the principle behind it. Normally, to execute a search warrant, a peace officer must approach a residence and announce his presence and his intentions. If, however, the warrant is directed toward the recovery of contraband such as narcotics, such contraband could be disposed of prior to his announced entry. To combat such activity, it would conceivably be necessary to enter without prior notice.

In one state the Drug Abuse and Prevention Control Act of 1970 authorizes any officer to: "Execute a search warrant relating to offenses involving controlled dangerous substances. . . . (He) may, without notice of his authority and purpose, break open an outer or inner door or window of the building provided that there is probable cause to believe that (a) the property sought may and, if such notice is given, will be easily and quickly destroyed or disposed of, or (b) the giving of such notice will immediately endanger the life or safety of the executing officer or other person. . . ."

It is within the parameters of substantive and procedural criminal law that the police agencies operate, but consideration must also be given to organizational roles.

Conflict in the Police Role

The police officer, in his day-to-day activity, is the representative of government with whom many citizens have the most frequent contact, and the only governmental official authorized to use force to carry out his assignments. This places the police organization and police officer in a difficult position. Although often needed, their authority, their use of force, and what they represent are at times resented by citizens. Historically, the police response to this resentment has been a tendency to become isolated from the community and to develop a strong occupational solidarity.

Within this context, it is now appropriate to discuss the concept of role. Both organizations and individuals have roles. The police organization has a role in the community, and the police officer has a role in the community and in the organization. Role can be generally defined as the expectations held concerning *what* an organization or individual is supposed to do and *how* it is supposed to be done.

In identifying the police role there are several sources from which expectations can be derived. Generally speaking, expectations for the police organization are derived from the law, the community, and the police organization itself. For the individual police officer, expectations can be derived from the same sources and, additionally, from fellow employees. The problem that develops from having so many sources anticipating specific behavior from police is that the expectations may not be clearly communicated, or that they may be in conflict. These differences in expectations create role conflict for police.

The basic source for expectations concerning the police role is the law. Criminal law is both substantive and procedural. Substantive law defines the elements of acts that are required or prohibited. For example, robbery, murder, and larceny are prohibited acts; having a driver's license, registering for the draft, or obtaining a license to sell liquor are required acts. Procedural criminal law concerns the correctness of the application of the substantive criminal law. In the crime of robbery, a suspect may be arrested only on probable cause and, if arrested, the suspect does not have to discuss the matter with police and may have an attorney if desired. These are some examples of the procedures the police must go through to enforce the substantive criminal law.

Role conflict for police exists in both substantive and procedural criminal law. Two factors create this conflict in the case of substantive criminal law. The first factor concerns the number of police available to enforce laws. Because of the number of police officers in most communities, the police must be selective in the laws they enforce. This is not necessarily a conflict, however, because a second source of police role expectations—the community—does not want some laws rigidly enforced. The conflict arises when there is a difference in what the police want and what the community expects. A case in point might be gambling for charitable purposes such as in a church bingo game: a "raid" would probably upset the community sufficiently so that the political leaders could demand that no such police action take place again. Another example is that of traffic laws. Citizens normally expect a certain tolerance in speeding cases and warnings instead of tickets in non-moving violations, such as faulty headlights and taillights. Again, if the police rigidly enforce traffic laws, the community, through its political leaders, might demand a return to a certain level of tolerance.

In communities where there is a consensus concerning which laws are to be selectively enforced and those in which tolerance is expected, the conflict between legal and community police role expectations is minimized. Such a consensus is most likely to occur in rural and suburban communities where a substantial majority of the population have the same socioeconomic and racial/ethnic backgrounds. In these communities, standards of community conduct are usually agreed on, and these standards are clearly communicated to the police. The community–police relationship in this type of community becomes personalized, because the police and citizens get to know each other rather well.

This is not always the case in many urban areas. Large cities tend to generate far more serious crime problems for police. This factor as well as the impersonal nature of urban life tend to create problems for the community in clearly communicating its expectations to police. This is made more difficult by the fact that cities usually have diverse populations with groups having a wide variety of socioeconomic and racial/ethnic backgrounds. This leads to differences within the urban community as to its expectations of police. From neighborhood to neighborhood in the urban city it is possible to find differences in expectations concerning the manner in which the police should handle such things as gambling, liquor law violations, traffic violations, disturbances, and juvenile matters.

Another role conflict that exists for police concerns procedural criminal law. Ideally, the police would never enforce substantive criminal laws except in the appropriate manner determined by procedural law. In other words, police should never make illegal arrests or searches of persons and property, nor attempt to coerce confessions. As a practical matter, however, these things do occur at times. The reason, again, relates to expectations concerning the police role. The law certainly precludes police activity involving violation of procedural rights of suspects, but the community expects the police to deal efficiently with the crime problem and may exert pressure, often through political leaders or the news media, to reduce the crime rate. This pressure has led the police, at times, to be more concerned with solving crimes and making arrests (enforcing substantive laws) than doing so in the proper manner (observing procedural criminal laws). Once again, the legal expectations and community expectations concerning the police role are in conflict, and the police organization must adjust to this conflict. The adjustment results in the development of a policing style.

Another important factor in role conflict for police comes from the expectations that are derived from the police organization itself. Historically, community police agencies have viewed the most important part of their job as dealing with major crimes like murder, rape, robbery, burglary, and larceny. This image is generally given support by the concern shown these crimes by the community, newspapers, movies, television, and books. Organizations—including police—have a tendency to want to be efficient in what they do. Since serious crime is of major importance to police, their organizations want to deal with crime as efficiently as possible. At times, however, this inclination is hampered, in the police opinion, by the procedures they must use to solve criminal cases. Many police officers criticize court decisions that they believe limit their ability to efficiently deal with crime. This attitude has been enhanced by police isolation from the community and the mistrust and suspicion some policemen have of nonpolicemen. The fact that many police departments have developed a strong orientation toward crime fighting, especially in the urban areas, has led to a disregard of procedural laws in some cases. In other words, the police may often feel a strong desire to catch criminals without a correspondingly strong desire to care how they go about doing it.

The role conflicts that exist for police organizations also exist for police officers. In addition, conflict as to role expectations also exists between the police organization and the policeman's fellow employees, or peers. Just as a police organization adjusts to role conflict by developing an organizational style, a policeman adjusts to role conflict by developing a style of policing. At the heart of the policeman's style is his discretion—how and for what reasons decisions are made.

Policing Styles

Role conflict for police organizations and officers requires that some type of adjustment be made in role performance. Given the fact that expectations may differ about performance (what is to be done by police and how it is to be done), how do the police respond?

In 1931, Hopkins described what he called the police "war theory" of crime control—a basic conflict between substantive and procedural criminal law.[5] According to Hopkins, considerable public pressure is exerted on police to control crime. This created a police attitude that supports the settling of matters with criminals in the streets and, at times, the use of excessive physical force was found to be involved. Hopkins found widespread police belief that crime was controlled by punishment and that the police job was to administer that punishment. And, if necessary, police illegalities involving excessive force and violation of procedural rights of suspects were justified by many officers.

From these observations, Hopkins developed his war theory of crime control: police believed they were waging a war on crime and that any methods were justified in winning that war. Westley, in his 1951 research in a Midwestern city, made observations similar to those of Hopkins.[6] Westley found that some police officers believed it permissible to use violence to gain citizen respect. However, this was not the case for the majority of police. Westley also noted that the policemen were publicly regarded as corrupt and inefficient and they, in turn, tended to view the citizens of the community as the enemy. The police also believed that the manner in which they wanted to perform their job was in conflict with that desired by the community. The adjustments made by the police to this basic role conflict were:

1. A tendency to withdraw from the community by isolating themselves and associating primarily with each other.
2. To disagree with what the community wanted because of the negative attitude of the public toward the police job.
3. The development of the belief that it was acceptable to use violence to gain respect from citizens (e.g., a person who "talks back" might get slapped or punched).
4. To apprehend as many criminals as possible in order to silence public criticism.
5. Use of violence and the violation of procedural rights of suspects was considered acceptable, especially in cases where information

---

[5] E. Jerome Hopkins, *Our Lawless Police* (New York: Viking Press, 1931).
[6] William A. Westley, "The Police: A Sociological Study of Law, Custom, and Morality." unpublished Ph.D. dissertation, University of Chicago Press, 1951. Published (Cambridge, Mass.: M.I.T. Press, 1970).

was required to apprehend a suspect, and to punish sexual criminals when reluctant witnesses would not testify in court.

Banton refers to Westley in his comparative study of American and Scottish police departments.[7] In the three American cities studied, two Southern and one Northeastern, Banton also reported an isolation of the police from the community. Because of the nature of police work there was a tendency for the officer to become separated from the community. This created some problems regarding how police officers made decisions or exercised discretion. Banton demonstrated this point by indicating that the police officer on patrol was more "peace officer" than "law enforcer."

A peace officer's role involves handling problems—many of which are minor offenses of the law—without making an arrest. According to Banton, much of the patrolman's time was spent as a peacekeeper instead of as a law enforcer. The peace-officer role is important in a discussion of styles, because it emphasizes community desire in regard to selective law enforcement, and also the police manpower limitations in enforcing all laws. The peace-officer concept is also important because it emphasizes the fact that policemen make decisions concerning offenses of the law in which the law is not used as a guideline. This is the exercise of police discretion and is related to style; how the organization handles peacekeeping situations is also related to the police style of the organization.

Another important contributor to the understanding of police adjustment to role conflict is Skolnick.[8] The adjustment that he describes concerns that of substantive and procedural criminal law. Skolnick, in 1966, studying two urban police departments, found a police tendency to emphasize a social-order role more than a legal-actor role. In other words, the police seemed to be more concerned with using substantive

---

[7] Michael Banton, *The Policeman in the Community* (New York: Basic Books, 1964).

[8] Jerome H. Skolnick, *Justice Without Trial* (New York: Wiley, 1967). Skolnick's distinction concerning the order-maintenance and legal-actor roles of police is similar to Herbert Packard's crime-control and due-process models. The former emphasizes social control and factual guilt instead of legal guilt and individual justice. Herbert C. Packard, "Two Models on the Criminal Process," *University of Pennsylvania Law Review, 113* (November 1964), pp. 1-68.

laws to maintain order than in doing so within the guidelines of procedural laws. Above all, says Skolnick, the policeman sees his job as "ferreting out crime" by being alert to it and by being ready to respond vigorously, and to decide later if arrest or search were justified.

Skolnick also believes that the development of police professionalism in the United States provides support for the social-order role of policemen. This is done by the administrator who advocates production in arrests, traffic tickets, and the like· In other words, police professionalism becomes related to managerial efficiency. The more arrests and tickets produced, the more efficient and professional the organization. The problem is that the police emphasis on social order through the apprehension of suspects is given support by this idea of professionalism. Skolnick sees policemen as being too concerned with controlling crime by any means necessary, and not concerned enough with the legal expectations of the role. The police organization's expectations of the role— with some community support—are to be efficient in making arrests and to be concerned about how the arrests are made only after the job is done.

Wilson has also made an important contribution in understanding the role adjustment of police agencies.[9] In a study of eight community police organizations, Wilson identified three basic policing styles: watchman, legalistic, and service. The differences in styles were based on how each police organization handled two basic types of situations confronting police—order-maintenance and law-enforcement situations.

Order-maintenance situations are those related to disturbances of the peace or minor conflicts between two or more people. These types of situations are similar to the peacekeeping activities identified by Banton. Examples of the former might be a noisy drunk, a panhandler, or a loud stereo; examples of the latter might be a tavern fight, a family disturbance, or a landlord-tenant dispute. In such situations it is not simply a matter of applying the law; instead, the law must be interpreted and an attempt must be made to determine who is wrong and what to do. The sanction of arrest might be used, but frequently this is not done.

Law enforcement situations usually involve more serious matters and are those circumstances where a regular pattern of police response has developed. In cases where robbery, burglary, or serious assaults are

---

[9] James Q. Wilson, *Varieties of Police Behavior* (Cambridge: Harvard University Press, 1968).

involved, there is little doubt that the officer will make an arrest if possible. Little interpretation of the law is required in such situations. This is also true of serious traffic violations, in the sense that some traffic violations (for example, speeding in a school zone) will automatically result in a ticket. In other words, although traffic violations are not as serious as robbery and burglary, some violations are serious enough so that the response of the police officer is pretty well predetermined.

Wilson found that there were different types of emphasis given, primarily to the order-maintenance situations. In the *watchman* style, the police tended to view the maintenance of order as their primary function. In this style there is a tendency to overlook, tolerate, or ignore many minor violations of the law, or to handle them short of arrest. The patrolman is encouraged by the organization to follow the path of least resistance. However, while many minor crimes are ignored, there is a tendency to take a "get tough" approach when the police think that certain activities are getting out of hand, such as juvenile fights developing into gang fights.

The second form Wilson identified was the *legalistic*. In this style the police organization encourages the patrolman to take a law enforcement view of as many situations as possible. In other words, the patrolman is encouraged to see every situation in terms of only legal alternatives. The legalistic department acts as if there was a single standard of conduct—the law—for the whole community, and generally only one appropriate solution—a legal one—for each situation.

Wilson's third style, the *service*, takes seriously all situations encountered. However, the service style does not formally apply the law as frequently as the legalistic style. Order-maintenance situations for the service style are taken seriously, but alternatives other than arrest are often used. The most common alternatives might be referral to some social service agency or the development of a special police program (traffic education, drug education, and the like) to cope with order-maintenance problems.

A useful example to contrast Wilson's three policing styles is their respective responses to order-maintenance situations involving juveniles drinking beer. The tendency of the *watchman* police organization would be to ignore the situation, or perhaps to confiscate the beer, pour it out, and tell the juveniles to go home. The *legalistic* police organization would probably arrest the juvenile and confiscate the beer for evidence. The *service* police department would probably confiscate the beer for evidence, take the juveniles home to their parents, and perhaps suggest attendance at an educational program on the problems relating to drinking. In a law enforcement situation involving a "robbery-in-progress call" all three organizations would attempt to arrest the suspect, since there would be little doubt as to what is expected of the police.

A Policing Styles Model

To enhance the student's understanding of the concept of policing styles, this section describes a model that can be used to analyze community police organization styles. The model is general in nature and should not be considered definitive or absolute; instead, it is a useful way of viewing the distinctive characteristics of police organizations in their adjustments to role conflict.

A basic assumption in model development is that the goal of police is to reduce crime and maintain order in a manner designed to establish a trusting relationship with the great majority of citizens, and by developing this trusting relationship, to insure community support in the effort to reduce crime. The legal expectation of the police role is reflected in the concern for crime; the need for community support reflects a concern for community expectations of the police role. The concern for the crime and order-related goals of police involves both the order-maintenance and law-enforcement situations described by Wilson, and the peace-officer and law-officer roles of Banton. How these activities are carried out determines the style of the police organization. Generally, their dealings with crime and disorder are affected by two broad causative factors: (1) the opportunity of the criminal to engage in the deviant behavior, and (2) his desire and reasons for engaging in the deviant behavior. The word motive will be used to apply to both the desire and reasons for the desire to engage in criminal or disorderly behavior.

The methods that police select to deal with crime and disorder can be directed at opportunity or motive, or both. From the standpoint of the general community, police methods can be generally classified as either positive or negative in nature. Positive methods are those that the general community tends to see as helping it to solve its problems, and encouraging, supporting, and assisting community efforts to deal with criminal and disorderly problems.

Negative methods are those the general community accepts as being related to police arrests or giving tickets; that is, providing negative sanctions for behavior. An example of a positive method would be to respond to a rash of juvenile traffic violations with a driver-training course; a negative method would be to issue more traffic tickets to juveniles. The former method places the police in a positive relationship with the community by helping, in a nonpunitive manner, to deal with the problems. The latter method places the police in an essentially negative relationship with the community by emphasizing punishment of the juvenile.

Six Police Methods

Some of the more typical methods employed by community police organizations are described below. They are certainly not all-inclusive. They can be categorized as being mostly positive or negative, or both, from a general public perspective, and directed at opportunity or motive, or both. Figure 5-3 identifies the relationship of police methods as to opportunity and motive, and general positive or negative impact on community perceptions of police.

Educational. The educating of the community to protect self and prop-

Figure 5-3. Categories of police methods: general community reactions.

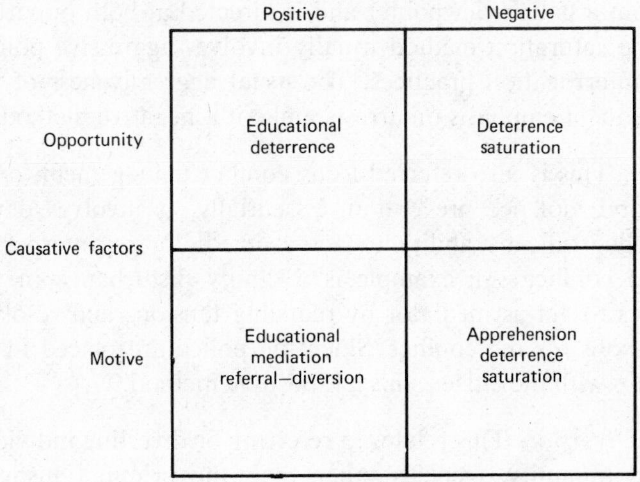

	Positive	Negative
Opportunity	Educational deterrence	Deterrence saturation
Causative factors		
Motive	Educational mediation referral—diversion	Apprehension deterrence saturation

erty, and keeping the community informed as to drug problems, the law, driving problems, and the like, are examples of this method. The contemporary concept of crime prevention often involves educational programs encouraging the citizen to engage in "target hardening" (i.e., increasing protection for home or business). This method can be related to both opportunity and motive. Educational programs designed to harden targets primarily concern opportunity; programs designed for drug education concern motive. This is essentially a positive method.

Apprehension. This involves making arrests or giving tickets and is the application of negative sanctions for behavior. It constitutes the "catching" role of the police and involves such aspects as normal investigations (in which the intent is to arrest), undercover work, stakeouts, raids, and the like. Generally, this method is negative in nature for the general community.

Deterrence. Deterrence relates to the visibility of the police in uniforms or marked mobile units. This method, commonly called patrolling, is designed to limit both the opportunity and desire for citizens to engage in deviant behavior. The uniformed walking beat officer, the marked police car, and the helicopter are the primary means of deterrence. This is both a positive and negative method because, although police presence reassures some citizens, it frightens or creates anxiety for others.

Saturation. This is an extreme form of deterrence and applies to "flooding" an area with police officers. It is usually directed at troublesome areas (from a police viewpoint) and is directed at both opportunity and desire. The saturation method usually involves aggressive police patrolling and interrogation practices. The usual aggressiveness of this tactic and its frequent emphasis on arrests make it a negative method.

Mediation. This is also referred to as conflict management, crises intervention, and violence prevention. Essentially, it involves development of the police officer's ability to act as mediator in interpersonal and intergroup conflict. An example is a family disturbance in which the officer tries to act as mediator by reducing tensions and resolving some of the reasons for the conflict. Since the police are placed in a helping relationship with the citizen, this is a positive method.

Referral/Diversion. This relates to referring or diverting individual problems to community agencies other than the criminal justice system.

Figure 5-4. The uniformed walking beat officer is a primary deterrent to crime.

A referral to a family counseling center might be an alternative for a family disturbance after the mediation has taken place. Diversion is most common in juvenile and drug cases. Both methods are designed to deal with the motive instead of the opportunity for inappropriate behavior. This is a positive method because of its helping orientation.

Counselor or Enforcer Roles

To assist in developing a policing styles model, the word counselor will be applied to the positive methods used by police, and the word enforcer will be used to apply to negative methods of police. The police, generally speaking, can be placed in counselor or enforcer roles in the community. Figure 5-5 uses these two basic police roles to create a matrix that identifies styles of community police organizations.

Depending on the degree of emphasis given to the enforcer and counselor roles of police, several styles of community policing can be

Figure 5-5. The counselor-enforcer model of policing styles.

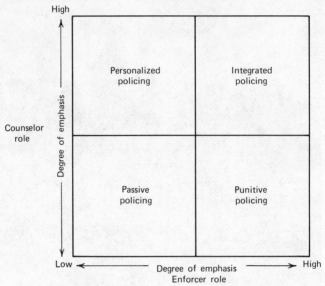

identified. Emphasis is defined as the tendency and willingness to use certain methods.

Degree of Emphasis	Policing Style
Low counselor and enforcer	Passive
Low counselor, high enforcer	Punitive
High counselor, low enforcer	Personalized
High counselor and enforcer	Integrated

Passive Policing. This is similar to the watchman style of Wilson. Generally, the police have a tendency to ignore many violations and avoid initiating any active programs to deal with crime problems. This is usually because of excessive political influence in the police department and the pressure placed on police when they become too aggressive. The other extreme occurs when police are politically pressured to do something about crime. The normal reaction of the passive police organization is to become punitive because of its traditional orientation of dealing with crime in an aggressive and punitive manner. Passive policing usually exists in moderate-to-large departments where concern for the "crime problem" can generate pressure for police action. An urban community, recently faced with a rising crime rate, pressured its passive police force to "control crime." The police response was to engage in aggressive saturation tactics to increase arrests. From an overall organizational perspective, punitive policing usually does not last long. Historically, as the police become more aggressive and negative, the community resists, and forces the police to again become passive. This passive-punitive cycle is not uncommon in many cities in which there is considerable political influence in the police department.

Personalized Policing. In a small community where police officers and citizens understand each other well, personalized policing can be extensive. In the smaller community, a citizen-police familiarity usually results in decisions based on the individual and the problem instead of on the problem itself. For example, in personalized policing, juveniles in difficulties are likely to be taken home to their parents instead of being arrested.

Personalized policing can also exist in larger cities with precinct or neighborhood police stations. Here, the people are more likely to know each other as individuals, thereby changing the manner in which decisions are made. The problem with personalized decisions is just what the name implies: the decisions made by police may often reflect a "helping" role (related to the counseling role), which may not be objective. It is one thing to refer a person to a family counseling center to help solve that person's problem; it is quite another matter to do nothing because the individual and the officer are friends. Another problem in personalized policing is that "favorite" groups may develop. In communities with diverse racial populations, middle-class whites may be known, favored, and treated favorably, while the racial minority might suffer from enforcer action. In these cases, the personalized policing represents the helping relationship only to selected groups, usually those who "run" the community.

Integrated Policing
A balance between the enforcer and counselor roles of police, this style usually comes into being when a community of whatever size desires

objective, impartial, and effective policing. This usually comes about when a community is "fed up" with one or a combination of the other three styles, and demands a change. Both enforcer and counselor roles are emphasized in the sense that the integrated style uses what is most effective in dealing with crime in order to maintain community support. The leadership in an integrated department is likely to use all the above described police methods as community problems dictate. Usually, the balance maintained ensures support by the great majority of the community.

Many police organizations are now attempting to move away from personalized, passive, and punitive policing. The word most often used to describe this change is professionalism. Two models of professionalism are emerging that are related to the integrated style. One is Wilson's service style which, at present, appears to be prevalent in suburban communities with homogeneous populations. These cities have no serious crime problems and demand a "professional" government. The other professionalism is that characterized by Skolnick as efficiency oriented. The primary thrust of this professionalism supports punitive policing by rewarding arrests, tickets, and negatively aggressive tactics. The "efficient" department has not yet rewarded the police officer for success in the counseling role. Until the professionally efficient police organization recognizes that enforcer and counselor roles must be balanced, and both rewarded by the organization, the integrated style will not develop, and *efficient* professionalism will not become *effective* professionalism.

The integrated police style is oriented toward effectiveness. It recognizes the following:

1. To be successful in crime control, an organization must develop community trust and support. The police will never be effective without the active support of the community.
2. There are many offenses of the law that can best be handled by positive counseling methods.
3. The legal expectations of the police role demand a strong commitment to strict observance of procedural rights of citizens.
4. The police role in dealing with crime and disorder should not be overemphasized. The basic responsibility for both lies primarily with the citizens of the community who can be encouraged by police officers to accept this responsibility.
5. Historically, the more punitive the police become in doing their job, the more restrictions are placed on them. If the police demands

to become "unhandcuffed" are to be heeded, they will have to find alternative methods to the enforcer role to be effective in meeting their share of the responsibility in reducing crime.

6. None of the above can be accomplished without a strong personal commitment to professional growth of the individual police officer. Only through personal development, via research, education, and training, will this professional growth take place.

There is a tendency, in discussing styles, to think of only one style for each police organization. This is not the case, since one organization can have several styles. These styles can follow shift lines (such as days or evenings), speciality (such as traffic or investigations), or neighborhoods in the community. This, of course, is the result of different expectations of performance within the police organization itself; and different expectations create role conflict for which adjustments are necessary.

Student Checklist

1. Can you identify the two primary areas of modern police power and authority?

2. Can you define the terms arrest and search and seizure?

3. Can you identify the two major categories of crime?

4. Are you able to recite the Fourth Amendment to the Constitution?

5. Can you list the three elements of penal code guidelines for arrests by a peace officer?

6. Can you define the term reasonable cause?

7. Are you able to identify the "no knock" principle?

8. Can you list the sources of expectation for identification of the police role?

9. Do you know what constitutes Hopkins's police war theory of crime control?

10. Are you able to list the six methods that a law enforcement agency uses to police a community?

Topics for Discussion

1. Discuss the major thesis presented by William A. Westley.
2. Discuss the three basic policing styles identified by James Q. Wilson.
3. Discuss the major thesis proposed by Jerome H. Skolnick.
4. Discuss the integrative policing concept.
5. Discuss the passive policing concept.

ANNOTATED BIBLIOGRAPHY

Banton, Michael. *The Policeman in the Community*. New York: Basic Books, 1964. A sociological study of the role of police in the United States and Scotland. Significant areas covered are control of interpersonal relations, conflict between police and private roles, and a discussion of the comparative isolation of the police from the community.

Bayley, David H., and Harold Mendelsohn. *Minorities and the Police*. New York: Free Press, 1969. A survey of the relationships between the police and minority groups in Denver, Colorado. The analysis of the police as an occupational group and the discussion of police attitudes toward Mexican-Americans and blacks are the important areas of concern.

Berkeley, George. *The Democratic Policeman*. Boston: Beacon Press, 1969. A comparative sociological study of police in the United States and selected Western European countries. The discussion of the apparent conflict between the idea of police and democracy is most interesting. The book includes discussion of recruitment and education, the policeman at work, policing the police, and police and society.

La Fave, Wayne R. *Arrest: The Decision To Take A Suspect into Custody*. Chicago: Little, Brown, 1965. A legalistic study of the implications of the arrest of suspects. A significant portion of the book concerns the legal implications of the use of discretion by police officers, and the impact of that discretion.

More, Harry, Jr., ed. *Critical Issues in Law Enforcement*. Cincinnati: Anderson Press, 1972. A book of readings covering several important contemporary issues in policing. Areas of most significance include a discussion of the police role, police professionalism, civil disorder, ethnic tensions, control of police conduct, and policy formulation.

Reasons, Charles, and Jack L. Kuykendall, eds. *Race, Crime, and Justice*. Pacific Palisades: Goodyear Press, 1972. A book of readings covering the relationship between the judicial system and minority groups. The section on police and minority groups is most valuable in understanding the dynamics of police-minority group encounters, and the exercise of police discretion in minority communities.

Skolnick, Jerome. *Justice Without Trial*. New York: Wiley, 1966. A sociological study of two urban police departments in the United States. Significant areas of discussion include the "working personality" of the policeman, the danger-authority conflict in the police role, and the differences between order-maintenance and legal-actor roles.

Wilson, James Q. *Varieties of Police Behavior*. Cambridge: Harvard University Press, 1968. This is a sociopolitical analysis of the management of eight municipal police agencies in the United States. The development of different styles of policing are discussed and a threefold typology is developed; the types are the legalistic, watchman, and service style.

The study of this chapter will enable you to:

1. Distinguish between the duties performed by British solicitors and barristers.
2. Write an essay that sets forth the functions performed by the Attorney General of the United States.
3. Compare the duties performed by the U.S. Attorney General and a typical state attorney general.
4. List the prosecutor's responsibilities in the criminal process.
5. Identify the advantages and disadvantages inherent in the high political orientation of the prosecutor's office.
6. Write an essay that identifies the problems of coordinating the prosecutorial functions within a state.
7. Describe the duties and responsibilities that could be performed by a state council of prosecutors.

6
Prosecuting Attorney

The American system of criminal justice has as its foundation the legal system of the English common law and Roman law from continental Europe. This is especially true as to the substantive criminal law that statutorily defines, in every state, those acts that are illegal and punishable as crimes. Most of these legislative pronouncements were also crimes at the English common law. There is, however, very little relationship in England and Europe to the criminal justice system function performed by American prosecutors.

Historical Precedence

In Europe, the prosecutor is a career official, permanently appointed, who has a close relationship to the court, which gives him far less autonomy than his American counterpart. The European prosecutor is generally not a member of a bar.

Although he is a key figure in the administration of criminal justice, his authority stems from being part of a central instead of a local government. In those states in the United States that have an integrated bar, membership in a bar association is required as a condition precedent to the practice of law.

At the British common law all criminal prosecutions were brought in the name of the Crown; in the United States today all criminal prosecutions are brought in the name of a state, commonwealth, or the United States, depending on which governmental body has jurisdiction. To represent the Crown in the early English prosecution, a general attorney (or attorney general, as the office became to be known) was appointed. He is a member of government and also a member of the bar, of which he is the ex-officio head. Prior to 1879 the attorney general was the only person in England who could be described as a public prosecutor. He had the power to proceed with or refuse prosecution of a criminal case referred by police, other governmental offices, or by a private citizen.

In 1879 the office of Director of Public Prosecutions was created, but the director acted in an advisory capacity only in regard to criminal matters. Between 1884 and 1908 the office of Director of Public Prosecution was merged with the office of the Treasury Solicitor who, prior to 1908, performed the solicitor side of the work necessary for criminal prosecution. In that year, a division of responsibility was made between government civil and criminal matters, with the latter being assigned to the Director of Public Prosecutions.

To understand this British system and its division of work—which greatly differs from the American system of criminal justice—a distinction must be made as to the duties of solicitors and barristers. The solicitor is an individual who has demonstrated by his education and office legal work a proficiency to practice law. He makes the decisions to prosecute and prepares cases for trial by doing the legal research and by drafting the pleadings necessary to get the case to court. At this point in the proceeding a barrister is employed to present the case in court. In short, the barrister is a trial attorney only. An individual can become a barrister only by graduation from one of the four Inns of Court, which are the British law schools. A senate composed of individuals of these four law schools controls the education and discipline of barristers.

In the United States there is no central coordination in the requirements for an individual's admission to the bar, and no special education or experience requirements for an attorney to be a trial attorney. In this respect, the American medical profession is far ahead of the American legal profession; a physician cannot specialize in a particular field without additional education and experience. Yet an individual who graduates from a law school, passes a state bar examination, and is admitted to the practice of law can be in court the next day prosecuting or defending a serious criminal case.

In England today the Director of Public Prosecutions is appointed by the Home Secretary. He acts, however, under the guidance and direction of the Attorney General, and in practice enjoys a great deal of independence. It is his duty to prepare and prosecute the more serious classes of criminal offenses—which are approximately eight percent of all criminal prosecution.

In effect, the Director of Public Prosecutions is the solicitor for the Crown, with the Attorney General or his staff serving as barrister for the most important cases each year. The remaining cases prepared by the Director of Public Prosecutions are presented in court by a group of barristers appointed by the Attorney General and known as Treasury Counsel or Crown Counsel. Another four percent of Britain's criminal cases are prepared and presented by other public bodies, such as the Post Office. The remaining criminal cases are police or public referrals for prosecution.

In 1935 a Solicitors Department was created in Scotland Yard to conduct all case preparation for police prosecution in the metropolitan area. These solicitors have a great deal of latitude and authority and can choose any barrister to present their case in court.[1] The majority of barristers are in private practice, and may choose those cases that they will accept for court presentment. Since the barrister is a professional advocate and has no part in the preliminary decisions as to whether to prosecute or what particular crime is to be charged, it is not uncommon that a barrister present a case for the prosecution one day and for the defense the next.

It can be readily seen that the British system of power, from the King or Queen to Attorney General to the police, might be used for oppression, as was the case during the reign of the Stuarts. It was with this background that the framers of the U.S. Constitution established a separation of power: the legislative branch, to define various acts that constitute crimes and establish penalties for their violation; and the judicial branch, to guarantee fairness in sentence and constitutionality of the law enacted by the legislative branch.

Types of Prosecutor

The Attorney General of the United States is the chief prosecutor for the federal government. The individual selected to hold this position is

[1] Patrick Devlin, *The Criminal Prosecution in England* (New Haven, Conn.: Yale University Press, 1958).

appointed by the President with the approval of the Senate. The Attorney General is a member of the President's Cabinet, and in addition to establishing policy for the U.S. Department of Justice (which he heads), he assists the President with the legal problems and questions necessary in establishing the domestic and foreign policy of the United States. The U.S. Attorney General is responsible for representing the government in all civil cases, both in trial court and on appeal, in which the United States is a party, and to prosecute to final judgment all violation of federal criminal statutes. There are approximately 140 Assistant Attorneys General in the Justice Department, located in Washington, D.C. This staff, which serves in one or more divisions of the Department of Justice, assists the Attorney General in disposing of government-appealed cases before the U.S. Supreme Court, giving legal opinions to other governmental agencies, and establishing policy, supervision of and assistance to the 93 U. S. District Attorneys who originate and prosecute federal criminal violations in their districts.

The largest divisions of the U.S. Department of Justice include the Criminal Division, the Civil Division, and the Anti-Trust Division. The Attorney General is also responsible for several federal administrative agencies. One of the largest is the Federal Bureau of Investigation— with its many agents in the field, its crime laboratory (which may be utilized by local agencies), the National Crime Information Center (NCIC), and its training academy located at Quantico, Va., which has successfully trained and graduated many thousands of local law enforcement officers. Another fast-growing agency under the Attorney General is the Law Enforcement Assistant Administration, created by the Omnibus Crime Control and Safe Streets Act of 1968 for the purpose of providing financial assistance and technical advice to local units of government. One of the most important functions of LEAA—based on the congressional finding that crime is a local problem and could be best solved on the local level—is the disbursement of many millions of dollars to states, and then to local governments, to assist in the improvement of law enforcement. It is with LEAA assistance that many law enforcement officers are able to attend college under the Law Enforcement Education Program (LEEP) loans or grants.

There is far more opportunity and authority for coordination of activities in the federal system than is available at the state or local level. The U.S. Attorney General directly controls the activities of the 93 U.S.

District Attorneys. Therefore, policy established in the Department of Justice is the same for, and is followed in, the U.S. District Attorneys' offices throughout the United States and its territories. A recent example of coordination, possibly only in the federal system, was the establishment of Strike Forces in some of the largest cities, staffed by investigators from the FBI, the Internal Revenue, Bureau of Narcotics and Dangerous Drugs, the U.S. Treasury, the Bureau of Customs, and other federal agencies, as needed.

Since criminal activities may encompass violations within the jurisdiction of several federal agencies, the Strike Force concept provided a coordinated investigative and exchange of information effort. To assist the U.S. District Attorney in whose jurisdiction a Strike Force was operating, several Assistant U.S. Attorneys General were assigned to prosecute individuals arrested by Strike Force officers. Based on the success of the Strike Force operation, a strong argument can be made for the establishment of one federal investigating agency instead of the many agencies now in existence to conduct investigation of criminal activity in one specific area. In July 1973, agents of the Customs Bureau, the Bureau of Narcotics and Dangerous Drugs, the Office for Drug Abuse Law Enforcement, the Office of National Narcotics Intelligence, and certain special agents of the Treasury Department were formed into the Drug Enforcement Agency, which will be responsible for all drug abuse law enforcement in the United States at the federal level.

The U.S. District Attorneys are appointed by the President to serve under the authority of the U.S. Attorney General as federal prosecutor in a geographically designated district. In the less populated areas of the United States the federal district follows the state boundary, whereas in the more populated states there are two or more federal districts in each state—such as the Southern District of New York, or the Northern District of California.

The 93 U.S. District Attorneys have authority to appoint assistants to carry out the duties required of their office. The majority of their time is spent in criminal justice functions, such as preparing search warrant affidavits; appearing as prosecutors before federal grand juries; and representing the federal government at criminal arraignments, preliminary hearings, and trials. Much of their time is spent working with and providing legal advice to agents of the FBI and other federal investigating agencies. Closely related to criminal work is the legal enforcement of the

Civil Rights Act. The remainder of the U.S. District Attorneys' duties are civil in nature and range from condemnations of land for roads and buildings to representing the government in negligence actions.

Although the opportunity exists for complete coordination and uniform policy establishment in the federal criminal justice system, there are some inherent weaknesses. The major problem lies with the appointments of the Attorney General, the U.S. District Attorney, and his assistants, based largely on political consideration, not on individual ability. It is extremely disrupting to the Justice Department to change all personnel in a district attorney's office upon the election of a President from another political party. This issue might be partially resolved by giving Civil Service status with career possibilities to the many assistant U.S. District Attorneys. It could be completely resolved by providing career status to all federal prosecutors.

Each state has an attorney general whose prime responsibility is to represent the state in all civil matters and, in most states, handle the appeal of the criminal prosecutions in the state supreme courts and in federal courts. The authority of the state attorney general varies from state to state. In Alaska, Delaware, and Rhode Island, for example, the attorney general has the full responsibility for all criminal prosecutions, and those who prosecute on the local level are assistant attorneys general. In other states the attorney general has absolutely no control over local prosecutions. In the majority of states, however, the attorney general has concurrent jurisdiction with the local prosecutor. This jurisdiction is rarely used to circumvent the prosecutor but is, as a practical matter, used to supplement the local prosecution service.

On the local level the prosecutor takes many names. He may be known as the district attorney, a prosecuting attorney, a state attorney, a county attorney.[2] Whatever he is called, however, the duties are essentially the same. It is the prosecuting attorney's responsibility to examine the facts presented to him by the police or a private citizen; to make a determination that a crime has been committed and that there is sufficient evidence to prosecute to a successful conviction; to file the necessary pleading; and to conduct the trial of the criminal case. Prosecuting attorneys are usually elected and have the authority to hire assistant

[2] Patrick Devlin, *The Criminal Prosecution in England* (New Haven, Conn.: Yale University Press, 1958).

prosecutors, based on the moneys available for salaries established by the county board or state legislature.

Also performing a prosecuting function are city attorneys. Most cities have a city attorney's office that handles the civil work for the city. Serving under the city attorney is a city prosecutor, whose responsibility is the prosecution of violations of city ordinances. In some situations the city attorneys and city prosecutors have the authority to prosecute under state statutes for misdemeanors, and to conduct preliminary hearings in felony cases. It is in this area that the most citizens have their contact with the criminal system, since the majority of traffic offenses—which for the most part are misdemeanors—are prosecuted by city attorneys.

Functions and Responsibilities

Earlier chapters have considered a number of the prosecutor's responsibilities in the criminal process, including his authority to determine whether an alleged offender should be charged and to obtain convictions through guilty plea negotiations. The decisions he makes influence and often determine the disposition in all cases brought to him by the police. The prosecutor's decisions also significantly affect the arrest practices of the police, the volume of cases in the courts, and the number of offenders referred to the correctional system. Thus, the prosecutor is in the most favorable position to bring about needed coordination among the various law enforcement and correctional agencies in the community.[3]

The prosecutor has the responsibility of presenting the government's case in court, and his skill as a trial lawyer can be a crucial determinant of whether an offender is convicted. And at a time when police practices are coming under increased judicial scrutiny, law enforcement agencies rely on the prosecutor to advocate their position in the courts.

Finally, the prosecutor is often an investigator and initiator of the criminal process. Prosecutors work closely with the police on important investigations. Many jurisdictions have found that investigations and prosecutions for homicide, consumer fraud, governmental corruption,

[3] The President's Commission on Law Enforcement and Administration of Justice: *Task Force Reports: The Courts* (Washington, D.C.: U.S. Govt. Printing Office, 1967), p. 72.

and organized crime, which typically involve difficult problems of proof and require lengthy and careful investigation, are best conducted under the direct supervision of the prosecutor's office. The extent to which such offenses are detected and successfully prosecuted depends directly on the prosecutor's diligence.

In many jurisdictions, unfortunately, the potential of the prosecutor's office is not realized. In many cities the prosecutor must operate under such staggering caseloads (with a small staff of assistants) that sufficient attention cannot be given to each case. In many lower courts prosecution is left to police officers. Meeting the day-to-day trial business of the office leaves little time for developing policies within the office, or for attempting to coordinate the efforts of other agencies. Responsibility for making charging decisions and trying cases is often delegated to inexperienced young assistants who have had insufficient training and who receive only limited guidance from their superiors. Yet needed changes frequently depend on the vigorous leadership of the prosecutor. Implementation of alternative methods of dealing with offenders for whom criminal prosecution is inappropriate, new procedures for the negotiation of guilty pleas, bail reform, regulation of statements to news media, and expanded pretrial discovery of evidence in criminal cases depend heavily on the support and sympathetic involvement of the prosecutor. They highlight the importance of improving the quality of the men who serve as district attorneys and their assistants.

Obstacles to Effective Prosecution

The district or county attorney in most states is a locally elected official. In larger communities the prosecutor has a staff of assistants (as many as 216 in Los Angeles County). But the majority of the country's more than 2700 prosecutors serve in small offices with one or two assistants; frequently all are part-time officials. Their official duties are to prosecute all criminal cases and in most jurisdictions to represent the local government in civil cases (see Table 6-1). But when not engaged on a case they are free to practice law privately. This pattern of outside practice is common in rural counties and smaller cities, although it may be found in our largest cities as well.

The conception of the prosecutor's office as a part-time position is

TABLE 6-1. **State Prosecutors: A Comparison.**

State	No. of Counties	Title of Prosecutor	No. of Prosecutors*	Duties
Alabama	67	District attorney	34	Criminal, civil
Alaska	4	District attorney	5	Criminal, civil, appeals
Arizona	14	County attorney	14	Criminal, civil
Arkansas	75	Prosecuting attorney	18	Criminal only
California	58	District attorney	58	Criminal, civil, except 26 counties
Colorado	63	District attorney	15	Criminal only
Connecticut	8	State's attorney	9	Felony, criminal, and appeals
		Prosecuting attorney	18	Misdemeanor, criminal
Delaware	3	Deputy attorney general	4	Criminal, civil, appeals
Florida	67	State attorney	17	Felony, criminal
		Prosecuting attorney	59	Misdemeanor, criminal
Georgia	159	County solicitor	8	Criminal, except capital offenses
		Solicitor general	40	Criminal, civil, appeals
Hawaii	4	County attorney	3	Criminal, civil, appeals
		Prosecuting attorney	1	Criminal, appeals
Idaho	44	Prosecuting attorney	44	Criminal, civil
Illinois	102	State's attorney	102	Criminal, civil, appeals
Indiana	92	Prosecuting attorney	82	Criminal only
Iowa	99	County attorney	99	Criminal, civil
Kansas	105	County attorney	105	Criminal, civil appeals

* Does not include assistants.

Source: The Prosecutor, Journal of The National District Attorneys Association Foundation, 2 No. 4 (July, August 1966), p. 192.

TABLE 6-1. **State Prosecutors: A Comparison** (continued).

State	No. of Counties	Title of Prosecutor	No. of Prosecutors*	Duties
Kentucky	120	Commonwealth attorney	46	Felony, criminal, appeals
		County attorney	16	Misdemeanor, criminal
Louisiana	64	District attorney	34	Criminal, civil
Maine	16	County attorney	16	Criminal, civil
Maryland	23	State's attorney	24	Criminal, civil
Massachusetts	14	District attorney	9	Criminal, civil, appeals
Michigan	83	Prosecuting attorney	83	Criminal, civil, appeals
Minnesota	87	County attorney	87	Criminal, civil, appeals
Mississippi	82	District attorney	19	Felony, criminal
		County attorney	82	Misdemeanor, criminal
Missouri	114	Circuit attorney	1	(St. Louis) Felony, criminal only
		Prosecuting attorney	115	Criminal only
Montana	56	County attorney	56	Criminal, civil
Nebraska	93	County attorney	93	Criminal, civil
Nevada	17	District attorney	10	Criminal, civil
New Hampshire	10	County attorney	10	Criminal, civil
New Jersey	21	County prosecutor	21	Criminal only
New Mexico	32	District attorney	11	Criminal only
New York	62	District attorney	62	Criminal, civil, appeals
North Carolina	100	District solicitor	21	Criminal only
North Dakota	53	State's attorney	53	Criminal, civil, appeals

* Does not include assistants.

Source: The Prosecutor, Journal of The National District Attorneys Association Foundation, 2 No. 4 (July, August 1966), p. 192.

TABLE 6-1. **State Prosecutors: A Comparison** (continued).

State	No. of Counties	Title of Prosecutor	No. of Prosecutors*	Duties
Ohio	88	Prosecuting attorney	88	Criminal, civil, appeals
Oklahoma	77	District attorney	27	Criminal
Oregon	36	District attorney	36	Criminal, civil, appeals
Pennsylvania	67	District attorney	67	Criminal, civil, appeals
Rhode Island	5	Attorney general	1	Criminal, civil
South Carolina	46	Circuit solicitor	15	Criminal, civil
South Dakota	64	State's attorney	64	Criminal, civil
Tennessee	95	District attorney general	21	Criminal only
Texas	254	County attorney	238	Criminal
		District attorney	63	Felony, criminal
		Criminal district attorney	16	Criminal only
Utah	29	District attorney	7	Felony, criminal
		County attorney	29	Misdemeanor, criminal, civil
Vermont	14	State's attorney	14	Criminal, civil, appeals
Virginia	98	Commonwealth attorney	123	Criminal, civil
Washington	39	Prosecuting attorney	39	Criminal, civil, appeals
West Virginia	55	Prosecuting attorney	55	Criminal, civil
Wisconsin	71	District attorney	71	Criminal, civil
Wyoming	23	County prosecuting attorney	23	Criminal, civil

* Does not include assistants.

Source: The Prosecutor, Journal of The National District Attorneys Association Foundation, 2 No. 4 (July, August 1966), p. 192.

one of the consequences, as it is one of the causes, of the low salaries paid to prosecutors and their assistants. In response to a recent survey conducted by the National District Attorneys Association, some prosecutors in 21 states indicated that their annual salary was less than $4000. Even in large cities the compensation of the district attorney and his assistants tends to be extremely low in comparison to the earnings of lawyers of similar experience in private practice. A high proportion of prosecutors in almost all states reported in the American Bar Foundation's 1964 survey that they did not receive adequate funds to operate their offices effectively. For example, the highest paid assistant in the State's Attorney's Office in Baltimore, an office with 32 assistants serving a city of almost a million persons, receives slightly more than $10,000, and comparably low salaries are common elsewhere.

Obviously, a talented attorney—even one dedicated to public service—cannot be expected to remain long at such a position if it is his only source of income. Many prosecutors and their assistants must and are expected to engage in private law practice. Pressures on a part-time prosecutor not to permit his public office to interfere with his private practice are inevitable. These pressures are strengthened by the economic reliance on private practice and by the widespread attitude that a prosecutor's position is a temporary stepping-stone in a political career.

While direct conflicts of interest between the prosecutor's public office and his private practice are clearly unlawful and, we may assume, rare, there are many indirect conflicts that almost inevitably arise. The attorneys he deals with as a public officer are the same ones with whom he is expected to maintain a less formal and more accommodating relationship as counsel to private clients. Similar problems may arise in the prosecutor's dealings with his private clients whose activities may come to his official attention. It is undesirable to place a prosecutor in a position in which he must always be conscious of this potential for conflict and be careful to avoid improprieties or the appearance of conflict.

The high political orientation of the prosecutor's office contributes to the problems of low pay and part-time service. In almost all states, local prosecuting attorneys are chosen by the votes of the community. Only four states and the federal system provide for the appointment of prosecutors, and even in these jurisdictions partisan considerations appear to play a vital part in their selection. In a few communities highly competent men have made a career in the office, but generally the incumbent moves on after one or two terms.

The prosecutors in most cities select a high proportion of their assistants primarily on the basis of party affiliation and the recommendations of ward leaders and elected officials. Highly qualified practicing lawyers and recent law school graduates may be prevented from entering the prosecutor's office because they are unable or unwilling to acquire political sponsorship. Lawyers who are considering a career in the prosecutor's office may be daunted, even if they have the required political support, by the likelihood of discharge if their party does not retain control of the office at the next election. Furthermore, the obligations usually attached to a patronage position—such as purchasing or selling tickets to fund-raising dinners, campaigning, or systematically contributing to the party—may be distasteful to many lawyers.

Political factors and noncareer tenure of prosecutors have certain advantages. Local election increases the likelihood that the prosecutor will be responsive to the dominant law enforcement views and demands of the community. Since he is not dependent on another official for reappointment, the prosecutor possesses a degree of political independence that is desirable for an officer charged with the investigation and prosecution of charges of bribery and corruption. The frequency of election, the turnover in the job, and the noncareer attitude toward it all have affirmative values. A new man is likely to come to the office without a comfortable acceptance of the status quo; turnover reduces the dangers of lower and lower achievement.

But many of these same factors interfere with the full development of the prosecutor's office. Political considerations make some prosecutors overly sensitive to what is safe, expedient, and in conformity with law enforcement views that are popular instead of enlightened. Political ambition does not encourage a prosecutor to take risks that are frequently required in reasoned judgments. In dealing with offenders, with the police and other law enforcement agencies, and with the courts, the prosecutor is safer sticking to the familiar and most limited connotation of his job.

The Prosecutor's Office as a Full-Time Career

The problems of low pay and part-time employment must be approached together. High-quality attorneys who should be encouraged to seek the position will do so only if it offers reasonable economic rewards. Full-time devotion to duty cannot be demanded unless salaries are based on the assumption that the prosecutor will not have a second income from an outside law practice. In most city offices there is little apparent justification for the continuation of part-time prosecutors. These offices are faced with very heavy workloads that require the fullest attention from men who are not distracted by other obligations and interests. Several cities have successfully established full-time offices in which neither the district attorney nor his assistants are permitted to practice law.

The smaller county presents other problems because there is generally not sufficient work to keep a prosecutor busy full time, even if he has civil law responsibilities. In part, this is an indication that the county unit of prosecution is too small to be efficient in such situations. Some states have moved to create district attorney's offices covering judicial districts larger than one county. Oklahoma, in 1965, eliminated the part-time office of county attorney and created in its place the full-time office of district attorney. Each district attorney is responsible for criminal prosecution in a number of counties comprising a prosecutorial district. Local influence over criminal prosecutions is maintained by requiring the district attorney to select one assistant, who may serve part-time, from each of the counties in his district.

It seems unlikely that the basic elective method of selecting prosecutors will soon be changed. The election of local prosecutors is ingrained in our political traditions. Moreover, experience in several large cities has shown that the elective process can produce dedicated career prosecutors who are highly professional and competent. Instead of replacing the elective method, steps should be taken to reduce some of the political pressures on the job.

First, political leaders in the community should raise their sights in selecting candidates and should give preference to men who see the office as a relatively long-term professional opportunity instead of as a short-term step to another office. In addition, the appointment of assistant district attorneys should be removed from political patronage. This might be accomplished through the traditional Civil Service method, which has been relatively successful in some large cities. Many communities may not find this approach desirable, however, nor would it appear to be the only way to deal with the problem. Certainly the appointment of assistants should not depend on political sponsorship. Assistants should be free from political obligations to campaign or to contribute, and prosecutors should be given full authority to appoint and discharge assistants on the basis of merit. Experience in New York and Los Angeles shows that this approach is feasible, provided only that political leadership recognizes that the patronage and political leverage surrendered by such a reform is more than compensated for by the greater potential for effective law enforcement.

Coordination of Prosecutorial Functions

Although each state has a single code of criminal laws, the state prosecutorial function, like the police and the courts, is fragmented among a number of independent agencies. The states are geographically divided into districts or counties, each of which has a prosecutor's office headed by an elected or appointed official. In many urban areas one prosecutor, typically the district attorney, is responsible for felony cases while another independent officer, perhaps the corporation counsel or city attorney, deals with less serious offenses and sometimes the early stages of felony cases. The number of county and local prosecutors may be as high as 317, in Texas, or as few as 4, in Hawaii. Each of these prosecutors' offices is virtually autonomous. Apart from informal communication there has often been little or no coordination among them.

The existing system is not without advantages. A local prosecutor is usually a product of the community in which he serves. He is locally elected and is likely to be responsive to his constituency. Most important, since marked variation in the crime problem and in community resources may exist from area to area within a state, he is in a position to adjust prosecutorial policy to local conditions.

But division of the prosecutorial function and lack of coordination among local offices within a single state is also likely to have deleterious consequences. A strict enforcement policy in one county may simply divert criminal activity into neighboring areas. A community's effort to deal with crime will be limited if criminal groups can operate from a nearby jurisdiction with relative impunity. This may be seen in large metropolitan areas where prostitution, gambling, and bootlegging become exceedingly difficult to suppress when they are operated from nearby havens.

The traditional notion that the criminal law will be applied within a state with a reasonable degree of uniformity is weakened by a fragmented system of prosecution. Prosecutors exercise enormous discretionary authority within their jurisdictions. They decide whether to prosecute and for what offense; they decide whether to negotiate a plea of guilty and on what terms. Exercise of this broad discretion by many prosecutors scattered through a state inevitably results in an uneven application of the law. While such subtle decisions cannot and should not be confined by rigid rules, sufficient policy coordination is desirable to ensure a reasonable degree of consistency. The challenge is to devise a system that strikes an acceptable balance between the needed flexibility and our traditional notions of evenhanded administration of the criminal law.

Closer communication among local offices within a state, and greater involvement by the state in their operations, would have a number of advantages. County prosecutors' offices frequently are too small to maintain specialized personnel and technical facilities. They are generally unable to maintain formal training programs of the sort that could be conducted on a regional or statewide basis. A state agency could make manpower and special services available to local prosecutors, including fingerprint experts, medical specialists, and technical assistance in the form of a central laboratory. Supplemental legal, investigative, and trial specialists could be provided to meet the demands of extraordinary caseloads or unusually difficult cases.

Another important aspect of the coordinated statewide approach to law enforcement would be to maintain a uniformly high caliber of personnel and quality of work throughout the state. To a large extent this would not require continuous overseeing of the internal operations of local offices. Statewide provisions could regulate matters like basic manpower requirements, perhaps described as a function of population or caseload; standards for selecting assistants; requirements and opportunities for preservice and in-service training; rates of compensation for assistants; permissibility of part-time employment; and programs for encouraging lateral movement from county to county within a state.

Law enforcement on the county level has occasionally faltered because of corruption or incompetence; a state agency with the power to intervene is needed. In most states the attorney general or the governor has the power to supersede local prosecutors or to appoint special prosecutors when the elected district attorney has not adequately performed his duties, a power exercised only in extreme cases. In situations short of outright misfeasance, state officers may be unwilling or unable to use such a drastic sanction, and in the absence of continuing contacts with local prosecutors, the state officers may find themselves without a remedy.

A better communication among prosecutors' officers within a state should contribute to the development of cooperation among local prosecutors' offices in different states and between local prosecutors' offices and federal agencies. Stronger state government participation could ease the problem of determining priorities and allocating resources in connection with a federal program providing financial assistance to local law enforcement. A state agency would provide a logical forum for consideration of joint law enforcement problems by prosecutors, police, correctional authorities, and the courts.

Existing Structures

As the highest legal officer in the state, the attorney general might be expected to provide needed leadership in developing ties among prosecutors within the state and with law enforcement agencies in other states and in the federal government. The powers of the various state attorneys general include a number of ways in which this leadership may be exercised. At one extreme, the attorneys general in Alaska, Delaware, and Rhode Island have full responsibility for all criminal prosecutions, and those who prosecute cases locally work under their direct supervision. At the other extreme there are a few states—Ohio, Tennessee, and Wyoming, for example—where the attorney general has no authority over local enforcement activities. In several states the attorney general has little involvement in any criminal matters; the attorney general of Connecticut is exclusively a civil law officer.

In most of the states, however, the attorney general has broad authority, through constitutional or statutory provisions or inherent common law powers, which provides a basis for coordination of the activities of local prosecutors. Some of these grants of authority include concurrent jurisdiction to prosecute or the power to supervise, assist, consult, or advise local prosecutors. In practice, however, there is little actual coordination. The attorneys general in a few states—Indiana, Kansas, Massachusetts, and Texas, for example—hold statewide prosecutors' meetings once or twice a year. California is divided into zones, and zone meetings called by the attorney general are held bimonthly.

In Ohio, the attorney general annually conducts two courses for county attorneys. Some attorneys general also require periodic reports from local prosecutors.

The prevailing pattern, then, is that most of the state attorneys general do possess formal authority to coordinate local law enforcement activity; that in most states this authority has not been exercised; and that even in those states where some coordination is attempted, much more could be done.

The lack of coordination of local prosecutors in the states may be compared with the organization of the prosecutorial function in the federal system. The entire country is divided into 93 federal districts, each of which has a prosecutor's office headed by a U.S. Attorney. As in many states, the U.S. Attorney General formally occupies the position of chief prosecution officer. Efforts have been made to coordinate and supervise the prosecutorial activities of U.S. Attorneys' offices by the Department of Justice Criminal Division, which furnishes research and manpower assistance, performs certain training functions, and establishes major prosecutorial policy for the entire country. It also assumes more direct responsibility for decision in certain kinds of cases when centralized control is deemed particularly important.

Problems of Developing Effective State Coordination

Recognition of the need for greater state responsibility for local law enforcement is not a recent development. The Wickersham Commission in 1931 called attention to the changing nature of this country's law enforcement needs:

> In the formative era we had a great and justified fear of centralization. But overdecentralization may be quite as bad as overcentralization. Under the conditions of transportation today and with the facilities for and coming of highly organized crime, the state is as natural a unit as the county or town was a century ago. . . .When but little in the way of administration was needed and legislative regulations were relatively few, occasional exercise of local private judgment as to enforcement of laws of statewide application did little or no harm. With the coming of great urban centers, the rise of industrial communities, and the development of communication and transportation, this private judgment on the part of local officials has become an obstacle to efficient administra-

tion. In more than one state refusal of local prosecutors to enforce state laws in the locality led to legislation providing for removal by some central authority long before the national prohibition act. But this is a crude substitute for a control over prosecutions by a central responsible office, beyond the reach of local politics, analogous to what obtains in the federal system.[4]

In the 44 years since the Wickersham Commission recommended greater state action, some halting steps have been taken by a few states, notably California and Alaska, but for all practical purposes the prevailing pattern remains substantially the same. Why has so little been done when the need has been so clear?

There are the inherent problems involved in promulgating constitutional or legislative enactments on the state level where that is required. Any proposals that require legislative action face the possibility of substantial delays. Any proposals for government reorganization, the establishment of new agencies, or the granting of new powers to old agencies inevitably meet resistance from vested interests.

The political dimensions of the problem should not be underestimated, even when no constitutional or legislative action is required. Local prosecutors' offices are often heavily involved in the intricacies of politics on the local government level. Similarly, the state attorney general or any similar state officer or agency that might be looked to as a focal point for coordination will also often be heavily involved in state politics. When attempts to coordinate law enforcement begin to be interpreted as involving state control and state supervision, friction may develop between state and local government.

While progress toward a more coherent law enforcement organization is beset by difficulties, the need to move in this direction is compelling. County prosecutorial lines that made little sense in the 1930s often make no sense today. The growth of enormous urban complexes that transcend county and even state lines, the rapid mobility of the modern criminal, and the increased incidence of organized criminal activity make the need for coordination of prosecutorial efforts greater today than it was 30 years ago. Realistic recognition of the difficulties, however, should be helpful in planning programs for action.

---

[4] The National Commission on Law Observance and Enforcement (Wickersham Commission), report published in 1931.

To accomplish the desired coordination, different administrative approaches may be desirable in different states, depending on the governmental structure and political practicalities. Consequently, it is not feasible to describe in detail the type of state machinery required, but it is possible to sketch the basic features of a state-level operation geared to policy coordination and the provision of services to local prosecutors.

State coordination of local prosecution implies involvement of a state office in local prosecutions. This state coordination could mean control of all prosecutorial decision-making by the state attorney general or a similar officer. It could mean that local prosecutors would be required to obtain approval from the state officer at each key point in processing a case, or that decisions would be made initially in the state capital or by agents sent out by the state office. Although this is the approach followed in a few small states, in most places it would present unacceptable disadvantages. It would be unduly cumbersome and inefficient, requiring a large investment of manpower at the state level and resulting in decisions by persons too far from the scene. Moreover, most of the advantages of locally centered prosecution would be forfeited.

There are, of course, certain instances where such detailed control by a state officer is desirable. The attorney general in some states has direct responsibility for the enforcement of certain laws, such as the antitrust laws or consumer fraud statutes. And, as already noted, in many states the attorney general may send in a special prosecutor to deal with cases of official corruption or with other cases of special importance. But these limited situations do not provide a basis for a general assumption of the prosecutorial function at the state level.

Coordination by the State Attorney General

A preferable type of coordination would involve the state attorney general in providing technical and statistical services, engaging in training operations, and developing rules of general applicability for the various kinds of discretionary decisions prosecutors make. Some examples of the kinds of policies that are appropriate for state formulation are:

1. A state attorney general, perhaps in response to developing court decisions or rules, might formulate guidelines on the circumstances under which local prosecutors should routinely make certain information and evidence available to defense counsel before trial.
2. A state attorney general, after consultation with state youth and

correctional authorities, might develop a program under which local prosecutors obtain probation reports before proceeding with the prosecution of certain classes of youthful offenders.

3. A state attorney general might establish rules requiring local prosecutors to reveal in open court the negotiations leading up to the tender of a guilty plea.

4. A state attorney general might formulate guidelines on the types of cases in which noncriminal dispositions should be pursued and the circumstances under which court approval should be obtained.

Under this approach there would often be a need for local prosecutors to formulate still more detailed rules. For example, local prosecutors might be required to make rules for preservice and in-service training of their assistants within broad state guidelines describing the extent and nature of the training. The state function in such an area would consist of establishing such guidelines; assisting the local prosecutors with curriculum development and providing training materials, specialized instructors, and other forms of technical assistance; and inspecting and reviewing the local operation to ensure compliance with the basic state standards.

There are other kinds of state policy coordination that might be adopted. The attorney general might perform a purely advisory or consultative function either for the individual cases or with respect to general policies. State involvement might be limited simply to requirements that local prosecutors develop policies covering given subjects. Such limited coordination might reduce existing fragmentation in many states, but it would not appear to strike the appropriate balance between centralized control and autonomous local prosecutorial operation.

State Council of Prosecutors

To assist in the development of prosecutorial policy, a council comprised of the attorney general and all the local prosecutors in the state would be desirable. Such a council would be helpful both in those states where the attorney general already has the power to promulgate policy and in those where it is not feasible, legally or politically, for him to do so. The state attorney general would ordinarily be an appropriate person to assume a large role in organizing the council. In Texas, for example, since 1951 the attorney general has annually called a statewide conference of county attorneys, district attorneys, and other law enforcement officers.

Such a council might simply be a group that meets periodically to exchange views on common problems. Although even this limited beginning might involve somewhat more statewide coordination than presently exists, it would be far better for the council to have a real policy-making function. The meetings of local prosecutors already established or provided for in California, Indiana, Kansas, Massachusetts, and Texas may be used as a limited model. However, it is not clear whether these bodies have a substantial policy-making function.

Creation of the council would tend to ensure adherence by local prosecutors to the state policies. Decisions made jointly by the participants will be more readily acceptable to independently elected officials. The council may also have the advantage of allaying the fears of local prosecutors that their authority is being undermined by a powerful state officer. Implementation is simpler when the policies and standards represent the consensus of those seasoned practitioners who must carry them out at the operating level.

The fact that the council could meet only periodically would limit its effectiveness. It could not, for example, assist in the day-to-day interpretation of previously formulated policies or deal promptly with problems that may arise. Nor could it perform other significant functions that require continuing activity or availability throughout the year. In all states, however, the attorney general's office could bring a continuity of effort that a sporadically meeting council cannot. His staff could give direction to the council's work by suggesting the areas in which statewide standards, programs, and policies are needed, and by providing the research and other assistance required. Review of how the standards work in practice could also be a function of the attorney general, with the council participating in efforts to obtain compliance from local prosecutors.

There is a need for a regular mechanism by which the state officer can ascertain the extent to which local prosecutors apply state policies. When the attorney general represents the state in criminal appellate litigation, as he does in many states, he will have a partial check through his control over the cases that are appealed. The development of statewide statistical and case-monitoring systems would provide additional sources of information. Limited auditing or inspection services for local prosecutors' offices might also be established. And if statewide policies are made public, it may be expected that deviations will arouse the attention of the bench or bar.

Enforcement of Statewide Policies

A difficult issue would be presented if a local prosecutor refuses to apply a statewide policy or consistently applies it in a way that distorts its purpose. It seems clear that a state body, whether the attorney general or a prosecutors' council, should have final authority on such an issue. Whether such authority already inheres in the general powers of the attorney general is a question that can only be answered on a state-by-state basis. To give a council of prosecutors such authority would clearly require constitutional or legislative action by the states.

In any event, direct confrontation between local and state officers on such matters may be expected to occur rarely. The interests on both sides normally tend toward accommodation, not confrontation, because political officers usually seek to avoid disputes calling into play basic questions concerning their ultimate powers. The possibility of conflict is minimized by the involvement of local officials in the policy-formulation process, and by their need for the kind of service and assistance that the state officer can provide.

In 1952 the American Bar Association Commission on Organized Crime and the National Conference of Commissioners on Uniform State Laws proposed a Model Department of Justice Act designed to clarify how the role of the state attorney general or a state director of criminal justice might be used to encourage cooperation among law enforcement officers, and to provide general supervision at the state level over prosecution within the state. It is a useful starting point for consideration of the types of problem that may arise.

Student Checklist

1. Do you know how to distinguish between the duties performed by British solicitors and barristers?
2. Can you write an essay that sets forth the functions performed by the Attorney General of the United States?
3. Are you able to compare the duties performed by the U.S. Attorney General and a typical state attorney general?
4. Can you list the prosecutor's responsibilities in the criminal process?

5. Can you list some of the advantages and disadvantages inherent in the high political orientation of the prosecutor's office?
6. Can you write an essay that identifies the problems of coordinating the prosecutorial functions within a state?
7. Are you able to describe the duties and responsibilities that can be performed by a state council of prosecutors?

Topics for Discussion

1. Discuss the advantages of centralized control of the prosecutorial function.
2. Discuss means of limiting the prosecutor's discretion.
3. Discuss the legal educational preparation of prosecutors.
4. Discuss the need for the prosecutor's office to become career-oriented.

ANNOTATED BIBLIOGRAPHY

The following authors appear in the same volume of *The Prosecutor, Journal of the National District Attorneys Association, 5,* No. 4, July, August 1969. Busch, Ted. "Prosecution in Baltimore Compared to the Houston System," p. 253; Fertitta, Robert S. "Comparative Study of Prosecutor's Offices: Baltimore and Houston," p. 248; Meglio, John J. "Comparative Study of the District Attorneys' Offices in Los Angeles and Brooklyn," p. 237; Skoler, Daniel L., and June M. Hetler. "Criminal Administration and the Local Government Crisis," p. 253; and Trammell, George W., III. "Control of System Policy and Practice by the Office of District Attorney in Brooklyn and Los Angeles," p. 242.

This issue provides a concise review of the prosecution function, comparing Los Angeles, Brooklyn, Baltimore, and Houston. Skoler and Hetler provide an analysis of the economic and political problems inherent in any attempt to improve the prosecution function.

American Bar Association Project on Standards for Criminal Justice. *Standards Relating to the Prosecution Function and the Defense*

Function. New York: Office of the Criminal Justice Project Approved Draft, March 1971. This volume of standards for the prosecutor and defense function is one of 15 volumes containing standards for the improvement of the criminal justice process. The standards relating to the prosecution function provide guidance for the prosecutor in his relationship to the defendant and his attorney, the press, the court, the police, the witnesses, the grand jury, the decision to prosecute, the trial jury, plea discussion, and the protection of the rights of the defendant and the public which he serves.

Kerper, Hazel B. *Introduction to the Criminal Justice System.* St. Paul: West Publishing, 1972. Covers the entire system of criminal justice with a brief introduction to criminal law and the elements of a crime that must be proved for a conviction. Oriented toward the process of the criminal justice system with special emphasis on the individuals who compose the system, their duties, functions, and problems. Mrs. Kerper also provides suggestions for improvements of the criminal justice system.

National Conference on Criminal Justice, Working Papers, Law Enforcement Assistance Administration, January 1973. These working papers, printed by the U.S. Government Printing Office, establish the first major standards for the improvement of the criminal justice system. They will replace as reference material The Task Force Reports and *Challenge of Crime in a Free Society* promulgated by the President's Commission on Law Enforcement and Administration of Justice. The National Conference Standards cover, in separate chapters: the police, courts, corrections, and community crime prevention, with standards or goals to be reached by each component.

Nedrud, Duane R. "The Career Prosecutor," *Journal of Criminal Law, Criminology, and Police Science 51* (1960) pp. 343, 557; *51* (1961) p. 649; *52* (1961) p. 103. A series of four articles covering all aspects and problems inherent in the establishment and application of the Model Department of Justice Act promulgated by the National Conference of Commissioners on Uniform State Laws in 1952. Mr. Nedrud examines the advantages and disadvantages of the Model Act as applied to state and local prosecutors' offices.

The study of this chapter will enable you to:

1. Identify the significant court decisions that contributed to the concept of the right to counsel.
2. List the reasons why a defendant needs a counsel in a criminal case.
3. Identify the purpose and functions of a lawyer reference service.
4. Write a short essay that describes the "criminal bar."
5. Compare the assigned-counsel system and legal aid societies.
6. Trace the history of the public defender system.
7. Identify the type of legal services provided by OEO/LSP.

7
Defenders

Whether a man is philosophically pondering the concept of justice or is under indictment for a crime, he is concerned with the issue of adequate representation. Present-day provisions for adequate counsel include: retained counsel, public defenders, assigned counsel, legal aid counsel, and mixed systems. Regardless of the type of counsel, the need is recognized. Mr. Justice Sutherland stated:

> *The right to be heard would be, in many cases, of little avail if it did not comprehend the right to be heard by counsel. Even the intelligent and educated layman has small and sometimes no skill in the science of law. If charged with crime, he is incapable, generally, of determining for himself whether the indictment is good or bad. He is unfamiliar with the rules of evidence. Left without the aid of counsel he may be put on trial without a proper charge, and convicted upon incompetent evidence, or evidence irrelevant to the issue or otherwise inadmissible. He lacks both the skill and knowledge adequately to prepare his defense, even though he have a perfect one. He requires the guiding hand of counsel at every step in the proceedings against him. Without it, though he be not guilty, he faces the danger of conviction because he does not know how to establish his innocence. If that be true of men of intelligence, how much more true is it of the ignorant and illiterate, or those of feeble intellect.*[1]

The Right to Counsel

English-speaking people have had an historical obsession with man's right to equal justice. In 1215, the Magna Carta conveyed the concept

[1] Powell v. Alabama, 287 U.S. 45 (1932).

of equal justice, and that same belief was carried by the early settlers along the Eastern Seaboard.[2] After the American Revolution and the development of the Constitution, the concept of equal justice was again set down and included within that concept the notion of an individual's right to the assistance of counsel when faced with a criminal prosecution.

So deep was the concern for the rights envisaged within the concept of equal justice that the rights of all Americans were amended to the Constitution in what was referred to as the Bill of Rights. The right of assistance of counsel spelled out in the Sixth Amendment stated, simply and without doubt as to the intention of its framers, that, "In all criminal prosecutions, the accused shall . . . have the assistance of counsel for his defense." The new federal government's limits were set. Each individual state also provided limitations on its actions and for the rights of its citizens.

The right to counsel established by the Constitution guaranteed that right only in federal courts, and only if the defendant wanted and could afford an attorney. In 1937 the Supreme Court interpreted the Sixth Amendment to mean that every defendant in a federal prosecution was entitled to a lawyer regardless of the ability to pay that attorney's fee.[3] It was another matter, however, if the person was accused of a crime relating to a violation of a state penal code.

The struggle of individuals in various state courts to be represented by counsel, particularly if the accused could not afford an attorney, has been resolved only recently. Several attempts had to be made before the Supreme Court ruled that the Sixth Amendment applied to all, regardless of financial standing or place of jurisdiction.[4] The issue of counsel in misdemeanor cases for the poor is still being resolved.

The first major breakthrough occurred in 1932. Having to decide whether nine black youths charged with rape, a capital offense, were entitled to effective counsel, the Court ruled that the right to counsel was

---

[2] In England the right to counsel as a part of the concept of equal justice developed slowly, and it was not until 1836 that an Englishman, charged with a felony, could be represented by counsel.

[3] Johnson v. Zerbst, 304 U.S. 458 (1937).

[4] Whether the limitations set down in the Bill of Rights were simple limitations on the powers of the federal government or whether they applied to all Americans in their relations with every level of government was reviewed in Barron v. Baltimore, 7 Ret. 243 (1833), and Betts v. Brady, 316 U.S. 455 (1942).

part of the idea of "due process of law" in capital cases, and established the right to counsel in capital cases.

> . . . where the defendant is unable to employ counsel, and is incapable adequately of making his own defense because of ignorance, feeble-mindedness, illiteracy, or the like, it is the duty of the court, whether requested or not, to assign counsel for him as a necessary requisite of due process of law.[5]

In 1942 the Supreme Court again considered the issue of right to counsel. While not allowing a poor person to obtain "free" counsel, the Court stated unequivocally that the absence of counsel constituted a denial of due process. Thus, the right to counsel in state courts was established, particularly for those who could afford the counsel.[6] But it was not until 21 years later that the issue of the right of counsel for the indigent was settled in state courts.

Right of the Indigent to Counsel

The sheer weight or number of cases and the escalation of crime has produced a processing machinery that has occasionally overlooked justice. The poor, lacking effective representation by counsel, have been particularly at the mercy of the mechanics of the system. In study after study, the story has been the same—an overloaded system discriminated against those who could not afford counsel; the rights of the individual, whether guilty or not, were not safeguarded.[7] The presence and advice of counsel were not for the sake of ritualism but were simply the essence of justice.[8]

The various state and municipal courts had long recognized this problem but it was not until 1963 that the Supreme Court took the step

---

[5] Powell v. Alabama, 287 U.S. 45 (1932).
[6] Betts v. Brady, 316 U.S. 455 (1942).
[7] See Lewis R. Katz, "Municipal Courts—Another Urban Ill." *20 Case W. Res. L. Rev.*, 87 (1968), pp. 101-105; Dallin H. Oaks and Warren Lehman, *Criminal Justice System and the Indigent: Study of Chicago and Cook County* (Chicago: University of Chicago Press, 1967); and Lee Silverstein, *Defense of the Poor in Criminal Cases in American State Courts.* 3 vols. (Chicago: American Bar Foundation, 1965).
[8] Kent v. United States, 383 U.S. 541 (1966).

that could accelerate the process of meeting those rights framed in the Bill of Rights. In *Gideon* v. *Wainwright*,[9] the Supreme Court ruled that anyone charged with a crime in a state court was entitled to an attorney even if he could not afford one. In a rapid expansion since then, the point at which counsel is obtained and whether the ruling applies to misdemeanors have been clarified, or are still in the process of clarification. The *Gideon* decision gave the Sixth Amendment's right to counsel a meaning for every citizen charged with a felony, regardless of financial status.

From the moment that one is suspected or arrested by a law officer, he, or she, is entitled to the assistance of counsel. Because each step in the criminal justice process can be crucial, the accused, even if indigent, is entitled to that assistance while being questioned[10] at preliminary hearing,[11] at arraignment,[12] and at any identification or lineup,[13] as well as during the trial. A person intent on a criminal act, however, cannot extend the right to the commission of that crime, nor can an attorney advise his client[14] prior to or during commission.

After the trial the convicted retains the right to counsel. The sentencing process and any appeals resulting from the process are vital steps that also require the assistance of an attorney. The procedures, for instance, involved in sentencing require that factual information be brought to the judge's attention. The presence of an attorney can assure that the convicted person's interests are safeguarded.[15] On the same day that the Supreme Court decided the *Gideon* case, it held that the failure to provide counsel for the indigent, when a person was entitled to an appeal, was a denial of due process.[16]

The relationship between the individual who has been sentenced and his rights is not severed. The growing area of peno-correctional law

[9] Gideon v. Wainwright, 372 U.S. 335 (1963).
[10] Miranda v. Arizona, 384 U.S. 436 (1966).
[11] White v. Maryland, 373 U.S. 59 (1963).
[12] Hamilton v. Alabama, 368 U.S. 52 (1961); see also Hessenauer v. People, 256 NE (2d) 791: Ill. (1970).
[13] United States v. Wade, 388 U.S. 218 (1967).
[14] Garcia v. United States, 364 F. 2d, 306, 10th Cir (1966); and In re Disbarment Proceedings, 321 Pa. 81.
[15] Townsend v. Burke, 344 U.S. 736 (1948).
[16] Douglas v. California, 372 U.S. 353 (1963).

stands in testimony to this. The key decision by the Supreme Court that recognized the concept of effective counsel where the possibility that the individual's rights may be impaired was *Goldberg* v. *Kelly*.[17] While not answering the question of furnishing an attorney to the indigent, the accused does have the right to retain counsel if he so desires and has the resources to do so. Another issue is whether such matters as parole and probation are trials in a sense of formality of evidence and "combat" of adversary attorneys.[18] A great deal of clarification is needed in the rights of the individual in the peno-correctional area of the criminal justice system. The guidelines are still being written.

The peno-correctional area is not the only area where the guidelines on the right to counsel are in a state of flux. The constitutional decision providing counsel for indigents in criminal cases (*Gideon*) has been assumed by some to be for felony cases only, while for others it applies to misdemeanors. Although the Supreme Court spoke in generalities, the states assumed that the Court probably meant misdemeanors that carried felony-length terms of imprisonment if they meant misdemeanors at all. In one instance, an Arkansas court sentenced a man to 30 days in jail and a $254 fine. He could neither afford an attorney nor pay the fine. Because of a "$1-a-day" rule the defendant received 254 additional days in jail. The Supreme Court denied *certiorari* to review the conviction.[19] Some states appoint counsels for the indigent—others do not. Some make the appointment at a point prior to the trial—others make the appointment only for the trial. This confusion is likely to continue for some time. Since the local jurisdictions have the problem of insufficient funds and lack of attorneys to provide counsel to indigents charged with misdemeanors, the Supreme Court must face the issue of the constitutionality of the matter. The grand jury system creates another problem area, since grand juries deny the right of a person to counsel. The Supreme Court has upheld the matter[20] but in actuality:

[17] Goldberg v. Kelly, 397 U.S. 254 (1970).
[18] Sostre v. McGinnis, 442 F. 2d 178 (2d Cir. 1971), *certiorari* denied 405 U.S. 978 (1972).
[19] Winters v. Beck, 239 Ark. 1151, 397 S.W. 2d 364 (1966), *certiorari* denied 385 U.S. 907 (1966).
[20] Commonwealth v. McCloskey, 443 Pa. 117, 277 A. 2d 764 (1971), *certiorari* denied 404 U.S. 1000 (1971); and Catalano v. United States, 444 F. 2nd 1095 (1971), *certiorari* denied 404 U.S. 1001 (1971).

. . . if the witness would like the benefit of counsel, he should make a request to the foreman of the grand jury. If the witness explains that he is ignorant of the proceedings and the law, and states that he should feel more at ease with a lawyer present, the foreman will frequently grant the request. The prosecutor cannot help but appear in a negative light if he argues against such a request. If the witness' request is denied, he can have his lawyer wait outside the proceedings and he may leave the room to consult with him at any time during the proceedings (before answering every question if he wishes).[21]

Two remaining problems involving the right to counsel are the questions of waiver of counsel and effective counsel. What if the defendant does not want to be represented by an attorney? The trial judge should ascertain whether the defendant possesses the capacity to handle the matter. It has been recommended that counsel be assigned on a standby basis to offer advice and to act if called on by the accused. The other question is a touchy one often avoided: what if the counsel hired or provided is incompetent? There have been cases where the defendant's attorney has been intoxicated or under the influence of drugs. The American Bar Association recommends that allegations of ineffective counsel be reviewed by another attorney and, if the charges have validity, appropriate action be taken on the defendant's behalf.[22] The concepts of equal justice and the right to counsel have progressed, but many controversial issues still exist.

The Need for Counsel

The process through which the accused must pass from arrest to appeal is a complicated one. Only an experienced attorney can assist his client. The attorney, for instance, must know all the facts, where to find them, and how to evaluate their importance in order to explore the available alternatives at preliminary examination, at arraignment, during interro-

[21] John Dominick, *The Drug Bust* (New York: The Light Co. 1970), p. 39.
[22] American Bar Association, *Standards Relating to the Prosecution Function and the Defense Function* (tentative draft) (New York: Institute of Judicial Administration, ABA, 1970), p. 170.

gation of his client, when bail is set, when plea bargaining is sought, during the trial, and in any postconviction proceedings. Each step is critical; the strategy and tactics employed depend on a variety of factors.

If the accused is, in fact, the perpetrator of what he was accused of doing, and the law enforcement and prosecution personnel did their work well, then the work of the counsel is limited to seeing that the rights of the individual are protected and that the state proves the matter. If the state presents a poor case or is negligent in putting the case together, the defense counsel must exploit the shoddy work. Shoddy workmanship is what convicts honest men, destroys reputations, and makes a sham of justice. It is defense counsel's duty to see that justice is done and that his client is protected from the transgressions and omissions of the state.

One of the first steps defense counsel can take is to have a precharge conference with the prosecutor to determine whether charges should be dropped and alternative methods, other than prosecution, can be found to achieve the rehabilitation and return to society of a productive person. For example, the client may have a chronic drinking problem and community treatment may be available. If the violation involved is of a minor nature and the client is willing to seek aid, the need for prosecution may be minimized. In more serious cases, where diversion is not practical, the defense counsel can increase his knowledge of the state's case, and may even influence the charges eventually brought against his client by bringing mitigating information to the prosecutor's attention.

Bail is another critical area. Counsel, if prepared, can supply the court with useful information to determine whether the client should have bail and at what figure it should be set. If counsel was recently retained, he can get a short delay to research the matter. It has been shown that having the client out on bail has a significant bearing on a successful defense.

The preliminary hearing is important, and often critical, in some cases. Since the arresting officers need "probable cause" to have made the arrest, counsel can obtain a dismissal if it is not shown. He can protect his client by watching for hearsay evidence. Where it is allowed, he may present witnesses. A good counsel, through cross-examination, will often discover the nature of the state's case, who the key witnesses are, and their reliability. By cross-examination, the testimony is recorded so that counsel can compare the testimony of the preliminary hearing with that later given during a trial. By "freezing" testimony at this stage, the counsel can later impeach the credibility of the witness if the testimony has changed. It may also give grounds later for having evidence suppressed if it was seized illegally, if identification was the result of improper police lineup, or if the confession was defective. The preliminary hearing is a critical point in the procedures. An effective counsel can determine if the state really has a case.

If the case is a highly emotional one with prejudicial publicity, the counsel can seek a continuance in order to allow publicity to die down. Or his case may be jeopardized by another case of a similar nature that has public attention. Counsel may even ask for a change of venue in order to have a trial in a community where emotions are not affected by adverse publicity or local issues. He can request that the trial be moved to a metropolitan area where a particular type of crime is commonplace, or the victim unknown, or attitudes not as hostile. A fair trial requires an atmosphere of calm and rationality, and it is counsel's duty to help obtain such an environment.

Sentencing of the convicted also requires the presence of an attorney, who must know which facts and circumstances could explain the accused's conduct, and perhaps mitigate punishment. Any errors in the presentation of the defendant's history must be corrected. The effective and well-prepared counsel will be able to assist in putting the presentence reports of probation officers in some perspective.

As can be seen by these examples, counsel and his choices of actions can assist the attainment of justice. There are, however, attorneys who manipulate the procedures to serve their own or their client's ends, and not those of justice. To the unethical a delay to achieve a fair trial in an atmosphere of calm and rationality can easily be used to allow testimony to be lost or become stale. A few ill-chosen phrases or temporary confusion at the preliminary hearing can later be used by the unscrupulous to discredit or undermine a witness who is telling the truth. One can easily see that possibilities exist for an unethical counsel to abuse or manipulate the criminal justice process.[23]

---

[23] The positive aspects of the need for counsel and the "manipulative" techniques available to counsel based on Robert M. Cipes, ed., *Criminal Defense Techniques* (New York: Matthew Bender, 1969, 1972); and F. Lee Bailey and Henry B. Rothblatt, *Successful Techniques for Criminal Trials* (San Francisco: Bancroft-Whitney Co., 1971).

Plea Bargaining

In most jurisdictions an informal process is available so that the defendant can be offered certain considerations if a plea of guilty is entered. Usually referred to as plea bargaining, the critical points for its occurrence are: the period following the initial hearing before the arraignment; the arraignment; and the interlude between arraignment and the trial. Very few cases go through to the stage of a jury trial.[24] The bargain arrived at often provides some reduction in charge or degree; for example, second degree murder to voluntary manslaughter, or robbery to grand larceny,[25] and the type or length of sentence in exchange for the accused offering a plea of guilty.

As conceptually structured, the system is intended to be an adversarial one—that is, one where the advocates of the state and the accused argue the fact before a neutral judge. In practice, the system is faced with mounting caseloads, inadequate staffing, and a lack of funds that reduce the adversary concept to a reality of being an exchange or bargaining system. Although it is not an evil in the full sense, it does alter the ideal and opens the way for abuses and injustices from time to time, particularly if the defendant is, in fact, innocent—or the charges made are unreal. For those who are actually guilty the bargain or exchange system means that the adversarial system does not occur in the courtroom before an impartial judge, but in the halls and offices of the courthouse.

The bargaining system offers some benefits to the participants. The prosecutor can get his conviction and devote his meager staff and time to other cases, the court can relieve the congestion of its calendar and not be caught up in lengthy trials, and the defense can put its energies into other cases. For the guilty, plea bargaining often reduces the time in jail prior to trial if they were unable to make bail, and allows them to get a "better deal" than was originally thought possible.

---

[24] Newman, *Pleading Guilty for Consideration: A Study of Plea Justice, J. Crim. L., C. and P.S.,* 46 (1956), p. 780.

[25] Eugene E. Siler, Jr., *Guilty Plea Negotiations,* Robert M. Cipes, ed. op cit., § 13.06.

Eligibility for Legal Assistance

To qualify for legal assistance, the defendant must establish eligibility. Generally, at arraignment, the judge or magistrate makes a few inquiries of the accused to determine his ability to hire counsel. After a few questions, counsel is assigned. Later, a financial affidavit, followed by investigation, determines if the defendant is incapable of hiring a lawyer.

The actual standards for eligibility will vary from jurisdiction to jurisdiction and from state to state. However, a few rough guidelines are standard. When it is determined that the accused is indigent, further evaluation occurs. The seriousness of the charge is considered and the duration and complexity of the case are estimated, to determine just what efforts by a counsel will be needed. With a knowledge of the fee schedule that would likely be operative in such a case, the financial resources of the accused can be measured against the likely expenses. The findings can then be applied to declaring the person eligible, partially eligible, or responsible for retaining his own counsel, depending on categories used in the different jurisdictions.

The Criminal Bar

For the individual who has financial resources and is thus deemed ineligible for free counsel, the only solution is to hire an attorney. The attorneys available to the defendant range from those who may occasionally take a criminal case to those who make their living solely from such cases. Generally, most attorneys shy away from criminal cases for a variety of reasons, ranging from the low prestige attached to such cases to the low income generally derived from this type of legal work. Some simply refuse to take such cases because they lack familiarity and experience in the criminal procedures, and feel that other attorneys can better serve the client. Some clients use their own attorney or are referred to a good criminal lawyer. Those lawyers who handle criminal cases on a regular basis are known to other lawyers who will then refer clients to them. These attorneys become known as the "criminal bar" because of the frequency with which they accept criminal cases.[26]

[26] Arthur L. Wood, *The Criminal Lawyer* (New Haven: College and University Press, 1967), p. 29.

There are essentially two types of criminal lawyers: nationally known attorneys who defend highly visible clients whose cases are emotional or involve controversy; and local attorneys who handle common types of cases in great volumes. The nationally known attorneys are familiar to most newspaper readers and television viewers—F. Lee Bailey, Jake Ehrlich, Edward Bennett Williams, and Louis Nizer. While prominent, these criminal lawyers do not service the vast majority of criminal cases that are the everyday drama of the courthouse. The real workload is carried by the local criminal bar.

The reputation of the attorneys in the local criminal bars is low. Because they are often forced to seek out their clients instead of having the client come to them, as is the case in prestigious law firms, they are referred to with contempt by their peers:

> . . . *referred to as the Fifth Streeters in the District of Columbia, and the Clinton Street Bar in Detroit. These designations identify members of the group within the legal profession who are found prowling the urban criminal courts searching for clients who can pay a modest fee. . . . This small group of practitioners is usually more poorly educated, works harder, and is in a more precarious financial situation than its brothers in corporate practice.*[27]

Despite the poor peer evaluation, the local criminal bar rated fairly high in the estimation of the consumers of New Haven, Connecticut.[28] What appears to fuel their peer group's disdain is the "pressure" that the criminal lawyer must exert to get paid, and what others claim is a lack of ethics. Harry Subin, in his examination of the Court of General Sessions in the District of Columbia,[29] describes the quest for money as coloring all the contacts between client and attorney. He describes "Rule One"—the collection of the fee. It pervades the relationship from beginning to end. Subin also indicated that the defense attorney is often lax in case preparation, investigative background, and contact with clients. Both the quest for fees and the lack of interest in the case can be seen to contribute to the low prestige of the criminal bar among their peers.

[27] George F. Cole, ed., *Criminal Justice: Law and Politics* (North Scituate, Mass.: Duxbury Press, 1972), pp. 29-30.
[28] Jonathan Casper, *Criminal Justice—The Consumer's Perspective* (Washington: NILECJ, Dept. of Justice, 1972), pp. 29-30.
[29] Harry I. Subin, *Criminal Justice in a Metropolitan Court: The Processing of Serious Criminal Cases in the District of Columbia Court of General Sessions* (Washington: OCJ, Dept. of Justice, 1966).

Among the general public, the prestige of defense attorneys fluctuates widely. The public sympathizes with the defense of the innocent, as has been so well documented in its response to television programs ("Perry Mason" and "Owen Marshall") and popular heroes who are charged with wrongdoings. At the other extreme, the public cannot comprehend how someone trained in such a noble and ancient profession can defend the "guilty" or even "associate" with seamy characters, and deal in what is classified as shady practices. The movies of the 1930s and 1940s had the James Cagneys, Humphrey Bogarts, and Edward G. Robinsons as society's public enemies, with a "shyster" close at hand to manipulate criminal procedures for the benefit of the evildoers, always at the expense of righteousness. The lawyers who defended accused Communists in the 1950s, despite the clients' difficulties in securing counsel, did not strike a responsive chord with the general public. The public supports the defense of the innocent and the popular cause, but strikes out at those who take the cases of those considered "guilty" or those who lack popularity.

Until recently, the accused who was required to secure his own defense attorney encountered difficulties. The average person usually does not know where to find an attorney to represent him. Since lawyers are not allowed to advertise, they cannot even list their specialty in the telephone book. The accused is often forced to depend on bail bondsmen, arresting officers, and jail trustees to refer him to a suitable attorney. The problem of making contact between the criminal lawyer and potential clientele often obliges attorneys to congregate in places where clients are accessible, or to engage in unethical practices, such as "kickbacks," for referrals. These behavior patterns can lead to disbarment.[30] Various bar associations recognize the problem and are attempting to deal with it.

One such method is a lawyer reference service in a populated urban area, a public service of the local bar association. It has been in operation since 1971, and is one of the first lawyer reference services to categorize member attorneys according to their legal areas of expertise and to set minimum qualifications. For example, to serve a client charged with a criminal offense, the attorney must, at a minimum, have handled two cases from preparation through jury trial to verdict. In addition, the

[30] In re Winthrop, 135 Wash. 135 (1925); and In re Ades, 6F. Supp. 467 (D.Md. 1934).

attorney must have appeared at least on ten occasions in the particular court in which he plans to practice, or he must demonstrate some form of equivalency. Once the attorney meets the criteria, he is placed on a list in which the names are rotated to assure an equal opportunity. When a defendant is arrested or charged he is supplied with the telephone number of the service. By calling the service, the accused is referred promptly and confidentially to an attorney who has the expertise and experience in the field. The attorney will consult with his client for the simple fee of $10, and arrangements for further service is then planned. Other such referral services are being developed and augmented elsewhere by other bar associations.

Despite the shortcomings of the criminal bar, Jonathan Casper in studying the criminal justice system in New Haven could report:

> The defendant with a street lawyer felt himself to be a real participant in the process, to be making choices, to have an advocate. This is not to say that all defendants with street lawyers were completely satisfied with their attorneys. None wanted to be in prison, and most of them were. Some didn't care for their lawyers personally, finding them cold or brash. Some felt that the attorney had other things on his mind and hadn't paid as much attention to their cases as he could have. Some felt that their attorneys were not as skilled in the criminal law as they might have been, and some felt they were not able to communicate as well as they wished. But still, they took it as a kind of given that the lawyer was on their side, cared what happened to them, and was willing to listen to them. The sources of these favorable reactions to the attorneys obviously are in part the product of the behavior of the attorney, for the street lawyers seem to have spent more time and appeared more concerned with their clients.[31]

Defense for the Indigent

Unless the defendant acts as his own counsel or has sufficient funds to hire one, there are just a few ways he can obtain counsel, depending on the jurisdiction (Table 7-1). An attorney can be secured through a legal aid society, a public defender's office, or be assigned a counsel by the

[31] Casper, *Criminal Justice,* pp. 31-32.

TABLE 7-1. **Defense for the Indigent.**

State	Assigned Counsel	Public Defenders	Legal aid Societies
Alabama	X		
Alaska	X		
Arizona	X	X	
Arkansas	X		
California	X	X	
Colorado	X	X	
Connecticut		X	
Delaware		X	
District of Columbia	X	X	X
Florida	X	X	
Georgia	X	X	X
Hawaii	X	X	
Idaho	X		
Illinois		X	X
Indiana	X	X	
Iowa	X		X
Kansas	X		
Kentucky	X		
Louisiana	X		X
Maine	X		
Maryland	X	X	
Massachusetts		X	X
Michigan	X		
Minnesota	X	X	
Mississippi	X		
Missouri	X	X	

court. "Going it alone" can present a multitude of problems for the uninitiated, and is generally avoided.[32]

The person without sufficient funds to obtain counsel who meets the various tests of eligibility, can have an attorney assigned to his defense. The court-appointed counsel system is the most widely used system of providing counsel for the indigent. It is found in almost every

[32] For an excellent review of the difficulties, see Gerald W. Smith, *A Statistical Analysis of Public Defender Activities* (Washington: NILECJ, Dept. of Justice, 1970), pp. 17-19.

TABLE 7-1. **Defense for the Indigent** (continued).

State	Assigned Counsel	Public Defenders	Legal aid Societies
Montana	X		
Nebraska	X	X	
Nevada	X		
New Hampshire	X		
New Jersey		X	
New Mexico	X		
New York	X	X	X
North Carolina	X	X	
North Dakota	X		
Ohio	X	X	
Oklahoma	X	X	
Oregon	X	X	
Pennsylvania	X	X	X
Rhode Island		X	
South Carolina	X		
South Dakota	X		
Tennessee	X	X	
Texas	X		X
Utah	X	X	
Vermont	X		
Virginia	X		
Washington	X		
West Virginia	X		X
Wisconsin	X	X	
Wyoming	X		
Federal courts	X		X

state, primarily in the most rural areas, and is probably the least expensive system for the less populated areas.[33]

The Assigned-Counsel System
The court-appointed counsel system is characterized by its lack of organization and the case-by-case approach. When the accused is arraigned,

[33] Richard L. Grier, "Analysis and Comparison of the Assigned-Counsel and Public Defender Systems," *49 North Carolina L.R., 705*, 1971.

the presiding judge appoints counsel to defend the indigent defendant, based solely on the most routine questioning as to financial status. The counsel may be an attorney who happens to be in the courtroom,[34] or the judge may select an attorney from a list of volunteers. The selection may be made randomly or on a rotating basis.

The system is well suited to the rural areas of America. In fact, some 2750 of the United States' 3100 counties use the assigned-counsel system, as do some cities. Ideally, the jurisdiction should maintain a list of qualified attorneys, provide adequate support and facilities for the program, develop some means of performance evaluation, and provide adequate compensation and expenses to be effective.[35] However, this can be a monumental financial burden in some communities and rarely becomes the reality.

First, there is a tendency for the system to be voluntary instead of compulsory. The young lawyers who are not yet blessed with sufficient clientele to assure a livelihood are ambitious to demonstrate their skills and become known in the community. Most are eager to have cases come their way. This availability becomes known to those who make counsel assignments and, therefore, the young lawyers tend to get assigned the bulk of the cases. In metropolitan areas this can be a problem because a young and inexperienced attorney may be dealing with an experienced prosecutor who specializes in criminal law. In rural areas this is not a problem. For example, in Latah County, Idaho, the position of prosecutor is a part-time one, filled by a succession of attorneys. Thus, if the defense is disadvantaged, the state often is as well. Because of the lack of cases and the number of attorneys in Latah County, the rotation is fair and equitable; elsewhere, the caseload may well be staggering, and there is a tendency to call on those who are ready and willing.

Second, few supports are provided for the attorney. To be effective, the defense counsel requires secretarial and investigative support. Investigators must be knowledgeable in their job in order to assist the counsel in the preparation of the case. Even social workers would be useful, since

---

[34] Subin, *Criminal Justice*, p. 91.

[35] Task Force on the Administration of Justice, the President's Commission on Law Enforcement and Administration of Justice, *Task Force Report: The Courts* (Washington: U.S. Govt. Printing Office, 1967), p. 60.

the attorney is often asked by the incarcerated to perform small tasks that help reduce personal worry. Few assigned-counsel systems take these factors into consideration. Thus, there is the reduced likelihood that these attorneys will be effective. Few, if any, records are kept, and measures of performance are totally lacking. The decentralized nature of the assigned-counsel system works to reduce its effectiveness.

Third, the provisions made for compensating the counsel for his activities are often inadequate. The Administrative Office of the United States Courts set down the compensation for defense counsels' assigned cases in federal courts at $30 per hour for time spent in court or before a magistrate, and $20 per hour for time expended outside court. If the local "going rate" is less, the judicial council of the circuit can set rates not to exceed the minimum hourly scale established by the local bar association. The maximum compensation cannot exceed $1000 in felony cases and $400 in misdemeanor cases under the federal system. Various other rates are set for federal appeals, posttrial motions, and probation revocations. Most states set their maximum amounts at $500 for felony defenses and $300 for misdemeanor defenses.[36] These amounts are not equivalent to the rates in private practice, nor do they meet the myriad expenses incurred by a counsel.

The advantages of the court-assigned counsel system merit review. First, it is probably the most logical system for rural America. It can be made effective for metropolitan areas by centralizing and remodeling to remove its shortcomings. The success of the Poor Prisoners Defense Act (1930) and the Criminal Justice Act (1967) in using assigned counsel in the United Kingdom should be examined for their potential use in the United States.[37] Since the assigned counsel often does not depend fully on criminal cases, he is not under the same courthouse pressures that harass the "criminal bar" or public defenders. And his occasional glimpse of the criminal justice system may stimulate him to a greater concern for change in the system.

---

[36] Robert M. Cipes and Philip H. Pennypacker, "Assignment of Counsel in State Courts," Cipes, ed., *Criminal Defense Techniques,* § 14.10(2b).
[37] C. F. Shoolbred, *The Administration of Criminal Justice in England and Wales* (London: Pergamon Press, 1966), p. 119; and *A Guide to Recent Criminal Legislation* (London: Pergamon Press, 1968), pp. 116-117.

The Public Defender

The underlying principle of the public defender is that the state has the duty to provide defense counsel for those who are unable to afford counsel. With the shortcomings of assigned counsel (in populated areas) and legal aid societies, some other means of coping with the mounting crime rate had to be found. Yet, the concept of state-provided counsel for the poor is neither new nor revolutionary.

In the third and fourth centuries the Roman Empire established the office of *Pauperus Procurator*; by the eighteenth and nineteenth centuries many European states possessed some form of legal services for the indigent.[38] The first true public defender offices in the United States sprang up in Oklahoma in 1911, and the most copied and successful one, the Los Angeles County Defender's Office, started in January 1914. A 1971 survey by the Advisory Commission on Intergovernmental Relations showed that 31 percent of all counties in the United States had a public defender. Of these, most were county supported, but 42 percent had a special tax levy, and 3 percent were supported by a user charge.[39] Six states have statewide defender systems (Florida, Connecticut, New Jersey, Massachusetts, Delaware, and Rhode Island), of which the oldest is Connecticut's system (1917). The decision as to location of the public defender's office is at the discretion of the various state legislatures. The most popular method is to permit the rural areas to choose between the public defender and assigned-counsel system; but to authorize the more populated districts or counties to establish public defenders. In Illinois, the state requires that all counties of over 35,000 population establish the public defender system.

The defender's office is normally under county control. In some cases, while still dependent on local government for funding, the actual direction of the office is the charge of a specially selected board who answer to the public, as do other regulatory agencies. More direct control can be exercised if the county commissioners/supervisors select the public defender themselves. There are counties, such as San Francisco County, in which the public defender is elected directly by the voters. Whatever the method, there are strengths and weaknesses in each. Budget-

[38] "The Public Defender," *Saskatchewan Bar Review 30:2* (1965), 110.
[39] Advisory Commission on Intergovernmental Relations, *Profile of County Government* (Washington: U.S. Govt. Printing Office, December 1971), Table 13, p. 23.

ing is always the crucial point: some interesting attempts to remove the public defender from the politics of the budgetary process have been attempted. For example, in Los Angeles County, the defender receives 60 percent of the amount approved for the prosecutor's budget.

There are many advantages to a public defender system of legal services delivery. As a result of the *Escobedo* v. *Illinois*[40] and *Miranda* v. *Arizona* decisions, counsel should be available at the earliest possible moment in the justice process. *Douglas* v. *California* held that counsel should be available through any appeal that might be forthcoming. If each step is handled by a single agency, continuity can be achieved. It is in the interest of the accused that counsel be appointed early, so that the attorney has sufficient time to prepare his case thoroughly.

From the public's viewpoint the public defender system is the most economical one available. In 1969, the North Carolina General Assembly experimented with various delivery systems and found that, in the four districts of their state where they conducted tests, the public defender system was the most economical.[41] Findings in other states confirm this.[42]

A valuable advantage of a public defender's office is that it is frequently staffed with the support personnel often lacking in other systems. It usually has trained investigators who search for all the facts in the commission of the crime, locate witnesses, and supply much of the relevant information needed by the attorney. Constant communication is maintained with psychiatrists, document analysts, pathologists, medical experts, and criminologists.

Criminal law and its procedures require that an attorney has expertise, experience, and the time to devote to his specialty. Because the attorneys in a public defender's office operate full time in criminal law, expertise and experience are quickly gained by the newly employed. Often a "zone defense" is employed so that each defender quickly becomes expert in every phase of the process.

A public defender's office has other values in a democratic society. Since the defenders have contact with all elements of criminal justice system, there is a constant check on district attorneys, police, judges,

---

[40] 378 U.S. 478 (1964).

[41] Grier, *Analysis and Comparison*, 709.

[42] Dulany Foster, "The Public Defender and Other Suggested Systems for the Defense of Indigents," *53:6 Judicature, 248* (1970) and Smith, *Statistical Analysis,* p. 26.

correctional personnel, and others. And since the defender's offices can hire more attorneys in more "respectable" surroundings, the influence of the criminal defense "establishment" will increase, and the rights of the individual will be better served.[43]

The size and growing influence of the defenders can be seen in some annual expenditures:

Chicago	$1,201,000
Detroit	$1,412,000
New York City	$3,729,000
Philadelphia	$1,187,000
San Francisco	$2,237,000
Los Angeles/Long Beach	$6,288,000[44]

These expenditures indicate the growing public interest in the criminal justice system, particularly in its defense activities.

Despite its many advantages, there are some criticisms levelled at the public defender systems. Its detractors argue that defenders do not provide a check on the activities of others, but become a part of the machinery that must compromise to keep the overloaded system from breaking down. Others claim that it is unhealthy for all of the participants in the process to be state employees.

There is no doubt that a social system exists in many courthouses. Some studies have shown that public defenders tend to work toward the goals of the system instead of those of the client.[45] But this is not proof that the defender's office is under anyone's thumb. As Skolnick points out, the public defender ultimately has the power to frustrate the entire system by delaying each and every case.[46] It is known that, like any other

---

[43] H. Reed Searle, "An Argument for the Public Defender System," 5 *Santa Clara Lawyer, 57* (1964).

[44] LEAA, Dept. of Justice, *Expenditures and Employment Data for the Criminal Justice System, 1969-70.* (Washington: U.S. Govt. Printing Office, 1972), Table 15, pp. 37-39.

[45] Jonathan D. Casper, "Did You Have a Lawyer When You Went to Court? No, I had a Public Defender." *1 Yale Review of Law and Social Action, 409* (1971); Abraham S. Blumberg, *Criminal Justice* (Chicago: Quadrangle Books, 1967); and Edward J. Dimock, "The Public Defender: A Step Toward a Police State," *American Bar Association Journal 42:3* (1956), p. 219.

[46] Jerome H. Skolnick, "Social Control in the Adversary System," *Journal of Conflict Resolution 11* (1967), pp. 52-70.

agency, defenders are overworked; overloading any system seems to create the conditions whereby principles can become compromised.

The consumer does not see the public defender as really "being on his side." Since those charged with a crime are usually quite suspicious and mistrustful—especially if they are poor and feel helpless—they simply do not trust the public defender assigned to their case.

> *They typically encountered their lawyer in the hallway or bullpen of the courthouse, or found themselves before the judge with a man beside them that turned out to be their attorney. The typical defendant reported that he spent a total of 5 to 10 minutes conferring with his attorney, usually in rapid hushed conversations in the courthouse. . . . Most of the men reported that the first words uttered were: "I can get you . . . if you plead guilty. . . ." Thus, the public defender is not "their" lawyer, but an agent of the state. He is the man with whom they had to bargain, not simply, the prosecutor. He is the surrogate of the prosecutor—a member of "their little syndicate"—rather than the defendant's representative. . . .[47]*

The concept of justice requires that all the participants, including the accused, feel that the system has been fair and equitable. The suspicion of collusion between state agencies, prosecutor and defender, does not help.

Mixed systems are often an attempt to prevent the defender from being too closely identified with the state while still achieving as many of the advantages as possible. Although called a legal aid program, the Province of Ontario's Legal Aid Plan is just such an attempt to avoid the problems encountered by public defenders' offices by resorting to what is called a mixed system. Set up under the Legal Aid Act of 1967, the Ontario Plan is a state-sponsored private attorney program. Headquartered with the Law Society of Upper Canada, there are branches throughout the province. The offices provide the normal support, but private attorneys are employed on a case-by-case basis. Once the accused person's eligibility is determined, he receives a certificate that can then allow him to "contract" a lawyer who has a criminal law specialty. This tends to reduce the closeness of defender and courthouse that is often the focal point of criticism. The Ontario Plan reported in 1971 that some 600,000 persons had been assisted, over 50 percent of whom were involved in criminal charges. The costs per case ranged from an average

[47] Casper, *Criminal Justice*, pp. 23-24.

of $1427 for unlawful homicide to $101 for drunk and impaired driving, figures that make the mixed system competitive with other forms of legal service delivery.[48]

Other mixed systems of indigent defense can also be found. Volunteer support of an established public defender's office in the Santa Clara County Public Defender Department helps to ameliorate the disadvantages described. Many programs involving college students and law students can be found. Intern programs, from assisting the attorney to working with investigators, are becoming more common, and in some jurisdictions, public defender's offices, legal aid societies, and assigned-counsel programs are all available. All contribute to providing defense counsel for the indigent.

Despite the shortcomings, the public defender system is a twentieth-century response to the ills of the criminal justice system in the United States. It will probably remain the chief response in urban areas, while assigned counsel will remain the rural response.

Legal Aid Societies

Probably the oldest forms of defense counsel for the indigent are the legal aid societies and the individual attorney involved in legal aid. The first such formal organization known was the *Deutscher Rechts-Schutz Verein* of New York City (1876), founded to assist German-speaking residents and emigrants on legal matters. Before long the Society began to assist people outside the German community. By 1888, legal aid societies had sprung up in Chicago, Pittsburgh, Philadelphia, and Newark. Today there are more than 173, of which only a few deal with criminal cases.[49]

The bulk of indigent criminal cases were handled by private attorneys who acknowledged their professional responsibilities in providing these services. Caseloads of these attorneys swelled. Those who made liberal and general interpretations of their fee charges in such cases were beseiged with requests for services. As a result, the time available for

[48] Law Society of Upper Canada, *Ontario Legal Aid Plan: Annual Report 1971* (Toronto: Law Society of Upper Canada, 1971), pp. 4, 21.
[49] Murray L. Schwartz, *Cases and Materials on Professional Responsibility and the Administration of Criminal Justice* (New York: Matthew Bender, 1962), pp. 95-96.

case preparation often was much less than the actual time needed, thereby creating conflicts of priorities for the concerned attorney.

Formal legal aid societies provided at least an alternative for those generous, but overworked, attorneys so that they could more effectively distribute their workload. Funds were solicited so that essential services could be provided; and the attorney who gave his time and skills could be supported by investigators and other staff. The legal aid societies, however, continued to face problems. Meager funding has been the chronic problem that has plagued the movement since its earliest day. Gifts of money, some governmental grants, and gifts that provided annual interest were not enough.

Another problem has been a prevailing attitude of indifference by both practicing attorneys and the general public toward legal service delivery to low-income individuals. The bar associations felt that legal aid programs would divert business from private practitioners. Occasionally, public wrath has been directed against the service in the form of arguments that the "guilty" one does not need protection, or when the society provides counsel in well-publicized and highly emotional cases.

In order to alleviate the inadequacies of staffing and funding, a few spirited attorneys have taken the legal aid concept to their organized bar associations and the colleges of law. One of the most successful programs developed has been that of the Houston Legal Foundation. Headed by Judge Sam Johnson, all lawyers under 50 years of age in Harris County, Texas, must rotate as counsel in criminal court. Supported by five local groups and the Ford Foundation, the criminal bar receives support from a staff that apparently brings realization to the Sixth Amendment.[50] In some areas, law students become involved in legal aid through local societies. The Universities of Utah, Chicago, Georgetown, Boston, Harvard, Wyoming, Kansas, and Pennsylvania are just a few. Not only do these students help provide legal aid to indigents accused of crimes, but they work with the incarcerated at correctional institutions.

The concept of a legal aid society program is far-reaching, humanistic, and professionally oriented. The working model has never been quite able to deliver the idealistic standards of operation as set down by the conceptual model, but it has filled a void. The problems are many:

---

[50] Howard James, *Crisis in the Courts* (New York: David McKay, 1971), pp. 132-133.

instead of volunteers backed up by support personnel, societies have had to face a lack of interest and a lack of funding; key staff members are often lacking or overworked; investigatory staffs receive requests from others not part of the society; turnover rates are high, and often the staff and attorneys are inexperienced; and local bar associations restrict the clientele by restrictive eligibility requirements and types of cases that may be accepted by the society. Local influences, politics, and general apathy all work to prevent the legal aid concept from becoming a reality. Some impact has been felt in criminal justice, but the bulk of the casework has too often been divorce and bankruptcy.

Legal Services: Office of Economic Opportunity

Although legal aid societies expanded their services for the indigent, legal representation still proved inadequate. In 1965, the Office of Economic Opportunity (OEO) initiated the Legal Services Program (LSP). The OEO/LSP provided funds for expanded legal services as well as for innovation and experimentation. The funds for this program were allocated to provide free legal service with eligibility based on income. The basic objective was to provide assistance to those people who could not normally afford legal services.[51]

OEO/LSP funds were limited in their usage. Grants were awarded to local services that met OEO requirements, or to provide those services not already available in existing legal aid societies. Programs were developed mainly to fill those gaps where no legal aid services existed or only volunteer programs operated. Neighborhood offices were established and were to be "tailored" to the community in which they were located and the clientele they were to serve. Store-front offices were opened in ghetto areas; mobile units, suitably equipped, served urban areas; circuit riders traveled in rural areas; Indian reservations received services. The gaps in legal services were to be met; but only in a limited sense were the gaps in criminal justice to be closed.

Two programs involved in serving the defendant were the New Haven Legal Assistance and the Legal Aid Society of Louisville, Ken-

[51] Judith H. Grimes, "Legal Aid in Idaho: The 'Public' Bar." 7 *Idaho L.R., 234* (1970).

Figure 7-1. A neighborhood legal aid service.

tucky. The New Haven Legal Assistance was supported by OEO, state funds, and foundation grants. Although OEO funding cannot be used for criminal defense, the fact that the program had other sources of moneys allowed the legal assistance attorneys to represent clients involved in criminal proceedings. The assistance received by defendants rated fairly high from the consumer's viewpoint.[52] The Legal Aid Society of Louisville, Kentucky operated with a staff of about 30, 17 of whom were attorneys. With an annual budget of $281,000, some 10,000 cases per year were handled by the Society, but only a few involved indigents accused of criminal offenses. A paraprofessional legal assistance unit was developed in cooperation with the University of Louisville's Kent School of Social Work to assist the clients by interviewing and directing them to

[52] Casper, *Criminal Justice,* pp. 32-33.

services, legal and other, that they required.[53] Many indigents requiring criminal defense were directed to sources of those services.

When OEO/LSP-sponsored agencies have entered the area of criminal justice, there has been considerable reaction. A few of the examples of adverse pressure on OEO/LSP and locally sponsored agencies were the 1970 incident involving the Western Center on Law and Poverty's efforts on behalf of the Coalition for Correctional Reform; the 1970 situation of representing black militants during bail hearings by the New Orleans Legal Assistance Corporation; and the Upper Peninsula Legal Services, Inc., of Michigan, in its defense of individuals charged with misdemeanors in 1971.

In order to understand the reasons why OEO/LSP has developed as it has and why it is open to criticism when it enters the criminal sector, one must take note of the legislation that made the greatest impact on its development. The 1963 Supreme Court decision in *Gideon* v. *Wainwright* extended a state's responsibility to provide counsel from their own funds; it became a state matter.[54] In 1964, the Criminal Justice Act stated that a federal court must supply legal defense for the indigent. These curtailed the activities of others in the field. It was not until 1968 that limitations were placed on the legal services program. The 1968 Amendment to the Economic Opportunity Act prohibited the handling of criminal matters through OEO-funded programs. Any violation would, of course, open the way for action against OEO/LSP attorneys and programs, and did.

The future of OEO/LSP appears uncertain. Originally funded until 1974, it was later marked for dismantling in June 1973, an action that was stayed by a district court. The loss of OEO/LSP has not been accepted with calm resignation. Outside pressure has caused Congress to halt the total dismantling of OEO. Bar associations and other interested parties have been advocating the revitalization in a new form. The suggestion most often put forward is for the creation of an independent legal service in the form of a governmental corporation. Such a corporation would be directed by 11 members who would be named by the President.

---

[53] David Holt, "A Formerly Sinking Ship is Sailing Smoothly Now," Louisville *Courier-Journal*, December 7, 1972, p. A23.
[54] Smith, *Statistical Analysis,* p. 25.

There would be no more than six from one political party, and the majority would be lawyers.

Among suggestions for the delivery of legal services were prepaid legal insurance—a type of judicare—and contracts with private law firms. The proposal contained various limitations, such as parental/guardian consent for minors receiving legal assistance, and the denial of services to anyone not in the job market. If the legal service corporation concept does develop, it will be interesting to see whether it will be allowed to operate in the areas of criminal justice.

Student Checklist

1. Can you identify the significant court decisions that contributed to the concept of the right to counsel?
2. Are you able to list the reasons why a defendant needs a counsel in a criminal case?
3. Do you know the purpose and functions of a lawyer reference service?
4. Can you write a short essay that describes the "criminal bar"?
5. Do you know how to compare the assigned-counsel system and legal aid societies?
6. Can you trace the history of the public defender system?
7. Can you list the type of legal services provided by OEO/LSP?

Topics for Discussion

1. Discuss the advantages of the public defender system.
2. Discuss the impact of the decision of the U.S. Supreme Court in the *Gideon* v. *Wainwright* case.
3. Discuss the disadvantages of the assigned-counsel system.
4. Discuss the importance of right to counsel.

ANNOTATED BIBLIOGRAPHY

Advisory Committee on the Prosecution and Defense Functions (ABA), *Standards Relating to the Prosecution Function and the Defense Function* (tentative draft). Chicago: American Bar Association, 1970. The setting of standards of conduct for the defense attorneys. Although aimed at the ideal, the suggested procedures do indicate the problem areas encountered by the defense.

Bailey, F. Lee, and Henry B. Rothblatt. *Successful Techniques for Criminal Trials*. San Francisco: Bancroft-Whitney, 1971. A text written for the practitioner in criminal law. Each section deals with techniques and the importance of each step in the process. Excellent step-by-step approach for those interested in defense techniques.

Baughman, Robert J. *Counsel for Indigents*. Frankfort, Ky.: Legislative Research Commission, August 1969. A short but concise analysis of the different delivery systems and background on the development of counsel for indigents, both in Kentucky and in the United States.

Carlin, Jerome. *Lawyers on Their Own*. New Brunswick, N.J.; Rutgers University Press, 1962. A study of the professional environment of the solo practitioner and the problems faced when attempting to secure cases and collect fees. Also gives insight into the relationship of the solo lawyer with the other members of the bar.

Casper, Jonathan D. *Criminal Justice—The Consumer's Perspective*. Washington: NILECJ, Department of Justice, 1972. Study based on interviews of 71 men charged with felonies in Connecticut. Chapter Four deals with the defendants' views on defense attorneys.

Oaks, Dallin H., and Warren Lehman. *Criminal Justice System and the Indigent: Study of Chicago and Cook County*. Chicago: University of Chicago Press, 1967. A study of the multistage screening process of who will be treated/punished for criminal behavior. Half of the book deals with the law and practice of legal assistance to the indigent criminal defendant.

Smith, Gerald W. *A Statistical Analysis of Public Defender Activities*. Washington: NILECJ, Department of Justice, 1970. A study that compares the different types of defense attorneys. Statistical study of who is served by public defenders, how public defenders dispose of their cases, and what happens to cases handled by public defenders.

Wood, Arthur Lewis. *Criminal Lawyer*. New Haven: College and University Press, 1967. An in-depth analysis of the "criminal bar" in New London, Connecticut; Brooklyn, New York; Jersey City, New Jersey; Birmingham, Alabama; and Madison, Wisconsin; and the role envisaged by the lawyer and others.

The study of this chapter will enable you to:

1. Identify the levels of the three-tier plan for state judicial systems.
2. Differentiate between the roles of state supreme court decisions and district courts of appeal decisions.
3. List the five types of cases handled in courts of general jurisdiction.
4. List the titles of eight different inferior courts.
5. Identify the three principal ways that a case reaches the U.S. Supreme Court.
6. Identify the concepts of the Missouri Plan that are fundamental to the selection of judges based on merit.
7. Write an essay that describes the duties performed by court administrators.

8
The Judiciary

The structure of the judicial system at the local, state, and federal levels reflects the influence of social and political growth. An examination of the historical development of any area will reveal how social and economic groups influenced laws and judicial operations. Like other branches of government, the court system is molded by its environment. In California, for example, the Court Act of 1851 reflected contemporary issues when it provided for the trial of lawsuits concerning mining claims. Justice-of-the-peace courts were given the right to conduct jury trials in these matters. This action had a significant impact on the historical development of American mining and water law. The Act reflected the economic and social needs of that state at that time.

General Characteristics

Care must be taken when referring to courts by name; consider only the functions and jurisdiction exercised by the individual court. Courts perform a combination of one or more of three functions: appellate jurisdiction, general jurisdiction, and limited jurisdiction.

Using this concept as a model, it is less complicated to compare the various state judicial systems, which are described as being a three-tier plan: (1) state appellate courts; (2) trial courts of general jurisdiction; and (3) inferior courts (those with limited jurisdiction). Although this description is essentially correct, it fails to consider two things. The first is the overlapping of jurisdiction between the three tiers. In some instances a state appellate court may have trial jurisdiction (this is usually very limited), or a court of general jurisdiction may have appellate jurisdiction over inferior courts.

Another type of judicial system is beginning to emerge that is reflective of a new direction in court reorganization and reform. Here, the states are eliminating the inferior courts. In 1969, for example, Idaho eliminated this level of trial court. Legislation has been introduced in several states to establish the two-tier system with only appellate and trial courts.

State Appellate Courts

All 50 states have provided a system of appeal from the decisions of trial courts. In most of the states the court of last resort is called the supreme court. In New York, however, this role is vested in the Court of Appeals, while the Supreme Court is a Court of General Jurisdiction. The New York Supreme Court hears both civil and criminal appeals. In Oklahoma and Texas there are two separate courts of last resort, one for civil and one for criminal cases.

Perhaps the term "courts of last resort" is a misleading one. The proper meaning is: the court that provides the last possible appeal of a judgment or finding *within the state judicial structure*. If there are federal questions, the interested party may appeal for relief to the federal court system in either criminal or civil cases.

Originally, the state supreme courts could easily accommodate all cases that the system produced. Most state supreme courts had a chief justice and two associate justices. As the number of appealed cases increased, the usual resort was to add additional justices, with the workload being assigned among them. This practice worked until it became apparent that there was a limit to the number of justices who could be accommodated on the bench. In the 1960s, New Mexico realized the folly of this approach when the legislature was requested to add additional justices. Instead, state lawmakers decided to create an intermediate appellate court. The objective was to limit the number of appeals reaching the docket of the New Mexico Supreme Court.

The intermediate appellate courts are organized on a regional basis. In large states, the appellate courts may be further subdivided. This regionalization creates a new problem—that of uniformity. While the state supreme court decisions are binding throughout the state, district courts of appeals are not, and their decisions may differ between districts.

In many states, the courts of general trial jurisdiction may exercise appellate jurisdiction over inferior courts within their geographic area. The appellate procedure in these courts can be of two types: trial *de nova* (a retrial) or formal appeal with briefs and all records. California, for example, uses both types of appeal procedures. The trial *de nova* might be considered a case of judicial instant replay. It is usually an appeal from a court not of record.[1] In small claims courts of California, appeals from this type of case are all heard *de nova*. A formal appeal process is initiated in all other types of cases. Judicial delay results when there is a wide range of cases that may be appealed in this manner. In some states, all cases from inferior courts may be appealed to a court of general jurisdiction that hears them *de nova*. Defense attorneys, in this instance, have used the lower court as a hearing session and appealed all guilty verdicts in traffic and criminal cases.

State Courts of General Jurisdiction

The state courts of general jurisdiction have broad authority to conduct litigation in both civil and criminal cases. Court titles include superior courts, chancery courts, circuit courts, district courts, criminal courts, and courts of common pleas. In states such as Arkansas, Delaware, Indiana, Maryland, Mississippi, New Jersey, Oklahoma, and Texas there is more than one court of general jurisdiction. There is a court of general jurisdiction for criminal matters, and another for civil.

Because of the lack of uniformity in judicial systems in the various states, it is difficult to generalize about courts. One must instead look at the functions of the court generally performed. This approach recognizes the fact that judicial systems in all states must handle the same types of litigation regardless of organizational differences. The California Superior Court is an example of a court of general jurisdiction with a full

---

[1] Courts of record are those whose acts and judgments are recorded. A court may be a court of record for some purposes, and not for others.

range of judicial functions performed. The Superior Court will try all cases not specifically assigned to a lower court. It is organized on a geographic basis, with each county having a superior court. In small, rural areas, there is usually one judge. Because of the state constitutional requirements, this can result in a judge who does not have a large enough caseload to keep him busy at all times.

In contrast, a county with a large population may have a number of judges assigned to its superior court. The size of the caseload may have a great determination on the amount of specialization. Courts with five or more judges will generally specialize in criminal, civil, probate, family law, and juvenile departments. If there are not enough cases to warrant a full-time judge being assigned to one of these categories, the judges may decide to schedule this type of case on certain days of the week, which results in a form of specialization.

Types of Cases

Criminal Cases. The superior courts in most states have constitutional authority in all criminal cases that are felonies, and in those misdemeanor cases not otherwise provided for by the legislature. In some states, the legislature has given jurisdiction over all misdemeanors to inferior courts—municipal and justice. In that case, a superior court may have no misdemeanor criminal jurisdiction. However, some states provide for concurrent jurisdiction in courts of general jurisdiction and inferior courts for state misdemeanor offenses. The law enforcement officer makes the decision regarding the court in which he should file the case. In many instances, the decision where to file is based on the amount of bail the defendant would have to post.

The major criminal workload of the courts of general jurisdiction are felony trials. This type of case originates in the court by the filing of either an indictment (hearing held by a grand jury) or an information (based on preliminary examination conducted by a magistrate).[2] Some

---

[2] The use of the preliminary hearing conducted by a magistrate has been used in California since 1879. California was challenged in Hurtado v. California 110 U.S. 516 (1884) on Fourteenth Amendment grounds that it did not provide the defendant with due process under the law. The states are not required to follow federal standards.

states require a grand jury hearing even though a preliminary hearing has been conducted.

Juvenile Cases. A number of states have established a separate juvenile court, and there has been an increase in the practice of giving jurisdiction over juveniles to the superior court. The juvenile court exists as a separate department of the court. One judge is assigned to hear this type of case under special rules specified by the legislature. The types of case generally handled are criminal acts, delinquency, child abandonment, and other miscellaneous provisions of the law. The juvenile court is given the authority to determine whether the juvenile is either a fit subject for action by that court or should be remanded to the department for trial as an adult.

Civil Actions. Civil actions constitute the largest single category of filings for the superior court. Civil filings in one state's superior courts for the year 1969–1970 amounted to 88,087, while criminal filings for the same period were 72,048.[3] This is generally the ratio in all states.

Filings for civil actions heard by the court are for return of money, breach of contract, to determine title to either personal or real property, to declare laws unconstitutional, and other actions. Civil actions are limited only by the imagination of the litigants. In contrast to the inferior court, all types of civil cases may be filed here. If inferior courts have not been given specific legislative authority to hear a case, jurisdiction is retained in the superior court.

Probate. Probate cases deal primarily with the estates of deceased persons. Wills are administered and the assets distributed. In California, the Superior Court has jurisdiction over probate hearings. In Michigan, as in some other states, probate jurisdiction is vested in an independent court.

Mental Incompetence. A number of superior courts also conduct hearings into the mental competency of individuals. At the conclusion of such a hearing, a judge may commit a defendant to a mental institution for safekeeping and treatment.

---

[3] Annual Report of the Administrative Office of the California Court, January 4, 1971, pp. 159, 160, 161.

The inferior courts (or lower courts, as they are also known) are extremely difficult to categorize. In contrast to courts of general jurisdiction, where matters heard are fairly uniform, the inferior courts in most states are completely fragmented. For example, prior to their 1972 constitutional change, Florida had ten different types of inferior court. Courts with the same titles had different jurisdictions depending on the county in which they were located.

The inferior court is a by-product of the historical development of the nation. Years ago, each county, ward, city, town, village, or township had to have a court to hear cases involving violations of the law. Because of transportation difficulties, small courts operating on a part-time basis met society's needs. In Table 8-1 the titles of inferior courts in existence throughout the country illustrate the fragmented structure. The name of an inferior court in one state may be the title of a court of general jurisdiction in another state.

TABLE 8-1.   **United States Inferior Court Titles.**

Courts of probate	Municipal courts
County courts	Courts of common pleas
Justice courts	Police courts
Recorders courts	Superior courts
Magistrate courts	Juvenile courts
City and town magistrates courts	Probate courts
Civil courts of record	Courts of ordinary
Courts of claims	Small claims court
City courts	Mayor courts
Family courts	Traffic courts
Court of criminal corrections	District courts
Surrogates courts	Land courts

What common characteristics do inferior courts share? They usually are small in size and workload, with a single part-time judge. In metropolitan areas inferior courts may have a higher number of filings and have several full-time judges. California requires municipal court judges to be practicing attorneys for a period of five years prior to sitting on the bench, but justice court judges are not required to be admitted to the practice of law. All that is required of the justice court judge is that he pass a written qualifying test administered by the California Judicial Council.

The California Inferior Court recently served as a model for other states as they have reorganized into a three-tier system. On January 1, 1952, California consolidated its inferior courts into municipal and justice courts. Prior to this date, a fragmented judicial system had been in existence with city, police, and justice-of-the-peace Class A and B courts. The entire state was divided into judicial districts—with two restrictions: a district had to be wholly within a single county, while a municipal court could hear cases that occurred in its own district or in any justice court's district in the county. Since in California there are uniform penal and traffic codes that take precedence over local codes, there is no real advantage to filing a case in one court instead of another. In some states, the discussion as to the choice of a municipal code violation over a state code violation is based on revenues that are returned to the city or county. The local jurisdiction usually receives more money from a local code violation.

The municipal court has a much higher civil jurisdiction than a justice court, and can also hear a wider range of cases. This is true also of the small claims jurisdictions.

The U.S. Constitution insures that two judicial systems—state and federal—operate within the nation. Article III of the Constitution outlines the specific jurisdiction of the federal courts; under the Fifth Amendment, all other cases are heard in the state courts.

U.S. Supreme Court

The Supreme Court is the highest court in the land. Its membership consists of a chief justice and eight associate justices. The number of associate justices has varied from four to nine during the history of the country. The current composition of the court was established in 1869.

Article III, Section 2, gives the Supreme Court both original and appellate jurisdiction. For practical purposes, the majority of the Court's work is appellate in nature. The appeal procedure is established by Congress. There are currently three principle ways a case reaches the Supreme Court. They are: (1) by appeal; (2) by *writ of certiorari*; and (3) by certification.

When considering appeals from state courts, the Supreme Court must accept cases that fall into two categories: the validity of a treaty or statute of the United States has been questioned, and it has been held invoked by a state court; or a state law has been questioned on the grounds that it violates the Constitution, laws of the United States or treaties, and a state court has upheld the law.

The Supreme Court also considers appeals from the courts of appeal. In certain instances, the Court will also consider direct appeals from district courts. The right to appeal to the Court is extremely limited, but Congress has given the Court almost unlimited power to decide which cases they will hear.

The Court may approve a *writ of certiorari* to require a lower court to send the record of the case to it for review. This is done only when at least four justices believe the issues important enough to warrant consideration.

The certification is a little-used device employed by lower courts to ask the Supreme Court to answer a question of law. Currently, only courts of appeal and courts of claim may use this process.

Federal Courts of Appeal

The federal courts of appeal exist for much the same reason that the state district courts of appeal exist—to relieve the Supreme Court of much of its workload. They were originated in 1891 as circuit courts of appeal and were given their current title in 1948. They hear appeals from district courts and independent regulatory agencies.

Federal District Courts

The U.S. District Courts are of original jurisdiction. They hear, with some exceptions, all cases and controversies involving federal questions, and they consider both criminal and civil litigations. The district court is the only federal court that has jury trials.

U.S. District Courts are located throughout the nation, and the more populous states may have one or more judicial districts. Each district court has a clerk, a U.S. Attorney, a U.S. Marshal, one or more

U.S. magistrates, referees in bankruptcy, probation officers, court reporters, and their assistants.

When a district court has more than one judge, the workload is divided between judges according to the rules and regulations of the court. When there is an excessive caseload in one district, the chief judge may temporarily assign cases from one district court to another in the same circuit.

Court Personnel

The judicial system is similar to any other system in which people have roles that, in some instances, conflict or complement each other. Some of the roles are truly adversary in nature and others are clearly supportive. Most people are familiar with the roles performed by judges, prosecutors, and defense counsels, but there are many other court functionaries who play a vital part in the judicial process, and each of these are discussed below.

Judges

In general usage, the justice or judge is a person who sits as part of an appellate court. There is usually a chief justice, or presiding justice, and two or more associate justices. In the federal system they are appointed by the President and confirmed by the Senate for life terms.

At the state level a justice or judge may be elected, appointed by the governor, or appointed from a list supplied by a nonpartisan commission composed of lawyers, judges, and laymen. There have been major criticisms of both the elective and appointive processes. The major objection to these processes is that they fail to identify men qualified to become judges. Both systems tempt candidates to play politics in order to obtain their appointments. During the past century, there has been an effort to avoid the defects of both the appointive and elective systems for the selection of judges. The Missouri Plan provides for selection based on merit and it has been adopted either partially or totally by several states. This concept includes:

1. A nonpartisan nominating committee or commission composed of members of the bar and laymen appointed by the governor, chaired by a judge.

2. A specified number of candidates nominated by the commission for each judicial vacancy.
3. A judicial vacancy to be filled by the governor from the list provided by the nominating committee.
4. A judge who will run for reelection solely on the question of whether he should be retained in his office.

The Missouri Plan is based on the concept that nonpolitical judges are apt to be more impartial than political judges. By eliminating the political process (either elective or appointive) in the selection of judges and by substituting the selection process of the Missouri Plan, it is believed that judges will be better qualified.

Until the 1960s the only method for removal of judges was by impeachment by the legislature or through the ballot box. Both are deemed inadequate for most needs, and this inadequacy created the impetus to supplement the traditional processes.

In 1960, California became the first state to pass a constitutional amendment providing for the retirement, discipline, and removal of judges. The amendment provides for a Commission on Judicial Qualifications. The Commission consists of nine members: two judges of the courts of appeal; two judges of the superior court; one judge of the municipal court; two members of the bar; and two nonlawyers. The judicial members of the Commission are selected by the California Supreme Court; the two lawyers are selected by the board of governors of the California bar; and the two nonlawyers are appointed by the governor and approved by the California Senate. The terms of office are four years.

Any California judge is subject to review by the Commission, and any citizen may complain about a judge to the Commission. The proceduce is that the Commission staff conduct an informal, confidential investigation. If the facts warrant, the Commission may hold formal hearings or order hearings before three special masters appointed by the California Supreme Court. The Commission can recommend to the State Supreme Court the removal, retirement, or censure of a judge, and the court will review the matter and render the final decision.

Attorney General

The attorney general is elected in 42 states, appointed by the governor in 6 states, appointed by the legislature in 1 state, and appointed by the state supreme court in another. Historically, this office has been an appointive instead of an elective post.

The attorney general's duties require him in some instances to represent the state in civil matters. He sues and defends in the name of the state on all litigation. He is usually required to give written advisory opinions on any questions of law. These are given to the governor, heads of state agencies, and to state legislators. Among his other duties, he supervises the department of justice in some states. He may supervise district attorneys, sheriffs, and local police, with the authority to direct the sheriff to perform investigations or, if he deems it necessary, he may appoint someone to perform the duties of the sheriff in conducting an investigation. In some states the attorney general can prosecute criminal actions if a district attorney is disqualified. He may also supersede a district attorney where he feels the laws are not being adequately enforced.

District Attorneys and County Prosecutors

The district attorney or county prosecutor is usually an elected official. He is required to have been an attorney for a period of time, the length varying from state to state. If his office is a large one, he may appoint deputies to assist him in his work. He has the authority to decide which cases to prosecute, but he does not usually have the power to terminate a case once it has commenced.

Marshal/Bailiff

Ohio and Iowa use the title of bailiff, which is comparable to the title of marshal used in some other states. Both are charged with carrying out orders of the court—serving warrants of arrest, writs, other civil processes, and maintaining order in the court while it is in session. They are often responsible for the custody of prisoners who are awaiting court action and, if necessary, in the transportation of prisoners to detention facilities. During jury trials, they are sworn to closet the jurors, maintain seclusion, and tend to their requirements during deliberation. The marshal or bailiff also escorts jurors to and from the courtroom during periods of deliberation.

Court Administrators

The position of court administrator (sometimes called court attache) is relatively new. The first court administrator was appointed in 1950 for the court of common pleas in Media, Pennsylvania, but the concept did not start to grow until the years 1964 to 1966. At present there are no uniform educational or experience standards established for court administrators, although several degree programs to train personnel in this field have recently been established. Some of the more important duties of the court administrator (similar to those of a court clerk) are: personnel management services; financial management services including preparation of the court's budget; management of physical facilities; information services with law enforcement and public agencies; intergovernmental relations assistance; jury administrative services; statistical recordings; systems analysis; calendar management; and conducting training seminars and providing manuals for day-to-day operations by deputies.

Traditionally, most of the duties of the court administrator have been performed by the clerk of the court. In addition to these, the clerk is responsible for all ministerial duties of the court. All papers and processes (except warrants of arrest) are issued in the clerk's name. There have been no uniform educational or experience criteria developed for this position. It may be filled either by election, appointment, or through a competitive Civil Service examination.

As with other departments associated with the courts, the number of court deputies depends on the business of a particular jurisdiction. In larger courts it is normally the practice to have three divisions consisting of civil (which includes small claim filings), criminal, and traffic. In smaller courts, however, the divisions may be handled by one or two deputies, requiring them to be adept at all phases of the handling of the processes of the court.

Student Checklist

1. Can you identify the levels of the three-tier plan for state judicial systems?
2. Are you able to differentiate between the roles of state supreme court decisions and district courts of appeal decisions?

3. Can you list the five types of cases handled in courts of general jurisdiction?
4. Are you able to list the titles of eight different inferior courts?
5. Can you identify the three principal ways in which a case reaches the U.S. Supreme Court?
6. Can you list the concepts of the Missouri Plan that are fundamental to the selection of judges based on merit?
7. Are you able to write an essay that describes the duties performed by court administrators?

Topics for Discussion

1. Discuss the advantages of a three-tier plan for state judicial systems.
2. Discuss the trend of consolidating inferior courts.
3. Discuss the functions performed by a court administrator.

ANNOTATED BIBLIOGRAPHY

Abraham, Henry J. *The Judicial Process*, 2nd ed. New York: Oxford University Press, 1968. It is a selective comparative introduction to the judicial process and seeks to analyze and evaluate the main institutions and considerations affecting the administration of justice. Included are discussions of staffing of the courts, courts of the United States, and courts of England and Wales.

Cardoza, Benjamin N. *The Nature of the Judicial Process*. New Haven, Conn.; Yale University Press, 1921. This work is a discussion by one of the most famous justices of the United States Supreme Court about the conscious and unconscious processes by which he decided cases. Major segments deal with history, tradition, and sociology.

Frank, Jerome. *Courts on Trial*. New York: Atheneum, 1969. Deals with the function of the courts. It analyzes procedural reforms, the jury system, the role of the judge, judicial training, and precedents.

Jacob, Herbert. *Justice in America: Courts, Lawyers, and the Judicial Process*, 2nd ed. Boston: Little, Brown, 1972. The three major sections of this book deal with the functions of the courts, the participants in the judicial process, and the structure and rules of the judicial system.

James, Howard. *Crisis in the Courts*, rev. ed. New York: David McKay, 1972. Deals with failures in the judicial system. Discusses such issues as trial delay, bail jurys, sentencing, and requirements for judicial education.

Karlen, Delmar. *Anglo-American Criminal Justice*. New York: Oxford University Press, 1967. Examines the similarities and differences between the British and American criminal justice system. This included an analysis of police, prosecution, defense, and courts, as well as systems procedures.

Roche, John P. *Courts and Rights: The American Judiciary in Action,* 2nd ed. New York: Random House, 1966. Covers the judicial process, structure of the federal judiciary, legislative courts, common law, Bill of Rights, and citizen's rights. The first section provides a good insight into the federal system.

Watson, Richard A., and Randal A. Downing. *The Politics of The Bench and the Bar*. New York: Wiley, 1969. This book is an empirical examination of the nonpartisan court plan. Covers the recruitment and selection process of judges, the Missouri Selection Plan, and judicial performance.

The study of this chapter will enable you to:

1. Contrast the differing philosophical bases of each of the correctional subsystems.
2. Write a short essay on the concept of community treatment.
3. List the steps involved in institutional rehabilitation.
4. Define the term furlough/release.
5. Compare the work release and the educational release programs.
6. List the features common to halfway house programs.
7. Write an essay on the concept of conjugal visitation.
8. Identify the two significant programs in which lay members of the community have become involved.
9. Describe the ways in which private industry can work with and assist governmental correctional institutions and agencies.

9
Corrections

The correctional reform movement in America is stronger today that at any time in the history of the nation's criminal justice system. The National Advisory Commission on Criminal Justice Standards and Goals, in its preliminary report of January 1973, said:

Corrections for too long has preferred to isolate itself from the purview of both the public and the other criminal justice system components. Corrections can, and needs to, speak from its own standpoint and experience about which offenders it can handle most effectively, and how earlier steps in the criminal justice process affect corrections. It is time that corrections verbalized some of the knowledge it has accumulated about criminal offenders and their treatment, both before and after conviction. Corrections alone cannot solve the problems of crime and delinquency, but it can make a much more significant contribution than it does now.[1]

Few are satisfied with the existing correctional system. The reform movement is powerful, but its direction is uncertain. And the movement to reform the corrections system is coming from all areas: from the press, the public, the police, the courts, the legislatures, inmate populations, and from practicing corrections personnel. Pressure is being brought to bear from all of these quarters, and from others, and there is a sometimes violent clashing of views among members of the "old guard" and those who would make corrections more effective in reducing crime by making it more responsive to the massive changes taking place in society.

---

[1] Report of the National Advisory Commission for Criminal Justice Standards and Goals, presented to the Law Enforcement Assistance Administration, January 1973.

Conflict is a way of life, in the nation's corrections system. But then, change always brings conflict. The tight security and limited freedom of the institution seems, at first glance, diametrically opposed to such programs as work release, halfway houses, probation, and parole. But prisons have failed miserably in their efforts to rehabilitate those who have been confined, and the high percentage of repeat offenders—between 70 and 95 percent, depending on whose statistics are being used as a yardstick —offers dynamic proof that institutionalization has failed to help reduce crime in America. For this reason, community treatment programs have been stressed in the last decade. Community treatment has been heralded by some as the panacea for correctional ills, and condemned by others as a mollycoddling approach to attempting to rehabilitate hard-core offenders. Among corrections practitioners there is a great variance of opinion and strong disagreement on the values and dangers of community treatment programs. This conflict exists at all governmental and institutional levels, and throughout the criminal justice system.

Prison guards at one institution in New England recently went to court in an effort to seek removal of the state corrections commissioner, who was attempting to establish changes in his prisons—changes that the guards felt were dangerous. The guards lost their case, but the administrator was later dismissed by the governor, who felt that the commissioner would be unable to perform his duties effectively in the hostile environment created by a guards versus boss situation. In a Southern state, a corrections commissioner resigned as a result of clashes with the state departmental official who was his immediate supervisor. The corrections chief was recognized throughout the American Correctional Association as a reformer whose thoughtful approach to penology had scored impressive changes in the state and had attracted bright, young, progressive administrators with high academic qualifications to his staff. The state official with whom he clashed over prison policies was a political appointee whose personal view toward incarceration and offenders was stricter.

This conflict of opinion is by no means confined to administrators. It is very much in evidence in many institutions, often between correctional staff personnel and line officers, and sometimes between guards who work on the same shift. Confusion and resentment are the common results of this conflict. It extends into the cells where men already confused (and possibly hostile) often react violently to administrative indecision.

Norman A. Carlson, Director of the Federal Bureau of Prisons, said recently that "The deeper an offender becomes involved in correctional processes, and the longer he has to be locked up, however humanely, the greater the costs to society and the more difficult will be his successful reintegration into the community."[2] Carlson feels that the idea of diverting from prisons those people with medical and social problems—who basically hurt only themselves and not society—holds much promise. Many in the system agree with him that not all offenders need to be confined in institutions.

A number of promising alternatives to detention are available. At the pretrial stage, it has been demonstrated that the use of summons in lieu of arrest and release on personal recognizance can be used for many minor, nonviolent offenders. Following conviction, there are also a number of alternatives to be considered. Carlson believes that probation is far less costly than imprisonment and, for many offenders, is more effective.

The acceptance of alternatives to incarceration is beginning to take hold at local and state levels of government in most states. The fact is that incarceration has failed to rehabilitate many of those offenders who have experienced the frustrations of being imprisoned, with little or no educational or vocational training, and with almost no opportunities for earning money while serving time.

The House Select Committee on Crime concluded, as a result of a series of hearings held in 1973, that changes in our present correctional systems involve certain risks in the light of presently held security concepts.[3] Nevertheless, the Committee stated, the painful lessons of the recurrent waves of prison riots, epitomized by Attica, Raiford, and a multitude of other disturbances, is that the present correctional system has created and nurtures serious threats to security and public safety because of the frustration and desperation that drives men to rebellion. Only through a drastic restructuring can we hope to correct our correctional system, the Committee concluded.

[2] Norman Carlson, "Corrections—The Changing Challenge," *Justice Magazine*, February 1972.
[3] "Reform of Our Correctional Systems," a Report by the House Select Committee on Crime, June 26, 1973.

Figure 9-1. The House Select Committee on Crime has stated that the present correctional system has failed to rehabilitate many offenders because of the frustration and desperation of those incarcerated.

Community Treatment

The average daily population in the nation's correctional institutions is projected to reach 1.8 million persons in 1975. Ninety-eight percent of those offenders will inevitably return to the community to live and work. It is difficult—perhaps impossible—to prepare a person who has been confined in an institution, for months or years, for the transition from incarceration to freedom in the community. Distrust and fear of the ex-offender by the citizenry poses a dangerous threat to the offender who, in turn, often approaches his release with severe anxiety, and sometimes with a sense of helplessness.

The President's Crime Commission focused on one aspect of the problem when stating:

Institutions tend to isolate offenders from society both physically and psychologically, cutting them off from school, jobs, families, and other supportive influences and increasing the probability that the label of criminal will be indelibly impressed upon them. The goal of reintegration of the offender into the community is likely to be furthered much more readily by working with the offender in the community than by incarceration. . . . With two-thirds of the total corrections caseload under probation or parole supervision, the central question is no longer whether to handle offenders in the community but how to do so safely and successfully.[4]

Programs such as work release, educational release, and the halfway house are examples of more traditional community-based corrections programs. They are used for the prisoner in custody or under the jurisdiction of the institution. But the modern correctional trend, which takes a radically different approach, is to program the offender into community-based alternatives prior to institutionalization; that is, to use community facilities instead of jails, prisons, reformatories and training schools. There now exists a wide range of community treatment programs and facilities for instituting community treatment programs for adults and juveniles, male or female, felon or misdemeanant, probationer or parolee, and for others. These new treatment programs are not, however, widely accepted in all communities, and the American Bar Association, the American Correctional Association, and other similar groups have tackled these and other correctional problems with great fervor in the early 1970s in an effort to reform the nation's correctional systems. Community treatment is not being billed as the panacea for all of the nation's problems in rehabilitation of offenders, but it is being advocated more and more by knowledgeable correctional and legislative officials as a step away from the archaic into the progressive areas of humanitarian and efficient reform.

The underlying premise for this new direction in corrections, as stated in the Task Force Report on Corrections of the President's Crime Commission, is that crime and delinquency are symptoms of failure and disorganization of the community as well as of the offender.

In particular, these failures are seen as depriving offenders of contact with the institutions in society that are basically responsible for assuring the development of law-abiding conduct. The task of corrections therefore includes building or rebuilding solid ties between the

[4] The President's Commission, *Challenge of Crime in a Free Society* (Washington, D.C.: U.S. Govt. Printing Office, 1967).

offender and the community; integrating or reintegrating the offender into community life by restoring family ties; obtaining employment and education; and securing in a larger sense a place for the offender in the routine functioning of society. This requires not only efforts directed toward changing the individual offender—which has been almost the exclusive focus of rehabilitation—but also the mobilization and change of the community and its institutions, the Task Force stated.

It is clear that the correctional focus is shifting from nearly complete reliance on treating the offender in isolation from the community, toward efforts that seek to engage society and social institutions in the rehabilitation process. There are a number of indications that corrections has started to embrace new ideas and concepts about the role of society, its neighborhoods and communities, as a powerful force in rehabilitation.

Models

Institutional rehabilitation as a phase of corrections can be seen as a process of transition in which, theoretically, there are certain steps to be traversed. These steps might be reduced to:

1. Incarceration: Total confinement 24 hours a day in a custody/security institution.
2. Furlough/Release: Confinement in a security/custody institution with an opportunity for work or education release during part of the day and/or special furloughs into the community to prepare for return to normal life in the society.
3. Halfway House: Physical separation 24 hours a day in a group home setting in the community, from which the individual seeks work or actually works; a form of self-testing in a reality situation prior to release or parole.
4. Parole: Life in the community as a free person, 24 hours a day, with parole supervision.

Incarceration

Intrainstitutional efforts at rehabilitation, no matter how well planned, financed, or implemented, are nonetheless subject to serious inherent limitations. They simply cannot overcome the existence of a deep division between what is relevant within the institutional structure and what is relevant within the community. In large measure, this division has spurred the growing use of the methods of work and educational release and halfway houses, to name the most significant efforts. There is a broad spectrum of other related activities being added: prerelease, job or school release, staff-escorted trips into the community, and even (in a few states) unescorted leaves or furloughs. The institution, with its 24-hour confinement, is gradually being relied on less and less for rehabilitation. And efforts such as work or educational release and furlough/release are becoming more prominent in achieving the goals of offender rehabilitation.

The Task Force Report on Corrections, issued in October 1973 by the National Advisory Commission on Criminal Justice Standards and Goals, recommended that all local detention and correctional facilities, both pre- and postconviction, should be incorporated under state systems by 1982. States should also develop community-based resources and coordinate planning for community-based correctional services on a state and regional basis, the Commission said.

In stating that "the prison, the reformatory, and the jail have achieved only a shocking record of failure," the Commission recommended a ten-year moratorium on the construction of correctional institutions except when an "analysis of the total criminal justice and adult corrections systems produces a clear finding that no alternative is possible." Some members of the Task Force Report on Corrections clearly disagreed and, although a minority or opposition report was not prepared, these dissenting views were made known in a series of statements and comments following publication of the Task Force Report on Corrections.

In its comments on juvenile delinquency, the Task Force suggested a prohibition against detaining juveniles in jails, lockups, or other facilities used for housing adults. "Use of state institutions for juveniles and youths should be discouraged," the Task Force Report on Corrections recommended. It called for a focus on diversion of young offenders from the system where possible and, when not possible, an emphasis on community programs as opposed to incarceration.

Furlough Release
Unsupervised periods away from the correctional facility for family visits, jobs or job interviews, and testing, is what is meant by furlough/release.

Work release or educational release, in which the offender leaves the institution on a regular basis, can be technically considered as furloughs. Furloughs are not the special leaves that most institutions have been granting for family deaths or crises. The important distinction between furlough and other types of leave is that the prisoners are on their own when on furlough, instead of under guard, as is customary with special leave.

Although furlough programs vary from state to state, most states grant furloughs on the basis of individual need. Such needs arise for a wide variety of reasons: job interviews, crises in the home, prerelease planning, medical care, and even, very recently, for participation in community functions such as crime prevention programs.

The family visit furlough has been used frequently and routinely with juvenile delinquents and will continue to be used with this population; but the adult offender has only recently been accorded these privileges. The compelling reason for family visit furloughs, whether for juveniles or adults, is to keep family ties intact whenever possible.

About half the states have provisions for furlough. In many other states, authorities are planning to implement such programs or are seeking appropriate legislation. It is estimated that in the near future, almost 90 percent of the states will have furlough programs. The effect of furlough programs on recidivism (repeat offenses) is not known. There has not been sufficient study of the question; moreover, those few studies that have been made have generally failed to state explicitly the criteria of success or failure according to which furlough programs are judged. But enough information is available to conclude that the various programs have generally operated with minimal problems. If, as reported, furlough has strengthened family ties and has assisted in reintegrating offenders into the community, the potential of the furlough idea would be proved on this basis alone, and much argument could be made for expanding the programs.

There remain to be explored more fully a number of special programs that are related to the furlough idea. These include work release, halfway houses, and the unique conjugal visitation program. Applications and variations of these ideas can be seen today throughout the country.

Work Release. The work release concept represents a giant step away from the punitive institutional control system. Work release programs assist the individual to develop the motivational resources necessary to function adequately in the freedom of society. Both the institution and the prisoner must make basic changes in their outlook and operations for such programs to succeed. The individual who is given the opportunity to deal with the outside world must develop the necessary inner discipline; the institution must make certain concessions, permitting the "half-free" status and its wide testing of options and discretion. Institutions must provide separate housing for work release prisoners apart from the general inmate population to avoid the informal, but damaging, inmate social system. And institutions must refocus to give the individuals the opportunity to express and test their own preferences in terms of vocational and social behavior.

Work release began with Wisconsin's Huber Law in 1913, which remained the only statewide program for 44 years. The term "work release" means private employment of an offender outside the correctional institution: the offender returns to incarceration at the end of the day. Such programs are now largely the prerogatives of the county jails and are run by the sheriffs. From the 1950s to the present, work release programs have expanded swiftly, now encompassing over half the state systems, the Federal Bureau of Prisons, and the District of Columbia.

It should be noted that the work release concept has been opposed by many sheriffs. Their opposition stems from such concerns as limitation of staff and facilities, lack of control over selection of prisoners to be placed on work release, and related administrative difficulties. There are also practical problems resulting from the operation of work release programs: transportation problems, security problems (some prisoners walk away from their jobs), and problems of conduct (i.e., prisoners returning drunk). The special handling required and the security problems created do increase institutional costs. In fact, some or all of these problems, in some form and to some degree, may be seen in any such program. The press has reported crimes committed by individuals on work release. And such individuals have also been caught smuggling contraband (i.e., drugs) into the prison, or acting as a messenger service between non-release inmates and the outside.

However, these disadvantages must be weighed against the advantages for the individual, the institution, and the community when the program works properly. For example, the program is seen, at least theoretically, as enabling prisoners to support their families while in jail, and possibly saving the taxpayers not only the cost of their incarceration but also the cost of maintaining other persons on welfare. When prisoners are able to support themselves and their families by regular employment in the community, the jail experience need not be as demoralizing.

Jobs for work release are obtained in different ways. Some prisoners retain jobs held prior to incarceration. Others obtain jobs from sympathetic friends or employers. Still others find work on their own initiative or take jobs found for them by the institution's staff.

In 1973, the director of the South Carolina Department of Corrections, William D. Leeke, testified before the House Select Committee on Crime that work release programs in his state were resulting in a lower recidivism rate. He said that, "Since 1968, when we began a series of community-based, prerelease centers, less than 10 percent of the people who have successfully completed work release have returned (to the department) for parole violations or the commission of a new offense. Consequently, our work release program appears to be effective as a deterrent to crime."

Leeke stated that inmates at five community-based prerelease centers earn an average of $98.24 a week. For the period from January 1968 to November 1, 1971, total earnings of inmates were $2,210,913.18. The inmates paid taxes of $326,477.53, and paid (to the South Carolina Department of Corrections) $3.50 per day for room, board, and transportation for a total of $560,424.39. The inmates also contributed over $330,000 to their dependents.

Other states have reported similar successes with work release programs, notably Ohio and California.

Educational Release. A significant attempt is now being made to apply the basic concept of work release to special educational release, primarily for prisoners wishing to attend colleges, community colleges, or technical schools. Great impetus was given to the educational release idea by the Office of Economic Opportunity's (OEO) program. There has been a surprising increase in the use of educational release, and colleges have become responsive to prisoners' needs for education beyond the high school. Correctional institutions have responded enthusiastically to such programs, developing new liaisons with the educational community.

Penologist Daniel Glaser stated that his study of the relationship between education and recidivism rates of federal prisoners indicates that there is a limited crime reduction effect from education in prison.[5] Glaser's judgment was based on the fact that even inmates who are allowed to go to school make poor prospects for postrelease rehabilitation because they still cannot find adequate employment to support themselves and their families. In addition, the educational classes offered sometimes compete with vocational training programs that may be more useful to the inmate after he is released from prison. Glaser also found that inmates may take education courses in prison for the wrong reasons: something to do instead of spending idle time in a cell; or to impress the parole board. Finally, Glaser concluded that education may frustrate the inmate's vocational aspirations by promising something that is not fulfilled on the outside.

The House Select Committee on Crime, in studying educational programs in the corrections system, concluded that prison educational programs will not contribute to the reduction of the recidivism rate unless the entire prison system adopts a rehabilitative operating philosophy.

Both work and educational release take a giant stride in linking the offender and the community. They offer the bridge the offender needs between the highly structured institution and the comparative freedom of the community. As corrections personnel have begun to value this important transitional stage between incarceration and freedom, furlough and work release have come to be accepted as a part of corrections instead of a special program with only a tenuous organizational attachment.

The Halfway House

A more recent development is the halfway house. Many prison systems have used such devices as a prerelease center, in which men and women are prepared for release. These may be located away from the institution, but more often are part of the institutional complex. The prerelease center is a kind of decompression unit where the prisoner may make a gradual transition to the community. Its most sophisticated form is the halfway house, which has been referred to as the forerunner of parole.

Although a halfway house may be under the administration of the institution, unlike the prerelease center it is physically and geographically removed and is located in the community. It is usually a large, private

[5] Daniel Glaser, *The Effectiveness of Prison and Parole System* (Indianapolis: Bobbs-Merrill, 1969).

residence converted for use as a group home. Halfway houses may offer treatment begun in the institution. They provide a practical and realistic opportunity to test the ability to deal with he outside world in a socially acceptable manner. A well-located halfway house can make maximum use of local community resources, including educational, religious, vocational, recreational, and medical services.

Programs in the houses vary considerably; nevertheless, some features are common to most programs. Each inmate usually has "civilian" clothes and is given a key to his or her own room and to the house. This radical and seemingly paradoxical departure from life in prison has many implications, including among them the possibility of enhanced responsibility and improved self-image for the inmates. Employment assistance is a primary focus of the halfway house program, with both group and individual counseling also provided. Prisoners perform household tasks until they find steady work. When they have been working for some time, and have otherwise shown the degree of responsibility necessary for life in the free community, they may request to leave the house and begin living on their own. With the approval of the parole officer, the last step in the process of returning to society is completed.

The halfway house idea was pioneered by private organizations, mainly religious. Some of the first in the field were St. Leonard's in Chicago (Episcopal) and Dismas House in St. Louis (Catholic). The halfway house concept was given great impetus in the early 1960s by Attorney General Robert Kennedy when the Federal Bureau of Prisons in the Justice Department opened four experimental centers in Los Angeles, Chicago, New York City, and Detroit. The program produced some failures, but was generally successful. It proved beyond a doubt the economic wisdom of the halfway house. The federal experiment was copied widely throughout the country. Halfway houses are found today in most states. Although there are many private organizations still in the field, formal ties and relations with the corrections system are much stronger than in the past. Moreover, the halfway house is a part of the corrections system in virtually all progressive state systems.

An interesting innovation, termed the halfway-in house, has been used primarily for youths whose treatment needs do not require the harsher institutional regimen, those who can safely be allowed to remain in the community in a group home. As a form of recognition of the need to direct away from the institution all those who can possibly be without danger to self or the society, the halfway-in house is especially appropriate.

Whether considering the traditional halfway house or the halfway-in house, all admittances should be made on the basis of assessment of the individual. Offense alone is an inadequate criterion to use for admission, but unfortunately this is still relied on heavily. Candidates for admission should have the capacity for participation in group living and group counseling therapy. In the house, peer influence and understanding are vital. Often the house members develop a strong esprit de corps. For some it may be the only time in their lives they have done so. This base, in a group of friends who have similar problems, is an important aid in adjustment.

Halfway houses, like many programs in corrections, have not been thoroughly evaluated in terms of repeat crime. There is good reason to feel that a significant degree of success can be attributed to the halfway house influence. It certainly does not contribute to increased recidivism. This, coupled with the obvious economic savings, is a sufficient endorsement of the concept. Robert F. Kennedy was quoted as saying, "It is an investment that we can ill afford not to make."

The Conjugal Visit. A unique and unusual program somewhat related to community treatment programs is the conjugal visit. In the programs of furlough/work release and halfway houses, one vitally important motivation is to keep individual family ties intact. The recurring deterioration of a person's family ties over a period of years is familiar to all correctional workers. In spite of rather extensive efforts in the institution to prepare the offender for normal community participation, including the resumption of normal family ties and responsibilities, the steady erosion of family ties seems inevitable. Home furlough, judiciously used, may be a powerful way to reverse this trend—but it has not been generally available, whether because of existing laws or general social sanctions against it. A unique approach to this situation is the conjugal visit, in which wives (and family) come to the institution and, in a special setting, are able to carry on family relationships to a degree, including conjugal relationships.

The conjugal visit has become a topic of great interest, a signal example of humaneness in a punitive and harsh prison reality. The very nature of such a program is to fly in the face of established mores—the degree to which this is so may be simply seen by the fact that it is never

recommended or used for women prisoners. The concept of conjugal visits, limited though it may be, perhaps can provide some very real benefits. It can be viewed as a program that helps keep marriages intact and reduces prison problems related to sex. Most experts agree that problems relating to sex are among the prison administration's greatest.

Whether or not the conjugal visit is a rehabilitation tool is still quite unclear. Whether marriages tend to be held together or not by conjugal visits, or aggravated somewhat when unwanted births result, is a problem for not only the husband or wife but also for society. Conjugal visits are not generally favored by prison administrators in the United States, or for that matter in most nations. The criticisms of conjugal visits are many and well taken. Conjugal visits do not accommodate the homosexual, or the single person in whom sexual tensions are at least as great and disturbing. Conjugal visits are antithetical to prevailing mores and the necessarily strong emphasis on the physical side of sex is difficult to reconcile in terms of either humaneness in prison or rehabilitation with the emphasis on mental or spiritual renewal.

The conjugal visit is still in the discussion stage, and only one institution in this country provides for conjugal visits. Its experience neither militates against the conjugal visit nor makes a clear case for its applicability through the prison population. Nevertheless, for that one institution—the Mississippi State Prison at Parchman, the conjugal visit is likely to endure—and it will endure in a manner and style to which it has only recently aspired.

Conjugal visits at the Mississippi State Prison are decidedly different today than its once shabby approach to relations between man and wife, which bore a close resemblance to commercial sex. The conjugal visit, as practiced today, makes it a truly unique institution. Only Parchman, of the nearly 400 adult correctional institutions in the United States, provides for conjugal visits. The prison is unique also in its buildings and grounds. It is a plantation, and functions as such. There is little resemblance to the usual state prison buildings. It is a paradox in prison philosophy that a prison that provides for conjugal visits as the measure of its humaneness, at the same time practices the most dehumanizing of human relations, segregation by race.

Parchman has over 2000 inmates who live in camps, each a separate, self-contained little community, operated in large measure by inmates themselves. Maximum security inmates live in a different situation than others in the camps, and for them the conjugal visit is not allowed. For the other married prisoners each camp has a building in which each inmate can have privacy and intimacy with his wife necessary to a conjugal relationship. Visits are allowed periodically on Sundays, and five to ten inmates in each camp have use of the rooms in the "red house."

Today the conjugal visit is part of a larger family visitation plan that includes children as well as wives. It is the family visit that is emphasized, and the conjugal visit is seen as a logical part of these visits. Although the conjugal visit began as an informal, unofficial project, it has become a strong and desirable part of the program today. The small camp groups and the construction of truly private and appropriate quarters for the visits led to an increase in the use of this privilege by many of the married men.

The conjugal visit at Parchman is an integral part of its operation. It is considered an important element in keeping morale of inmates at a manageable level, and there has developed the feeling that the conjugal visit is a critically important facet of the program. This opinion is shared by inmates and staff alike. Whether or not it is a satisfactory program for other institutions to incorporate is not clear. Parchman is small, its camps are isolated, and its work programs are entirely outside work. All of this contributes to what appears to be a uniquely successful program in an unusual institution. Whether other prisons and penitentiaries can or should utilize the conjugal visit is a question that requires considerable further study.

The Community

Crime and its correction are a major concern of the American public. Both anger and fear are reflected in the populace—anger at the seeming inability of the system to deal effectively with crime and criminals, and fear of the encroachment of crime on all citizens. Nevertheless, a kind of ambivalence is prevalent among our citizens. We tend to glamorize certain misconduct, and many people, as a source of entertainment, will engage in all sorts of illegal behavior. The apathy of the public in recent years has been seen repeatedly in its failure to react suitably at the scene of a crime.

In a 1969 Lou Harris survey, done for the Commission on Correctional Manpower and Training, the following attitudes were conspicuous:

- The American public is aroused over the growing incidence of crime in this country.
- A general feeling prevails that our system of law enforcement does not really discourage people from committing crimes.
- Only half of the adult public (51 percent) believes that the nation's prison systems have done a good job in helping to deal with the problem of crime.
- Although 48 percent feel that rehabilitation is the major focus of prisons today, 72 percent feel that this should be the main emphasis.
- Similarly, 24 percent feel the main emphasis in prisons today is protection of society, but only 12 percent say protecting society is what the emphasis should be in the future.
- Only 7 percent feel that the main emphasis in prisons should be punishment.

- The public understands and supports rehabilitation as the primary goal for correctional agencies, yet only 5 percent feel that corrections has been "very successful" in rehabilitating criminals. However, 49 percent say "somewhat successful."
- One in five believes that "time in prison will often turn someone who is not really bad into a hardened criminal."

These points are more an indicator of the public's understanding of the problem than of its willingness to participate in doing those things necessary to reintegrate the offender into the community. Typical of the public's demeanor in this regard is the general verbal acceptance of community-based halfway houses. Yet invariably every effort to institute such a program in the community is met with active resistance. People simply do not want it in their neighborhood. In spite of this indictment of the community, there is evidence of real interest and concern, both in the community in general and in the private sector.

Two significant programs in which the lay community has been involved heavily, and with apparent good results, are the volunteer programs and programs for the indigenous paraprofessional (living in the corrections environment).

While the citizen volunteer should never be seen as a replacement for the professional, his role as a member of a team directed by the professional is extremely valuable. Aside from alleviating the professional's heavy caseload, the volunteer working in direct contact with the offender can provide services on a regular basis that would have been impossible for the professional to provide. The volunteers or their friends are likely to assist in the entry into jobs, schooling, recreation, and other activities, which could otherwise be blocked by persons not in sympathy with the plight of the offender. Aside from the direct services volunteers provided, they are opinion makers in the community and can influence more favorable attitudes toward the offender and the corrections system.

Volunteers generally are members of middle-class families of above-average income. They have education above that of the average citizen and are frequently professionals in the fields of teaching, medicine, and the law. Unlike correctional professionals generally, nearly 50 percent of volunteers are women.

Volunteers whose social and economic backgrounds are similar to the offenders frequently can help the individual offender more because of their better understanding of the problems and pressures. Often the life-styles of offenders run strongly counter to those of the middle-class person. As a result a social distance is maintained between the offender and the middle-class volunteer or professional. This social distance can be reduced dramatically by the indigenous paraprofessional, who can play a very effective role.

Use of indigenous paraprofessionals has gained in popularity, and its logical extension has been the use of the ex-offender in corrections. This use of the ex-offender has not achieved a marked degree of popularity, but its significance has caused a number of departments to develop programs using indigenous ex-offenders as paraprofessionals in corrections. The use of nonprofessional volunteers and paraprofessionals has confirmed operational feasibility and there is mounting evidence that an effective and productive service can be provided.

The Private Sector

Recent developments have focused on ways in which private industry can collaborate more effectively to cope with urgent correctional problems. The mounting interest in solving the problems of crime has thrust the public and the private sectors together into a new and growing national sense of social responsibility.

In the past the private and governmental sectors were seen as distinctly separate entities, but in the climate of the country today, it is often difficult to see where government leaves off and private industry begins in any endeavor. Sometimes it is more efficient and profitable for one or the other of the sectors to perform certain functions and to provide certain services. At other times, it seems more desirable that collaborative relationships be formed in order to solve particular pressing problems together.

For corrections, this trend means that the range of its sources of assistance has greatly increased. While few correctional agencies have as yet availed themselves of private industry's ample resources, the potential range of assistance to corrections is clear. Some evidence of industry's involvement is seen in JOBS, the large-scale, public-private, cooperatively sponsored program of the National Alliance of Businessmen, whose objective is to bring 500,000 of the nation's hard-core unemployed into meaningful occupations. The so-called hard-core unemployed are often clients of corrections or, if not, they are likely to be so if work opportunities are not made available.

In addition to such efforts, many firms today are capable of providing services to corrections if the field can find sufficient funds to purchase them. Areas in which private industry can become regularly and effectively involved include vocational training and work-experience programs, basic education, research and development, and ongoing staff development.

The U.S. Chamber of Commerce and its affiliates, with a membership of 5 million, has identified crime and its correction as a major problem of such significance that it warrants special treatment. It has convened national panels on the subject and has developed, published, and distributed two extremely popular publications, *Deskbook on Organized Crime* and *Marshalling Citizen Power Against Crime*. These efforts and others point to the Chamber's involvement as a potent force in endorsing community corrections concepts and in making employment available to the rehabilitated ex-offender and selected parolees and probationers.

The community must involve itself in corrections, or corrections will fail. Leadership is developing, and the move toward implementation of community-based corrections is on.

Parole

Estimates indicate that 60 percent of all adult felons are released on parole prior to the expiration of their sentence. Like probation, parole has proven to be successful as an alternative to imprisonment, especially in relieving the chronic overcrowding in the nation's prisons. Unfortunately, parole services suffer from extremely large caseloads for parole officers, poor pay, and undertraining of personnel. As a result of the lack of quantity and quality of supervision, too many parolees get in trouble while on parole, causing a recidivism rate that, with proper supervision, could be much lower.

In its 1973 report on "The Reform of Our Correctional Systems," the House Select Committee on Crime said that the supervisory problem is not the only problem with our parole system:

> *The lack of uniformity in the decision-making process and the lack of*
> *expertise of board members draw resentment from inmates and*
> *criticism from experts. The parole board hearing ideally should be*

based on the inmate's prior history, progress in the institution, readiness for release, need for supervision and assistance in the community, and attitude and general conduct during the hearing before board members. However, by and large, the hearing is often a retrial of the inmate's crime, and the inmate is not given the opportunity to properly present his case. Also there are frequently no definite standards by which a parole board makes a decision to grant or deny parole, and often no explanation is given for denial of parole. In some jurisdictions the inmate does not even have the right to be present during the hearing.

Another problem with the parole system, the Crime Committee reported, is that associated with parole revocation in some jurisdictions. Until the recent Supreme Court case of *Morrissey* v. *Brewer*, a parolee could be returned to prison without a hearing for minor rule infractions during his parole. The parolee ordinarily does not have the "right" to an attorney either at the parole revocation hearing or at the initial hearing to determine whether or not the inmate is to be given parole. An inmate on parole in New York, for example, may be returned to prison for such infractions as being seen with another ex-inmate having a drink in a bar or for living with a woman to whom he is not married.

The result of these overly strict and self-defeating conditions of parole is that a large percentage of parolees are returned to prison, adding to the overcrowded conditions that already burden the corrections system. Proper supervision of parolees and less restrictive conditions of parole would go far in implementing the greater use of parole as a viable alternative to incarceration.

Summary

Plans to help start pretrial diversion programs in 10 to 15 major United States cities were announced in Washington, D.C. during the summer of 1973 by the American Bar Association's Commission on Correctional Facilities and Services. Commission Chairman Richard J. Hughes reported receipt of a manpower grant from the U.S. Department of Labor to fund the pretrial diversion effort, to be cosponsored by the National District Attorneys Association.

These and other humane, innovative programs are being instituted for and in many of the nation's correctional systems, and supported by such groups as the American Bar Association, the American Correctional

Figure 9-3. One innovative rehabilitation program is an inmate council meeting in a South Carolina prison.

Association, the National Council on Crime and Delinquency, and the U.S. Chamber of Commerce.

The failure of prisons to rehabilitate offenders is well known. One of the major reasons for that failure, according to the Task Force Report on Corrections, National Advisory Commission on Criminal Justice Standards and Goals, is that "the offender has had too little contact with the positive forces in the nation: good schools, gainful employment, adequate housing, and rewarding leisure time activities." In affirming the position that the failure of major institutions to reduce crime is "incontestable," the Task Force Report on Corrections said that the "mystery is that they have not contributed even more to increasing crime."

Writing in the foreword of the American Bar Association's 1972 "Compendium of Model Correctional Legislation and Standards," Chief Justice Warren E. Burger states: "When society confines its offenders, it has disabled them in large part from acting to change themselves. At that point, society takes on an obligation to help the offender to help himself to begin again." And that is what corrections is all about—or should be.

Student Checklist

1. Are you able to contrast the differing philosophical bases of each of the correctional subsystems?
2. Can you write a short essay on the concept of community treatment?
3. Can you list the steps involved in institutional rehabilitation?
4. Do you know how to define the term furlough/release?
5. Can you compare the work release and the educational release programs?
6. Can you list the features that are common to halfway house programs?
7. What is the concept of conjugal visitation?
8. Are you able to identify the two significant programs in which lay members of the community have become involved?
9. Can you describe the ways that private industry can collaborate with governmental correctional agencies?

Topics for Discussion

1. Discuss the concept of conjugal visitation.
2. Discuss the conflict between security and rehabilitation in correctional institutions.
3. Discuss the advantages of community treatment.
4. Discuss the trend of lay member involvement in corrections.

ANNOTATED BIBLIOGRAPHY

Empey, LaMar T. *Alternatives to Incarceration*, U.S. Department of Health, Education, and Welfare Social and Rehabilitation Services, Office of Juvenile Delinquent and Youth Development. A basic statement of the diversion approach to delinquency in which a "diversion position" is stated followed by specific materials as it relates to pretrial, posttrial, and postincarceration diversion. Valuable for a solid grounding in this important approach to offender treatment.

Johnson, Elmer Hubert. *Crime, Corrections, and Society*. Homewood, Ill.: The Dorsey Press, 1964. A well-conceived and thoroughly presented basic text depicting corrections and correctional thought. Readable and detailed with studied approach to practice and procedures.

President's Commission on Law Enforcement and Administration of Justice, *Task Force Report: Corrections*, Washington, D.C.: U.S. Govt. Printing Office, 1967. A comprehensive and penetrating view of correctional operations in this country. Assertions and recommendations regarding corrections in the United States based on data from nationwide surveys and 25 action research studies.

Periodicals

National Council on Crime and Delinquency, *Crime and Delinquency*, 44 East 23rd Street, N.Y., N.Y. A professional forum for the expression and discussion of all competent points of view in the field of crime and delinquency. It is presented five times a year and its contributors and contributions explore every phase of the justice system's operations and philosophy.

Probation Division of the Administrative Office of the U.S. Courts, *Federal Probation*, Supreme Court Building, Washington, D.C. A primary journal in the field that is published four times a year and contains articles of current interest by and for those actively engaged in the field. In recent years it has provided some of the best thought on work release, furlough, halfway houses, and related subjects. It is a periodical that is basic reading for all who seek to keep up with the field.

Part Three

The Processes of Justice

The study of this chapter will enable you to:

1. Identify the multiplicity of roles that the prosecutor performs.
2. List the four charging options available to the prosecutor.
3. Identify the four basic situations confronting a prosecutor in the charging decision that will usually result in a decision not to charge, not to charge fully, or not to continue criminal proceedings.
4. Identify the factors that a prosecutor considers when charging a juvenile.
5. List the seven types of cases that a prosecutor will normally handle by selecting a no-charge alternative.
6. Compare the screening criteria of the American Bar Association and the National Advisory Commission.
7. Differentiate between plea bargaining and a tacit bargain.
8. Identify the formal means of holding a prosecutor accountable.

10
Prosecution

The prosecutorial process, as opposed to what might be called the trial process, occurs after the commission of a crime but before trial. It involves prosecutorial decisions on whether to charge, what to charge, whether to allow a noncriminal disposition of the case as an alternative to charging, and whether to grant charge-reduction or sentence-recommendation concessions in return for an agreement by the offender to plead guilty. The power to prosecute, with control over the two major elements of the prosecutorial process—charging and nontrial adjudication, is the power to subject an individual to the risks of a criminal prosecution, including potential loss of liberty or attachment of other undesirable sanctions, and to the personal costs of being subjected to the criminal process, such as adverse publicity, economic hardship, inconvenience, and the stigma of guilt that often attaches regardless of the outcome of the case.

The prosecutorial process is largely veiled, conducted often without the knowledge or scrutiny of the public or even other agents of the criminal justice system. The prosecutor has the virtually unfettered discretion to dispose of a case as he deems appropriate. The traditionally uncontrolled, discretionary nature of the prosecutorial process was aptly described by K. C. Davis:

> . . . The reality is that nearly all his [city or county prosecutor] decisions to prosecute or not to prosecute, nearly all of the influences brought to bear upon such decisions, and nearly all his reasons for decisions are carefully kept secret, so that review by the electorate is nonexistent except for the occasional case that happens to be publi-

cized. The plain fact is that more than nine-tenths of local prosecutors' decisions are supervised or reviewed by no one.[1]

Roles of the Prosecutor

The prosecutor performs a multiplicity of roles in this stage of the criminal process, all involving considerable discretion: he acts as a legislator, a system manager, a judge, a presentence or probation officer, an advocate for the defendant, and a major enforcer of the criminal law. As a legislator, he selects charges and grants plea-bargaining concessions to reflect what he thinks the law should be or how it should be applied in individual cases. Offenses with overly severe penalties or other undesirable effects are often charged or reduced to improve or avoid these consequences. As a systems manager, the prosecutor functions as an administrative official to ensure that the criminal justice system operates as efficiently as possible. Support and encouragement of the plea-bargaining process or a program for diverting offenders from the criminal process often reflect an interest on the part of the prosecutor to ensure that limited available prosecutorial and court resources are not overloaded or misdirected, but allocated to serve best the objectives of the system.

The prosecutor, in his role as judge, participates in a process by which the great predominance of convictions are obtained, not as a result of a trial before a judge or jury, but as a result of pleas of guilty. The plea-bargaining system is essentially a nontrial procedure. The prosecutor acts in a judicial role when he selects a charge, or agrees to make charging concessions or sentencing recommendations in consideration for a guilty plea, in order to control the sentencing discretion of the judge.

The prosecutor, when he decides to divert a convictable offender from the system or recommend a sentence to the court, must perform the background information-gathering and assessment functions usually performed by a presentence investigator in a probation department. Appropriate disposition of offenders without trial is dependent on accurate, complete information about the offender and the correctional or rehabilitation programs available.

[1] Kenneth C. Davis, *Discretionary Justice* (Baton Rouge: Louisiana State Press, 1969), pp. 207-208.

As an administrator of justice, the prosecutor has a duty to protect the interests of the offender, to see that the offender is afforded all procedural safeguards, and to ensure that the disposition selected promotes not only the interests of society, but the individual needs of the offender. The prosecutor traditionally serves as a major law enforcement official in his community. His charging decisions and policies have both a direct and indirect influence on enforcement agency practices. The major enforcement responsibility of the prosecutor is, of course, the duty to prosecute violators of the criminal laws.

All these functions require the day-to-day, largely discretionary, decisions of a prosecutor and his staff. The criminal process is not, and was never intended to be, applied to all law violators. For, as Judge Breitel noted:

> If every policeman, every prosecutor, every court, and every post-sentence agency performed his or its responsibility in strict accordance with rules of law, precisely and narrowly laid down, the criminal law would be ordered but intolerable. . . .[2]

The prosecutorial process, with the prosecutor at its center performing a variety of functions and roles normally associated with other decision makers in the system, operates much as a microcosm of the criminal justice system itself. These activities act as the bridge between the enforcement and judicial processes and provide the real focal point of the system.

Charging Authority and Options

The charging decision has been called the heart of the prosecution function. It involves the prosecutorial determination whether and to what extent the criminal process will be applied to a suspected law violator. A decision to commence prosecution is accomplished by the issuance and filing of complaints either to serve as a basis for an arrest warrant or summons, or as the charging document after arrest.

The charging decision historically has been considered a discretionary power of the prosecutor, subject to minimal constitutional or

[2] Charles D. Breitel, "Controls in Criminal Law Enforcement," *The University of Chicago Law Review, 27,* p. 427.

statutory restrictions and controlled by a few ineffectual and seldom-used control measures. Because of the low visibility of the charge decision and the opportunity for arbitrary action or inaction, there has been wide-spread condemnation of the charging system in existence in most jurisdictions:

> Viewed in broad perspective, the American legal system seems to be shot through with many excessive and uncontrolled discretionary powers but the one that stands out above all others is the power to prosecute or not to prosecute. The affirmative power to prosecute is enormous, but the negative power to withhold prosecution may be even greater, because it is less protected against abuse.[3]

Prosecutors do not prosecute all cases of criminal conduct brought to their attention by private citizens, police officers, or other investigative officials. Although the mandate of the prosecutor is full enforcement and prosecution of the laws, it has always been understood that prosecution is not a ministerial, hard-and-fast function; discretion must be exercised to conserve the limited resources of the criminal justice system, temper unreasonably punitive laws, and ensure that justice is provided in all cases.

Available to the prosecutor are a number of charging options:

1. No charge.
2. Alternatives to charging.
3. Less than full charging.
4. Full charging.

The considerations involved in rendering an appropriate charging decision have been well documented in an analysis of the charging process in the United States.[4]

There are four basic situations confronting a prosecutor in the charging decision, which will usually result in a decision not to charge, not to charge fully, or not to continue criminal proceedings:

1. Doubt exists as to the suspect's guilt.
2. No doubt exists as to the suspect's guilt, but the law precludes admission of evidence of guilt.
3. No doubt as to the suspect's guilt, but the judge or jury probably will not convict.
4. No doubt as to the suspect's guilt or the ability to secure a conviction, but prosecution is not considered in the community's interest.

---

[3] Davis, *Discretionary Justice*, p. 188.
[4] Frank W. Miller, *Prosecution*, (Boston: Little, Brown, 1969).

The first task the prosecutor must face when reviewing a request for initiation of criminal process is to determine if sufficient probability of guilt is present and, if there is, whether there is sufficient probability of conviction (that is, will a judge or jury confirm the prosecutor's estimation of guilt). If there is doubt that the suspect committed the act in question, no charge usually should be made. However, when there is no dispute as to the commission of a certain act by the suspect, the prosecutor must decide the legal consequences of that act—did the actions constitute a crime? Cases of borderline criminality, as in certain kinds of fraud and nonviolent property crime cases, are common. The reviewing prosecutor must insure that the weight and probative value of the evidence is sufficient to convince a trier of fact (the judge or jury). In cases of circumstantial evidence and witnesses of doubtful credibility, the prosecutor will be inclined not to prosecute if the probability of conviction is not high.

In many situations confronting the prosecutor, the evidence is convincing as to a suspect's guilt, but the law precludes its consideration. The exclusionary rules of evidence restrict the admission of certain relevant, trustworthy evidence of high probative value. When only hearsay evidence is available to support proof of an essential element of the crime, when there is no independent proof of a crime other than uncorroborated confession or admission, or when crucial evidence consists of illegally seized items, the prosecutor may not proceed until additional evidence is discovered.

The prosecutor's knowledge that the judge or jury will not convict despite sufficient evidence of guilt, in order to avoid the consequences of a harsh law, permits him to conserve resources by not charging.

The determination that, although an offender is convictable for a particular crime, it is in the best interest of the community not to charge fully, not to charge at all, or to terminate criminal proceedings represents the area of greatest discretionary latitude for the prosecutor. Charging decisions based on this general rationale are supported by a number of specific policy considerations for exercising prosecutorial restraint.

The prosecutor may be confronted with the unavailability or uncooperative attitude of an indispensable party: the victim of the criminal act, a key witness, or the defendant himself. The desire of the victim for the prosecutor not to charge or to discontinue prosecution, even though the victim's consent is not required, is a compelling influence, particularly if the probability of securing a conviction is diminished. In the case of physical assaults between members of certain cultural subgroups and intrafamilial fights, the victim does not always assist voluntarily in the prosecution of the offender. The prosecutor will often accede to the wishes of the reluctant victim and decline prosecution.

In the case of the "guilty victim," an individual who was the victim of a crime while himself engaging in illegal or undesirable behavior (for example, a visiting businessman is bilked by a prostitute), the prosecutor may not charge because of the difficulty in obtaining a conviction and his personal perception that prosecution in this class of cases is not desirable.

Prosecution is infrequent in cases of statutory rape. The charging decision is affected by the attitude and insistence of the victim and her parents. Negative considerations, such as the unpopularity of such laws, the harm a conviction for a sex offense would do to the offender, the willingness of the couple to marry, and the effect of prior promiscuous behavior by the female in lessening the chances for conviction, usually induce a no-charge decision.

The attitude and availability of an indispensable witness, such as an eyewitness to the criminal act, will affect the charging decision or continuation of prosecution. The availability of the defendant himself is an obvious factor in charging; if the defendant is deceased, in jail, being tried elsewhere on more serious charges, cannot be found, or cannot be extradited, then termination of criminal proceedings or no charging is likely.

The prosecutor may assess the cost to the system in pressing charges and find that the cost in economic terms or loss of public support outweigh the value of prosecution. In some extradition cases the costs of returning an offender from another jurisdiction for prosecution are prohibitive in terms of limited financial and manpower resources available. This cost must be balanced against the desirability of prosecuting the particular offender, especially in cases involving serious offenses. Extradition is seldom sought for misdemeanants.

Public opinion does have an impact on enforcement and prosecution practices. Prosecutors may not charge if the statute violated is extremely unpopular, if the offender is a person of standing in the community, and if prosecution would reflect adversely on the prosecutor or other criminal justice agency. Prosecutors are responsive to their constituencies; public approval and respect is desired.

In situations where the results of prosecution will cause undue harm to the offender in relation to the social benefit to be gained, in light of the particular criminal conduct involved or the socioeconomic status of the violator, there is often no charge filed. Second and subsequent prosecutions for offenses known to the prosecutor prior to the first prosecution are usually foregone after the initial case is concluded. An unfavorable disposition of the first prosecution may result in successive prosecutions if the prosecutor is particularly displeased with the disposition of the first case. Prosecution for minor offenses, such as a traffic violation or public intoxication, may not be initiated because of the relatively minor nature of the violations, the time and expense of prosecution, and possible harm to the offender's reputation in the community.

The prosecutor does not always charge all offenses or even the most serious offenses supported by the facts, in order to reduce or avoid harm to the offender. A major reason for this practice is the desire to spare the offender an unnecessarily harsh punishment or collateral harm. Such charging leniency occurs in instances of relatively minor offenses, such as underage drinking or attendance at a social club's annual stag show—the first offense perhaps involving youthful offenders without prior criminal records, and the second offense perhaps committed by respectable members of the community.

The stigma that attaches to a conviction for a sex offense is often a consideration for prosecution on less serious charges or charges with less offensive connotations. The decision may also reflect the intent of the prosecutor to limit the judge's sentencing discretion if the possible punishment for the sex offense is considered too severe.

The prosecutor, either in his charging policy or as a result of plea discussions, attempts to provide some flexibility in traditionally restrictive sentencing structures in most states. By utilizing the charge selected, the prosecutor can effectively establish the limits of the judge's sentencing authority. A particularly harsh statutory mandatory minimum sentence can be avoided by reduction of the potential charge to a lesser charge. The minimum required sentence for a violation—such as sale of narcotics—may be considered prohibitive for certain first-time offenders, resulting in the selection of a charge with less severe sentencing possibilities, such as possession of narcotics. This practice of undercharging to maximize sentencing discretion or avoid unduly severe sanctions is also employed to increase the probability of probation and increase the probability of a more lenient sentence generally. A common method for attaining these objectives is the selection of a misdemeanor charge instead of a felony with its usually harsher consequences.

The decision not to charge is reached in some circumstances when the offender can be incarcerated by methods other than the criminal process. If the offender will be confined regardless of the outcome of the prosecution of the case and for an acceptable length of time, the prosecutor is encouraged to use those methods for incarceration that allow him to commit the least resources for accomplishment and that best provide for the personal needs of the offender. Four situations in which alternative procedures may provide adequate incarceration potential are: (1) civil commitment of insane offenders; (2) civil or criminal commitment of sexual psychopaths; (3) revocation of probation or parole when the offense constitutes a violation of the conditional release; and (4) release of the offender to another jurisdiction for criminal prosecution or revocation of probation or parole.

There are additional formal alternatives to prosecution that the prosecutor has available to avoid the imposition of undue harm to an offender and yet retain the offender within the criminal justice system. In the case of juvenile offenders, the prosecutor may have a choice of allowing the offender to enter the juvenile justice process or attempting to divert him into the criminal justice system and treating him as an adult. The prosecutor must weigh a range of considerations: (1) the seriousness of the offense; (2) the desirability of avoiding a criminal record; (3) the rehabilitation potential for the youth in both systems; and (4) the location of the authority for initiating the appropriate disposition, that is, commitment for treatment.

No-Charge Alternatives

No-charge decisions are occasionally made when there are civil remedies that are considered more effective than invocation of the criminal process. The prosecutor in many states is empowered to initiate civil proceedings to control vice. This civil authority may include provisions for abatement of nuisances, such as brothels and gaming houses. The "padlock laws" permit the closing of premises used for proscribed vice activities. Confiscation of a motor vehicle used for illegal operations dealing with gambling, liquor, prostitution, or narcotics is another civil sanction provided by state statute, which may be invoked in addition to charging or as an alternative to charging. Revocation of liquor licenses of certain offenders is another common alternative to criminal prosecution for frequent liquor-law violators.

Offenders willing to assist in the achievement of other enforcement objectives by acting as informants customarily receive charging concessions, including immunity from arrest, for their cooperation. The assistance required may be regularly providing information on criminal activity; engaging in police-supervised purchases of contraband such as narcotics from other persons; and acting as a witness against other offenders, often codefendants with the informant in a criminal case.

In many cases, selection of no-charge alternatives to prosecution cases serves more satisfactorily to attain the objectives of the criminal justice system and relieve the demand on system resources and time. Informal administrative procedures for diverting offenders from the criminal process are used by prosecutors in such cases as: (1) nonsupport, (2) disorderly conduct, (3) family and neighborhood assaults, (4) the exhibition of obscene materials, (5) minor juvenile offenses, (6) statutory rape, and (7) minor property offenses. In the first five cases the noncriminal dispositions are designed to prevent recurrence of the offense, with the threat of prosecution for future offenses the inducement for compliance. In the last two instances, informal resolution is sought through conciliatory measures—such as marriage or restitution—designed to satisfy all parties.

Full Charging

Full charging is the practice of charging the most serious and the greatest number of charges for which the evidence suggests a reasonable probability of conviction. This "on-the-nose" charging may simply reflect the preliminary assessment of the case by the prosecutor with or without any real interest in ultimately securing conviction for the full charges. Full charging, when engaged in as a regular practice by a prosecutor, often reflects his fair assessment that full enforcement of the law and prosecution for all supportable charges should be pursued. Frequently, however, full charging is not the common practice of the prosecutor. Prosecutors have been faulted for overcharging and for arbitrary full charging.

Prosecutors engaging in the practice of overcharging initiate a greater number of charges than they intend to prosecute to judgment (horizontal overcharging), or a charge more serious than that for which conviction is expected (vertical overcharging). Prosecutors defend this practice as simply fulfilling their professional duty to charge the greatest number and most severe offenses warranted by the evidence. Overcharging provides greater assurance that the offender will be convicted of some charge. In some jurisdictions, overcharging results because the prosecutor must make the charging decision at an early stage of the proceedings when he does not have the full information necessary for the precise charge for which he will seek conviction. Elsewhere, the control of the initial charging decision by the police instead of the prosecutor results in overcharging. In too many cases, the actual purpose of excessive charging is to provide the prosecutor with leverage in the plea-negotiation process to induce the defendant to plead guilty to a smaller number of offenses or a less serious offense.

Occasionally prosecutors will deviate from a policy of charging for a lesser offense and opt for full enforcement in charging. When pressure from the news media and the public is exerted for charging with a more serious or a greater number of offenses than is the normal practice of the prosecutor, it is often expedient to adjust charge decisions to the public demand, even though the sentences imposed ultimately do not differ significantly than those imposed under normal charging practices.

Charging to the full extent may, in fact, provide a social service for the offender or the victim. The classic illustration of this situation is the acquiescence of the prosecutor to the request of homeless public inebriates to be incarcerated during cold-weather months for their own protection. A full-charging decision is rendered when the prosecutor desires to rid the community of particular offenders. If the offense is especially odious, full charging is likely. If the offender is a frequent nuisance or scofflaw in the community, a professional petty thief or vice offender with a past criminal record, or a higher-up in an organized crime enterprise, prosecutors are inclined to consider full charging despite a customary practice of less-than-full charging or not charging for the particular behavior involved.

The practices of prosecutors are now being influenced by the recommendations and standards endorsed by a number of eminent national organizations and commissions attempting to improve the American criminal justice system. That these bodies do not always concur as to the appropriate justification for exercising prosecutorial discretion is a manifestation of the controversy that surrounds the activities comprising the prosecutorial process.

Charging Standards

The American Bar Association's recommended standards for performance of the prosecution function provide guidelines for the fair and uniform use of the prosecutor's broad discretion in making the charging decision. It is considered unprofessional conduct for a prosecutor to institute criminal charges when he knows they are not supported by probable cause. However, he is not required to press all charges that the evidence might support; even when evidence may exist to support a conviction, he may, with good cause consistent with the public interest, decline to prosecute. Among the appropriate factors suggested for consideration in exercising discretion in the charging decision are:

- The prosecutor's reasonable doubt that the accused is in fact guilty.
- The extent of harm caused by the offense.
- The disproportion of the authorized punishment in relation to the particular offense or the offender.
- Possible improper motives of a complainant.
- Reluctance of the victim to testify.
- Cooperation of the accused in the apprehension or conviction of others.
- Availability and likelihood of prosecution by another jurisdiction.

The ABA standards urge prosecution in cases involving serious threats to the community, even though juries in the community tend to acquit for the criminal violation in question. All prosecutors are admonished not to bring or seek a greater number or more severe charges than can reasonably be supported by evidence at trial.

In supporting these guidelines for exercising prosecutorial charging discretion, the commentator for the American Bar Association standards notes:

> *Differences in the circumstances under which the crime took place, the motives or pressures activating the offender, mitigating factors of the*

*situation or the offender's age, prior record, general background, his
role in the offense, and a host of other particular factors require that the
prosecutor view the whole range of possible charges as a set of tools
from which he must carefully select the proper instrument to bring
charges warranted by the evidence. In exercising discretion in this way,
the prosecutor is not neglecting his public duty or discriminating among
offenders. The public interest is best served and even-handed justice
best dispensed, not by a mechanical application of the "letter of the
law," but by a flexible and individualized application of its norms
through the exercise of the trained discretion of the prosecutor as an
administrator of justice.*[5]

The American Bar Association standards also suggest that the
prosecutor explore the availability of noncriminal disposition when making the charging decision. Formal and informal programs of rehabilitation should be identified. The offenses of many first-time offenders may
warrant consideration for noncriminal disposition or diversion from the
criminal justice system.

The National Advisory Commission on Criminal Justice Standards
and Goals has endorsed the practice of prosecutorial screening, the discretionary decision to stop, prior to trial or plea, all formal proceedings
against a person subject to the criminal process; and diversion, the halting or suspending of formal criminal proceedings before conviction on
the condition or assumption that the individual will do something in
return. The Commission considers screening to be appropriate only when
neither diversion or conviction is desirable, or when there is insufficient
evidence to support a conviction; however, the deterrent value of conviction should be considered as well as the probability of conviction.
Screening because of insufficient resources to prosecute all violations
should be eliminated.

Criteria for screening individuals out of the criminal justice system
or deciding not to charge are presented by the Commission; many are
in contrast with the American Bar Association charging criteria. Subjects
should be screened out of the system if they are unconvictable, that is,
there is no reasonable likelihood that the evidence admissible against
them would be sufficient to obtain a conviction and sustain it on appeal.

---

[5] American Bar Association Project on Standards for Criminal Justice, *Standards
Relating to the Prosecution Function and the Defense Function*, Approved Draft,
1971, New York: Institute of Judicial Administration, 1968, p. 94.

Individuals who are considered convictable may not be charged if the benefits to be derived from prosecution or noncriminal diversion are outweighed by the social costs associated with those actions. The important factors to be considered in the screening decision are:

- Any doubt as to the accused's guilt.
- The impact of further proceedings on the accused and those close to him, especially the likelihood and seriousness of financial hardship or family life disruption.
- The value of further proceedings in preventing future offenses by other persons.
- The value of further proceedings in preventing future offenses by the offender.
- The value of further proceedings in fostering the community's sense of security and confidence in the criminal justice system.
- The direct cost of prosecution, in terms of prosecutorial time, court time, and similar factors.
- Any improper motives of the complainant.
- Prolonged nonenforcement of the statute on which the charge is based.
- The likelihood of prosecution and conviction of the offender by another jurisdiction.
- Any assistance rendered by the accused, including aid in the apprehension or conviction of other offenders.
- Socially beneficial activity engaged in by the accused that might be encouraged in others by not prosecuting the offender.

Diversion, which the Commission viewed as a legitimate and appropriate activity of the criminal justice system, allows the prosecutor to adjust for overcriminalization, is more economical than formal processing through the system, increases the available resources for appropriate disposition of the offender, and permits more effective utilization of those limited resources. Diversion of offenders into noncriminal programs before formal trial or conviction is considered appropriate if there is a substantial likelihood that conviction could be obtained and that the benefits to society from channeling an offender into an available noncriminal diversion program would outweigh any harm or cost to society by the decision not to prosecute.

Among the factors considered relevant to a favorable decision for noncriminal diversion are:

- The relative youth of the offender.
- The willingness of the victim not to have the offender prosecuted.
- Any likelihood that the offender suffers from a mental illness or

psychological abnormality that was related to his crime and for which treatment is available.
- Any likelihood that the crime was significantly related to any other condition or situation, such as unemployment or family problems, that would be subject to change by participation in a diversion program.

On the other hand, factors considered as unfavorable by the Commission for an affirmative diversion decision are:
- Any history of the use of physical violence toward others.
- Involvement with syndicated crime.
- A history of antisocial conduct indicating that such conduct has become an ingrained part of the offender's life-style and would be particularly resistant to change.
- Any special need to pursue criminal prosecution as a means of discouraging others from committing similar offenses.

In making this decision the prosecutor should consider whether the extent of the offender's having been processed in the criminal justice system has sufficient deterrent value to warrant consideration for diversion.

The Commission identified two common prerequisites for diversion: (1) criminal prosecution is undesirable because of the possibility of undue harm to the offender or his underlying problem, because prosecution is probably inffective in preventing future offenses, or because the needs of the victim are not met by prosecution of the offender; and (2) the appropriate assistance, such as treatment, counseling, or mediation procedures, are available. Diversion is an appropriate alternative to criminal prosecution only if the programs do not unjustifiably impair the deterrent impact of criminal punishment; the offenders are carefully selected to ensure that diversion provides protection against future commission of crimes by the offender; and offenders who are not convictable are not forced to participate in diversion programs under the threat of formal prosecution. Situations in which noncriminal diversion might be employed are public intoxication, assaults involving husband and wife, mentally ill offenders, fraud, drug abuse, youthful offenders, and unemployed offenders.

The President's Commission on Law Enforcement and Administration of Justice analyzed the charging process and developed its recommendations for its improvement:

Prosecutors should endeavor to make discriminating charge decisions, assuring that offenders who merit criminal sanctions are not released and that other offenders are either released or diverted to non-criminal methods of treatment and control by:

> *Establishment of explicit policies for the dismissal or informal disposition of the cases of certain marginal offenders.*
>
> *Early identification and diversion to other community resources of those offenders in need of treatment, for whom full criminal disposition does not appear required.*[6]

The Commission viewed the charging process, not from the standpoint of who can be tried and convicted, but how the system should handle people with special needs and problems. This focused attention away from the criminal process toward the dispositional alternatives appropriate to the offender. The Commission believed that individuals with a need for special therapeutic treatment, such as mentally disordered or deficient offenders, should be diverted as soon as possible.

Nontrial Adjudication

Approximately 90 percent of all convictions are the result, not of a trial before a judge or jury, but of a plea of guilty or what is called self-adjudication, nontrial adjudication, or conviction without trial. The offender in most criminal cases, with or without inducement, usually pleads guilty, thereby waiving an array of protective constitutional rights, such as the right to a trial by jury, thereby relieving the prosecuting attorney of the administrative burden of presenting his case at trial. The reasonably efficient functioning of the criminal justice system is predicated on a regular and significantly large number of guilty pleas to pending charges.

Nontrial adjudication often is the result of pretrial resolution through the much maligned process of plea bargaining. Plea bargaining has been the target of considerable controversy within the past few years. This method of securing guilty pleas has been viewed both as "an essential, indeed indispensable, part of the administration of justice"[7]

---

[6] The President's Commission on Law Enforcement and Administration of Justice, *The Challenge of Crime in a Free Society* (Washington, D.C.: U.S. Govt. Printing Office, 1967), p. 134.

[7] American Bar Association Project on Standards for Criminal Justice, *Standards Relating to the Prosecution Function and the Defense Function*, pp. 102-3.

on one hand, and on the other, "as a pernicious process ready for extinction."[8]

Plea bargaining (or as it is called in various jurisdictions, "plea negotiation," "trading out," and "compromise of a criminal case") is the process by which the prosecutor and the defendant, usually represented by his attorney, determine the value of a plea of guilty, that is, what charge or sentencing concessions will the prosecutor grant in exchange for the plea. Plea bargaining assumes many forms, depending on the time the plea bargaining occurs, the nature of the original charge, the caseload of the prosecutor and the courts, and the flexibility of the sentencing structure in the jurisdiction.

Charging concessions usually include reduction to a charge less serious than is supported by admissible evidence or permission to plead guilty to a lesser-included offense or the less serious of several charges filed. Charge bargaining is sought by the defendant in order to control the sentencing discretion of the judge. The defendant may desire to limit the maximum potential sentence, avoid a mandatory minimum sentence, or create an opportunity for the granting of probation. Charge bargaining also allows the defendant to avoid the stigma of conviction for an offense with an undesirable label, as is associated with most sex-related crimes.

Plea bargaining for sentence concessions from the prosecutor is common in jurisdictions with a flexible sentencing structure. Where the judge has considerable latitude in the imposition of sentence, the ultimate charge assumes lesser importance. In sentence bargaining the prosecutor promises to recommend a particular sentence or to refrain from making or opposing a particular disposition.

One further form of plea bargaining has been identified—the so-called tacit bargain. When the defendant is aware of the customary practice of the court to be more lenient to defendants who plead guilty or to apply more lenient sentences for guilty pleas to particular offenses, the defendant pleads guilty with the expectation that the tacit bargain will be fulfilled. To a lesser degree, the practice of the prosecutor to make or not oppose sentencing recommendations may be anticipated by the defendant in entering a guilty plea.

---

[8] National Advisory Commission on Criminal Justice Standards and Goals, *National Conference on Criminal Justice* (Working Papers), January 1973, p. Ct.-5.

The value of the plea-bargaining process in the American system of criminal justice was considered by the President's Commission on Law Enforcement and Administration of Justice:

> *The negotiated guilty plea serves important functions. As a practical matter, many courts could not sustain the burden of having to try all cases coming before them. The quality of justice in all cases would suffer if overloaded courts were faced with a great increase in the number of trials. Tremendous investments of time, talent, and money, all of which are in short supply and can be better used elsewhere, would be necessary if all cases were tried. It would be a serious mistake, however, to assume that the guilty plea is no more than a means of disposing of criminal cases at minimal cost. It relieves both the defendant and the prosecution of the inevitable risks and uncertainties of trial. It imports a degree of certainty and flexibility into a rigid, yet frequently erratic system. The guilty plea is used to mitigate the harshness of mandatory sentencing provisions and to fix a punishment that more accurately reflects the specific circumstances of the case than otherwise would be possible under inadequate penal codes. It is frequently called upon to serve important law enforcement needs by agreements through which leniency is exchanged for information, assistance, and testimony about other serious offenders.*[9]

Balanced against the value of the process are the costs that it imposes on the criminal justice system and the individual offender:

> *At the same time the negotiated plea of guilty can be subject to serious abuses. In hard-pressed courts, where judges and prosecutors are unable to deal effectively with all cases presented to them, dangerous offenders may be able to manipulate the system to obtain unjustifiably lenient treatment. There are also real dangers that excessive rewards will be offered to induce pleas or that prosecutors will threaten to seek a harsh sentence if the defendant does not plead guilty. Such practices place unacceptable burdens on the defendant who legitimately insists upon his right to trial. They present the greatest potential abuse when the sentencing judge becomes involved in the process as a party to the negotiations, as in some places he does.*[10]

[9] The President's Commission on Law Enforcement and Administration of Justice, *The Challenge of Crime in a Free Society*, p. 135.
[10] Ibid.

American Bar Association Standards

The American Bar Association considers the practice of plea bargaining to be proper when used to achieve limited worthwhile objectives and when the defendant is provided certain safeguards to assure his plea is knowing, voluntary, and accurate. The standards adopted by the ABA to guide the process whereby adjudication is accomplished without trial have the express objective to formulate procedures that will maximize the benefits of conviction and minimize the risks of unfair or inaccurate results instead of attempting to eliminate the plea-bargaining procedure. Plea-bargaining discussions are considered proper if it appears that the public interest in the effective administration of justice would be served by these discussions. Among the factors to be weighed in this determination are:

- The defendant by his plea has aided in ensuring the prompt and certain application of correctional procedures to him.
- The defendant has acknowledged his guilt and shown a willingness to assume responsibility for his conduct.
- The concessions involved will make possible alternative correctional measures that are better adapted to achieving the rehabilitative, protective, deterrent, or other purposes of correctional treatment.
- The concessions will prevent undue harm to the defendant from the form of conviction.
- The defendant has made public trial unnecessary when there are good reasons for not having the case dealt with in a public trial.
- The defendant has given or offered cooperation when such cooperation has resulted or may result in the successful prosecution of other offenders engaged in equally serious or more serious criminal conduct.
- The defendant by his plea has aided in avoiding delay (including delay due to crowded dockets) in the disposition of other cases and thereby has increased the probability of prompt and certain application of correctional measures to other offenders.

In addition to the guidance offered for determining under what circumstances plea bargaining is appropriate, the ABA standards also prescribe the concessions or terms that are proper for a prosecutor to offer in the bargaining process. As may be dictated by the circumstances of a specific case, the prosecutor may, if the defendant agrees to enter a plea of guilty or *nolo contendere* (no contest), make or not oppose favorable recommendations as to the sentence that should be imposed; seek or not oppose dismissal of the offense charged if the defendant pleads to another offense reasonably related to the criminal conduct involved; or seek or not oppose dismissal of other charges or potential charges. Prosecutors are required to afford similarly situated defendants equal plea-agreement opportunities.

The National Advisory Commission on Criminal Justice Standards and Goals recommends the abolition of plea bargaining as soon as possible, but no later than 1978. It is the opinion of the Commission that plea negotiation not only serves no legitimate function in the processing of criminal defendants, but it also encourages irrationality in the court process, burdens the exercise of individual rights, and endangers the right of innocent defendants to be acquitted. Until plea bargaining is abolished, the process should be modified to provide procedural safeguards for all defendants, including formulation by the prosecutor of written plea-bargaining policies and practices.

The prosecutor, in developing these written procedures, should consider the following factors in plea bargaining:

- The impact that a formal trial would have on the offender and those close to him.
- The role that a plea and negotiated agreement may play in rehabilitating the offender.
- The value of a trial in fostering the community's sense of security and confidence in law enforcement agencies.
- The assistance rendered by the offender—in the apprehension or conviction of other offenders, in the prevention of crimes by others, in the reduction of the impact of the offense on the victim, or in any other socially beneficial activity.

The weakness of the prosecution's case must never be used as the reason for granting plea-bargaining concessions.

This Commission also condemned overcharging practices by prosecutors to induce pleas of guilty. It is considered improper to charge or threaten to charge for offenses for which the available admissible evidence is insufficient to support a conviction, or for offenses that are not ordinarily charged in the jurisdiction for the particular conduct engaged in. The prosecutor should not threaten that a more severe sentence will result for pleading not guilty than is ordinarily imposed on defendants pleading not guilty.

The President's Commission on Law Enforcement and Administration of Justice presented a third viewpoint about plea bargaining. It urged improvement of plea-bargaining procedures in those jurisdictions where plea bargaining is an ordinary occurrence; it did not advocate expansion of plea bargaining into jurisdictions able to deal with criminal caseloads without reliance on or encouragement of guilty pleas. Existing plea-bargaining procedures should be reexamined to ensure that the discussions are more careful and thorough, broader in scope, and conducted early in the criminal process. Plea discussions should involve a thorough assessment of the factual basis of the prosecution's case, a consideration of the offender's personal history and correctional needs, review of the dispositional alternatives available for the particular offender, and attention to the specific charge to which the offender will plead guilty.

Through adoption of these recommendations and others, the Commission believed that plea negotiations can be conducted fairly and openly, can be consistent with sound law enforcement policy, and can bring a worthwhile flexibility to the disposition of offenders.

The Prosecutor's Accountability

The awesome power of a prosecutor, the pivotal figure in the criminal justice system, to control the destiny of all suspected and actual violators of the criminal laws has not gone unrecognized, despite the general lack of knowledge and understanding about the prosecutorial process. The potential for abuse in the exercise of the vast discretionary authority vested in the prosecutor in both the charging and nontrial adjudication aspects of the prosecutorial process, and the need for control of this authority, have caused increased attention to be devoted to ensuring that the prosecutor is accountable for his activities.

The Code of Professional Responsibility promulgated by the American Bar Association and adopted in most states defines the professional norms or standards of professional conduct expected of all lawyers. Public prosecutors who are attorneys are subject to these professional norms. The Code provides that a public prosecutor shall not institute or cause to be instituted criminal charges when he knows or it is obvious that the charges are not supported by probable cause. The unique position of the prosecutor in the criminal justice system is recognized; his duty is not merely to convict, but to seek justice. Prosecutors are advised to use restraint in the selection of cases to prosecute and in the discretionary exercise of other governmental powers.

Proper prosecutorial conduct is also prescribed by state legislatures and state attorneys general with supervisory authority over local prosecutors. Court rules frequently prescribe acceptable prosecutor behavior in criminal cases.

National standard-setting bodies have proposed additional standards of conduct to guide the use of prosecutorial discretion. Prosecutors are generally urged to adopt written regulations or guidelines available to the public to ensure the uniform application of reasonable and fair procedures for decision making during the prosecutorial process. Recommendations range from advocating the preparation of written regulations establishing policy guidelines, standards, and procedures for charging, noncriminal diversion, plea-discussions, and screening or precharge conferences—to requiring the submission of a written statement to the court of reasons for a decision not to charge or a decision to dismiss existing charges. These national standards permit the prosecutor to exercise his discretionary power in handling criminal cases, requiring only that such discretion is properly confined, structured, and checked; and conducted as a visible process in which all offenders are treated equally and fully under the law.

Both direct and indirect formal, legal control measures may be invoked against prosecutors; however, these direct controls are infrequently applied and rarely successful. Adverse charging decisions are subject to challenge through an assortment of direct legal remedies, intervention by the attorney general being one example. Continuing unwillingness or inability of the prosecutor to enforce the criminal code as the community expects or is contemplated by the law can be controlled by indirect but severe measures, such as removal from office.

The remedies involving removal from office are disbarment or disenrollment from the practice of the law by the agency responsible for the discipline of attorneys; criminal prosecution for misfeasance, malfeasance, or nonfeasance; initiation of a *quo warranto* action or an ouster suit; and suspension or supersession of the prosecutor by the legislature, the governor, or the attorney general. Such remedies are seldom successful except in instances of gross behavior or physical incapability. As long as the prosecutor exercises his charging discretion in good faith in accordance with the resources available to him, his judgment will seldom be subject to successful challenge.

Direct controls are applied in situations where the prosecutor's charging decision in any particular case is not acceptable to a citizen, the judiciary, the governor, or the attorney general of the state. Private citizens may proceed with an action called *mandamus*, whereby the prosecutor can be compelled for cause to continue prosecution of a criminal case. Judges in some states can compel continuation of prosecution, either by the prosecutor, a substitute, or the state attorney general.

Administrative control of local prosecution activities by the state attorney general varies. The attorney general and local prosecutors may have concurrent or overlapping jurisdiction; the attorney general might have supervisory control over the prosecutor; he may be authorized to intervene in local prosecution; he may be able to supersede local prosecutors' decisions; and he may have direct control over all local prosecutors in the state. In the remainder of the states the attorney general has little or no control over local prosecutors.

The prosecutor's conduct is also influenced by the actions and attitudes of other members of the criminal justice system. Police enforcement practices, the officers' personal charging preferences, the nature and completeness of investigative reports, and police selection of a deputy prosecutor to approve charges all affect charging decisions. The judge, through his pattern of acquittal, dismissal, and sentencing decisions, and personal preferences and attitudes toward particular offenses or classes of offender, affects subsequent prosecutor decisions in charge selection, plea bargaining, and trial strategy.

The prosecutor also responds to informal influences from the community. The wishes of crime victims or their relatives toward prosecution of charges, as in statutory rape cases or family assaults, are given consideration. Since prosecutors are usually elected officials, they are subject to the same pressures exerted on all public officials by their constituency. The constant attention of the communications media, the desires of influential or vocal community leaders and organizations, and the preferences of observers within the criminal justice system affect the prosecutor's perception and the performance of his job.

Student Checklist

1. Can you identify the variety of roles that the prosecutor performs?
2. Are you able to list the four charging options available to a prosecutor?

3. Can you identify the four basic situations in the charging decision that will usually result in a decision not to charge, not to charge fully, or not to continue criminal proceedings?

4. Can you list the factors that a prosecutor considers when charging a juvenile?

5. Are you able to list the seven types of cases that a prosecutor will normally handle by selecting a no-charge alternative?

6. Do you know how to compare the screening criteria of the American Bar Association and the National Advisory Commission?

7. Do you know how to differentiate between plea bargaining and a tacit bargain?

8. Can you identify the formal means of holding a prosecutor accountable?

Topics for Discussion

1. Discuss the problems incurred by a reviewing prosecutor when he must insure that the weight and probative value of the evidence is sufficient to convince a trier of fact.

2. Discuss the practice of overcharging—horizontal and vertical.

3. Discuss the American Bar Association recommendations in exercising discretion in the charging decision.

4. Discuss the process of plea negotiation.

5. Discuss the standards of professional conduct expected of prosecutors.

The study of this chapter will enable you to:

1. Identify the four major statutes that were historical antecedents of the English bail system.
2. List the individuals who are involved in the bail decision.
3. Define the term money bail.
4. Identify the role of the professional bondsman.
5. List the two principles set forth in the Bail Reform Act of 1966.
6. Define the term personal recognizance.
7. Identify the primary function of court-administered bail.
8. List the four criticisms of preventive detention.

11
Bail: Release or Detention

When a person is arrested on suspicion of a crime, the date of his trial—if he has one—may be a year or more away. During the period between arrest and trial the defendant may have several concerns: supporting himself and often his family as well; locating witnesses and working with his lawyer to prepare a defense; and putting his affairs in order in the event that he is found guilty and sent to prison. The community, on the other hand, has two demands to make of the defendant: that he appear at his trial; and that he refrain from endangering other people in the interim period.

The interests of the defendant and the community in this pretrial period occasionally conflict. In the overwhelming majority of cases, the device used by American courts to accommodate these varying concerns is still the anachronistic and inappropriate system of money bail. Today this system is under increasing attack for not serving the best interests of either the community or the defendant.

The problems inherent in the current bail system are becoming fully documented with each study that is conducted. It is well established that the present bail system discriminates against the poor defendant. Whether or not a man ever sees the inside of a jail often depends on his financial situation. Studies have shown that the defendant who remains free prior to trial has a lesser chance of being convicted, and if convicted, has a greater chance of receiving a lighter sentence. Moreover, bail has been shown to be ineffective in its primary purpose of guaranteeing a

Source: The National Commission on the Causes and Prevention of Violence, *Law and Order Reconsidered*, Report of the Task Force on Law and Law Enforcement. (Washington, D.C.: U.S. Govt. Printing Office, 1968), pp. 247-267.

defendant's appearance at trial, and very few defendants make their court appearances out of fear of forfeiting bail.

This chapter explores the historical antecedents of the monetary bail system, the nature and the problems of the present bail system, and alternatives to the bail system that are being instituted in various parts of the United States.

History of Bail

Our bail system most likely has its derivations in the ancient institution of hostageship developed in England by the Germanic Anglos and Saxons. As a war tactic, a hostage would be held until another person's promise was fulfilled or some desired consequence achieved. Eventually, the site of the practice shifted from the battlefield to the courtroom. A third person—a relative, friend, or clergy—would come to court and vouch for a defendant's trustworthiness. The defendant would be released in the custody of the surety.

A bail system like the one used in the United States today developed during the first thousand years A.D. in England. Judges traveled on circuits, and their visits to a given area might be several years apart. Until the judges arrived, prisoners were held in the custody of local sheriffs. Prison conditions were atrocious. Prisons were also insecure, and inmates frequently escaped. Maintaining the prisons was a financial burden. Thus, the sheriffs were happy to have others assume the responsibility of maintaining custody of defendants, and they frequently released defendants into the custody of sureties, usually friends or relatives of the accused. If the defendant failed to appear for trial, the custodian was required to pay over a sum of money. This liability of the surety for the appearance of the defendant, and the ability to discharge the liability by the payment of a sum of money, remains the basis of our present system of bail.

In 1275, an extensive inquest by a hundred jurors exposed many fraudulent practices in the sheriffs' administration of the release of prisoners on bail. As a result of the inquest, Parliament passed the first statute governing bail practices. The Statute of Westminster I established those crimes that were bailable on the presentation of sufficient sureties, and those that were not.

The historical antecedents of the Eighth Amendment to the U.S. Constitution go back to the efforts of the English to implement the promise of the thirty-ninth chapter of the Magna Carta that "no free-man shall be arrested, or detained in prison . . . unless . . . by the law of the land." Despite that provision, when five knights thrown in prison by Charles I in 1627 brought an action for *habeas corpus*, release was denied on the basis that the protection of the provisions did not extend to the pretrial period. Parliament responded to the case by declaring that "the cause of imprisonment must be known, else the statute will be of little force. . . ." and went on to adopt the Petition of Right, which, after reciting various abuses of the power to imprison, prayed that "no freeman in any such manner as is before mentioned, be imprisoned or detained."

The Habeas Corpus Act of 1679 provided for a procedure to free "many of the King's subjects (who) have been and hereafter may be long detained in prison, in such cases where by law they are bailable. . . ." Nevertheless, judges continued to thwart the purpose of the Act of 1679 by setting impossibly high bail. Parliament therefore declared, in the Bill of Rights it drew up in 1689, that "excessive bail ought not to be required. . . ."

Thus, the English protection against pretrial detention eventually comprised three separate but essential elements: the determination of whether defendants had the right to release on bail; the *habeas corpus* procedure developed to implement defendants' rights; and the protection against judicial abuse by the excessive bail clause of the 1689 Bill of Rights.

Professor Caleb Foote, who has done extensive historical research into the origins of bail, has concluded that the particular words in which the subject of bail is dealt with in the Eighth Amendment are the result of historical accident, and that the most plausible interpretation of the words, "excessive bail should not be required," is that they were intended to grant a constitutional right to bail.[1] Professor Foote's interpretation is that the framers of the U.S. Constitution intended to include all three elements of the English protection against unwarranted pretrial detention. While the English principle of *habeas corpus* found its way into our counterpart *habeas corpus* provision (Article 1, Section 9) and the

---

[1] Caleb Foote, "The Coming Constitutional Crisis in Bail," *113 U. of P. L. Rev., 959* (1965) p. 1125.

excessive bail language was incorporated into the Eighth Amendment, the fundamental, substantive right to bail itself, which these other remedial rights were intended to supplement, was inadvertently omitted.

Professor Foote's explanation of the oversight is that the phrasing of the Eighth Amendment was derived almost verbatim from the Virginia Declaration of Rights of 1776, whose author, George Mason, was not an attorney and probably knew little about the technical legalisms of the fundamental law of bail. Professor Foote concluded that any intent to omit this basic right from the Constitution—and to legislative discretion—would have been an anomaly in view of the primary purpose of the Bill of Rights to protect the people from abuse by the legislative branch of government. Without some right to have bail set, the protection against "excessive bail" would be meaningless. Professor Foote's research would seem to indicate that all defendants have the absolute right to bail. This view has generally been adopted by the courts except for capital offenses. Thus, the Federal Rules of Criminal Procedure provide:

> A person arrested for an offense not punishable by death shall be admitted to bail. A person arrested for an offense punishable by death may be admitted to bail by any court or judge authorized by law to do so in the exercise of discretion, giving due weight to the evidence and to the nature and circumstances of the offense.

This section of the Code is undergoing revision as a result of findings by the Supreme Court that the death penalty, *as administered*, was unconstitutional; and that persons charged with capital offenses do have a right to bail.

State constitutions contain similar provisions under which an exception is made to the general guarantee of bail: only when he is charged with a noncapital offense does a defendant have the right to be released on bail.

The Bail Decision

One of the purposes of a defendant's initial appearance before a judge is the setting of bail. The judge determines the amount of bail, but his decision has traditionally been influenced by the investigator, the prosecuting attorney, and the defense counsel. The investigator or the prosecutor will often confer with the judge prior to arraignment proceedings in an attempt to influence his decision as to the amount of the bail to be set. This would normally be done by disclosing to the judge the defendant's previous criminal record or other facts that would tend to indicate that an accused may be a "poor flight risk." Many of the facts cannot be brought out in open court, or not at an early stage in the criminal proceedings. The prosecutor alone will sometimes contact the judge in an attempt to influence the bail decision, but normally only upon request of the law enforcement agency.

In cases where the defendant is represented by counsel, his attorney will frequently argue vigorously that his client be set free on a nominal bail or on his own personal recognizance. There are many advantages to a defendant being free on bail. First is the obvious advantage of temporary freedom. In addition, the accused is often able to contribute significantly to his own defense by gathering evidence and locating witnesses. Also, freedom gives the defendant an opportunity to rehabilitate himself and demonstrate to the court that he has turned away from his criminal behavior pattern.

Many defense attorneys agree that "time is the best defense." This expression suggests that the further away the trial date from the alleged offense, the lesser the chance of conviction and, in the event of a conviction, the greater the chance for a lenient sentence. This theory is predicated on the following: the defendant can establish ties in the community and demonstrate that he is responsible and stable, the prosecution may be more apt to consent to a guilty plea to a lesser charge or even a dismissal of the charge; and a judge may be less likely to apply a harsh sentence should the defendant be convicted.

Bail and the Poor

The abuses of the money bail system have received considerable national attention in recent years. But despite empirical studies showing the extent of detention based simply on the failure of the poor defendant to make bail (and the hardship such detention produces); despite demonstrations by the Vera Institute of Justice in New York that for many defendants bail is not only inequitable but unnecessary; and despite public response to conferences, articles, books, media coverage, Congressional hearings, and a new federal law, money bail remains the method of release used most often in the United States today.

The system of money bail is based on the assumption that the threat of forfeiture of his money or property will act as an effective deterrent to a defendant's temptation to flee before his trial. But, as Supreme Court Justice Douglas has pointed out, this theory is based on the assumption that a defendant has property. In fact, many defendants do not have property they can put up for bail: a defendant who cannot post bail must go to jail.

Pretrial detention of an accused who, were it not for his poverty, would remain at liberty pending trial, is not only bad policy; it may also violate a constitutional right to equal protection of the laws. The Supreme Court has held that neither the federal government nor a state can convict an indigent of a serious crime without providing him counsel at the government's expense. Nor can a government fail to provide an indigent with a free transcript of his trial, where a transcript is necessary to an appeal, and the type of appeal a convicted defendant is given cannot in any way be made to hinge on whether he can pay for the assistance of counsel. But the Supreme Court so far has not applied the equal protection guarantee to questions of pretrial detention. Too often, American citizens are committed to prison cells for prolonged periods of time prior to trial, only to be later acquitted of any wrongdoing. And, too often, the only reason a person may have been forced to serve a pretrial "sentence" is that the individual was poor or friendless.

Whether or not the phrase "excessive bail" in the Eighth Amendment was intended to provide a constitutional right to bail, the excessive bail clause should at least be interpreted consistently with the Supreme Court's other decisions prohibiting financial discrimination against an accused. The Eighth Amendment proscription of excessive bail, together with the Fourteenth Amendment guarantee of equal protection, should be interpreted as requiring recognition that the imposition of any bail can be excessive when it is beyond a defendant's means to provide it. In such a case, some nonfinancial means of assuring the defendant's attendance at trial must be found.

Bail and the Unpopular

In addition to discriminating against the poor, the wide discretion allowed in setting bail enables the judge, usually on behalf of the police, to punish the unpopular defendants prior to the trial. The setting of money bail in amounts that the arrested person obviously cannot pay is used all too often as a method of preventively detaining suspected habitual criminals pending their trials. Judges have also changed the security requirements in order to assure that certain defendants cannot meet them. For example, if the unpopular defendant had the cash to post bail, he may then additionally be required to put up property as security. If the defendant happens to own property, it may be further required that said property be unencumbered. Finally, it is possible to avoid bail altogether by indicting for more severe, nonbailable offenses. In Georgia, civil rights demonstrators who marched in public were charged with attempting to incite insurrection, a nonbailable offense, even after similar charges in other cases had been found unconstitutional.

The Bondsman

Even if such abuses did not exist, the money bail system could be condemned simply because it has spawned the world of bondsmen. When a judge has decided in favor of pretrial release and has set bail in a reasonable amount, it is the bondsman who ultimately holds the key to the jailhouse. He may in effect veto the decision of the judge by refusing to provide bail for good reasons, for bad reasons, or for no reasons. With few exceptions, bondsmen have refused to handle cases arising out of civil rights demonstrations. Even where they have provided bail, they have been known to charge higher fees in these unpopular cases.

The professional bondsman has been given a major role in the criminal process only in the United States and the Philippines. The bondsman is a creature of the frontier conditions that existed in early America. The comparative intimacy of smaller, more homogenous England had given birth to a bail system that was based on personal trust. In America, on the other hand, many people lacked personal friends or relatives who would provide the bail necessary for their pretrial release; the vast, unoccupied areas to which a defendant could flee made it difficult, if not impossible, for private sureties to assure their attendance at trial. Thus, paid sureties came to take the place of personal sponsorship. Although the names of large, respectable insurance companies appear on bail bonds, these companies delegate the actual conduct of the bonding business to their agents, the local bondsmen, who retain the ultimate power over detention. That the companies comply with state insurance laws has little relation to any state control over the writing of bail bonds. And the companies have little to lose; because of requirements of collateral, they run no risk of default.

Some states limit the fees that bondsmen may charge for writing bonds; others have no such limitations. Even though premiums may be regulated, there are no controls on the collateral a bondsman may require. And the character of bondsmen rarely is effectively regulated. Their unpopularity is reflected in the following by Ronald Goldfarb:

> . . . The bail bondsman is an unappealing member of society. He lives on the law's inadequacy. . . . Our system created him. Bondsmen are products of our uniquely commercialized administration of justice, just as Prohibition created the racketeers who preyed on the society that gave them birth. It is our national disgrace that our system of justice should allow a group . . . to thrive and profit from its inadequacies.[2]

The Costs of Bail

A poor person who must remain in jail until his trial suffers a heavy toll in human costs. During this period the defendant loses his earning capacity and often his job. This economic burden on the defendant and his family may have irreversible effects. His home will be disrupted and his family humiliated. His incarceration may be permanently damaging to his relations with his wife and children. Frequently, families are involuntarily forced to seek welfare or financial relief. All of this punishment is brought about without determination of his guilt. But because he is poor, he is treated as though he were a convicted criminal serving his sentence.

The cost to the taxpayers can also be cumbersome. Society must pick up the bill for the additional welfare relief for the defendant's family. Without the defendant's ability to work and pay for his attorneys' fees, a public defender is used, and his fees are paid by the taxpayers. The cost to the public for the maintenance and care of those incarcerated

[2] Ronald Goldfarb, *Ransom: A Critique of the American Bail System* (New York: Harper & Row, 1965), p. 102.

is somewhat staggering. The average daily population of federal prisoners awaiting trial in places of detention is 3300. The government must pay $3.39 per day for each of them—the total costs come to about $4 million a year. In addition, the federal government often will not have facilities of its own, and will have to house its prisoners in local jails on a rental basis. These agreements cost the government more than its own prisons. "In some instances we are paying as much as $7.50 a day for the care and custody of a federal prisoner; for juveniles, it may run two or three times that high."[3]

Bail's Effect on Justice

In addition to the bail system's discrimination against the poor and unpopular, its cost to the defendant and the public, and its surrender of law enforcement functions to bondsmen, studies have shown that defendants who can afford bail plead guilty less frequently, are convicted less frequently, and if convicted, receive shorter or nonjail sentences more commonly than those who must spend the pretrial period in jail.

The period before trial plays a crucial part in the administration of criminal justice. The Supreme Court early recognized that the time between the institution of formal charges and the trial is "perhaps the most critical period of the proceeding . . . when consultation, thoroughgoing investigation, and preparation are vitally important. . . ."[4] But only in limited ways can the jailed defendant help his attorney prepare his defense. He may be detained at an inconvenient location or have insufficient time available for working with the attorney, or with investigators or witnesses. He cannot make amends with the complaining witness in an effort to have the charges dropped. He cannot help locate witnesses or evidence. He earns no money that could be used to help his case.

Pioneer studies of bailed and unbailed defendants in Philadelphia and New York give support to the hypothesis. The Philadelphia study showed that defendants who came to court from jail received less favorable treatment as to both the proportion of those convicted and those

---

[3] Ibid., p. 44.
[4] Powell v. Alabama, 287 U.S. 45, 57 (1932).

receiving prison sentences.[5] The contrast between the disposition of jail and bail cases was so striking that it raises a strong inference that the handicap of jail status is a major contributing cause for the difference.

The New York study concluded that being in jail operates to the disadvantage of the defendant at every stage of the proceedings.[6] Defendants who were free on bail stood a better chance of being freed by a grand jury, being acquitted at trial, or receiving suspended sentences. Of course, some of the factors (such as a long criminal record or strong evidence of guilt) that lead to high bail and detention may also lead to a finding of guilty and a prison sentence instead of probation. But a more recent study concluded that the 47 percent greater likelihood of a defendant's receiving a prison sentence if he spent the pretrial period in jail could not be explained by differences in the backgrounds of defendants who were detained, as compared to those who posted bail.[7]

Often, unbailed defendants who are sentenced by the court to probation will have lost much of the benefit of that disposition. Ironically, one of the purposes of having convicted offenders, particularly those who are young or without a prior criminal record, serve their sentences on probation in the community is to avoid the degrading, and frequently corrupting, effects of jail.

Bail Reform

In 1966, in response to a growing national interest in bail reform, Congress enacted the Bail Reform Act, the first major overhaul of federal bail law since 1789. The Act established two primary principles: (1) that an accused shall be released pending trial unless good reasons exist why he will probably not return to stand trial; and (2) that a person's ability to post money bond shall be irrelevant to a pretrial release decision. A defendant may be released on his own recognizance or on the execution of an unsecured appearance bond. A judge who determines

[5] 102 *U. of P. L. Rev., 1031* (1954).
[6] 106 *U. of P. L. Rev., 685* (1958).
[7] Wald, "Pretrial Detention and Ultimate Freedom: A Statistical Study," *39 N.Y.U. L. Rev., 631* (1964).

that such a release will not reasonably assure the defendant's appearance has the authority to impose any one or more conditions (most of them nonfinancial) that are calculated to deter flight. The defendant's appearance at trial—not his possible danger to the community—is the only consideration that may be taken into account.

A defendant who continues to be detained 24 hours after the release hearing as a result of his inability to meet the conditions of release may have the conditions reviewed by the judicial officer who imposed them. Unless the conditions are changed and the defendant released, the judge must state in writing his reasons for imposing these particular conditions. The statute provides for prompt appeal of release conditions.

It is more difficult to secure release in a capital case or after conviction pending an appeal. The rationale for changing the presumption of release in these cases is that a defendant who is charged with an offense punishable by death or who has already been convicted is more likely to flee. Hence, a judge is authorized to order detention in those situations where he has reason to believe that "no one or more conditions of release will reasonably assure that the person will not flee or pose a danger to any other person or to the community."[8]

In the Bail Reform Act, Congress recognized that it is an anachronism to make freedom pending trial depend on a defendant's ability to pay. As the Senate Judiciary Committee pointed out: "Respect for law and order is diminished when the attainment of pretrial liberty depends solely upon the financial status of an accused."[9] Since the passage of the Bail Reform Act of 1966, many states have passed legislation adopting nonfinancial alternatives to money bail. There remains a great need, however, for further bail reform at the state and local levels, where the great majority of defendants are tried. Prosecutors and judges in too many jurisdictions continue to recommend and set bail in dollar amounts with little or no articulation of reasons why these amounts are required. There is either a conscious intent to detain, or an apparent lack of concern as to whether detention will be the result of requiring money bail.

[8] 18 U.S. Code Sec. 3148.
[9] 5 Rept. No. 750, 89th Cong., 1st Sess. (1965).

Release on Personal Recognizance

One possible alternative to the current bail system is release on *personal recognizance*. A defendant released by these means is allowed to remain free until his trial, conditional only by his promise to appear; no money bail is required.

Formally conducted experimentation by the Vera Institute of Justice in New York found that for many defendants, such release, removing the necessity for the posting of collateral or supervision by the court, is both efficient and humane.[10] Many—perhaps most—defendants are trustworthy and have sufficient ties to their families, jobs, and communities to prevent them from fleeing before their trials.

Release on personal recognizance obviously cannot be used in all cases. Thus, the method of determining those defendants who may safely be released on their own trust is crucial. A judge often lacks the time and resources to conduct those investigations of defendant's backgrounds that are essential to intelligent release decisions. The Vera Institute hoped to fill this gap in the background information available to the judges and to convince them to adopt alternatives to money bail.

In the Institute's first project, the Manhattan Bail Project, law students were hired to interview arrestees in detention pens just prior to arraignment in the Manhattan Criminal Court. Interview questions were designed to determine the defendants' community ties and whether they could be trusted to return for trial merely because of a promise to return. Defendants' answers were scored on a weighted system according to such factors as residence stability, welfare and medical care, family ties, community contacts, employment, and previous criminal record. The answers were verified for accuracy by a Vera staff member. If the defendant was determined to be a good risk, the information was summarized and made available to the prosecuting attorney, the defense attorney, and the arraigning judge.

Vera found that, with its recommendations and verified information to support them, judges were willing to release defendants on their own recognizance. Of the first 300 cases in which Vera recommended release, 200 were released on recognizance. Of those, only two did not

[10] Ares, Rankin, and Sturz, "The Manhattan Bail Project," *38 N.Y.U. L. Rev., 67* (1963).

appear for trial. This nonappearance rate was better than the rate for those defendants who were released on money bail.

The Manhattan Bail Project served to show that the characteristics of persons likely to appear if released can be identified. Similar projects have since been initiated in other cities, using specially created bail agencies, police, sheriffs, welfare departments, public defenders, probation departments, or VISTA to fill the release advisory role. The reported nonfinancial release programs have shown success wherever they have been tried.

Court-Administered Bail

Alternatives to the release on personal recognizance programs have appeared in various parts of the nation. In Illinois, state legislation allows a defendant to post with the court an amount equal to premium for a bond (normally 10 percent of the total bail). Once the defendant posts this amount, he may go free until his future court appearances. If the defendant returns for trial, all but 1 percent of the total bail is returned to him. This 1 percent is withheld by the court for administrative costs. Under previous systems, the defendant would lose the entire 10 percent premium to a bail bondsman, plus a possible administrative fee.

The Illinois plan further provides that credit must be given for any time spent in jail prior to sentence. Also, the defendant is compensated for this detention against any fine imposed upon conviction. This procedure returns the administration of bail to the courts, where it belongs. It also saves bailed defendants most of the money previously lost to the bondsmen. It fails, however, to solve the problem of the poor defendant who, lacking the necessary premium, may still go to jail.

Citations and Summonses

Even more promising than release on recognizance or other alternatives is the use of summons. The summons is commonly used in minor cases to expedite disposition. In the case of the most frequent example, the parking ticket, a person is charged with an offense and quickly released without jail, bail, or even arrest. The defendant simply is notified to appear for trial at a certain date. The summons can, however, replace arrest and imprisonment in nontraffic cases as well. A summons may be used by the police on the spot instead of a formal arrest, or it may be issued by the police desk officer in the stationhouse shortly after an arrest. A number of jurisdictions authorize the use of an on-the-spot citation by a police officer, especially in traffic offenses. Many jurisdictions also employ a street citation or mail summonses for cases involving municipal code violations.[11]

The extensive use of citations for all misdemeanor offenses in Contra Costa County, California, offers a model that is being adopted by other jurisdictions. Unless an arrest is necessary to protect the community, the processes of the court, or the defendant, a misdemeanor suspect is released at the scene of the offense if he can satisfactorily identify himself. Thus, a summons is the norm in petty theft, minor assault, and municipal ordinance cases. If the arresting officer decides on use of the summons, he first checks with his station by radio to determine if the subject is wanted. If he is not, the summons is issued immediately.

There are some situations that do require an arrest. If the crime is serious, if there is danger of flight or of further criminal conduct, or if the offense is in progress when the police arrive, the need to arrest might be great. In many cases identification, booking search, questioning, fingerprinting, and photographing may be required immediately, but continued detention should be avoided whenever possible.

Preventive Detention

The current bail debate revolves largely about the special problems presented by dangerous or unreliable defendants. At present, statutory authorization or pretrial detention in the United States is extremely rare. In a great majority of states, present constitutional and statutory provisions grant an absolute right to bail, at least in noncapital cases. Yet pretrial detention, in a disguised form, is commonly achieved by judges who set money bail at unreasonably high amounts.

Although detention without conviction of crime has precedents in dealing with the mentally ill and juveniles thought likely to become criminals, the adoption of any system of pretrial detention is beset with diffi-

---

[11] The President's Commission on Law Enforcement and Administration of Justice, *The Task Force Report: The Courts.* (Washington, D.C.: U.S. Govt. Printing Office, 1967). pp. 40-41.

culties that are both theoretical and practical. On the theoretical side, many have argued that pretrial detention is precluded by the presumption of innocence, by the excessive bail clause of the Eighth Amendment, and by the due process clauses of the Fifth and Fourteenth Amendments.

The presumption of innocence, expressly mentioned in the constitutions or codes of most states, has generally been considered as a rule of evidence designed to secure a fair trial by requiring the prosecution to prove its case beyond a reasonable doubt. If the presumption of innocence precludes any predictions of future wrongful conduct before a defendant has been convicted, it bars both pretrial detention and conditions of release. It is doubtful, however, that any court would adopt such an interpretation.

In 1970 Congress enacted a law that established a preventive detention plan for the District of Columbia. This crime bill authorized judges to consider a defendant's "danger to the community" as well as the "likelihood of flight" in setting release conditions. If no condition of release is considered adequate to protect the community, the judge could order a detention hearing for a defendant charged with a "dangerous crime" or a "crime of violence." The bill enumerated the specific types of crime falling into these categories. To order detention, which is limited to 60 days, in most cases the judge must find "clear and convincing evidence" that the defendant has committed a dangerous or violent crime.[12]

In March 1972 a study was published on the effectiveness of the Washington, D.C. crime bill and how preventive detention had been applied. Surprisingly, during the first 10 months that the law was in effect, the prosecution attempted to invoke the preventive detention provisions in only 20 of the 6000 felony cases that entered the process. Of the 20, only 10 were ordered detained by the lower judge, and 5 of these were reversed on appeal.[13]

Further studies on the subject of preventive detention indicate that the basic assumptions on which the philosophy of preventive detention rest may be faulty. A National Bureau of Standards study undermines

[12] U.S. Senate Committee on the Judiciary, *Preventive Detention,* hearings before the subcommittee, 91st Congress, 2nd Sess. May 20–June 19, 1970 (Washington, D.C.: U.S. Govt. Printing Office, 1970).
[13] John Kaplan, *Criminal Justice: Introductory Cases and Materials* (Mineola, N.Y.: Foundation Press, 1973), p. 324.

the assumptions of preventive detention on several points. First, the study found that the amount of pretrial crime was very low (about 17 percent) when misdemeanor and felony arrests were considered, and only about 5 percent when only serious felony arrests were counted. The second conclusion was that there was no correlation between the type of crime for which the first arrest was made and the severity of a second offense. The third finding was that most bail recidivism does not occur in the immediate postarrest period, or in the 60 to 90-day period after arrest in which preventive detention would cause the man to be held. The last major finding was that not enough correlation existed between any one of the 10 characteristics listed in the crime bill, if taken singly, to support it as being a reliable predictor of bail recidivism. The characteristics were not tested as a group, however, and therefore this finding is not complete.[14]

While the Bail Reform Act of 1966 has been lauded as a revolutionary step toward progress, the concept of preventive detention has come under much criticism. Many experts view it as a conservative backlash reaction to the "liberal" Bail Reform Act. Much of the criticism has centered around the following arguments:[15]

1. It violates the Eighth Amendment right to reasonable bail.
2. It denies due process of law—that is, it punishes for anticipated criminal conduct instead of actual conduct.
3. It violates the presumption of innocence.
4. It convicts on "substantial probability" instead of "beyond a reasonable doubt."

While the idea of protecting society from the continued criminal activity of dangerous offenders sounds appealing, the concept of using preventive detention to accomplish this end is plagued with problems. There have been suggested alternatives to preventive detention that would possibly accomplish the same purpose, but without the detrimental side effects. Possible alternative solutions to pretrial crime are expedited trials, restrictive conditions of release, forfeiture of the right to bail following pretrial crime, and stricter sentences for offenses committed during the pretrial period.[16]

[14] American Bar Foundation, *Preventive Detention: An Empirical Analysis.* Reprinted from *Harvard Civil Rights–Civil Liberties Law Review, 6,* No. 2 (1971), pp. 294-297.
[15] Ibid., p. 298.
[16] Ibid., pp. 359-368.

It is understood that these suggestions do not represent foolproof methods of eliminating pretrial crime, but they do appear to be closer in harmony with the traditional American system of justice than the concept of preventive detention is. Despite painstaking studies that have been made, all currently available prediction methods have a relatively low ability to predict criminal behavior. Any system of preventive detention of accused persons poses dangers to cherished individual rights. Any alternative solutions to pretrial crime that lessen the threat of infringement on individual rights should be explored.

Student Checklist

1. Can you list the four major statutes that were historical antecedents of the English bail system?
2. Are you able to list the justice-actors who are involved in the bail decision?
3. Do you know how to define the term money bail?
4. Can you identify the role of the professional bondsman?
5. Can you list the two principles set forth in the Bail Reform Act of 1966?
6. Do you know how to define the term personal recognizance?
7. Can you identify the primary function of court-administered bail?
8. Can you list the four criticisms of preventive detention?

Topics for Discussion

1. Discuss the impact of bail on the poor.
2. Discuss the impact of bail on the unpopular.
3. Discuss the problems of incarcerating all those who are accused of committing a crime.
4. Discuss the use of citations.

ANNOTATED BIBLIOGRAPHY

Abraham, Henry J. *Freedom and the Courts*. London: Oxford University Press, 1967. The basic problem of drawing lines between the rights of the individual and the rights of the community are well described in this text.

American Bar Foundation, *Preventive Detention: An Empirical Analysis*. Reprinted from the *Harvard Civil Rights Law Review 6*, no. 2 (March 1971). This report is an empirical analysis of preventive detention. The report first discusses how preventive detention was brought out, as a conservative backlash to the Bail Reform Act, and proceeds to build a case for the unconstitutionality of this concept.

Bailey, F. Lee, and Henry B. Rothblatt. *Successful Techniques for Criminal Trials*. San Francisco: Bancroft-Whitney, 1971. Each section of this book deals with the significance of each step in the process, including the bail system.

Goldfarb, Ronald. *Ransom: A Critique of the American Bail System*. New York: Harper & Row, 1965. A text identifying the injustices, outmoded, and unworkable system of monetary bail. Experiments, research, and reported cases are described in detail, along with a comparative analysis with other countries. Alternative solutions to bail are evaluated by the author.

Kaplan, John. *Criminal Justice: Introductory Cases and Materials*. Mineola, N.Y.: The Foundation Press, 1973. This text is a comprehensive and up-to-date study of the criminal justice system. It offers a section on the history, nature, current trends, and alternatives to the bail system.

President's Commission on Law Enforcement and Administration of Justice. *The Task Force Report: The Courts*. Washington, D.C.: U.S. Govt. Printing Office, 1967. This study thoroughly examines all aspects of the court function of the criminal justice system and various other court-related topics.

Report of the Task Force on Law and Law Enforcement to the National Commission on the Causes and Prevention of Violence. *Law and Order Reconsidered*. Washington, D.C.: U.S. Govt. Printing Office, 1968. This report includes a detailed study on the nature of our present bail system and how it has evolved. The injustices and inconsistencies of bail are closely examined.

Tappen, Paul W. *Crime, Justice, and Corrections.* New York: McGraw-Hill, 1960. A sound, basic text written by a proponent of returning legal safeguards to correctional clients.

The study of this chapter will enable you to:

1. List five arguments in favor of the grand jury system.
2. Identify some of the arguments that set forth the reasons for abolishing the grand jury.
3. Identify two methods utilized in the selection of grand jurors.
4. List the qualifications that an individual must possess to become a juror.
5. Contrast the type of evidence that can be received by a grand jury with that which can be presented in a trial.
6. List the requirements of an indictment.
7. Distinguish between a True Bill and a No Bill.

12
Grand Jury

Authorities disagree as to the precise date of birth of the grand jury. More readily agreed on is the belief that the grand jury can be traced to the so-called Frank Pledge system, which established the responsibility of each man for his neighbor. The inception of the present grand jury system seems to have been during the reign of Henry II of England in the twelfth century. He ordered that 12 knights or other trustworthy men of every 100 from every village were to disclose, under oath, the names of those residents of their village believed guilty of criminal offenses.[1]

The grand jury originated as an instrument of the British Crown, but slowly evolved into the voice of the people themselves and became a shield against royal persecution. In 1681, the grand jury refused to indict Lord Shaftesbury for treason despite the insistence of Charles II. By the close of the seventeenth century the grand jury had established itself as an important protector of the rights and privileges of the English citizen.

During the seventeenth and eighteenth centuries the colonists brought the grand jury system—along with other institutions of England—to the New World. There it proved to be an important part of the direction taken by local government by making known the wishes of the people. The first colonial grand jury was seated in September 1635, in the Massachusetts Bay Colony. Although patterned after their English forebears, the grand jurors of the Massachusetts Bay Colony were not appointed by a sheriff, but were elected at the various town meetings by

---

[1] Richard D. Younger, *The People's Panel* (Providence: Brown University Press, 1963), p. 1.

their fellow citizens. These early jurors usually involved themselves in seeking out such crimes as wife beating and capital crimes, but others sought out abuses in local government.

The period of the American Revolution stands as an example of the strength of the grand jury system and of its ability to echo the wishes of the people. In 1765, the grand jury of Boston refused to indict participants of the Stamp Act riots; and in 1768, the grand jury of Suffolk resisted the threats of the chief justice of Massachusetts, who demanded that they indict the editors of the *Boston Gazette* for libel against the governor. Realizing the power of the grand jury, the governor sought the support of the secretary of state for the colonies, who suggested to the governor that the power enjoyed by the grand jury might be removed by reverting to the English method of sheriff's appointment of jurors. Fortunately, there was insufficient support for the suggestion in the House of Commons to change the procedure.

Of such significance was the grand jury to the framers of the Constitution that it became a part of the Bill of Rights. The Fifth Amendment specifies that "no person shall be held to answer for a capital, or otherwise infamous crime, unless on presentment or indictment of a grand jury." While the federal government may not bring to trial anyone so accused, the states are not bound to use the grand jury, although most of them do for capital crimes.

In England Jeremy Bentham attacked the grand jury system as "an engine of corruption"—"systematically packed" on behalf of the upper classes. Bentham also opposed it on the grounds that it was an inefficient element in the administration of criminal justice. He recognized the incompetence of a body of men untrained in the law. He believed that a professionally trained prosecutor could perform the functions of a grand jury with far greater efficiency, with far less expense to the people, and with less bother to the courts. The noted English statesman, Robert Peel, was among the first to suggest that a responsible public prosecutor would be in a much stronger position to expedite the processing of criminal cases without the intervention of a grand jury. The grand jury system was abolished in England in 1933 for reasons of economy, and in order to promote greater efficiency in the administration of criminal justice.

In the United States the grand jury system has been under attack many times. It is still high on the list of controversial subjects. Immediately following the Civil War, the movement to abolish the grand jury in this country steadily gathered momentum. Raising the banners of economy and efficiency, as they did in England, opponents of the grand jury brought its use to a successful conclusion in many states and curtailed it in others.

Critics in the United States, 1792 to the Present

In 1792, Judge Alexander Addison of Pennsylvania observed that he was fearful of the danger of giving jurors an almost unbridled license in the conduct of their investigations. He stated that restrictions should be placed on grand jury operations, and that jurors could embark on the investigation of a criminal case only when a matter came directly to the attention of one of them, or when the judge or district attorney initiated the action by submitting a criminal case for their consideration. The effect of this judicial pronouncement was to place these juries almost entirely under the control of the court.[2]

In Connecticut the grand jury had almost ceased to be an investigating body. It no longer met as a body unless summoned by a court. Furthermore, indictment by a full jury was mandatory only in the case of crimes punishable by death or life imprisonment. When information was received in all other categories of crime, it became the practice for individual jurors or the district attorney to sponsor the complaint. Gradually, through disuse of the grand jury in most cases, this body lost most of its broad powers of initiating investigations.[3]

In 1849, Edward Ingersoll, a prominent member of the Pennsylvania Bar, published an essay on the general subject of grand juries in which he condemned the institution as being incompatible with the American constitutional guarantee of freedom. He was in favor of placing limitations on their investigative powers on the grounds that their power to indict on the basis of the knowledge of their own members, together with the secrecy of their deliberations, was not in agreement with all modern theory of judicial proceedings.[4]

The grand jury issue became the subject of debate on the floors of

---

[2] Alexander Addison, *Reports of Cases in the County Courts of the Fifth Circuit* (Washington, 1800), Part II, pp. 37-46.

[3] Statutes of Connecticut, 1784, p. 94.

[4] Edward Ingersoll, *The History and Law of the Writ of Habeas Corpus With an Essay on the Law of Grand Juries* (Philadelphia, 1849), p. 47.

state constitutional conventions for the first time in 1850, supplementing materials that had already become available on the pages of the law journals and textbooks. In that year, constitutional conventions were held in three states to revise their constitutions and, in each instance, the abolition of the grand jury system was high on the agenda.[5]

At the Indiana constitutional convention in Indianapolis, the future of the grand jury in that state became the subject of heated debate. Those delegates seeking abolition of the grand jury system encountered stiff competition and in the face of a determined opposition, they managed to obtain the adoption of a clause authorizing the legislature to continue, modify, or abolish it at any time. Establishing a precedent, Indiana became the first state to include such a provision in its constitution.

In federal courts, the jury tended to become more and more a mere extension of the court. As part of an economy measure, Congress in 1856 gave the power to federal judges to discharge jurors when in their opinion such action would best serve the public interest.

In 1857, delegates gathered in Salem, Oregon, to draft a constitution for statehood. Delegate David Lodan, a member of the territorial bar, placed on the agenda of the convention a resolution to replace the grand jury system with professional prosecutors who, because of their legal background, were in a much stronger position to initiate and process criminal cases. His proposal met with serious opposition on the ground that Oregon was a frontier territory with dangerous criminal elements in evidence. The opposition held to the belief that a secret method of filing complaints was in the best interests of the people. Antijury forces failed in their attempt to abolish the grand jury system outright, but they did succeed in getting the convention to adopt a constitutional provision empowering the legislature to nullify the system at any time.[6]

Antijury adherents made the first successful attempt to abolish the system by legislative action in Michigan in 1859. Since the state constitution no longer guaranteed the right to a grand jury indictment, the legislature was left free to take whatever action it deemed advisable. The

[5] *Journal of the Convention of the State of Indiana to Amend the Constitution* (Indianapolis, 1851), pp. 28, 60, 116, 964.

[6] Richard D. Younger, *"A History of the Grand Jury in the United States,"* Doctoral dissertation, University of Wisconsin, Madison, 1954, and a condensed version under the title, *"The Grand Jury Under Attack,"* Journal of Criminal Law and Criminology, 46, No. 1 (May–June 1955).

judiciary committee of the Michigan Assembly gave its unqualified support to a proposed plan to end the use of inquests, characterizing them as "a crumbling survivor of fallen institutions . . . more akin to the star chamber." Spearheaded by Alexander W. Buell, a Detroit attorney, the committee placed before the legislature a proposal to abolish the grand jury system as an institution dangerous to individual liberty. The committee called attention to the lack of legal background on the part of most jurors, and the inability of the courts to control the nature and direction of their investigations. The efforts of the committee proved so successful that it gained legislative support for a bill abolishing the grand jury system in the state of Michigan. In February 1859, the legislature provided for the prosecution of all crimes based on the information given by a district attorney. By the same token, only a judge could summon a grand jury for the purposes of an investigation.[7]

In 1886, Eugene Stevenson, a New Jersey public prosecutor, condemned the grand jury as an arbitrary, irresponsible and dangerous part of government that long ago should have come "within the range of official responsibility." He much preferred the efficiency and decisiveness of a public prosecutor, observing that the summoning of a new body of jurors at each term insures an unfailing supply of ignorance.

In 1889, Idaho, Montana, Washington, North Dakota, South Dakota, and Wyoming were admitted into the Union. During the constitutional conventions that prepared them for statehood, opponents of the grand jury seized the opportunity to carry forward with their message, and with virtually complete success. In the Idaho convention, the expense of the juries received major emphasis—a potent factor in view of the limited resources of the state at that time.

The views of a member of the Supreme Court helped fuel the movement to abolish the grand jury system in this country. At the annual convention of the Ohio State Bar Association in July 1892, Justice Henry B. Brown proposed abolition of the inquest as a means of simplifying criminal procedure, observing that public prosecutors offered a far more efficient method of bringing criminal offenders to trial. Previously, in 1872, the Wisconsin Supreme Court handed down a decision that the

---

[7] Report of the Judiciary Committee of the House of Representatives on recommending the passage of the bill to provide for the trial of offenses upon information, Michigan House Document No. 4, 1859.

Fourteenth Amendment did not prevent states from ceasing to use the indictment procedure. The decision remained under attack until the United States Supreme Court brought the controversy to a halt in 1884. In the case of *Hurtado* v. *California*, L 10 U.S. 516 (1884), the defendant had challenged his murder conviction on the ground that he had come to trial on an information instead of a grand jury indictment. The Court gave judicial approval to states that desired to abolish the grand jury. The Court held that due process of law included any system of prosecution that preserved liberty and justice and was not limited to indictment by a grand jury.

In 1899 the state of Oregon, under the provisions in its constitution, authorized the substitution of information for the indictment in criminal proceedings. Missouri, in 1890, turned over the duties of the grand jury to district attorneys.

Annual meetings of bar associations set the stage for bringing into sharper focus the movement to abolish the grand jury. In 1905, the Committee on Law Reform of the Iowa Bar Association recommended to the convention a resolution calling for prosecution upon information, and it was adopted. Justice Henry B. Brown of the Supreme Court reaffirmed his opposition to the grand jury system in an address to the American Bar Association in 1905. George Lawyer, an Albany attorney, called on the New York State Bar Association to abolish the grand jury. In Texas, emphasis was placed on the waste of time and money that grand juries entailed. Describing the system as a useless and unnecessary piece of legal machinery, H. N. Atkinson, a Houston lawyer, told members of the Texas Bar Association that it cost the taxpayers of Texas counties between $100,000 and $200,000 each year, in addition to the loss represented by men being taken away from their homes and businesses to perform a function that could be discharged with much greater efficiency by one man, the prosecutor. Using the same argument, Aaron Hahn of Cleveland called on the 1912 Ohio Constitutional Convention to purge the grand jury system in that state.

Writing in the American Bar Association Journal for February 1963, Melvin P. Antell, Judge of the Essex County District Court (Newark, New Jersey), authored an indictment of the grand jury that its supporters would find very difficult to answer. He states in part, "We are told by its apostles that it (the grand jury) is a 'bulwark of liberty and law,' 'the conscience of the community,' 'a guardian of justice.' Let alone being 'bulwark,' 'conscience,' and 'guardian,' we hear also that it is the 'cornerstone of our criminal jurisprudence.' "

This brief review of the historical development of the grand jury system reflects strong support for and against the system, but it is still an integral part of the judicial process.

In order to proceed further, one must understand exactly what the function of the grand jury is. The grand jury is a body of citizens of a jurisdiction, legally selected, empanelled by lot, and sworn to inquire into abuses in government and crimes committed in that jurisdiction. Whereas the grand jury has county jurisdiction in each of the states, federal grand jury jurisdiction consists of a district, of which there are 91.

Grand Jury Proceedings

Generally, two methods are involved in the selection process of grand jurors. One form is by lot, drawing from a list of the tax rolls or the voter registration list. The preferred technique is the selection by a public official who can exercise a certain amount of discretion in the selection process. In most of the states, lists are prepared by a jury commissioner or by the board of supervisors. In California, a jury commissioner presents the presiding superior court judge of the county with a list of qualified jurors from which a selection of names is made by the judge. Each January the list of those selected is then given to the county clerk, who places the names from the list on individual slips of paper and places them in a "grand jury box" for random selection.[8] Those selected to serve as members of the grand jury are usually "blue ribbon" citizens, prominent members of the community above the caliber of those selected for trial juries in terms of education, experience, and training. It is not uncommon to find doctors, engineers, banking officials, and corporate executives on any given grand jury, yet they are rarely found on trial juries.

Qualifications vary from state to state, but usually call for a grand juror to be a person of high integrity, good moral character, and sound mind and body, who displays sound judgment. He must be a citizen of the United States, reside within the jurisdiction for which he will serve,

[8] Penal Code (of California), Sections 895-912, Legal Book, Los Angeles, 1969.

*Figure 12-1. A grand juror must be a person of high integrity, good moral charac-
ter, in sound mind and body. Those selected to serve are usually "blue ribbon"
citizens: physicians, engineers, or corporate executives, who are rarely found on
trial juries.*

and be at least 21 years of age, although the age requirement will no
doubt be challenged soon. He must not have been convicted of any
felony and in many states may not serve on a grand jury if he is an
elected public official. He may not serve on a grand jury if he has been
discharged as a grand juror within a specified time period—usually one
year—nor if he is currently serving as a trial juror.

While most state statutes are silent as to the racial issue in grand jury selections, case decisions as early as 1939 addressed themselves to that matter. In *Pierre* v. *Louisiana*, 306 U.S. 354 (1939), the U.S. Supreme Court held that:

Protection against racial discrimination is secured by recent holdings that if, in the selection of grand jurors, the members of a race are intentionally *and* systematically excluded *from grand jury service* solely on account of race, *the conviction of a* member of that race *will be reversed as a denial of equal protection of the law as guaranteed by the Fourteenth Amendment. (emphasis added)*

This decision was reaffirmed in *Smith* v. *Texas*, 311 U.S. 128 (1940).

A more recent case decision has been handed down by the Supreme Court that specifies that *any* subsequent conviction resulting from grand jury action is in danger of being reversed if *any* minority group member is purposefully discriminated against in grand jury selections [*Whitus* v. *Georgia*, 394 U.S. 545 (1967)].

Although the number varies, historical precedent has held that the number of grand jurors empanelled be from 12 to 23. Usually, 23 members sit on a federal grand jury. Sixteen are required to be present to hear a case, and 12 are required to return an indictment.

The tenure of the grand jury is usually 12 months in most states, although Rule 6(g) of the Federal Rules of Criminal Procedure specifies that a grand jury shall serve until discharged by the court. The maximum time that they may serve, however, is 18 months. Usually, only one grand jury is empanelled at any one time within a jurisdiction. Rule 6(a) of the Federal Rules allows the court to order one or more grand juries to be convened, "at such times as the public interest requires." The Organized Crime Control Act of 1970 has, for special cases, expanded the powers of the federal grand jury. Although the average tenure of a grand jury is 12 months, the actual time varies from one jurisdiction to the next, depending on the amount of business to be conducted. A rural county grand jury in a state with a sparse population may convene for only a few months each year, but the grand jury of a highly urbanized county in a heavily populated state such as New York may be kept busy for its entire 12-month tenure. Furthermore, where a grand jury is abusing its power, the court of that jurisdiction may see fit to discharge its panel. The instances of such occurrences are rare, however.

Time and time again throughout the history of the grand jury, its role as a protector against the arbitrary acts of government or of judges who bend to governmental influence is found in the continued use of such words as, "responsible citizen," "high integrity" and "sound judgment" in the requirements for the selection of grand jurors. Each time a grand jury is empanelled, its members are thoroughly instructed that their duty as grand jurors is to screen accusations that have no foundation and to formally accuse only those persons against whom the evidence appears to be sufficient to warrant a trial.[9] The grand jury must base its decision on the sufficiency of the evidence and not the sophisticated manner or enthusiasm of the prosecutor. Nor can its decisions be based on the lack of sophistication or enthusiasm, for political pressure can be brought to bear in an effort to influence a presentation. That is why the grand juror must possess those virtues previously cited, so that he might inquire where a question is left unanswered.

The oath administered to members of the grand jury bears repeating. However, there are occasions when the real value of an oath may be somewhat limited:

> *You do solemnly swear that you shall diligently inquire and true presentment make of all such matters and things as shall be given you in charge. The government's counsel, your fellows' and your own you shall keep secret. You shall present no one for envy, hatred, or malice; nor shall you leave anyone unpresented through fear, favor, hope of reward or gain. But you shall present all things truly as they come to your knowledge, according to the best of your understanding. So help you God!*

Secrecy of Proceedings

One of the elements under which the grand jury functions that lends it the greatest strength in the investigations it conducts and in the cases it hears for indictment is the element of secrecy. All business conducted by the grand jury is "behind closed doors." Although the prosecuting attorney is present to exhibit that evidence and those witnesses upon which he hopes to secure an indictment, he is prohibited from being present during the grand jury's deliberations and voting—as are all other persons.

---

[9] Paul B. Weston and Kenneth M. Wells, *The Administration of Justice*, 2nd ed. (Englewood Cliffs, N.J.: Prentice-Hall, 1973), p. 14.

A judge may be present at various times during a hearing, but only when the grand jurors seek his legal opinion. In some states a court recorder is present to take minutes, but only during the proceedings when evidence is presented or witnesses are heard. Witnesses called to testify, of course, know only what occurred or was said during the time they were presenting their testimony. They are then immediately excused from the room. It has been pointed out by one observer that the courts have justified the Exclusionary Rule on the basis of two issues: judicial economy and the secrecy of grand jury proceedings. Furthermore, these traditional justifications rely on the general policy of the necessity for grand jury secrecy and the interests that are protected.[10]

Mr. Justice William J. Brennan of the Supreme Court has outlined four reasons for the necessity of the secrecy in grand jury proceedings:

1. To prevent the accused from escaping before he is indicted and arrested or from tampering with the witnesses against him.
2. To prevent disclosure of derogatory information presented to the grand jury against an accused who has not been indicted.
3. To encourage complainants and witnesses to come before the grand jury and speak freely without fear that their testimony will be made public, thereby subjecting them to possible discomfort or retaliation.
4. To encourage the grand jurors to engage in uninhibited investigation and deliberation by barring disclosure of their votes and comments during the proceedings.

As a rule, a grand juror cannot be required or even allowed to testify to those matters discussed in the jury room during deliberations. A grand juror cannot be required to disclose how any individual grand juror voted or, for that matter, how the entire body voted. A grand juror cannot be required to disclose what opinions were expressed during deliberations, or to state what evidence was examined that resulted in an indictment, or even to state whether or not an indictment was considered in a particular matter. A grand juror cannot testify that a particular indictment did not receive the required number of votes, or that the evidence presented did not support an indictment.[11]

[10] Roger T. Brice, "Grand Jury Proceedings: The Prosecutor, The Trial Judge and Undue Influence," *The University of Chicago Law Review, 39,* No. 4 (Summer 1972), p. 772.
[11] Lester B. Orfield, *Criminal Procedure from Arrest to Appeal* (New York: New York University Press, 1947), p. 167.

Perhaps the most often challenged issue with regard to the grand jury (and which is held to be its greatest strength) is its privilege of secrecy. In the course of a routine investigation by the police, a complaint may be filed in the municipal court and the accused, through the right of pretrial discovery, may learn what evidence the police hold at the time of the preliminary examination. He can thereby prepare a defense accordingly well in advance, should he be held to answer before the superior court. No such privilege is afforded the accused who has been charged through indictment because of the secrecy of the grand jury procedure. The accused will have little time to formulate a defense or to attempt to intimidate or otherwise influence witnesses who might testify against him at the trial.

Evidence

The evidence received by a grand jury during an investigation or hearing at the state and federal level must have been legally obtained, just as is the evidence presented at preliminary examination in municipal and trial courts. Through the complaint and information process, evidence seized as a result of a violation of constitutional guarantees cannot be introduced in court. Not only can illegally obtained evidence not be introduced, but should it later be determined that such evidence was used, a conviction could be overturned [*Mapp* v. *Ohio*, 367 U.S. 643 (1961)].

That is where the distinction must be made with regard to the grand jury. In most of the states and at the federal level, there is no such requirement binding upon grand jury indictments. Although the grand jury may receive only legally obtained evidence, an indictment based on the introduction of illegal evidence will nevertheless be held valid unless it can be shown that there was no other evidence on which the indictment was returned. If there was other evidence reviewed by the grand jury that established a case against the accused, the indictment will be upheld. Some states have varied this somewhat, and illegally obtained evidence may be vulnerable, but the federal rule holds that such evidence will not jeopardize the indictment.[12] In *Blue* v. *United States*, 384 U.S. 251

[12] B. James George, *Constitutional Limitations on Evidence in Criminal Cases* (New York: Practicing Law Institute, 1969), p. 182.

(1965), the Supreme Court ruled that no one may control evidence received by the grand jury.

Over the years, many witnesses have chosen to exercise their Fifth Amendment right to refuse to testify for fear of self-incrimination. Because the grand jury relies heavily on the testimony of witnesses, such refusals have hampered investigations. The courts have ruled, however, that where a general investigation is being conducted and the scope of that investigation has yet to be narrowed to such a degree that a particular witness has been classified as a defendant, the privilege against self-incrimination does not apply. The witness, therefore, is compelled to testify under penalty of contempt for which he can be jailed for the duration of that grand jury's term. Such was the ruling of the Supreme Court in 1906 in *Hale* v. *Henkel*, 201 U.S. 43 (1906) and of the Michigan Supreme Court in 1943 in *People* v. *Robinson*, 306 Mich. 167 (1943). Other states have held that, where the sole purpose of securing evidence from a witness through his testimony is to obtain an indictment against him, such a witness may exercise his Fifth Amendment rights without fear of being compelled to answer incriminating questions. Such has been held by New York, *People* v. *De Foe*, 308 N.Y. 597 (1955) and by California, *People* v. *Calhoun*, 50 Cal. 2d 137 (1958).

Indictment Requirements

The indictment, a written accusation charging a person with the commission of a crime and presented to the court having jurisdiction by its grand jury is, in effect, the same as an information filed by the prosecutor after the accused has been bound over by a municipal court judge as a result of a preliminary hearing. The difference lies in the manner by which each is initiated. The indictment, when presented to the grand jury for consideration, is drawn into a document called a Bill. If, after hearing all of the evidence, the grand jury determines there is sufficient evidence to bring the accused to trial, the bill is endorsed as a True Bill. Should the grand jury determine there is insufficient evidence on which to base an indictment, the bill is endorsed as a No Bill and no further action is taken in the matter. While the indictment is an accusation presented by another person, usually the prosecutor, a Presentment is an accusation or investigation initiated by the grand jury of its own accord, since the grand jury can initiate its own investigations on the basis of information supplied by one or more of the grand jurors themselves.

It is not the function of the grand jury to decide the guilt or innocence of the accused, but merely to decide whether or not sufficient evidence has been presented to warrant that person being brought to trial to answer the charges against him. Should the grand jury decide there is a *prima facie* case, a True Bill is issued. There is a great deal of difference between the extent of evidence necessary to constitute a *prima facie* case and that necessary to convict an accused at a trial. In order to convict, the trial jury must be convinced that the accused is "guilty beyond a reasonable doubt." This matter has caused some concern to grand jurors, and it is something that each grand juror must continually keep in mind during an indictment hearing.

Further requirements of an indictment are that the accusation be clearly stated; the jurisdiction, time, and place of the crime be stated; and that the full name of the accused be stated. In those cases where the true name of the accused is unknown, such facts must be so stated in the indictment, and an accurate physical description be included in a John Doe indictment. When the true name of the accused is learned, that information must be entered into the court records. The indictment must spell out, in much the same manner as an information, the violations of the law alleged. Where there is more than one chargeable offense, each one must be listed separately and is termed a *count* of the indictment. For example, an indictment of a gang of armed bank robbers may result in multiple counts. First degree robbery, carrying loaded weapons, assault with deadly weapons, and conspiracy may be charged. In such a case, there would be four counts to the indictment of each of the accused, for all the responsibles may not be listed on a single indictment. A separate indictment is required for each participant in the crime, be they 2 or 20.

The indictment, once a highly technical and complicated document that few could understand and until 1733 was written in Latin, is now written in English and in a form that can be clearly understood by the average citizen. A Bill of Particulars is an additional document of an indictment. It specifies, in more detail than is specified in the indictment itself, the facts surrounding the nature of the accusations. The defendant must request that a Bill of Particulars be prepared, as it is not completed as a matter of course.

Although the federal government is obligated to the grand jury indictment process by way of the Fifth Amendment, some states have limited their use of the indictment. Since 1884 there has been a steady increase in the use of the information method of preferring charges. In that year the Supreme Court ruled that the Fourteenth Amendment did not guarantee indictment by a grand jury in the state courts [*Hurtaldo* v. *California*, 110 U.S. 516 (1884)]. While some states have limited their use of indictments, most continue to utilize the grand jury in capital and infamous crimes. Infamous crimes are those offenses that could result in punishment by imprisonment; capital crimes are those that (before the *Furman* decision) could result in the death penalty. No doubt offenses classified as capital crimes will continue to be acted on by the indictment method, since legislators in many states are revamping their statutes to conform with the specifications established in the *Furman* decision. Tennessee still utilizes grand jury indictments for offenses involving fines of more than $50 or imprisonment.[13]

The question of a waiver of the right to an indictment by the grand jury has not posed a serious problem since the U.S. Supreme Court upheld the validity of a waiver of a jury trial in 1930, in *Patton* v. *United States*, 381 U.S. 276 (1930). Thus, a serious challenge of a waiver of the grand jury indictment should not arise.

Although the information method may appear to be more popularly utilized today and may seem to be more functional, the right to an indictment by grand jury still remains at the federal level and has been established in several state constitutions as well. England, the birthplace of the grand jury, abolished the use of indictments in 1933. Some authorities feel strongly about the right to grand jury indictment, believing that no one should be prosecuted for capital or infamous crimes except by grand jury indictment, because it, "protects one of the established procedures of the common law from further inroads on the part of government attorneys with their informations."[14] Another question of interest is that of the propriety of a resubmission of evidence to the grand jury after an initial failure to indict the accused. Since the doctrine of double jeopardy does not apply to grand jury proceedings, there is no bar to such a procedure. As a general rule, however, the evidence submitted for

[13] Richard G. Sheridan, *Urban Justice* (Knoxville: The Bureau of Public Administration, The University of Tennessee, 1964), p. 70.
[14] J. A. Grant, *Our Common Law Constitution* (Boston: Boston University Press, 1960), p. 18.

reconsideration must be substantially different from that previously submitted in order to be considered.

In some cases, usually those that are highly involved, a sealed indictment may be granted to the prosecutor. This would be permissible where there can be demonstrated a strong risk of flight by the accused, or the high probability that an attempt at reprisal against witnesses will be made. When the court permits such an indictment, it is not disclosed until after all arrests that resulted from the indictment have been made.

Investigative Powers

Grand jury proceedings are *ex parte*, that is, on behalf of only one party in an action. Grand jury proceedings are conducted in behalf of the prosecution. The accused is not permitted to introduce evidence nor to present witnesses in his own behalf. Although he may volunteer to testify, he must do so without the assistance of his attorney. The attorney may remain outside the grand jury room and may be consulted each time the questioning moves to a different area, but the attorney is never allowed into the proceedings with his client. In such instances, the person waives his right against self-incrimination and must answer all questions put to him or be held in contempt.

The grand jury's power to compel witnesses to appear gives it a tremendous advantage (in conducting investigations) over the police and the prosecutor, neither of whom can compel anyone to appear for questioning unless they have been arrested. While the standard methods of conducting investigations work well enough for the police and prosecutor in routine matters, such methods are virtually useless where the more sophisticated types of crimes are to be dealt with. Bribery, blackmail, conspiracy, extortion, and the work of organized crime, as well as the investigation of corruption in office, racial issues, and riots, require the more sophisticated capabilities of the grand jury. Here the prosecutor is better able to learn the views of a representative group of people.

The grand jury has the power to compel the production of records, and has access to experienced investigators and accountants who can delve into hidden facts and figures. An experienced prosecutor can extract valuable testimony from reluctant witnesses who, but for the secret proceedings, might never arrive at a preliminary hearing in open court.[15] While such a witness may choose to exercise his Fifth Amendment rights, the grand jury can grant immunity in order to compel testimony. In such cases, the witness will be protected from prosecution for crimes revealed as a result of his testimony.

The grand jury also enjoys several privileges not permitted trial jurors. Where a trial juror may be disqualified through challenges, for cause, or through peremptory challenges because of prior knowledge concerning a case, a grand juror will not be disqualified.[16] Having a prejudice in a case, as in *Coblentz* v. *State*, 264 Md. 558 (1933), or having previously formed or expressed an opinion about a case, as in *Commonwealth* v. *Woodward*, 157 Mass. 516 (1893), will not disqualify a grand juror.

In a few states, the subpoena power of the grand jury has been taken control of by the courts themselves, but in most states, such as under New York and California statutes, the grand jury may direct the prosecutor to issue as many additional subpoenas as it feels is necessary to conduct its investigation.

The decision of a grand jury not to indict an accused on the charges presented does not prevent it from indicting that person on different charges if the jurors feel that procedure to be more advantageous. The grand jury may issue an indictment for more serious charges, for lesser charges, or may indict the accused at some later date when it has gathered further evidence against him. In a manner of speaking, a grand jury can keep a rein on too eager a prosecutor in this fashion. When the proceedings are taken out of the hands of the prosecutor, the so-called runaway grand jury determines the direction of the investigation. Though rare, such instances have occurred and with successful results.

Even the best laid plans can run afoul through outside influence, however, as in the case of a grand jury investigation and indictment in New York in 1959. There, the resulting conviction was overturned because of the method in which a confession was obtained. An acquaintance of the defendant, a police officer, took part in an extensive and deceptive interrogation after the indicted defendant surrendered himself to

---

[15] Lewis Mayers, *Shall We Amend the Fifth Amendment* (New York: Harper and Brothers, 1959), p. 38.
[16] People v. Looney, 314 Ill. 150 (1924).

the police on the advice of his attorney. Although the defendant repeatedly requested to see his attorney, the interrogation continued until a confession was elicited. The Supreme Court ruled that the absence of an indicted person's attorney directly impairs that person's constitutional guarantee under the Sixth Amendment, as in *Spano* v. *New York*, 360 U.S. 315 (1959).

As a practical matter, there are no time constraints imposed on an investigation, although they are usually not longer than the term of the grand jury itself. If a complicated investigation is involved, however, a grand jury may pass the investigation on to a succeeding jury, which will continue that investigation as its own. The grand jury must observe the statute of limitations, as do the police and prosecutor. Since the majority of the grand jury's investigations involve infamous or very sophisticated crimes—for which the statute of limitations is usually three to six years—there is little concern about time constraints. There should be a distinction made, however, in that once an indictment is issued, the Sixth Amendment requires that the defendant be brought to trial as quickly as possible. Any unnecessary delay could undo months of precise and costly investigation.

The grand jury plays a greater role, and is employed more consistently, at the federal level than at the state level. Federal statutes do not often deal with crimes of violence. They are concerned with the regulatory and tax statutes that frequently involve the conspiratorial efforts of several persons and over a lengthy period of time. The more advanced capabilities of the federal investigative agencies (any of whom may be called in to assist in a phase of the investigation), combined with the advantage of secrecy and the power to compel both the appearance and testimony of reluctant witnesses, lend an invaluable and positive effort toward the furtherance of justice by our court systems. And if a witness refuses to testify, he may be jailed for contempt until he decides to answer the questions put to him. While the commitment is usually specified, such as four months, the remainder of the time will be cancelled when the witness agrees to testify. Should he serve out the full commitment, he will again be brought before the grand jury and can be recommitted should he continue to refuse to testify. As has been pointed out, some states have permitted the accused to invoke his right against self-incrimination if subpoenaed before the grand jury. Still other state courts have held that if the purpose for issuing a subpoena is merely to gather evidence on which to base an indictment against that person, he may obtain a quashing, or voiding, of the subpoena. The same holds at the federal level, although the defendant may still be called before the grand jury. In such cases, the prosecutor is required to advise him that he may refuse to answer incriminating questions without fear of being held in contempt. Such a warning is not required of other witnesses. When the grand jury's investigation is still in its preliminary stages, and a witness called to testify is not yet considered a defendant but is subsequently indicted, that indictment will stand although he was not advised he could withhold incriminating testimony. The reason given is that he was, at the time he gave his testimony, not a defendant but merely a witness.

The grand jury is not limited to the investigation of criminal matters; it delves into civil matters as well. Part of its function is to conduct periodic inspections of such public institutions as county hospitals and jails, in an effort to determine the methods being employed in the management of public funds and to look into the conditions under which the facilities are being maintained. Such investigations would not normally result in an indictment, but in a presentment. Their findings are of value in that, once made public, there is usually sufficient influence and public interest to result in quick action being taken to correct poor or improper conditions, revitalize poor management techniques, or restructure the allocation of expenditures. Some states, by statute, direct that the grand jury conduct annual audits of county governmental agency records and accounts. They may employ experts, such as accountants, auditors, and appraisers, to assist them in their investigations. They may also review the salaries of county officials, such as the district attorney, county assessor, county auditor, and board of supervisors, to determine the needs for increases or decreases.

In most states the grand jury is also required by statute to present a final report outlining all of their findings with respect to the county government, and to present that report to the presiding judge of the superior court and the board of supervisors at the end of their term. The board of supervisors is then required, within a specified time period, to comment on the findings of the grand jury; all elective officials of the county involved must report to the board of supervisors on the findings relevant to their offices. All of these reports are then presented to the presiding superior court judge who empanelled that grand jury, and a copy of their findings is placed on permanent file in the office of the county clerk.

In a sense, then, of its two primary functions—investigating criminal charges and conducting periodic inspections and investigations of public institutions—the function in which the grand jury spends the majority of its time today is in its role as a "watchdog" of county governmental affairs.[17]

[17] Bruce T. Olson, "The California Grand Jury: An Analysis and Evaluation of Its Watchdog Function," Unpublished Masters Thesis, The University of California, Berkeley, 1966, p. 3.

Student Checklist

1. Can you list five arguments in favor of the grand jury system?
2. Are you able to list four arguments that set forth the reasons for abolishing the grand jury?
3. Can you identify the two methods utilized in the selection of grand jurors?
4. Can you list the qualifications that an individual must possess to become a juror?
5. Are you able to contrast the type of evidence that can be received by a grand jury with that which can be presented in a trial?
6. Can you list the requirements of an indictment?
7. Are you able to distinguish between a True Bill and a No Bill?

Topics for Discussion

1. Discuss the reasons for secrecy in grand jury proceedings.
2. Discuss the extent of the investigative powers of the grand jury.
3. Discuss the advantages of the grand jury.
4. Discuss the qualifications needed to serve on a grand jury.

ANNOTATED BIBLIOGRAPHY

Abraham, Henry J. *The Judicial Process*, 2nd ed. New York: Oxford University Press, 1968. This book analyzes and evaluates the main institutions affecting the administration of justice.

Brice, Roger T. "Grand Jury Proceedings: The Prosecutor, the Trial Judge and Undue Influence," *The University of Chicago Law Review, 39,* No. 4 (Summer 1972). Explores the role of the prosecutor and the trial judge in the proceedings of the grand jury. Takes neither the pro nor the con arguments regarding the overall merits of the grand jury, but instead reviews these key figures in view of the undue influence that could be brought to bear in *ex parte* proceedings. Explains how the courts have dealt with bias asserted through the undue influence doctrine.

Frank, Jerome. *Courts on Trial.* New York: Atheneum, 1969. Deals with court functions. A good analysis of procedural reforms, the jury systems, and legal precedents.

Lamb, Karl. *The People Maybe: Seeking Democracy in America.* Belmont, Calif.: Wadsworth Publishing, 1971. The author examines the more ignoble features of the American tradition in the hope that such examination may help us to avoid the repetition of past mistakes.

Nagel, Stuart S. *The Rights of the Accused.* Beverly Hills: Sage Publications, 1972. The defendant's rights from before his first court appearance to his posttrial rights, are thoroughly explored.

Organized Crime Control Act of 1970, Public Law 91-452, Washington, D.C.: U.S. Govt. Printing Office, 1970. As a result of the increased sophistication of organized crime in the United States and the difficulty in dealing with the ever-increasing problem, the Congress sought to find a method by which to better combat the problem. That method evolved into Public Law 91-452 and was enacted into law on October 15, 1970. It expands the use of grand jury proceedings in special cases that are defined as are immunity grants, compelled testimony, and sources of evidence.

Olson, Bruce T. "The California Grand Jury: An Analysis and Evaluation of Its Watchdog Function." Unpublished Masters Thesis, The University of California, Berkeley, 1966. An extensive treatment of the civil investigative side of the grand jury as it operates in California. Discusses the origin of this all-important function as well as the organization, selection, empanelling, and financing methods involved. Presents an analysis of the final reports submitted by the grand jury in each of California's 58 counties. Describes the grand jury as an institutional hybrid.

Report of the January 1970 Grand Jury, United States District Court Northern District of Illinois Eastern Division, Washington, D.C.: U.S. Govt. Printing Office, 1970. A report of the role of the grand jury in the investigation of the December 4, 1969 killing of two Black Panther Party members in Chicago by law enforcement officers. Contains the findings of the grand jury after hearing nearly 100 witnesses and examining more than 130 exhibits. Presents recommendations on possible solutions to the law enforcement problems disclosed by the investigation.

Tafoya, William L. "The Grand Jury and the Watergate Case," *Administration of Justice Journal 1*, No. 1 (Spring, 1973). Expresses the opinion that the grand jury is not an outdated institution of the court system. Suggests that although the "information" is beneficial to the administration of justice, it cannot be regarded as a utopia. Suggests that grand jury proceedings are free of the kind of political pressure that can be brought to bear in routine investigations. Highlights the ramifications of the grand jury investigation of the Watergate Case.

Younger, Richard D. *The People's Panel*, Providence: American History Research Center, Brown University Press, 1963. Presents the development of the grand jury from twelfth-century England and draws it forward in time. Special treatment is given to its momentum in America by reviewing important stages in its maturation; its Colonial, Revolution, and post-Revolution growth, as well as its gain in power through the transition of a new nation struggling with frontier America, the slavery question, Civil War, Reconstruction, and implications of the twentieth century.

The study of this chapter will enable you to:

1. List six advantageous derivatives of the judicial process.
2. Define the term complaint.
3. Distinguish between an indictment and an information.
4. Identify the five ways that an individual is subject to the jurisdiction of a state.
5. List the four major areas of jurisdiction for the federal government.
6. Identify the various types of pleas.
7. Differentiate between posttrial discovery and posttrial motions.

13
The Judicial Process

Our judiciary system gained recognition, validity, and power when the U.S. Constitution was enacted in 1787. Through social acceptance, this judiciary system has not only remained independent of alien forces, but has strengthened the basic constitutional concepts that all men are created equal and are guaranteed equal protection under the law. What has been developed and tempered over the years is a legal system constructed in such a manner to protect those who are innocent, and to formally exercise proper action in the case of the guilty.

There are basically two positions that society may take in dealing with one who is accused of a crime: ". . . either by presuming his innocence until it has effectively succeeded in proving him guilty under due process of law, or by presuming his guilt unless he successfully disproves that assumption under similar process."[1] Thus, instead of being of an inquisitorial nature wherein the judge is the leading figure and the accused is presumed guilty until proving himself innocent, our system of criminal procedure in America is essentially accusatory. The accusatory system is one in which demands are made on the government to ". . . establish guilt by evidence independently and freely secured and may not by coercion prove its charge against an accused out of his own mouth."[2] Sometimes referred to as the adversary system, this type of process ". . . presumes that both sides will be vigorously represented so that a neutral judge can arrive at the truth."[3]

[1] Henry J. Abraham, *The Judicial Process* (New York: Oxford University Press, 1962), p. 98.
[2] Ibid., p. 99.
[3] Stuart S. Nagel, *The Rights of the Accused* (Beverly Hills: Sage Publications, 1972), p. 18.

The American court system proceeds in a manner referred to as a judicial process. This is a process whereby the matter being disputed is heard and acted on by a court. The matter involves one or more parties. Many different sources may activate the machinery of the judiciary, including the plaintiff, petitioner, applicant, "the people" (the legal title for a group of people seeking court action), and the defendant himself. According to Roscoe Pound, in *Justice According to the Law*, there are six advantageous derivatives of our judicial process. These are as follows:

1. It is a process of applying a logical and systematic approach to a body of knowledge developed by both reason and experience.
2. Guidance is provided by a judge whose legal training relates actions in specific cases to known principles and standards.
3. Judicial decisions are subject to review by other legally trained persons, often sitting *en banc* (as a group) to mitigate individual prejudices and misconceptions.
4. Case records of judicial action are public.
5. Decisions as well as the grounds and reasons for them are published by appellate courts for the information and guidance of every interested person or agency.
6. Judges can resist public excitement and hysteria.[4]

Accusatory Pleadings

"In most criminal proceedings, the sequence of events begins with the arrest of the defendant by a police officer,"[5] which, in many instances, is proceeded by a trial. However, if the complaint of the arresting officer is not sufficient to proceed to the trial stage, formal proceedings must be taken by the prosecutor or by a grand jury. (The trial will usually follow in misdemeanor or minor offense cases, whereas the formal accusation process is usually required in more serious offenses.) These stages of formal accusations may take the form of an indictment or an information.

[4] Paul B. Weston and Kenneth M. Wells, *The Administration of Justice* (Englewood Cliffs, N.J.: Prentice-Hall, 1967), p. 121.
[5] Lewis Mayers, *The Machinery of Justice* (Englewood Cliffs, N.J.: Prentice-Hall, 1963), p. 52.

Complaint

The original complaint may be made by persons other than the police, including the victim of the criminal act, the prosecutor, or any private person. This complaint is usually superseded by a formal complaint. "The formal complaint is a charge, preferred before a magistrate having jurisdiction, that the person named (or an unknown person) has committed a specified offense, with an offer to prove the facts, to the end that a prosecution may be instituted."[6] The complaint must clearly state all the facts constituting the offense charged, since it is the evidence by which a warrant will be issued. According to the legal encyclopedias, "The term complaint has been characterized as a technical term descriptive of proceedings before magistrates and may be defined as meaning cause of action, also the story of the cause or causes of action, and specifically as a formal allegation or charge against a party made or presented to the appropriate court or officer as for a wrong done or a crime committed."[7] Although the original complaint may have been signed by an officer, citizen, or victim, the formal complaint is signed and issued by the prosecutor.

Indictment

The indictment is "a written accusation of a crime drawn up by the public prosecuting attorney and submitted to the grand jury, and by them found and presented on oath or affirmation as a true bill."[8] The grand jury is authorized to find the indictment when prima facie evidence is revealed in such a manner that would warrant a conviction by a trial jury.[9] The indictment is issued by the grand jury and it is signed by its foreman. The object of the indictment is to fairly inform the accused of the charge(s) against him so that he may adequately prepare his defense. *Corpus Juris Secundum* states that a defendant may, upon receiving the indictment, "avail himself of his conviction or acquittal as a protection

---

[6] Francis J. Ludes, ed., *Corpus Juris Secundum* (Brooklyn: The American Law Book Co., West Publishing, 1967), pp. 356-357.

[7] Ibid., pp. 116-117.

[8] Ronald J. Kiser, ed., *Corpus Juris Secundum,* Vol. 42 (Brooklyn: The American Law Book Co., West Publishing, 1944), pp. 835-836.

[9] Weston and Wells, *The Administration of Justice,* p. 72.

against further prosecution for the same cause; and to inform the court of the facts alleged so that it may decide whether they are sufficient to support a conviction, if one is to be had."[10]

The indictment should describe the defendant by his full name (or description), state the place of the offense, state the time of the occurrence, and all other supporting facts constituting the crime. A common state constitutional provision is that "a grand jury indictment is required in all felony cases, with an information by the district attorney being the ordinary method of accusation for misdemeanors."[11] However, about 40 percent of the states give an option to the prosecutor to proceed by information in lieu of grand jury indictment. For example, in California, where such an alternative is allowed, informations are used in 97 percent of all felony cases.[12]

A presentment is another type of accusation that is similar to the indictment. A presentment is "a notice taken by a grand jury of an offense from its own knowledge or observation, or of its own motion on information from others."[13] The indictment, different from the presentment, is preferred at the request of the government, and it is usually initiated by a prosecutor to a grand jury. The grand jury will then either find the allocation to be true (True Bill) or it is rejected (ignored—No Bill).

Information

An information is a written accusation of a crime preferred by the district attorney or other public prosecuting officer without the intervention of the grand jury.[14] The information is the "formal notification to the accused of the exact charge(s) against him,"[15] given to him so he may prepare his defense. One difference between the indictment and the information is that the former is presented by a grand jury on their oath, whereas the latter is presented by any public prosecuting officer on his oath with-

---

[10] Kiser, *Corpus Juris Secundum*, p. 836.
[11] Delmar Karlen, *Anglo-American Criminal Justice* (New York: Oxford University Press, 1967), p. 150.
[12] Ibid., p. 149.
[13] Ludes, *Corpus Juris Secundum*, p. 492.
[14] Kiser, *Corpus Juris Secundum*, p. 851.
[15] Marshall Houts, *From Arrest to Release* (Springfield, Ill.: Charles C. Thomas, 1958), p. 97.

out grand jury intervention. The information must state the location of the offense charged as well as the location of the trial, the day the offense was committed, the names of the accused, plus other supporting information.

The complaint, indictment, and information are all formal accusations. They constitute the formal charge to which the defendant must respond at his arraignment before the magistrate who issued the warrant.[16]

Jurisdiction and Venue

Jurisdiction is the power of a governmental agency to deal with some legal matter. Specifically pertaining to the judicial process, jurisdiction is the authority of the court to hear and determine a case. Section 1917 of the California Code of Civil Procedure states that the jurisdiction sufficient to sustain a record ". . . is jurisdiction over the cause, over the parties, and over the thing, when a specific thing is the subject of the judgment."[17] A person can be prosecuted in a state when he is subject to its jurisdiction. One is subject to the jurisdiction of the state when:

1. He has committed an offense in whole or in part in the state.
2. He has committed an inchoate in the state to be completed in another state.
3. When his conduct outside the state constitutes an attempt to commit a crime within the state.
4. When his conduct outside the state constitutes a conspiracy to commit a crime within the state and the act is committed within the state in furtherance of the conspiracy, or when the presence of a conspiracy in the state is in furtherance of the criminal design.
5. When the conduct of a citizen outside the state is prohibited by the law of the state of which he is a citizen and its courts obtain *in personam* jurisdiction over him.[18]

Generally, federal courts have jurisdiction over those cases that

---

[16] Edward Eldefonso, Alan Coffey and James Sullivan, *Police and the Criminal Law* (Pacific Palisades: Goodyear Publishing Company, 1972), p. 49.
[17] State of California, *California Justice Court Manual* (California: Judicial Council of California, 1969), p. 5.
[18] M. Cherif Bassiouni, *Criminal Law and its Processes* (Springfield, Ill.: Charles C Thomas, 1969), p. 329.

involve crimes committed within the United States, its territories and possessions, and on ships of our nation. The state courts have jurisdiction over those cases that involve crimes committed within the state against its statutes. Thus, the geographical location of the offense often determines which court will hear the case. The federal courts have criminal jurisdiction only when it is specifically expressed by Congress. Congress has conferred jurisdiction on the federal government to punish for the following:

1. Offenses against the laws of nations.
2. Offenses against the federal sovereign government.
3. Offenses against the person of individuals and property.
4. Offenses against public justice.[19]

Venue should be regarded as a procedural matter affecting both the location of the trial as well as the location in which the jury is selected. "Generally, a person has a right to be tried where the offense took place unless he waives that right by failing to object to the change of trial location or by asking to have the trial changed to a place where he feels he can get a fairer trial."[20] It should be mentioned that venue, unlike other rights of a defendant, is a privilege and not a right. Yet if the defense can prove that their case was prejudiced because of the venue, the outcome may be reversed and render the decision voidable, whereas if a violation of a jurisdiction rule is revealed, the decision is nullified. Venue is also basically the same for both federal courts and the states courts except that the former is regulated by federal legislation. Changing venue is also a privilege given to the accused in order for him to have his case transferred before trial, so that he may obtain a fair and impartial trial.[21] In this case, the jurisdiction would remain the same affecting only the location. The reason for a change would simply be a prejudiced court or community.

Types of Jurisdiction

Several types of jurisdiction affect criminal procedure. They are jurisdiction of subject matter, jurisdiction of the person, and territorial jurisdiction.

[19] Ibid., pp. 332-333.
[20] Neil C. Chamelin and Kenneth R. Evans, *Criminal Law for Policemen* (Englewood Cliffs, N.J.: Prentice-Hall, 1971), p. 24.
[21] Bassiouni, *Criminal Law and its Processes*, p. 335.

Jurisdiction of Subject Matter. Before one can stand trial in a court, that court must have jurisdiction over the subject matter. Usually, the nature of the offense stated in the complaint determines the jurisdiction. The legislature, limited by constitutional principles, determines which court may hear which matters. "It is possible for the legislature to confer subject matter jurisdiction on their courts in such a way as to create overlapping jurisdiction or concurrent jurisdiction."[22] If this occurs, jurisdiction is given to the first court that assumes responsibility over the matter. Subject matter jurisdiction in some states is decided merely on a differentiation between a felony and a misdemeanor. Other states, which may not be consistent in distinguishing the felony from the misdemeanor, will specifically state jurisdiction. A common practice, then, would be decided jurisdiction based on the possible penalty. The first court in which a case can be heard is referred to as a court with original jurisdiction. If an appeal materializes, a court with appellate jurisdiction then takes control over the case.

Jurisdiction Over the Person. No court can validly try a man for a crime unless that defendant is in the courtroom and is known to the court.[23] The court may acquire jurisdiction over the defendant by arrest with or without a warrant. Jurisdiction may also gain validity if the defendant voluntarily appears in court after a citation or like document is presented to him. He may consent to legal jurisdiction of the court by waiving all rights to complain of an illegal arrest. However, unless the court has jurisdiction of the subject matter, the consent is invalid.

Territorial Jurisdiction. Territorial jurisdiction is granted to that state in which the offense was committed, and in accordance with that state's laws only. But exceptions are always found. For example, if a crime involves two or more states, the territorial jurisdiction, as stated previously, would be difficult to determine. Some modern statutes have changed the common law rule by enacting statutes providing, in effect, that any crime begun in that state but completed in another is a chargeable crime in the completing state.

[22] Chamelin and Evans, *Criminal Law for Policemen*, p. 22.
[23] Ibid., p. 21.

Extradition

With the increase of both criminal activity and mobility, extradition has become an important part of our judicial process. Extradition, or interstate rendition, is the process through which one state by virtue of a legal process surrenders to another state an individual accused or convicted of an offense outside the jurisdiction of the asylum state and within the jurisdiction of the requesting state that is competent to try and punish him and, accordingly, demands his surrender for that purpose. This may also pertain internationally.

Article IV of the U.S. Constitution cites the need for each of the states to recognize with "full faith and credit" the public acts, records, and judicial proceedings of every other state, and specifically provides for a procedure of extradition and rendition among the states: "A person charged in any state with treason, felony, or other crime, who shall flee from justice, and be found in another state, shall on demand of the executive authority of the state from which he fled, be delivered up, to be removed to the state having jurisdiction of the crime."[24]

Interstate extradition or rendition may be implemented by a written application to the executive officer of a state—its governor—by the proper prosecutor, asking for a requisition upon another state for the return of the person sought. The application must contain all the pertinent information on the matter, including name and description of the person charged, the offense, the time and location of the offense, as well as a certification that the ends of justice require the arrest and return of the accused to the requesting state.

International extradition is honored if it is specifically negotiated between the nations. According to international law, a duty is imposed on any country to return a person who has sought asylum in that country for protection against facing criminal charges of another country if it is within the policy and procedures of their treaty. As of January 1, 1968, the United States was party to extradition treaties with 84 nations.[25] The application for international extradition should be directed to the Secretary of State of the United States, with a descriptive outline similar to

---

[24] California State Senate, *Constitution of the United States* (California: California Office of State Printing, 1972), p. 48.

[25] B. James George, Jr. and Ira A. Cohen, *.The Prosecutors Sourcebook,* Vol. 2 (New York: Practising Law Institute, 1969), p. 483.

that of a state extradition application. With regard to international extradition, uniformity of offenses does not exist and each nation, in its separate treaty, will outline which offenses will activate an extradition process. When a new nation is to be included in an established treaty, a retroactive effect will occur. This is where a criminal will be returned for prosecution to the party asking (usually where the offense occurred) whereas before the criminal could not be extradited.

Court Appearances and Proceedings

There are several transactions that one may make regarding court proceedings and appearances. These transactions will be discussed in the following pages.

Purpose: Rights of the Defendant
The basic purpose of a court proceeding is to determine if the defendant is guilty or not guilty of the crime charged. Through a court of law the person shall be entitled to both due process of the law and equal protection under law in the determination of guilt or innocence. According to Article I, Section 13 of the Constitution of the State of California, "In criminal prosecutions, in any court whatever, the party accused shall have the right to a speedy and public trial; to have the process of the court to compel the attendance of witnesses in his behalf, and to appear and defend, in person and with counsel."[26] It further states that "no person shall be twice put in jeopardy for the same offense; nor be compelled, in any criminal case, to be a witness against himself; nor be deprived of life, liberty, or property without due process of law."[27] The U.S. Constitution, in the Fifth and Sixth Amendments, expresses the same rights for the accused.

"Due process of the law" is probably the most important phrase when we speak of a defendant's rights. Arthur Blumberg, in *Criminal Justice*, simplifies the rights and privileges of a defendant. The due proc-

[26] State of California, *Constitution of the State of California* (California: Government Printing Office, 1971), p. 129.
[27] Ibid., p. 129.

ess requirements, as they have been wrought in the courts and through statutes and the federal and state constitutions, may be stated as follows:

1. Definiteness of penal statutes and codes.
2. Accusation must give notice.
3. Arraignment with all possible speed.
4. The privilege against self-incrimination.
5. The right to the assistance of counsel.
6. Trial by jury.
7. Right to call witnesses and confront adverse witnesses through cross-examination.
8. Right to an impartial judge and prosecutor.
9. Right to reasonable bail.
10. A presumption of innocence.[28]

The Wickersham Crime Commission, in its report, points out similar rights and privileges that need to be granted to the defendant in a criminal proceeding.

Arraignments

The arraignment is usually the first step in a formal trial process. "If an indictment or information is filed against the defendant, he is required to appear before a judge of the court which has jurisdiction to hear and dispose of the case."[29] The purpose of the arraignment is both to inform the defendant of the charge against him and to obtain a reply. Due process of law does not require that a formal arraignment take place in order to gain a valid conviction, therefore, the arraignment is one of the rights of a defendant which may be waived. The formal complaint, present-ment, indictment, or information is read to the defendant, and he is asked to respond in the form of a plea.

Types of Plea. Usually unknown to the layman, there are several alterna-tives that a defendant may utilize in the plea stage of the arraignment. These pleas may be guilty, not guilty, *nolo contendere* (no contest), stand mute, or motions of abatement, demurrer, quash, or dismissal.

"A plea of guilty is an admission of every material allegation in

---

[28] Abraham S. Blumberg, *Criminal Justice* (Chicago: Quadrangle, 1967), pp. 22-25.
[29] Ronald L. Carlson, *Criminal Justice for Police* (Cincinnati: W. H. Anderson, 1970), pp. 2-3.

the accusatory pleading."[30] "The guilty plea has become an important factor in the administration of American criminal law,"[31] and it is stated that guilty pleas are most common in both federal and state courts. A guilty plea is only held valid if given voluntarily. "The import of this requirement is that the plea reflect the considered choice of the accused, free of any inducement or factor that unfairly influences or overcomes his will. A guilty plea induced through coercion or promises, or otherwise unfairly obtained, or given through ignorance, fear, or inadvertence is involuntary and inconsistent with the due process of law."[32]

Not guilty is another common plea of the defense whereby the defense is denying the accusations made against him. The plea of not guilty would indicate that the accused demands a trial in a court of law to prove his innocence. The defense may make a plea of not guilty with stipulations on the plea such as insanity, self-defense, a provable alibi, intoxication, statute of limitations, or double jeopardy. These defenses can only be proven through the trial process.

Nolo contendere is a plea accepted in some jurisdictions in which the defendant asserts that he does not wish to argue or contest the issue of guilt or innocence. "This operates as a plea of guilty and authorizes the court to enter judgment and sentence upon the plea. The advantage of entering such a plea is that the defendant may subsequently assert his innocence in other criminal or civil proceedings and it will not be considered an admission of guilt."[33]

Standing mute (the defendant says nothing), is another indirect plea. If the defendant refuses to plea when he is arraigned, the court automatically enters a plea of not guilty.

The defendant may plead abatement, file a demurrer, move to quash, or to dismiss the accusation. The purpose is to say that the accusation is defective and that because of the defect the court can not properly charge the defendant.

Negotiated Plea. The negotiated plea (plea bargaining) is usually used for deserving defendants, but this is not the only reason for negotiating

---

[30] Ibid., p. 49.
[31] Livingston Hall et al., *Basic Criminal Procedure* (St: Paul: West Publishing, 1969), p. 569.
[32] Bassiouni, *Criminal Law and its Processes*, p. 457.
[33] Ibid., p. 458.

a plea. Plea bargaining gives numerous advantages to the administration of the court. The two primary concerns here would be cost and time consumption of supporting a criminal trial. The three major types of plea bargaining that would benefit the defendant are (1) recommendation of sentence, (2) plea of guilty to a lesser included offense, and (3) "the dismissal of charges in the indictment or other charging paper in return for certain considerations such as a promise to become a prosecution witness."[34]

Preliminary Examination

Being provided for by the constitution, statute, or by the rule of court, most states assert that any person arrested on a criminal charge is entitled to a preliminary examination (judicial inquiry) before a magistrate and without unnecessary delay. The purpose of such an examination is to determine "whether a crime has been committed in fact, and if so, whether there is probable cause or good reason to believe that the accused is guilty of its commission."[35] The preliminary examination does not determine the guilt or innocence of the accused, but merely the validity and existence of probable cause. This process is not a criminal prosecution; it is simply designed to prevent escape until the legal body can decide on the probable cause and guilt issues. If, after the preliminary examination and investigation, probable cause can not be found to exist against the accused, the charge(s) must be dismissed and the accused released. This stage also guarantees that the courts will mediate between the defendant and the source of prosecution to insure the integrity of the adversary system.

Grand Jury Indictment

According to the U.S. Constitution and many state constitutions, the grand jury is the main accusatory body. Historically, the grand jury is responsible for two primary duties:

> 1. To determine if the accused should stand trial because there is reason to believe that he had committed a felony.

---

[34] Bassiouni, *Criminal Law and its Processes*, p. 459.
[35] George and Cohen, *The Prosecutor's Sourcebook*, p. 435.

2. To protect the innocent from unfounded accusations and harrass-
ment by the state when there is no reason to believe that a felony has
been committed.[36]

The prosecutor will serve as an advisor or moderator to the grand
jury. The grand jury inquiry will call witnesses who are placed under
oath and questioned by any juror or the prosecutor to ascertain facts
pertinent to issuing an indictment or finding no ground to issue one. This
whole process excludes the public, the defense counsel, the defendant,
and in some cases, the witness' attorney. After the grand jury hears the
witnesses and completes the investigation, it will decide if there are sufficient grounds to issue an indictment. A majority of no less than 12 jurors
must vote. If evidence shows that action should be taken, the foreman of
the grand jury will write on the indictment "A True Bill" and sign his
name. If lack of evidence is the result and the grand jury refuses to issue
an indictment, "Not A True Bill" will be written on the document.

Right to a Speedy Trial

The right to a speedy trial is guaranteed by the federal and most state
constitutions. The U.S. Constitution deals with this matter, incorporated
as part of the due process clause, in the Sixth Amendment. The purposes
served by the Sixth Amendment guarantee was delineated in *United
States* v. *Ewell.* As stated in this case as an important safeguard, "To
prevent undue and oppressive incarceration prior to trial, to minimize
anxiety and concern accompanying public accusations, and to limit the
possibilities that long delays will impair the ability of the accused to
defend himself."[37] It is important to add that, "The right of a speedy trial
is necessarily relative. It is consistent with delays and depends upon circumstances. It secures rights to a defendant. It does not preclude the
rights of public justice."[38]

States guarantee the right to a speedy trial in procedural statutes.
Thus, in most cases, the setting of a time limitation is incorporated into
the general clause and basic right to a speedy trial. There is no specific

[36] Bassiouni, *Criminal Law and its Processes,* p. 449.
[37] Joseph G. Cook, *Constitutional Rights of the Accused* (Rochester: The Lawyers
Co-Operative Publishing Company, 1972), p. 499.
[38] Lloyd L. Weinreb, *Criminal Process—Cases, Comment, Questions* (Mineola:
The Foundation Press, 1969), p. 505.

time limitation for this right in the U.S. Constitution and the violation of a speedy trial will depend on the nature and circumstances of the delay. Up until 1967, "the right to a speedy trial in state courts was not available under the Sixth Amendment to the U.S. Constitution, but was looked upon rather as a matter of fundamental fairness and due process."[39]

Pretrial Discovery

Pretrial discovery is a process where one party may attempt to learn of evidence in the other party's case. It was only a recent charge that pretrial discovery was an allowable practice in the courts. Reasons for limiting pretrial discovery varied. It was thought that this process may enable the defense either to acquire perjured testimony or to alter or fabricate evidence that would be used in the case.

The landmark decision in *People* v. *Riser,* 47 Cal. 2nd 566 (1956) stated that, "For the prosecutor to keep evidence undisclosed partakes of the nature of a game rather than judiscial procedure. The state in its might and power ought to be, and is, too zealous of according the defendant a fair and impartial trial to hinder him in intelligently preparing his defense and in availing himself of all competent, material evidence that tends to throw light on the subject matter of the trial."[40] In California, pretrial discovery is an ordinary procedure between the prosecution and defense. Today, all it takes to disclose the opponent's evidence is a written or oral request, which is granted in almost all cases.

The Trial

The trial is no longer a process for the accused to prove his innocence by ordeal. The trial today is a humane process where the defendant is innocent until proven guilty. Bound by numerous proceedings, the court and trial process is complicated. Two basic methods of trial exist in our court system. One is the trial without a jury, usually for misdemeanant cases or nonserious offenses, and the other is trial by jury, which applies to all

[39] Bassiouni, *Criminal Law and its Processes*, p. 479.
[40] Weston and Wells, *The Administration of Justice*, p. 78.

serious cases. In the event that a case is heard without a jury, the judge will make the decision.

Briefly and simplified, the following is the chronological order of a jury trial proceeding:

1. The empaneling, examining, and administration of oath of a jury.
2. The opening statements (facts) of the prosecution.
3. The opening statements (facts) of the defense.
4. Prosecution presents its evidence with direct examination by the prosecution of its witnesses and cross-examination of the witnesses by the defense.
5. Defense presents its counterattack with direct examination of its witnesses and cross-examination by the prosecution of the witnesses.
6. Reopening of case if necessary.
7. Closing arguments of defense and prosecution.
8. Jury given instructions.
9. Jury returns the verdict.
10. Judgment is entered.

Discovery at Trial

Evidence in most criminal cases is produced orally and is based on recall of what took place. Real evidence (bullets, weapon, merchandise) and written evidence (such as records or documents) may also be introduced, although not as readily as oral evidence. Every litigant is responsible in the elucidation of the truth, which may be done by presenting all possible evidence.

> Nothing can be treated as evidence which is not introduced as such, although that which is necessarily obvious to them is evidence although not presented in the usual manner. The assumptions and suggestions of counsel do not take the place of evidence.[41]

Both the defendant and prosecution should be allowed to introduce any evidence relevant to the case, especially when one has a right to question the issue. Evidence or discovery at the trial is usually accepted if its introduction does not cause delay, hinder the proceedings, or cause prejudice to the opponent.

[41] Ludes, *Corpus Juris Secundum*, p. 156.

Posttrial Discovery

In some instances new evidence is discovered after the trial is over. Generally, in this situation the case will stand closed and the defendant will not be allowed to be retried. However, there are exceptions to the rule. For example, some states provide a certain amount of time after the trial for defense motions of this nature. Usually, this time stipulation for the posttrial motion is limited. The Federal Rules and Procedure for the U.S. Magistrates states that in misdemeanant cases, there is a six-month time allotment for motions for a new trial based on newly discovered evidence.

Sentencing Hearing

After a defendant pleads guilty or is found guilty by the court or jury, the next step in the trial proceedings is the sentence. At the sentencing hearing, the defense counsel will usually argue in favor of a specific sentence for his client—one that is usually of a lenient nature. The defendant is also given a chance to address the judge and speak in his own behalf. The judge, at such a hearing, is given many alternatives in sentencing the defendant. One alternative may include suspending an already imposed sentence of incarceration pending good behavior of the defendant. Other alternatives may include levying a monetary fine, merely sentencing the defendant to the stipulated sentence, or granting the defendant probation. The judge will use his discretion in sentencing the defendant, always seeking the best alternative available in the best interest of the defendant, the court, and society. In cases where the indeterminate sentence is applied, the judge may sentence the defendant to the maximum, leaving the discretion in the hands of the parole board.

Court Role of the Probation Officer

The presentence investigation is usually where the probation officer becomes involved with the court. In determining the best sentencing alternative available for the defendant, a probation officer will usually investigate the background of an offender and present the results of that investigation to the court. Thus, the judge, by the time of sentencing, will have had a chance to review information about the defendant. The background investigation will include many aspects of the defendant's personal life; for example, the defendant's prior criminal record and personal composition, including areas of economic condition, family status, education, employment history, residential stability, military history, religious practices, medical status, and other pertinent information. This investigation is referred to as the presentence report.

The utilization of the presentence report shows no historical consistency. Some courts order an investigation whereas others refuse to let a presentence report influence their decision. Sometimes manpower shortages or a lack of funds will prevent the court from obtaining such a report. In such a case, since the proceeding is an informal hearing, character witnesses may be presented in lieu of a report. In most cases, as one can readily see, the sentencing hearing is primarily for the benefit of the defendant—especially when presentence reports are used.

Posttrial Motions and Appeals

Motions are usually in order after the deliberation and verdict is pronounced. Two common motions are moves for a new trial or for a mistrial. Common mistakes that may cause a new trial or mistrial are numerous. The judge may have instructed the jury improperly; evidence may have been wrongfully excluded or included; misconduct of the jury; the defendant may have been absent during a portion of the trial; plus many other technicalities that may have occurred during the course of the trial.

The appeal is a process of obtaining a review of the proceedings of a lower court by a superior or higher court. An appeal is based on a question of law usually stemming from the procedure of the trial itself. The appellate court, in deciding the appeal, does not assume the defendant innocent, as he was before the original trial. The reason for the appeal is to decide if the jury could draw a conclusion with the evidence presented during the judicial process. It also examines if the conclusion may have been arrived at erroneously. The end result should be the prime concern, however. If a case is appealed in an inferior court the case will probably be tried in a court of general jurisdiction. If the case is appealed in a court of general jurisdiction the appeal will be heard in a state appellate court. If the appeal arises in a state appellate court the case is heard in the state supreme court.

Generally the decision of the state supreme court is final. In some instances, however, the case may be considered in the U.S. Supreme

Court. The decisions open to the appellate court vary. It may affirm or reverse the judgment, or it may modify or reduce the degree of offense or punishment. The court may also set aside, affirm, or modify the proceedings around judgment, and it may even order a new trial.

Postconviction Hearings

The purpose of a postconviction hearing act "is to provide adequate nontechnical procedures by which persons incarcerated in penal institutions can obtain a hearing for review of alleged denials of substantive rights which resulted during their incarceration."[42]

A specific format is designated for those who wish to have their case reviewed. Stipulations such as form, information needed, and time limitation for submittal are laid down and must be strictly followed. If one fails to comply with the set stipulations, his chance for review may be terminated. "Many jurisdictions do not afford adequate means for review of questions of due process or denial of constitutional rights after regular methods of appellate review have been exhausted. Foreclosure of the convict's rights in these instances is based upon a claim of *res judicata* (final settlement of dispute by court), even though the constitutional issue was not raised or was not known at the time of appeal, and on the lack of statutory postconviction procedures for the review of such matters."[43]

Student Checklist

1. Can you list six advantageous derivatives of the judicial process?
2. Are you able to define the term complaint?
3. Do you know how to distinguish between an indictment and an information?

[42] Bassiouni, *Criminal Law and its Processes,* p. 511.
[43] Ibid., p. 510.

4. Can you identify the five ways that an individual is subject to the jurisdiction of a state?
5. Can you list the four major areas of jurisdiction for the federal government?
6. Can you list the various types of pleas?
7. Do you know how to differentiate between posttrial discovery and posttrial motions?

Topics for Discussion

1. Discuss the implications of a plea of *nolo contendere*.
2. Discuss the importance of jurisdiction over the person.
3. Discuss the limitations of an information.
4. Discuss the importance of an independent judiciary.

ANNOTATED BIBLIOGRAPHY

Abraham, Henry J. *The Judicial Process*. New York: Oxford University Press, 1962. Thoroughly covering numerous aspects of both international and domestic judicial processes, this book serves as an excellent comprehensive introduction to its readers. The informative facts covering terminology, structure, and the processes of various court systems are often touched with flavorful opinions.

Bassiouni, M. Cherif. *Criminal Law and Its Processes*. Springfield, Ill.: Charles C. Thomas, 1969. This book discusses principles and theories of the criminal law, legal defenses, and numerous specific crimes. The criminal process is examined from the accusation to review of the conviction. Because it is complete about the procedure of the criminal process, this book gives one an excellent overview of criminal law and its processes.

Carlson, Ronald L. *Criminal Justice Procedure for Police*. Cincinnati: W. H. Anderson, 1970. This book covers numerous aspects of the criminal justice procedure. Opening with a general overview of the system, a discussion continues with a description of the preliminary hearing process, bail, accusatory pleadings, the trial and posttrial process. Judicial decisions in the latter part of the book clarify many points previously made.

Chamelin, Neil C., and Kenneth R. Evans. *Criminal Law for Policemen*. Englewood Cliffs, N.J.: Prentice-Hall, 1971. This book is a general discussion on the relationship between the police and legal principles. Successfully achieving its claim to explain the "what" and "why" of this relationship, the book makes informative reading for both the layman and the policeman. Opening with the historical background of criminal law, the book progresses with topics such as jurisdiction, the criminal act, the mental element, and other specific related criminal offenses.

Eldefonso, Edward, Alan Coffey, and James Sullivan. *Police and the Criminal Law*. Pacific Palisades: Goodyear, 1972. Dealing extensively with the relationship between criminal law and law enforcement personnel, this book provides excellent basic fundamentals for the reader. Procedures and explanations in areas of arrest, search, seizure, and evidence, as well as other police related functions are thoroughly examined.

Nagel, Stuart S. *The Rights of the Accused*. Beverly Hills: Sage Publications, 1972. This book emphasizes the rights entitled to one accused of a criminal offense. Nine areas of the criminal procedure are explored beginning with the rights prior to the first court appearance and concluding with posttrial rights of the defendant.

Weston, Paul B., and Kenneth M. Wells. *The Administration of Justice*. Englewood Cliffs, N.J.: Prentice-Hall, 1967. This book covers the entire administration of justice system in the United States, from the arrest to the final disposition. Areas within the system discussed include the role of the police, prosecutor, judicial system, and corrections. The book serves as a good introduction to the readers with its general overview of United States law enforcement.

The study of this chapter will enable you to:

1. Trace the historical antecedents of the juvenile court.
2. Compare the alternative schemes for juvenile court organizations.
3. Contrast between the handling of the incorrigible and the juvenile who has committed a felony.
4. Write an essay on the proper age differentiation between juvenile court and criminal court jurisdiction.
5. Describe the impact of *Gault* and judicial procedures in juvenile courts.
6. Describe the role of defense attorneys in juvenile court.
7. Identify the alternatives available at the intake process.
8. List the grounds for holding a juvenile in detention before his adjudicatory hearing.

14
Juvenile Justice

The first juvenile court law was passed by the Illinois Legislature in 1899. It established a separate, noncriminal procedure for children in Cook County who had violated the criminal law, or children who had been brought to the attention of the court as neglected, homeless, or otherwise disreputable. The juvenile court movement soon spread throughout the United States, and some special legal provisions for delinquent and neglected youth had been passed in virtually every state by the 1920s.[1]

The juvenile court statutes were early attacked as unconstitutional on the grounds that they deprived children of such basic criminal law rights as the right to appear with counsel, the right to a jury trial, and the right to remain silent in the fact of an accusation of crime. These efforts failed; the appellate courts looked upon the juvenile court process as a "civil inquiry, to determine whether, in a greater or lesser degree, some child should be taken under the direct care of the state and its officials to safeguard or foster his or her adolescent life." Since the proceeding was in the child's interests, following this reasoning, procedural niceties, such as letting the child know why he was being taken away from home, were not essential. As the Pennsylvania Supreme Court put it, "The natural parent needs no process to temporarily deprive his child of its liberty . . . to save it and to shield it from the consequences of persistence in a career of waywardness, nor is the state, when compelled, as *parens patriae* (in substitution for parents), to take the place of father

---

[1] Herbert H. Lou, *Juvenile Courts in the United States* (Chapel Hill: University of North Carolina Press, 1927), pp. 13-31.

for the same purpose, required to adopt any process as a means of placing its hands upon the child and lead it into one of its courts."

It must be recalled that in the early decades of this century, procedural due process was not a meaningful protection in the criminal law field, for either children or adults. In the federal system the privilege against self-incrimination, the right to a jury trial, and the right to assigned counsel in major cases were all recognized during this time, but the state court systems were relatively free to operate as they would, bound only by their own constitutions and state court interpretations. For example, the first right-to-counsel case coming from a state court to be decided in favor of the accused by the U.S. Supreme Court occurred in 1932. Therefore, the lack of procedural progress through the appellate courts in relation to the rights of children is understandable, if not excusable.

In removing children from the jurisdiction of the criminal court by establishing the juvenile court, the intent was to do away with both the punitive philosophy of the criminal court as well as the method of trial and punishment. A new philosophy was developed. The child was regarded as immature and not wholly responsible for its acts. The child was entitled to protection, rehabilitation, or retraining. The juvenile court was to act as a wise parent who would plan for the total welfare of the child instead of punish the child for a specific act.

A recent historical study of the development of the juvenile court argues that the founders of the juvenile court movement considered themselves involved in humanitarian work; however, their accomplishments contradict their libertarian and humanistic intentions.[2] Instead of developing as intended, the juvenile court became a paternalistic and punitive system paralleling the impact of a criminal court. Platt argues that, in many ways, the juvenile court movement was a step backward instead of the progressive move its founders believed in and sought.

In the 1940s and 1950s, a shift toward formalism in the juvenile court became apparent. Courts required that the child and his parents be notified of the allegations of the petition, and began to look critically at the use of hearsay evidence in the adjudication. Courts tightened up their

---

[2] Anthony M. Platt, *The Child Savers: The Invention of Delinquency* (Chicago: University of Chicago Press, 1969), p. 230.

interpretations of statutes defining delinquent behavior, requiring proof of a pattern of antisocial activity, and occasionally reversed commitments because the evidence did not justify such harsh treatment.

Legislatures realized that many of the due process procedures hammered out in the criminal law are not mere formalisms or historical accidents, but are essential aids in uncovering the truth in any court and in giving any person a fair chance to present his side of a case. Many states drew on the Standard Juvenile Court Act, published by the National Council on Crime and Delinquency and endorsed by the National Council of Juvenile Court Judges, and the United States Children's Bureau, as models of fair procedure in the juvenile court context.

Wisconsin and Minnesota revised their juvenile codes in the late 1950s, including elaborate notice requirements and controls over the admission of hearsay testimony. Oregon and California rewrote their juvenile court laws to provide a full code of juvenile practice, governing intake, detention, and social reports, as well as the hearing itself.

The Juvenile Court

At the outset of the juvenile court movement, the court itself was conceived of as nothing more than a different set of procedures for dealing with youths. Thus, there were no "juvenile courts" as separate judicial entities. In recent years, several alternative schemes for juvenile court organizations have been tried. Some states have established statewide juvenile courts, with their own judiciary completely separate from the civil and criminal courts of the state. Other states have established separate divisions of their highest courts of general trial jurisdiction to deal solely with juvenile cases. Both patterns are approved in the Standard Juvenile Court Act. In other states the juvenile court remains a part of the misdemeanor trial courts, although separate operational provisions are provided by statute.

Since the juvenile court is empowered to deal with such vital issues as felony-grade allegations against children and termination of parental rights leading to adoption, maintaining the juvenile jurisdiction in an inferior court is indefensible. Furthermore, there is a need to encourage uniformity of juvenile court practice throughout a state; this is best accomplished through the device of a board of juvenile court judges, which is only practicable where the juvenile court is either a separate court or is within the highest trial court.

While the juvenile court may well have been the focus for research programs, rarely has the juvenile court itself been the focus of research. In a recent study, Emerson provides a detailed description of the operations of a juvenile court and describes the impact of the court on those children coming to the court, as well as the wide range of social and institutional pressures impinging on the court.[3] The study describes the court's personnel and their relations with the institutions comprising the working environment (schools, police, churches, social welfare agencies), and how these relations shape court activity. Against this background, the study describes how the court deals with its caseload and focuses on the procedures by which the moral character of a child is defined. The study highlights the tension between exercising authority over a delinquent and at the same time trying to help a delinquent.

Vinter, in a similar study of one Michigan juvenile court, describes it as a people-processing organization concerned with children and youth whose behavior or whose situations violate the moral norms of the community. Court processing of a child can result in a new public identity or social situation with long-term consequences for the person processed. On the other hand, court processing can result in a youngster's obtaining services otherwise seldom available.[4]

Aaron V. Cicourel presents a detailed view of the everyday practices of the police, probation officials, and the juvenile court, and points out how these agencies can actually generate delinquency by their routine encounters with juveniles.[5] The conventional view that assumes delinquents are "natural" social types distributed in some ordered fashion is challenged. The organizational workings of the police, probation departments, the courts, and the schools are all viewed as contributing to the formation of the original events leading to contact with the law. This

[3] Robert M. Emerson, *Judging Delinquents, Context and Process in Juvenile Court* (Chicago: Aldine, 1969), p. 293.
[4] Robert D. Vinter and Rosemary C. Sarri, *The Juvenile Court: Organization and Decision-Making,* Paper 1 (Ann Arbor: The University of Michigan, Institute for Juvenile Hearing Officers, 1964), p. 20.
[5] Aaron V. Cicourel, *The Social Organization of Juvenile Justice* (New York: Wiley, 1968), p. 745.

creation of facts in turn leads to improvised interpretations for the particular case of character structure, family life, and future possibilities, so that particular cases are often justified as falling under an appropriate legal statute or precedent even before judicial litigation is begun. By means of this construction of cases, entitled the "creation of history," the particular case is exposed to a series of retrospective-prospective interpretations within, and disengaged from the social contexts relevant to what actually happened. The organizational workings producing delinquency are examined in a study of the activities of two police and probation departments of approximately the same size. Variations in law enforcement are traced by examining cases from low- and middle-income families. Thus, differences in the administration of justice are demonstrated, and the method by which community political structures influence juvenile justice is presented.

Juvenile Court Law

Juvenile court law has traditionally been defined as covering criminal conduct, misbehavior, and neglect, as these categories are presented to juvenile courts. This means that juvenile court law is primarily procedural, and not substantive, since it does not in and of itself proscribe or prescribe activities. To find out what is illegal, one must generally look to the criminal law. Juvenile court law merely decrees how persons of certain ages are to be processed if they act illegally (delinquency jurisdiction), or if they are the victims of others' illegality (the neglect jurisdiction).[6]

Beginning with the New York Family Court Act of 1962 and the California Juvenile Court Act of 1961, increased attention has been paid to the one group of juvenile "offenders" for whom juvenile court law does proscribe acts—misbehaving children. Older laws include within the criminal jurisdiction such acts as truancy and absconding, acts that, if committed by adults, are not criminal. Similarly, one finds old laws proscribing fornication and consumption of alcoholic beverages by

[6] The terms delinquency and neglect are often omitted in the statutes; see Standard Juvenile Court Act, Section 8.

minors, where these actions are typically not punishable when engaged in by adults. Finally, the delinquency statutes included a general category of children who are "incorrigible," who, in the words of the Tennessee Act, are "beyond the control of (their) parents or guardian or other lawful custodian."[7]

What these old laws said, essentially, is that children would be punished for acts that are permissible for adults. The new laws ostensibly recognize that this is something qualitatively different from merely handling children in a different court and correctional system. Thus, the New York law created the category of "persons in need of supervision" for noncriminal but illegal conduct, and the California law placed such conduct in a different provision of the juvenile court law than that covering criminal acts. But the new nomenclature makes no difference whatsoever. In New York, persons in need of supervision may be committed to training schools, as may delinquents; in California, the noncriminal miscreant may not be committed to the Youth Authority (which runs the California training schools) directly, but may, and often does, wind up there as a probation violator, still without having been adjudicated on the basis of a criminal act.

The lack of necessity for this "incorrigibility" jurisdiction and the lack of effective distinction between delinquent and nondelinquent behavior have been enunciated in several recently published articles. Delegates from 84 nations attending the Second United Nations Congress on the Prevention of Crime and Treatment of Offenders in 1960 took the same position. The only noticeable trend, however, is to retain jurisdiction over nonlaw violators, and to continue to deal correctionally with delinquents and misbehavers in the same institutions. Thus, the ostensible trend toward separation of criminal and noncriminal jurisdictional bases for dealing with children is more fiction than fact.

McKay has pointed out that since juvenile courts have jurisdiction not only over children guilty of acts that would be criminal if committed by an adult, but also over certain children who have not committed any specific criminal act at all (typically described as "incorrigible" or "beyond the control of their parents"), they may receive the same dispo-

[7] Tennessee Code Annotated section 37-242-5; see also Ohio Code section 2151.02 (repealed 1969).

sitional treatment as the juvenile who has committed a felony.[8] The *Gault* decision (1967), which held that due process requirements must be satisfied in juvenile courts, implied that the juvenile court jurisdiction over children who have committed no specific criminal act and yet face a period of incarceration would be subject to constitutional challenge on several grounds. Juvenile court statutes that use such terms as "incorrigible" or "disobedient" are similar to the status offenses (such as vagrancy), and are subject to criticism on the same grounds of vagueness as are the vagrancy statutes. The Supreme Court decision in *Robinson* (1962) indicated that the cruel and unusual punishment clause might be held to invalidate juvenile court jurisdiction over "incorrigible" children. The juvenile statutes governing noncriminal children also might be attacked on the grounds of "status crime," in which the alleged offense is a personal condition instead of a specific act, or on the grounds of equal protection of the laws. The *Gault* decision has brought about needed procedural reforms and may eventually result in a total reexamination of the entire court system.

The degree to which an offense committed by a juvenile influences the severity of the treatment decided on at the probation investigatory level and at the adjudicatory level was examined in California. Weighting systems were devised for both probation determinations and court dispositions. The data used in the study were derived from reports of 1965 activity as submitted to the California Bureau of Criminal Statistics by 56 county probation departments. The findings were interpreted as indicating that the severity of the treatment has a direct relationship to the severity of the offense and that the juvenile delinquent is treated in much the same way as the adult; that is, more severe treatment is given to juveniles in cases where the offenses involved would demand heavier penalties for adults as prescribed by the criminal code.

Outside the misbehavior area, one finds that juvenile courts have been vested with more areas of jurisdiction than has formerly been the case. The Standard Juvenile Court Act, for example, recommends that the juvenile court have exclusive original jurisdiction over custody determinations, adoption, and the treatment or commitment of mentally defec-

[8] Malcolm V. McKay, *Juvenile Court Jurisdiction over Noncriminal Children* (unpublished legal survey).

tive or mentally ill minors. Most new laws have adopted the broader jurisdiction. In addition, several states have adopted family court acts, based more or less on NCCD's Standard Family Court Act. A family court includes, in addition to the juvenile jurisdiction described above, jurisdiction over matrimonial actions and criminal conduct committed between members of a family. New York, Hawaii, and Rhode Island have adopted the family court model. In states in which all family jurisdiction is in one court, such as Oregon and Washington, a family court division of the court of general trial jurisdiction can be established administratively, and there can be one social service-probation agency handling all family cases. It is very likely that a further consolidation of jurisdiction along the lines of the family court will be seen in the future.[9]

Over the years, a continuing controversy has existed over the proper age differentiation between juvenile court and criminal court jurisdiction. The Standard Juvenile Court Act and most existing state legislation set 18 as the age below which a child is subject to the jurisdiction of the juvenile court. However, a number of states have maintained a lower age for the delinquency jurisdiction—in Illinois it is 17 years, in New York and North Carolina it is 16—while keeping the neglect jurisdiction at age 18. On the other hand, California has extended jurisdiction in the juvenile court to age 21, there being concurrent jurisdiction between the juvenile and the criminal courts over the 18 to 21 age group.

The difficult question of what to do with the older adolescent who commits an offense has been dealt with in several jurisdictions through the youthful offender concept. In some states, a separate judicial procedure has been established, either by statute as in New York or by practice as in Chicago and Baltimore, for some minors between the ages of 16 and 21. In the New York system, minors between the ages of 16 and 18 are eligible for youthful offender treatment in criminal court. This means that, if approved for such treatment, no criminal record is entered and any institutional commitment is to the reformatory instead of to the penitentiary. A more common differentiation is in the correctional area.

---

[9] The family court concept is explained in Sol Rubin, "The Standard Family Court Act," *1 J. Fam. L., 105* (1961); William H. Sheridan and E. Brewer, "The Family Court," *4 Children, 67* (1957). See also E. D. Dyson and R. B. Dyson, "Family Courts in the United States," *8 J. Fam. L., 505* (1968).

Figure 14-1. In some states, a separate judicial procedure has been established for minors. If the minor is eligible for youthful offender treatment, a criminal record may be averted.

Several states, including Indiana and Virginia, have established separate institutions for young felony offenders.

Judicial Procedures

As originally conceived, the juvenile court hearing was to be an informal inquiry into a child's acts and his social strengths and weaknesses, with any resulting disposition aimed primarily at increasing his conformity to behavioral norms and enhancing his maturation. While never fully accepted as a viable goal, this concept of the juvenile court process was dealt its death blow by the U.S. Supreme Court in the decision of In re *Gault*, 387 U.S. 1 (1967). There, the Supreme Court noted that commitment to an institution, whatever its purpose, amounts to imprisonment, and may be justified only by a hearing that conforms to constitutional requirements of due process.

The *Gault* case dealt only with children charged with behavior that, under the applicable state law, could result in an institutional disposition. The case established four rights: the right to adequate note of the acts allegedly giving the court jurisdiction over the child; the right to appear by counsel and to have counsel appointed if indigent; the right to remain silent in face of an accusation; and the right to confront and cross-examine witnesses against him. Left undecided in *Gault* were two crucial trial rights, the right to a trial by jury and the right to have one's involvement in illegal activity proved by a high standard of proof. These latter issues are the subject of current litigation; the courts have decided both ways, but there is an increasing trend in both appellate decisions and in new legislation toward establishing a high standard of proof, either proof by clear and convincing evidence (used in civil law for issues of special gravity) or to require proof beyond a reasonable doubt (the criminal law standard). Fewer courts and fewer statutes have adopted the jury trial requirement, and it may be argued that, if all other juvenile court proceedings are fair and a high standard of proof required, the safeguard of a jury may not be essential.[10]

The pattern of a juvenile court hearing is emerging in such standard-setting publications as the *Model Rules for Juvenile Court*, the *Uniform Juvenile Court Act*, and the *Legislative Guide for Drafting Family and Juvenile Court Acts*, as well as in recent juvenile court law revisions in several states. Adequate notice of the charges is assured by a requirement of serving a summons and a copy of the petition upon the child and his parents, custodian, or guardian. A notice of the right to retain counsel—including the right to have counsel appointed if the child is unable to afford it—is served with the summons. Under the new Kansas statute, counsel is nonwaivable; if a child does not appear with counsel of his own choosing, counsel will be appointed for him.

In contested adjudicatory hearings, one finds the petitioner represented by a legal officer of the state more and more frequently. With attorneys on both sides, the contested hearing takes on more of the flavor of the adversary criminal trial, with the judge maintaining a neutral role as fact finder instead of actively engaging himself in the eliciting of

---

[10] On juvenile court procedural rights in general, see Norman Dorsen and D. A. Rezneck, "The Future of Juvenile Law," *1 Fam. L.Q., 1* (1967), and B. J. George, "Juvenile Delinquency Proceedings: The Due Process Model," *40 U. Colo. L. Rev., 315* (1968).

testimony. Recent decisions have brought into the juvenile court process such refinements of the criminal law as the requirement that the testimony of a witness under a certain age be corroborated and that no social or otherwise irrelevant testimony be produced before the finding of guilt or innocence.

An interesting study was made of the effect of the 1961 California Juvenile Court law to determine the possibility of changing behavior patterns by legislation. Attempts at measuring certain consequences of the law were unsuccessful because of confusion over the definition of arrest and concurrently changing factors affecting the police and the courts, and because the effects of the law could not be separated from normal growth factors. It was, however, possible to assess the success of the new law in giving attorneys formal entry into the juvenile court. The evidence that representation by counsel more often resulted in a favorable disposition was impressive. Proportionately, dismissals and informal probation were ordered nearly three times as frequently in attorney as in nonattorney cases; wardships were more often declared in nonattorney cases, and, with no attorney on hand, children under wardship were more likely to be placed away from home. Private attorneys were somewhat more successful in obtaining dismissals than were public defenders. The new role of counsel gave rise to new adaptations among the participants in the juvenile court process that could defeat the intent of the law. It was concluded that, while formal structures are changeable in anticipated directions, the detailed forms taken by the new roles in these structures were less subject to change.

In a study of the Chicago court, 51 private attorneys who had represented juvenile clients in the juvenile court were interviewed in relation to defense work in the court system. In addition to the interviews with attorneys, hundreds of hours were spent in observing juvenile court practices. The findings indicated that private lawyers in juvenile court were typically small-fee practitioners who earn their livings from minor criminal and civil matters, and that the juvenile court generated its own system of complicity that did not encourage the kinds of informal bargaining arrangements that were found in the criminal courts. Among the occupational hazards found to exist in the juvenile court were modest and undependable fees; the lack of significance of informal bargaining and negotiated pleas; lack of fringe benefits; and a possible conflict of interest between serving the client and the client's parents. The research supported the proposition that lawyers in juvenile courts will be co-opted into a powerfully entrenched welfare system and pressured into abdicating their adversary functions in order to minimize conflict. The research also suggested that small-fee lawyers readily subscribe to a policy of benign paternalism. The findings supported the conclusion that private lawyers do not enhance the bargaining power or rights of young offenders, but instead help to consolidate their dependent status.

Another study analyzed the role of the public defender representing juveniles in a large Midwestern city. In 1966, "Metro's" juvenile court handled a total of 11,636 delinquency cases (25 percent were "adjusted" by administrative officers and were not referred to the courts because of a lack of evidence or seriousness). In one year, the public defender handled 345 delinquency cases representing 4 percent of the total court caseload of 8920 cases. These cases account for 87 percent of his total caseload during the year. The average client was a 14½-year-old black male. Juveniles with records who were charged with serious offenses were more likely to be assigned to the public defender. Analysis of individual cases showed that the public defender (1) rarely appeared at detention hearings; (2) made oral instead of written motions (in 83 percent of the cases he made no motions at all); (3) had no continuances in one-third of his cases; (4) held only one client conference prior to the court hearing in almost one-half of its cases; and (5) had no witnesses in over one-half of his cases. Relatively few of his cases—3½ percent—were dismissed on the motion of the state's attorney. Prosecutors were apparently unwilling to release juvenile defendants even though concrete evidence for a conviction might be lacking. The public defender in juvenile court was formally discouraged from plea bargaining, and he pleaded fewer clients (25 percent) than did his counterparts in criminal courts (30 percent). Because the rule of reasonable doubt did not apply, prosecutors won juvenile cases with minimal evidence. Research, however, supports Skolnick's assertion that the public defender can often be more effective than a private lawyer in obtaining dismissals or light sentences.

A growing trend in juvenile court practice is the separation or division of the adjudicatory hearing from the dispositional hearing. Juvenile court law is coming to realize that the factual issues at stake in a contested adjudication are indistinguishable from those at issue in a contested criminal matter, and consequently the fact-finding processes in the two systems are fast becoming identical. However, the rehabilitative and individualized aspects of juvenile court jurisprudence maintain their full validity at the dispositional stage of the juvenile court process. Here, an attorney for the state is rarely present, the rules of evidence are not in effect, and the atmosphere, ideally, is one of cooperation between all parties toward discovering the best treatment pattern for the child. It should be noted that such an approach does not differ in theory from that underlying sentencing in the criminal process. However, it is historically true that more attention is paid to a child's individual needs and problems than in the criminal context.

What then is the effect of these procedural reforms on the juvenile court? Some studies have reported lower commitment rates, but a greatly increased detention problem, and a marked slowdown in juvenile court work.[11] It is suspected, however, that any increase in complexity and consequent slowdown in the adjudication process brought by procedural reform can be, and has been, offset by reduced referral of children for official court action and increased diversion of children from the court.

Pre-Judicial Procedures

Along with procedural formalities, there has been a shift away from viewing the juvenile court as a catchall social agency and toward viewing the court as the governmental agency of last resort in dealing with children. The emphasis now, in many courts, is toward maximum diversion of cases; discouraging the police from arresting children for minor misbehavior, in favor of stationhouse adjustment instead of court referral, in favor of refusing court action at the intake stage, and in favor of dismissing petitions rather than placing children on "paper probation." How much of this diversion is actually occurring is difficult to assess; there are cities in which almost every child is proceeded against on a formal petition, and other localities where the formal juvenile court process is almost never invoked.

The trend toward diversion blossomed in the report of the President's Commission on Law Enforcement and the Administration of

[11] B. S. Alper, "The Children's Court at Three Score and Ten: Will It Survive Gault?" *Albany L. Rev.*, 46 (1969).

Justice. That body recommended the establishment of a new entity, the Youth Service Bureau, which would take children who otherwise would enter the formal juvenile court process and develop a comprehensive social plan for them. As conceived by the Commission, the Bureau would not primarily provide services to children, but rather see that services are provided, on a coordinated basis, by other community agencies. Several bureaus, modeled more or less on the crime commission proposals, have been set up and studied; the major problem seems to be that coordination of resources—where there are no resources—does not help things very much.

The procedural revolution in juvenile court law has had its effects on the pre-judicial process. It is now quite clear that the requirements of *Miranda* v. *Arizona* bind the police in dealing with youthful law violators. Furthermore, because of the presumed immaturity and inability of children to protect their own rights, several courts and NCCD's *Model Rules for Juvenile Courts* have provided that a child's statement to police or probation officers without the advice of counsel is inadmissible at the juvenile court hearing, unless his constitutional rights were competently and intelligently waived both by the child and by his parent or guardian. The practical effect of this rule is uncertain. On the one hand, police may be encouraged to follow the commands of almost every juvenile court statute and immediately deliver any child taken into custody to the court, while on the other hand, police may feel forced to set up their own quasi-judicial hearing processes to deal with children—without court referral at all.

With the increased importance of the intake process—which under the new doctrine is to serve as a screening and filtering device and not merely as a unit to prepare cases for court—has come increased attention to possible abuses of children's rights at this point. Probation officers, like police, must inform the child and his parent of their rights to counsel and to remain silent, and, in order to encourage the free flow of information at the intake point, several statutes and the *Model Rules* provide that statements made at intake may not be used in the court proceeding. Although "informal adjustment" (the provision of probation-type services without a court adjudication) is still encouraged, a number of states have provided that such activity be limited to a three-month period, and also have insisted that a child who maintains his innocence has the right to a court hearing and need not accept the benevolent and sometimes irritating offers of assistance from probation officers.

Detention

Under juvenile court law, a child may be held in detention before his adjudicatory hearing on several grounds that he is a potential runaway; that he must be held for pending proceedings in another jurisdiction; and most controversially, that he constitutes a danger to himself or to the community. In other words, juvenile court law has traditionally recognized the legitimacy of preventive detention.

While there is no trend to narrow the grounds for detention, emphasis has been placed on procedural controls over the detention process. In the judicial area, many states have established detention hearing provisions, either mandatory, or on request after notice of the right to a hearing. These hearings must be held promptly after admission to detention—usually within 24 or 48 hours—and have served as an important screening device to reduce detained populations. An effective detention hearing system, with counsel provided to children not privately represented, has proved to be an adequate substitute for the adult system of bail hearings, and few appellate courts have required that bail be made available if this alternative system is operative. Furthermore, it is generally accepted that there is no need for formal arraignment in the juvenile court system, for the task of making out the *prima facie* (at first view) case in the juvenile system is delegated to the probation department, which must pass on and approve any petition for formal court action.

Transfer to the Adult Criminal Justice System

In all but a handful of states, certain children under the juvenile court age may be transferred to the adult criminal justice system, either before the juvenile court hearing or after entry into the juvenile correctional system. The Standard and Uniform Juvenile Court Acts provide, for example, that a child 16 years of age or over who is charged with an act that, if committed by an adult, would constitute a felony, may, after a full investigation and hearing, be transferred from the juvenile court to the criminal court for prosecution as an adult. Under the U.S. Supreme Court case of *Kent* v. *United States*, such a transfer must be preceded by a judicial hearing, with counsel, testing the necessity for the transfer; the state must exhaust all possible juvenile correctional alternatives before denying the child the benefits of the juvenile justice system.[12]

The strict age and charge limitations of the standards have not been widely adopted. In many states, transfer is possible for children as young as 14, and may also occur in cases not of felony-grade allegations. There is substantial doubt as to whether this loosening is justified; for example, the state of New York has no transfer provisions, and California has operated adequately under the standard criteria.

In many states, transfer to adult correctional institutions is possible after a child has been committed to the juvenile institutions. The loosest statutes in this regard permit administrative transfer, with no judicial control, for any child in a state juvenile training school, whether or not he was originally adjudicated on the basis of law violation. This purely administrative system has been held unconstitutional in several decisions, although the cases go both ways. However, transfer with judicial approval has generally been upheld, and is supported, in rare cases, by the legislative standards of the U.S. Children's Bureau.

The Standard Juvenile Court Act, on the other hand, forbids all correctional transfer. Under this view, the only child in an institution who is possibly in need of adult treatment is one who commits a felony while in the institution. If this is the case, he can be the subject of a new petition and a transfer hearing, thus affording him all the rights of other children his age.

Recently, several courts have entertained legal proceedings involving children already committed to institutions or awaiting court action in detention. This phenomenon stems from two sources: the expansion of concern by the courts with prisoners' rights, as manifested in the U.S. Supreme Court case of *Johnson* v. *Avery* and many lower federal court decisions dealing with prison discipline, right to worship, to correspond with the court, and the like; and the new concern with the so-called right to treatment of persons involuntarily confined for rehabilitative purposes. While few cases on behalf of juveniles have been brought directly under the prisoner's rights doctrine, there is no doubt that this approach is equally valid in the juvenile as in the adult area. Already, segregation in training schools has been invalidated, and a great expansion of court

[12] Kent v. United States, 401 F. 2d 408 (D.C. Cir. 1968).

review of the conditions of confinement in training schools and detention facilities is anticipated.

The major breakthrough in this general area has been, however, in the "right to treatment." This doctrine was developed in regard to involuntary hospitalization of the mentally ill, where it had become established that confinement of nondangerous mental patients is legal only if adequate efforts at cure are made. Courts have held that a child in detention must get psychiatric treatment where indicated, or be released. In one case, a deaf child was ordered released unless special educational arrangements were made for him pending court disposition. A number of cases have been brought to require juvenile correction systems to raise the level of services, particularly educational services, in their juvenile institutions. And cases are being brought seeking release, not merely new services, when services for children are inadequate.

While these cases are new, the Standard Juvenile Court Act and statutes modeled on it have provided a vehicle for testing the adequacy of institutional care—a vehicle that has rarely if ever been used. The Standard Act provides:

> *A parent, guardian, or next friend of a minor whose legal custody has been transferred by the court to an institution, agency, or person may petition the court for modification or revocation of the decree, on the ground that such legal custodian has wrongfully denied application for the release of the minor or has failed to act upon it within a reasonable time, and has acted in an arbitrary manner not consistent with the welfare of the child or the public interest.*[13]

This provision should provide an excellent opportunity for creative litigation, since it seems to give a right to release if the institution is not acting in a manner consistent with the best efforts to promote the early return of the child to society and his family.

Conclusion

The battle for procedural reform of the juvenile court has basically been won; there remains an extensive mopping-up operation to drag recalcitrant courts, judges, and staffs into the world of due process. But the

[13] Standard Act §26.

victory does not really mean very much. It will, it is true, be more difficult to send a child who has not committed a crime to a training school,
particularly if he has a good lawyer and the offense alleged cannot be
magically turned into an allegation of "incorrigibility." This is important.
But nothing in the procedural revolution will keep runaways out of the
institutions, renovate homes that are unfit for habitation, or persuade
parents to stop filing complaints of ungovernability against their children.
The juvenile courts will continue to serve as the public repository of the
private sector's failures.

The need now is to examine seriously those conditions that produce an unjust system—racism, economic class oppression, arbitrary
power in the hands of irresponsible bureaucracies, and confinement as
the treatment for persons who challenge the stability of the existing
national power distribution. Until delinquent behavior by children and
neglect of children by parents cease to be a rational response to life in
America, the trends outlined herein will have little effect on the better-
ment of justice. Neither will the opportunity exist to learn how to
provide services that enhance desirable youth development and life
experiences.

Student Checklist

1. Can you trace the history of the juvenile court?
2. Do you know how to compare the alternative schemes for juvenile
   court organizations?
3. Are you able to compare the handling of the incorrigible and the
   juvenile who has committed a felony?
4. Are you aware of the proper age differentiation between juvenile
   court and criminal court jurisdiction?
5. Can you describe the impact of *Gault* on judicial procedures in
   juvenile courts?
6. Do you know what the role is of a defense attorney in juvenile court?
7. Can you list the grounds for holding a juvenile in detention before
   his adjudicatory hearing?
8. Do you know what alternatives are available at the intake process?

Topics for Discussion

1. Discuss the current role of the juvenile court.
2. Discuss the philosophy of the juvenile court.
3. Discuss the disadvantages of extending criminal court procedure to the juvenile court.
4. Discuss the importance of the intake process.

ANNOTATED BIBLIOGRAPHY

Cicourel, Aaron V. *The Social Organization of Juvenile Justice.* New York: Wiley, 1968. This text is a comprehensive analysis of the social aspects of the justice system as it applies to juveniles. Emphasis is placed on the everyday practices of the police probation officers and the court.

James, Howard. *Crisis in the Courts.* New York: David McKay, 1968. This study thoroughly examines many of the critical issues of the courts. It is a series of articles.

National Council on Crime and Delinquency. Council of Judges. *Model Rules for Juvenile Courts.* New York: NCCD, 1969. A report that delineates all of the procedural rules that apply to the juvenile courts. Emphasis is placed on broadening of jurisdiction.

U.S. Children's Bureau, *Standards for Juvenile and Family Courts,* by William H. Sheridan in cooperation with the National Council on Crime and Delinquency and the National Council of Juvenile Court Judges. Washington, D.C.: U.S. Govt. Printing Office, 1966. This study sets forth comprehensive standards for family and juvenile courts. It is a synthesis of legal and social standards.

Part Four

Trends Within the System

The study of this chapter will enable you to:

1. Identify the two areas in which diversion is a conscious policy.
2. List three arguments against informal pre-judicial processings.
3. Identify three major criticisms of civil commitment.
4. List four contemporary beliefs that have converged around compulsory treatment.
5. Compare civil commitment and compulsory treatment.
6. Identify the methods by which narcotic addicts can be treated under the medical model.
7. List the three recommendations for the postarrest diversion of alcoholic offenders.
8. Describe the process of a blacklist of multiple petty misdemeanant offenders.

15
Diversion from the System

The diversion of persons from the criminal justice system has been practiced for as long as law enforcement activities have existed. This practice exists primarily because the system allows—in fact, requires—considerable discretion on the part of the police.[1] This is especially evident in regard to decisions to arrest, to dismiss in court, to refer, or to resolve by informal disposition. Considerable discretion is also practiced by the prosecutor or intake worker relative to official or unofficial processing. In fact, diversion from the justice system may occur at any stage of the judicial process. Concern over the tremendous burden placed on courts, and the injustices associated with the inability of the courts to handle the volume of cases—compounded by evidence that criminal processing often does more harm than good—have resulted in a focus on diversion of certain groups of offenders prior to court processing.

Informal preadjudication disposition occurs in both the juvenile and the adult justice systems for many of the same reasons. First, even with the best legislative formulation, definitions of criminal conduct are likely to be ambiguous. The decision to divert an individual from judicial proceedings is affected by many factors, such as the nature of the offense, the circumstances of its commission, the attitude of the victim, and the character of the accused.[2] The use of discretion is affected also by the consideration that the stigma of official processing might seriously limit

[1] Primary source: National Institute of Mental Health, *Diversion from the Criminal Justice System* (Washington, D.C.: U.S. Govt. Printing Office, 1971).
[2] President's Commission on Law Enforcement and Administration of Justice, *Task Force Report: Juvenile Delinquency and Youth Crime* (Washington, D.C.: U.S. Govt. Printing Office, 1967), p. 10.

the accused's social and economic opportunities, or impose on him a deviant role that may lead to further antisocial acts. In addition, the large volume of cases would seem to require some screening of those less serious cases in order to allow concentration of law enforcement resources on what are considered to be major crimes.

The issue of screening out less serious cases is pertinent to the two areas in which diversion, as a conscious policy, currently is given most attention: minor noncriminal "delinquent" behavior; and adult conduct that is socially disapproved, but might be more appropriately handled by social agencies. While it is clear that many persons are diverted from the criminal justice system as a result of official discretion, the assumption that less serious offenders are screened out is questionable. Available arrest data and court statistics indicate that "most of the cases in the criminal courts consist of what are essentially violations of moral norms or instances of a known behavior rather than of dangerous crimes"[3] and that many juveniles contacted by police for truancy, waywardness, or incorrigibility end up in juvenile court with an adjudication of delinquency. Diversion does occur, but its use is so informal that it tends to depend on the personal inclination of the individual official making the initial or subsequent contact.

Arguments against informal pre-judicial processing are: (1) the broad powers of discretion may be abused; (2) enlarged discretionary power may result in inconsistent law enforcement and disrespect for law; and (3) discretion may be used to further staff convenience at the expense of other goals of crime prevention and control. These are valid criticisms of diversion as it might operate if informal discretionary powers were merely extended. The proponents of diversion, however, are not suggesting the extension of informal discretionary powers. Instead, they are advocating that: (1) pre-judicial disposition be made a conscious and clearly defined policy; (2) the processes of diversion be given some procedural regularity; and (3) decisions be based on explicit and predetermined criteria.

Whatever the reason for diversion from the criminal justice system, it occurs primarily because of official concern that application of the full criminal process is not always possible or appropriate. In the past, consideration of the need for diversion and special handling of some classes

[3] Ibid.

of deviants led to the creation of the juvenile court and a noncriminal procedure to be used in the interest of the child, as well as the sanctioning of civil commitment for treatment of mentally ill offenders (either adjudged incompetent to stand trial or after dismissal of criminal charges because of insanity). Experience with these measures has demonstrated that humanitarian intentions do not necessarily guarantee more humane treatment or successful rehabilitation of the individual. Juvenile court procedures have frequently been found to infringe on the rights of the child. In addition, adjudication of a person as mentally ill proved to involve problems of stigma as harmful, or more harmful, than a criminal record. In addition, several commitment procedures have been attacked for their failure to protect individual rights, and on the grounds that adequate treatment is often not provided and the custody involved generally becomes the equivalent of penal incarceration. Despite these criticisms, however, there has been considerable interest in broadening the use of civil commitment as an alternative for narcotic addicts and alcoholics. Since the early days of the juvenile court there has also been an increased use of delinquency adjudication for relatively minor misbehavior or for such vaguely defined statutes as incorrigibility.

Recently, there has been a noticeable shift in emphasis from lightening the impact of either civil or criminal court processing on certain groups of social deviants to removing such persons entirely from the judicial process. Generally, the American system has a tendency to rely too heavily on the law and legal process for the solution of pressing social problems. In other words, the arbitrary assignment to the criminal law of a variety of human conduct and conditions has come to be regarded as a problem of overcriminalization. The problems associated with overcriminalization have resulted in some experimentation, such as direct referral to community agencies, transfer of responsibility for certain groups to public health authorities, and legal reforms to remove certain kinds of minor misconduct or victimless crimes from the criminal statutes. (See Chapter 16 for a full discussion of overcriminalization.) Attempts to find alternatives outside the legal process have been most evident in the cases of juveniles brought to court for noncriminal misconduct.

Three types of social response to deviant but not clearly criminal behavior can be distinguished according to degree of involvement of the units of the criminal justice system: (1) penal sanction and criminal processing; (2) legal reform and transfer to public health authorities or social welfare agencies; and (3) the compromise solution, which is civil processing and compulsory commitment. From the literature on both latter practices, several issues emerge as predominant: civil commitment or compulsory court-ordered treatment; the use of health resources and other nonpenal measures for purposes of social control and individual treatment; and constitutional and statutory reform.

Civil Commitment

Civil commitment generally is described as a noncriminal process by which a sick or otherwise dependent person is involuntarily committed to a nonpenal institution for care and treatment. It is often represented as a useful and humane means of diverting selected types of deviants from the criminal justice system. However, closer inspection reveals that the affirmative aspects of diversion exist only in theory.

The rationale for civil commitment is at first difficult to resist. The reputed offender is diverted to a noncriminal proceeding and subsequently hospitalized for treatment instead of sentenced to prison. Concurrently, society is protected against whatever dangers such persons might present if left at liberty and, through rehabilitation, against the possibility of repetition of disapproved behavior upon release. Since few people support the punishment of ill persons or children, such a plan of treatment appeals to contemporary notions of justice.

Why, then, is civil commitment the subject of such controversy? Much of the criticism has been focused on the lack of adequate procedural safeguards, the absence of the treatment that is supposed to justify commitment, or the injustice of the longer confinement often imposed under civil as compared with criminal law. Although these are important areas of concern, the emphasis is unfortunate in that attention to specific problems of procedure and adequacy of treatment tends to mask or at least divert attention from the more basic issue of the validity of civil commitment itself.

The courts usually have been willing to support the legislatively determined distinction between civil and criminal commitment. Usually, however, they do so without careful scrutiny. The Supreme Court, in *Robinson* v. *California* (1962), decided that drug addiction is a disease and that an addict cannot constitutionally be dealt with as a criminal on the basis of his addiction. While it found penal imprisonment for addiction to be cruel and unusual punishment, the decision did not rule on the civil commitment of these same individuals.

The decision only implies that civil commitment of a sick person would be proper, but its language on this point is merely asserted, and no precedents are cited.[4] While the decision states that "a state might establish a program of compulsory treatment for those addicted to narcotics . . . (which) might require periods of involuntary confinement . . . (and) penal sanctions might be imposed for failure to comply with established compulsory procedures," the Supreme Court still has not handed down a decision on the civil commitment of ill offenders, and the substance of civil commitment statutes has not been examined to establish its "civil" nature. Meanwhile, the persistence of the "civil" label attached to procedures to commit ill persons for compulsory treatment— even though they may have not been proven to be dangerous or incompetent—leads to the belief that these persons are being properly diverted from the criminal justice system.

The case for civil commitment of ill persons in lieu of criminal processing is seriously challenged by the Supreme Court decision in *Powell* v. *Texas* (1968). In this instance, the Court upheld the criminal conviction of Powell, an alcoholic, on the grounds that he had committed an illegal act—being drunk in public—whereas in *Robinson*, the issue had been that of a condition—being an addict—which could not in itself be viewed as criminal. Most interesting was the cautionary attitude of the Court toward civil commitment as opposed to penal incarceration.[5] The Court in *Powell* claims that "one virtue of the criminal process is, at least, that the duration of penal incarceration typically has some outside limit." Therapeutic civil commitment, on the other hand, lacks this feature; one is typically committed until one is cured. It is also objected that there is as yet no known generally effective method of treating alcoholics, and the facilities for their treatment are woefully lacking. Thus, in the space of a few years, the court has moved from a position of invitation to one of deep suspicion. As Rubin points out, each of the Court's

[4] President's Commission on Law Enforcement and Administration of Justice, *The Challenge of Crime in a Free Society* (Washington, D.C.: U.S. Govt. Printing Office, 1967), p. 14.
[5] Sol Rubin, "Civil Commitment of Addicts and Alcoholics." Paper presented to the Governor's Conference on Drug and Alcohol Abuse, January 12-13, 1970, Miami Beach, Florida (New York: NCCD, 1970).

objections to civil commitment of alcoholics holds true for the true addict.[6] The case of civil commitment, both in terms of legality and of social value, obviously is still unsettled.

Compulsory Treatment

Civil commitment is not the only sticky problem in the diversion of individuals from the criminal justice system. Several contemporary beliefs have converged around compulsory treatment. These are: (1) that offenders should be treated instead of punished; (2) that some conditions, such as alcoholism and addiction, are not criminal but manifestations of illness; (3) that some persons, because of their condition (youth, mental illness), should be given special consideration or dealt with less severely; and (4) the belief that the state has a right and obligation to intervene where the individual or society is endangered. The civil commitment, juvenile court procedure, or compulsory treatment of the noncrime enforced by the prospect of penal processing for a crime came into operation to satisfy the requirements of these beliefs. The supposed diversion of persons to civil processing whose condition of behavior is held noncriminal appears to be an attempt to have it both ways. That is, the individual, not being criminal, is not being subject to penal sanction but, for the protection of all concerned, he may be subject to dissimilar measures classified as nonpenal.

The point on which this whole structure must rest is the power of the state to intervene in situations where no penal sanction exists. This is a power that should be limited by the requirements that there be sufficient danger either to the individuals or to the populace, and sufficient helplessness of the individual. More clearly stated, it is necessary that dangerousness and helplessness be clearly distinguished from the existence of a condition such as addiction or mental illness. The fact that the states' power to intervene in civil cases is clearly limited must be recognized for two reasons. First, because ignoring this fact leads to abuse. Second, because without constant attention to the weaknesses in such thinking, given a particular value system, any behavior might be convincingly described as harmful to self or others.

[6] Ibid.

It is impossible for society to have it both ways. If a specific deviate behavior is to be defined as not criminal, then it would seem that an individual should not be compelled to accept treatment for that condition unless the condition is ruled inherently dangerous. In addition, the person should only be committed after it has been determined that he is dangerous or helpless. If society believes that certain nondangerous offenders should be diverted from the criminal justice system, then that same society should not be satisfied with the substitution of measures that differ only in their description as "nonpenal" or "treatment."

There are other alternatives for handling the noncriminal juvenile, the narcotic addict, the alcoholic, and the nondangerous deviants. These should be discussed together, since the principle is essentially the same. In the case of a noncriminal deviant, where the individual is not otherwise committable under state power, he may be released to the community. Where a crime has been committed and the defendant is also a noncriminal deviant, he may be dealt with by the penal process for his offense.

Narcotic Addicts

In reality, there has been relatively little experimentation in the United States relative to the diversion of addicts from the criminal justice system. The ruling that an addict cannot constitutionally be labeled a criminal for his addiction would suggest a step in this direction. In practice, however, this has not been a large concession. Civil commitment statutes have functioned to retain the states' ability to incarcerate or otherwise intervene in the lives of both the addict offender and the addict non-offender. Instead of reducing the number of persons subject to state intervention, civil commitment ironically has greatly increased this number by bringing into the system that population of otherwise noncriminal persons whose only offense is their illness.

The states with the largest addict populations are California and New York. These states have enacted civil commitment statutes and both have developed extensive rehabilitation programs based on civil incarceration. While both the California rehabilitation center program and the program of New York State's Narcotic Addiction Control Commission are described in terms of rehabilitation, treatment, and hospitalization of patients, neither is based on the medical model. Both programs depend for their identification as nonpenal and medical on a distinction between treatment and punishment, with no apparent recognition of the fact that treatment can be provided as well in a penal institution. There is nothing inherently nonpenal about a treatment facility.

An Alternative: The Medical Model

In Great Britain, the addict is viewed as an ill person and, if he feels the need, may be treated by the medical profession. Of significance is the fact that the addict must seek the help. Statutorily, this may exist in the United States, but such is not in practice. The legislative enactments of both countries appear the same, since narcotic drugs may be prescribed by physicians for the treatment of addiction. The primary difference is that in Britain the determination of proper treatment of addiction rests with the medical profession, while in the United States the definition of professional practice has been rigidly established by nonmedical authorities.

The medical model, in which the medical profession has the authority to determine and to administer proper treatment to ill persons, is clearly prescribed—in regard to narcotics addiction—by the present law. It is only the nature of administrative enforcement by the Bureau of Narcotics and the collaboration of the American Medical Association that deters physicians from administering drugs to treat addiction. The Supreme Court in *Robinson* stated that "the narcotic drug addict is a sick person, physically and psychologically, and as such is entitled to qualified medical attention . . . as are other sick people."[7] This decision is a significant advancement in its prohibition of penal imprisonment for addiction. However, it has done nothing to enhance the treatment of addicts as sick people. Addicts will not receive the treatment to which they are entitled until the regulations of the Bureau of Narcotics and Dangerous Drugs (now part of the Drug Enforcement Administration) are amended to conform with the law. This will then encourage physicians to feel free to provide qualified medical attention to addicts, just as they do to other ill people.

Unfortunately, most communities in the United States would not

[7] Robinson v. California, 370 U.S. 660 (1962).

be prepared to deal with addiction as a social problem if the medical model and its voluntary aspect were immediately put into effect. Hospital and clinic facilities are, at present, generally lacking, and private physicians would be unable to handle the large number of addicts needing help. Existing facilities would not be capable of handling the influx of people needing treatment.

Little impact on the problems of drug dependence will occur unless the medical share of the responsibility is accepted, and programs commensurate with the magnitude of the problem are instituted. One approach to this situation is the community mental health center. The success of such a center, however, is still completely dependent on the acceptance of responsibility by the medical profession. In the medical health center the goals of treatment would be expressed in terms of the individual's diagnosed level of disfunction in different areas. Improved adaptation or functioning becomes a central goal, with particular phased subgoals assigned on the basis of individual characteristics. Addiction would be viewed as a chronic condition, and success in treatment defined individually. This approach is in stark contrast to the present requirements of compulsory treatment programs in which one relapse is taken to denote failure.

Other types of treatment facilities are residence facilities, hospital programs, and outpatient treatment in clinics. In addition, an increasing number of state and municipal hospitals are adding local hospitalization facilities specifically for addicted persons who are admitted voluntarily. In the community program of New York City's Metropolitan Hospital, addicts are detoxified by the methadone-substitution method and placed in a rehabilitation ward for four weeks, although they may sign themselves out at any time.[8] Major emphasis is placed on after-care including financial, family, housing services, legal advice, recreation, and vocational counseling. More recent is the experience with outpatient care of addicts. At New York's Bernstein Institute of Beth Israel Medical Center, addicts are given daily dosages of liquid methadone, which eliminates the craving for heroin while breaking the effects of any opiates if they are taken.[9]

[8] Alfred H. Freedman, Clifford J. Sager, and Edward L. Rabiner, "A Voluntary Program for the Treatment of Narcotic Addicts in a General Hospital" (New York: Metropolitan Hospital Center, 1972).
[9] Vincent P. Dole and Marie Nyswander, "A Medical Treatment for Diacerylmorphine Addiction," *J. Amer. Medical Assoc., 193,* No. 8 (1965), pp. 646-650.

These are only some of the ways in which addiction might be handled as a public health program by medical authorities without the use of civil commitment or other compulsory or penal measures. In conclusion, it is important to stress that drugs need not be legalized for the treatment of addiction to be carried out in the community. The legal basis for the administration of narcotics to addicts under a physician's care already exists, and it is necessary only to make enforcement conform to law.

Chronic Drunkenness Offenders

Although alcoholism and drug addiction may be considered together for the purpose of designing a public health approach to prevention and treatment, alcoholism presents a slightly different problem for the diversion of offenders from the criminal justice system. Alcoholism itself is not an offense, but being drunk in public almost always is, and it is the public drunkenness charge that provides the basis for intervention to control alcohol consumption. While removal of drug addicts from the justice system requires primarily a change in enforcement practices and the development of community facilities for treatment, in the case of the chronic drunkenness offender diversion requires a change in law. Civil commitment is not as popular a solution for the public drunk, since the drunkenness offender is usually put in jail.

Legal reform to remove public drunkenness as an offense is now a respectable and widely voiced recommendation. While commission of a criminal act by an intoxicated person requires criminal handling, the problem of drunkenness requires effective treatment, not an adjudication of guilt. It is now being argued that it may be more sensible to take a protective shelter-maintenance approach to the problem. That is, it is suggested that the costs involved in obtaining minimal success in attempting to cure the alcoholic require a different approach. It may be that neither the sick role nor the bad role is appropriate, and the state should rethink its function along the lines of providing temporary shelter for those who are rendered temporarily helpless as a result of being drunk. Obviously, this approach is novel and controversial and needs a great deal of additional thought and research.

The arguments against compulsory civil measures for narcotic addicts also apply to the alcoholic. However, until civil commitment of the drunk becomes acceptable practice, the major problem is not civil incarceration, but compulsory treatment for an illness condition manifested by the existence of a behavior closely related to those that are considered to be crimes. Compulsory treatment involves placement on probation under conditions of abstention and requires attendance for treatment, or it involves suspension of criminal charges in exchange for participation in treatment and its successful completion.

Not only is involuntary treatment for alcoholism a questionable practice, but there are indications that it is also ineffective. There have been various reports of municipal court programs in the United States that use such approaches as probation with referral to clinic treatment, Alcoholics Anonymous, court-sponsored honor classes, halfway houses, and camps instead of jail sentences. However, studies have indicated that enforced referral to treatment was no more effective than no treatment at all. One explanation offered for this is that the conditions of court-imposed referral confronted the offender with an anxiety-producing situation that may have increased the likelihood that he would resume his previous drinking pattern.

What are the alternatives? The Presidential Commission Task Force on Drunkenness recommended that communities establish detoxification units as part of a comprehensive treatment program to which inebriates might be brought by police for short-term detention under the authority of civil legislation. The Commission also recommended that drunkenness not be treated as a criminal offense, thus bringing up the problem of compulsory civil detention for a noncrime.

Experimental programs in the United States, operating under the premise that most chronic inebriates *require* compulsion to accept treatment, are not well founded; they also refute the argument that police arrest is necessary as a case-finding tool. Through the concerted efforts of public and private social agencies, a large number of alcoholics may be provided voluntary treatment and welfare services before an offense has been identified by police. If an essentially unavoidable situation is no longer treated as an offense, a greater number of these persons might be diverted from the criminal justice system.

In areas where health has been extended to the "skid-row" alcoholic by such organizations as the Salvation Army, the need for arrest and detention in order to provide social services and "control" of the situation has been considerably reduced. Were such services and facilities supplemented by other public and private agency efforts, including aggressive casework types of case finding, and treatment offered on a voluntary basis to this group, prearrest diversion might be successfully implemented on a large scale.

Postarrest diversion presents other problems, similar in principle to those involving the commitment for treatment of the addicted offender. The literature on the alcoholic offender reflects a growing support for the postarrest diversion of offenders, for purposes of treatment, to institutional or other compulsory treatment. Most widely recommended are: (1) brief, involuntary detention in civil detoxification centers following arrest, (2) involuntary commitment to an inpatient facility for treatment, and (3) enforcement of treatment of offenders on probation. These measures may be found effective in getting the alcoholic offender to accept treatment, or even to cure him, and they may be an improvement over the usual jailing and punitive detention. However, they cannot really be considered a diversion except in name, and a compulsory nature may well be unjustified if a right to refuse treatment is established. Closer examination reveals that these measures involve the use of community resources and penal treatment, the adoption of treatment orientation and correction, or the substitution of nonpenal hospital/patient terminology, instead of actual removal of the offender from the justice system. The goal of providing humane treatment should not be confused with diversion.

Examination of current practices and proposals concerning alternatives to penal sanction of the alcoholic offender supports the conclusions suggested by the literature on the narcotic addict: (1) civil incarceration is not a diversion or alternative, and thus it is difficult to justify; (2) commitment or other compulsion for purposes of treatment rather than because of dangerousness is questionable; and (3) there are voluntary alternatives involving a considerable saving in police, court, and correctional resources, which are more consistent with a policy in diversion.

Of course, prerequisite to the removal of the drunk or alcoholic offender from the justice system will be the development and expansion of community resources, such as medical welfare and other assistance. The nonoffender drunk then may be referred directly to social agencies for voluntary treatment or other services. An alcoholic who has committed an offense may be handled by the penal system, in which treatment for his condition might be offered. If his offense is not considered serious, he might be routinely handled in a special program for misdemeanants, involving police warning instead of arrest, and referral to community agencies for voluntary treatment or other assistance.

Petty Misdemeanant Offenders

It is well known that the overload on the courts is caused largely by the huge volume of minor offenses. In addition, the fact that penal sanctions do not seem to deter such offenses makes the petty misdemeanant offender the most obvious case for removal from the criminal justice system. It is widely accepted that new procedures for handling these offenders could and should be devised. Hugh Price recommends a procedure that is relevant to the misdemeanor problem of its recognition of the social class bias of many arrests for petty offenses. Price proposes the establishment of neighborhood police offices in ghetto areas. These offices would be staffed by community affairs officers and several neighborhood aides.[10] All persons arrested for petty offenses would be brought initially to a neighborhood office where the officer would check the police blacklist of multiple offenders who are not to be handled by the informal procedure. A person would be blacklisted if he has been detained and released by the police or prosecutor three or more times in the previous year, or if he has failed to appear for a prosecutor's or family relations hearing during the past year. A blacklisted offender would be formally booked and presented in court for prosecution. But an offender who is not found to be blacklisted would be recorded in a police log book, yet not formally booked, so no arrest would be entered on a criminal record card. The community affairs officer would meet with the offender and attempt to determine the problems that led him to commit the violation. Once the community affairs officer has assessed the severity of the offense and the nature of its origin, he may recommend that the party contact a mental health, employment, or legal aid agency, but such referrals would not be binding on the party. The officer may choose among several dispositions, such as outright release, release with warning, or referral to the prosecutor or family relations officer for conference.

The last disposition would be used in cases where the facts of the violation are more serious, or where the offender has committed the limit

[10] Hugh V. Price, "A Proposal for Handling of Petty Misdemeanor Offenses," *Connecticut Bar Journal, 42*, No. 3 (1968), pp. 55-75.

violations prior to blacklisting. At these hearings further possibilities for referral to social, legal, or other agencies would be explored. Again the dispositions of release, release with warning, and referral to other agencies are available. At this second stage, the hearings officer also would be authorized to issue an order for an arrest. Up to this point, however, no arrest would have been recorded. The purpose of this proposal is to minimize the impact of petty crimes on the courts and on the offender without impairing the ability of the police and courts to maintain law and order. It is also a means of reforming the unequal and discriminatory manner in which petty offenses now are processed at the police station.

This proposed model is a true example of diversion of offenders from the criminal justice system. Every attempt is made to handle the minor offender in alternate ways before an arrest is made. Where the offenses of public drunkenness or vagrancy are not removed from criminal statutes, and to the extent that case finding and provision of services are not offered before police contact, such a procedure exists as a possible alternative. One runs the risk, however, that by implementing this sort of program, one also reduces the possibility of removing some of these questionable laws from the books.

Noncriminal Juveniles

Even though the juvenile court was established as a means of removing the juvenile offender from the criminal justice system, this nonpenal alternative has functioned in such a way as to draw even more persons into the system of control by state intervention. That the juvenile justice system has not fulfilled the need for an alternative to the penal system is demonstrated by the current demand for new ways of handling the problem juvenile through diversion from juvenile court processing.

The concern of the juvenile court with this position in the interest of the child has necessitated the use of broad discretion by police and court officials and has resulted in the present informal system of pre-adjudication of many potential subjects of formal court action. A study of differential handling by police and selection of juvenile offenders for court appearance in four different Pennsylvania communities revealed wide variations in rates of arrests and court referral.[11] This position,

[11] Nathan Goldman, *The Differential Selection of Juvenile Offenders for Court Appearance* (New York: NCCD, 1963).

including whether a juvenile was diverted from formal processing, was related not only to offense, but to age, race, sex, and residence. Differential handling was found to be related to attitudes of the policemen toward the juvenile, his family, the juvenile court, his own role as a policeman, and his perception of community attitudes toward delinquency.

Many critics of the existing system of informal disposition have argued that the observed arbitrary and discriminatory factors in the selection process be eliminated through professionalization of the police. They suggest, among other things: (1) the setting of explicit standards by police departments; (2) the training of officers in juvenile behavior; (3) police community relations programs; (4) police juvenile liaison schemes; or (5) other means of improving police discretionary judgments. Since the police are often the first to come in contact with juvenile misconduct, such efforts are certainly of great importance. It is believed, however, that the screening of serious offenses from simple misconduct or other nonserious behavior should not be primarily a police responsibility. This is a home function, and it is questionable how much authority the police should have in the areas of child discipline, guidance, moral instruction, and protection.

Much of the literature on the removal of juveniles from the jurisdiction of police in the courts recognizes the extent of community responsibility in the area of social control. Many writers urge that the definition of delinquency be narrowed to exclude a variety of behaviors that, if committed by an adult, would not constitute a violation of the law. This implies not only that court processing for such conduct is unjust, but that handling of noncriminal deviants by community agencies and individuals is more appropriate. It also has been suggested that judges simply stopped accepting the dependent, neglected, or nondangerous child for detention, probation, or commitment, thus diverting such children to family and child welfare agencies or social and mental health services. This would force the public to accept the responsibility for their problems instead of turning them over to the police. It is common knowledge that many children throughout the United States who have not committed crimes are being drawn into the correctional system. It is believed that this is a serious detriment to both the child and the system itself. If it is public apathy or tacit acceptance of this situation that allows it to continue, then a broad effort should be made to make it understood that existing practices are neither effective nor necessary.

One alternative is to establish youth services bureaus within the communities. These bureaus would provide and coordinate programs and services for delinquents and nondelinquents alike. The purpose of the bureaus would be to facilitate the diversion of children and youth from judicial processing to social services.[12] Naturally, the nature of the services provided would relate directly to each community, thus some variants would exist. Presumably, local definitions of delinquency and interpretations of situations that require intervention will also affect the nature and extent of services.

Conclusion

Diversion of offenders from the criminal justice system is of paramount concern to most judicial areas across the nation, and several are deeply involved in such programs. But standards in the approach, selection, maintenance, and evaluation are needed if the maximum benefits are to be received both by the system and by the offender. Research on pretrial diversion programs is necessary and vital. In the summer of 1973, the National Science Foundation awarded a financial grant to the American Bar Association under the Foundation's Research Applied to National Needs program. The purpose of the grant is to review research on pretrial diversion programs that are adaptable both to adult and juvenile defendants as a community-based alternative for reversing criminal careers.

Few diversion programs are more than four years old and, as more metropolitan and municipal court systems consider adopting such projects, there is a serious need to examine research on the initial demonstrations and the policy implications and issues indicated by experience thus far. The project, to be conducted by a research evaluation study unit of the ABA National Pretrial Intervention Service Center, was funded to conduct a six-month evaluation of all available research relating to intervention programs. The project is expected to result in the preparation of a number of publications to assist municipalities, policy makers, and the research community in relating research findings to their

---

[12] Milton G. Rector, Statement Before the U.S. Senate Subcommittee to Investigate Juvenile Delinquency, *Crime and Delinquency, 16,* No. 1 (1970), pp. 93-99.

specific needs and interests. It is hoped that projects such as this will provide more complete answers on the best possible diversion programs available for inclusion on a regular basis in the nation's justice system.

Student Checklist

1. Can you identify the two areas in which diversion is a conscious policy?
2. Are you able to list three arguments against informal pre-judicial processings?
3. Do you know what the three major criticisms of civil commitment are?
4. Can you list four contemporary beliefs that have converged around compulsory treatment?
5. Can you determine the difference between civil commitment and compulsory treatment?
6. Do you know the methods that can be used to treat narcotic addicts under the medical model?
7. Can you list the three recommendations for the postarrest diversion of alcoholic offenders?
8. Are you able to describe the process of a blacklist of multiple petty misdemeanant offenders?

Topics for Discussion

1. Discuss the advantages of diversion from the justice system.
2. Discuss the need for civil commitment.
3. Discuss the disadvantages of compulsory treatment.
4. Discuss the police problems in handling the alcoholic offender.
5. Discuss the application of discretion to other areas of criminal violations.

The study of this chapter will enable you to:

1. Define the term overcriminalization.
2. List the three major categories of overcriminalization.
3. Differentiate between moral statutes and nuisance statutes.
4. Identify the two major types of criminal activity that are covered by illness statutes.
5. Identify the moral costs of overcriminalization for each category.
6. Contrast the consequences of repealing the nuisance and illness statutes.
7. List the consequences of repealing the moral statutes.

16
Overcriminalization

Overcriminalization can best be defined as the misuse of criminal sanction, a misuse that contributes to disrespect for the law and damages the ends that law is supposed to serve. It criminalizes conduct regarded as legitimate by substantial segments of the society; initiating patterns of discriminatory enforcement, and draining resources away from the effort to control more serious misconduct. Overcriminalization includes, for example, laws dealing with moral issues, such as various types of sexual activities and abortions; laws criminalizing certain illnesses, such as drunkenness and narcotics addictions; and the nuisance laws relating to such issues as pornography, obscenity, gambling, and vagrancy.

Categories of Overcriminalization

Moral Conduct
Any sexual conduct between married adults—except that conduct which is generally accepted as "normal"—is illegal! Probably no laws are broken more often, even by those sworn to enforce them or those who give them legislative existence. Such laws thus become organized hypoc-

Primary Source: National Commission on the Causes and Prevention of Violence, *Law and Order Reconsidered* (Washington, D.C.: U.S. Govt. Printing Office, 1969), pp. 551-556.

risy on a national scale. If all violators were prosecuted and punished, the majority of the adult population of the United States would be in prison. These statutes punish sexual conduct between unmarried adults in private, adultery, and consenting homosexual activity between adults in private. Prostitution enjoys a higher degree of justification, but none-theless is punishable under the criminal law, as are abortions in many states.

Morals have changed considerably in recent years, particularly those of younger people, and the standards of conduct embodied in these laws are being dissented from by an ever-increasing segment of our society. The general failure to enforce these laws is probably the only factor preventing an immediate vocal demand for their repeal.

Category of Illness

The law weakens its moral authority when it punishes an illness as though it were a crime. This category includes alcoholism and narcotics addiction, and it is not to be confused with other criminal activities related to drunkenness or addiction. Society's motivation is frequently that of protecting the offender from himself. The arrest of alcoholics frequently gets them out of harm's way on the streets and, particularly in the winter months, is probably the only thing that keeps many of them alive. Also, arrest is often the only method of preventing the drunk from becoming a public spectacle and from bothering other citizens.

Drug addiction is not to be confused with the criminal acts of possession, sales, or even use of narcotics. Once hooked, there is nothinig voluntary about the narcotic addict's need for drugs, and he is clearly a slave to his addiction. History has shown that criminal prosecution for addiction simply has not worked. Treatment in a noncriminal or civil setting should be available for all those who seek out such treatment.

High-intensity enforcement of simple possession of such nonaddictive drugs as marijuana is largely a myth. That is not to say, however, that statistically there is not an ever-increasing number of charges brought for these offenses. But more often than not, there is another reason for the arrest—and the nonaddictive drug is often discovered during the course of the arrest. Evelle J. Younger, Attorney General of California, in a law enforcement forum in Modesto in April 1973 stated, "approximately 90 percent of all the arrests in California for marijuana began with an original arrest for another criminal offense. The marijuana was found after the defendant was already in custody."

Category of Nuisance

The category of statutes identified as nuisance laws typically penalizes pornography, obscenity, gambling, and vagrancy. The laws punishing pornography are closely related to the moral laws dealing with printed matter and movies depicting nude bodies and various sexual acts. Both sale and possession are illegal, even if viewed in private. The obscenity laws deal with indecent exposure in public, topless and bottomless waitresses and entertainers in places both open and closed to the general public, and vulgar language in the presence of women and children.

The gambling laws are as diverse as any group of laws in existence. They cover racetracks, cardrooms, and casinos. In some jurisdictions it is legal to bet on the horses at the tracks but illegal to operate a cardroom. Some jurisdictions require only that a gambling establishment obtain a business license and pay taxes on the income. Generally, people who want to frequent such places are willing to travel the distances to those areas where the conduct is within the meaning of the law. The paradox seems to be that if it is, in fact, detrimental to the public good to gamble in one jurisdiction, the nature of the act is not changed by traveling the short distance into another jurisdiction. Prostitution may well fall into this paradox also, since there are jurisdictions where prostitution is legally sanctioned.

Many of the old vagrancy laws are being overturned by constitutional interpretation. In some jurisdictions, however, it is still a crime to wander aimlessly about without visible means of support or to lead a "lewd, idle, or immoral life." The constitutional lever being used to overturn many of these statutes is the vagueness or ambiguity of the meanings of the words or phrases. If leading an idle life was strictly enforced, a large segment of our youth would become involved criminally as vagrants.

Sensibly worded, such laws *can* serve a clear community interest. They help protect community tranquility and prevent undue annoyance of the majority of citizens by the pugnacious, the shiftless, the noisy, and the vulgar. The police use such statutes as weapons against prostitutes, gamblers, and others whose apprehension is difficult because of problems of proof, and as legal underpinning for their general peace-keeping and order-maintaining responsibilities.

Costs of Overcriminalization

The criminal sanction is optimally functional when it serves the greatest good of the greatest number. A single-factor analysis of monetary cost of applying such sanctions would be an oversimplification—and only a partial consideration. The other major cost consideration is the ethical cost to society. Consider both of these costs in each of the three categories of overcriminalization: moral statutes, illness statutes, and nuisance statutes.

Moral Statutes

Laws such as those against consensual fornication are rarely if ever enforced and are seen as prohibitions that are not seriously intended to be enforced. In this same vein one finds deviations from "normal" sexual activity between consenting adults in private. In those rare instances where enforcement is sought, the penalties become a discriminatory club against the unwary. The monetary cost would, of course, be minimal. The ethical cost is greater. If rules are unreasonable and are not taken seriously by lack of enforcement, they should be eliminated. If moral (sexual) sanctions are necessary, then they should be evenhandedly and enthusiastically enforced.

The moral statutes that are most often enforced are those against homosexualty. The monetary cost of vice squad operations nationwide is quite high. But the highest, and probably the most serious, cost is the degrading experience of the police officer who loiters in places where homosexuals are thought to frequent in order to make arrests. Public jury trials of these cases are also embarrassing to all concerned.

Policing of prostitutes is an involved operation that uses a great deal of police beat patrol time that could be better spent elsewhere. Therefore, the monetary cost is high. The ethical cost is somewhat of a paradox since, in most jurisdictions, only the prostitute is liable under the criminal laws. Those paying for her services are not subject to arrest —a flagrant inconsistency. If prostitution continues to be a law violation, it would seem that both parties to this criminal act should be prosecutable.

The moral questions about legalized abortion continue to generate much conflicting debate. The cost in enforcing these statutes against women probably is not as great as the ferreting out of the abortioner. The abortioner poses the serious ethical cost, because his existence is created by a set of archaic laws that prevent many competent medical personnel from performing abortions.

Illness Statutes

The amount of money spent in arresting, booking, taking to court, and housing the drunks in this country is astronomical. If the amount of time away from normal patrol functions that is spent handling drunks were to be computed on an hourly basis nationwide, the figure would defy belief. Presently, many jurisdictions allow for the handling of drunks as a medical problem where facilities permit. The time and money saved is considerable, and the ethical savings are that a multitude of sick persons are being more humanely treated.

The vast majority of marijuana arrests are made after the defendant comes to the attention of the police for other reasons. In terms of dollars, the actual costs of hunting down addicts per se is comparatively minimal.

In some jurisdictions, the person who is addicted to narcotics is on a par with those addicted to alcohol. That is to say, the physical condition is not illegal in and of itself; however, being "under the influence" will invoke criminal sanctions. There is growing evidence that these contradictions in treating and handling alcoholics and addicts are being resolved in some communities.

Nuisance Statutes

The monetary waste in undercover investigations of pornography—both movies and printed material—is large, but it represents a small fraction of the court costs of prosecution. Seemingly, all those arrested for pornography offenses become involved in extensive trials simply because, in many jurisdictions, there is no adequate definition of what constitutes pornography. The courts are split on this issue, and court calendars are almost hopelessly bogged down with this type of case. And the general public seems to be losing faith in the ability of the legal system to deal effectively with the problem of pornography prosecutions.

Obscenity laws dealing with live nude entertainment and bottom-less and topless waitresses and dancers are in much the same predicament as the pornography statutes. Again, there is no clear agreement on what is obscene. Those who frequent such establishments certainly do not agree with the legal situation; those who do not approve have the option of avoiding these establishments. This seems to be the growing attitude of the general public, thus making the monetary cost of enforcement even more enraging to citizen and law enforcement official alike.

Gambling laws throughout the nation are contradictory and para-doxical. If the citizens of California use the gambling establishments of Nevada in droves, Nevada reaps the wealth of California's citizens, who can bet on the horses in their own state, but are forbidden to have gam-bling casinos. Organized crime is firmly entrenched in gambling opera-tions, as well as in narcotics and prostitution, and will continue to flourish, partly because of present attitudes and practices in criminalizing these types of behavior.

The Consequences of Repeal: The Moral Statutes

The repeal of laws that penalize various sexual activity between consent-ing adults in private is long overdue. Emphasis must be placed on the meanings of the terms consent and private. The term adult has a legal definition in the attainment of a certain number of years. But in examin-ing the term consent, certain prerequisites would have to be present, such as willingness and mental capacity to give consent knowingly. Inducing consent by the use of alcoholic beverages or narcotics would be other than willing submission. The term private means in a place so as not to offend or outrage the public decency.

The criminal penalties resulting from homosexual activities seem to be a greater evil than the activities themselves. Again, borrowing the terms consent and private as used above—wherein the general public is not offended—perhaps such laws are more an invasion of privacy than criminal.

Suggestions for repeal of laws against prostitution ordinarily are accompanied by proposals for control and regulation or licensing. This would require each prostitute to register with the health department and have regular medical checkups, thus reducing and controlling venereal diseases. Income taxes could be collected from these establishments in the way they are collected from other service-oriented businesses. The fear of legalized prostitution seems to be that communities will immediately suffer increased prostitution and venereal disease epidemics and provide organized crime with fruitful increases in revenue. Reason seems to dictate the opposite.

History has shown that eradicating or even reducing prostitution is an impossibility. This is especially true when efforts to eliminate prostitution by use of the criminal sanction have been attempted. In those parts of the world where the sexual climate is more permissive and the welfare state has eliminated poverty, prostitution is virtually nonexistent. In comparison, the dominant puritan culture creates a market for the services of the prostitute. It is possible that the much-heralded sexual revolution in the United States may alleviate much of the prostitution problem. But it is not probable!

If the only support for the nation's abortion laws is a particular religious doctrine, then the First Amendment to the Constitution would argue decisively against such support. Abortion could be treated as a medical matter between the patient and doctor, thus eliminating the "abortion mills" that too frequently are underwritten by organized crime.

The Consequences of Repeal: The Illness Statutes

Laws against intoxication and addiction are under attack throughout the nation. Our statutory law embodies the common law principle that an act must be voluntary to be criminal. Although there is nothing voluntary about the need of alcoholics and addicts, one could argue that most alcoholics and addicts began their use voluntarily. But to criminalize and punish that which can only be termed an illness invokes the cruel and unusual punishment clause of the Eighth Amendment.

The police should remain the clearinghouse in determining whether the individual is merely a sick person or a drunken criminal. Law enforcement experience shows that many wanted criminals have come to the attention of police agencies by virtue of their drunkenness or conduct while drunk.

Establishment of treatment facilities is the necessary first step in combating narcotics addiction. Unfortunately, voluntary commitment to

Figure 16-1. Visiting "facility" for addict prisoners, in which no physical contact is allowed.

such facilities has been disheartening, and involuntary commitment seems justified. Since voluntary commitment is, for most addicts, unrealistic, this means that the addicts, more often than not, come to the attention of law enforcement while involved in narcotics traffic. Even though criminally arrested and convicted, the criminal sentences resulting from these convictions can be suspended, and the persons can be committed (diverted) to a narcotics treatment facility on a civil commitment. If the addict rehabilitates himself, then criminal charges can be dismissed against him.

Adequate follow-up care on outpatient status should be main-

Figure 16-2. A treatment center within a prison.

tained, however. Vocational and educational programming should be made available for those who are truly attempting to help themselves. Treatment programs, such as methadone maintenance, should continue to be explored and implemented. Various drug-free, self-help groups have experienced a great deal of support in some parts of the country, and should receive support and encouragement as their programs register successes and become more widely known. If such programs gained widespread support and implementation, narcotics traffic would shrink. Again, organized crime would be dealt a blow, and other satellite crimes—such as prostitution and theft—would be reduced proportionately.

The issue of the nonaddicting or hallucinogenic drugs poses a different problem and requires a different solution. Educational programs handled on a realistic and factual basis seem indicated. Treatment in the physical sense is not needed, except perhaps in cases of malnutrition and venereal disease. Strict controls on the manufacture and sales of such drugs should be rigorously maintained according to the now defunct House Select Committee on Crime.

The Consequences of Repeal: The Nuisance Statutes

The last group of statutes are those used to punish conduct deemed to be a nuisance to particular segments of society or to the police themselves: pornography (both written and on film), obscenity, gambling, and vagrancy. The chief questions raised by these laws is whether or not the majority of the public is offended by this type of conduct and whether or not the interest in maintaining the laws is strong enough to override public sentiment.

In most jurisdictions the criminal law punishes the sale, dissemination, and possession of obscene books, films, pictures, and the like. These laws place an obvious restraint on freedom of expression. The courts have continuously had to wrestle with the problem of whether or not there is a First Amendment violation. The basic rule previously was that the material was pornographic if it appeared to be utterly without redeeming social value. As a result of the June 1973 rulings on five separate pornography and obscenity cases, however, the Supreme Court seemingly reversed this guideline, and made pornography and obscenity a matter for "local community" regulation. Again, we are confronted with what the term pornography means to any given community. The nation may well soon see the creation of "porn cities" where the sale and purchase of such materials is legal—much like the situation that now prevails in the legality of gambling in Las Vegas.

One could probably gain support for the argument that materials alleged to be pornographic should not be publicly displayed on newsstands, nor should pornographic movies be shown in public establishments where minor children would have access to them. Instead, the arguments hold that such materials should be limited to private membership clubs, adult bookstores, and other facilities not generally subject to scrutiny by an unsuspecting passerby. Even if the pornography laws were to be repealed, however, there is still the matter of the promotion of such materials. There should be no invasion of the privacy of those who do not wish to receive or view such materials. Activities such as unsolicited mailings of flyers to the home, door-to-door sales, billboards, and the like would have to be strictly controlled.

Repeal of the laws relating to "obscene" acts in nightclubs has many of the same complications as the pornography issue. One should have the right not to be confronted with sex acts in public. (Topless sunbathing on a public beach and nude sunbathing out of the public view are different issues.) Public advertisement of live sex acts inside private clubs should be viewed critically. Bars, nightclubs, and theaters that charge admission for the viewing of acts that include nude bodies would necessarily have to be shielded from public view.

Repeal of the gambling laws would eliminate some of the hypocrisy that exists. This hypocrisy is best illustrated in areas where a state board controls and taxes racetracks, but forbids and makes the operation of casinos and cardrooms illegal. By legalizing this type of activity it could be controlled, taxed, and taken out of the hands of organized criminals, who have demonstrated their uncanny ability to operate and control gambling operations in defiance of the law. Law loses its credibility when some jurisdictions sanction gambling and others do not. If it is illegal to gamble in California, is Nevada immoral?

Laws against vagrancy and disorderly conduct are defended as a necessary peacekeeping tool by law enforcement agencies, who believe that the threat of arrest assists the officer in maintaining peace and tranquility in his community. Perhaps the real tragedy in laws governing vagrancy and disorderly conduct is the failure by lawmakers to officially recognize police discretion. In most states the statutes read that the police will arrest "all" violators and enforce "all" criminal laws. If these laws are not repealed outright, they should be amended to permit selective enforcement, depending on the circumstances. The issue is clear that the police do not, nor could they ever, arrest all violators of all laws—assuming that it would be physically possible for them to do so. The fact is that the police do exercise their judgment and do not always arrest, even when there is violation of law. This would legitimize an accepted practice and recognize the police as being responsible agencies. Yet enforcing and arresting "all" has been seen by some law enforcement agencies as an excuse not to exercise any discretion. This has been a problem, particularly in the past few years, in the handling of the civil rights and antiwar demonstrations. Enforcement of the "arrest all" doctrine has escalated many demonstrations to disastrous ends.

Police exercise of discretion and selective enforcement has been defended as necessary to fair and effective law enforcement. The test should be whether the exercise of discretion is fair and promotes justice. Decisions based on race, color, and political affiliations would fail the test.

In regard to the enforcement of the laws against vagrancy and disorderly conduct, few believe the guidelines will solve the problems of enforcement, but they may tend to temper them. Police officials contend that these laws are the only methods of controlling drunks, addicts, prostitutes, and gamblers. Ironically, the laws defining these groups as criminals may well be repealed too, thus eliminating much of the present usage of the vagrancy and disorderly conduct laws.

Complexity of the Problem

The problem of overcriminalization is an extremely sensitive and complex one. The views discussed in this chapter will invoke a variety of responses. Many will agree—and feel that the socialization of the laws suggested herein do not go far enough. Some will read with contempt; still others will be apathetic or unconcerned. Many would prefer to support and perpetuate the myth that Americans are one large group of like-minded people. We would like to believe that, in our society, there are time-tested values that are held sacred by all our people. Nothing could be farther from the truth. We have a heterogeneous society, rich with varied value systems and life-styles.

Historically, Americans have resented being told what to do. Attempts by the power structure to modify behavior are, more often than not, met by great resentment. In response to this so-called governmental interference with basic freedoms, however misconstrued in many instances, we see various cults or movements spring up and insulate themselves against the rest of society. American society has become more and more pluralistic. Until we recognize this fact and use it as a guideline in implementing social controls, the system will be self-defeating.

The criminal law is our most drastic measure in regulating conduct. When it is used to regulate morals, or is viewed by substantial segments of our society as cruel and inhumane or arbitrary and capricious, then it breeds contempt and hostility. In other instances the law becomes a means for arbitrary or abusive police conduct. Both are equally wrong.

Many of the criminal codes in the United States are over 100 years old. These codes have been amended over the years, but the basic structure that embodies the common law is hopelessly out of step with the times. The law is a living thing that should change and grow with the times, lest it lose its credibility with the people it is designed to serve. Repeal of the laws suggested in this chapter has begun in some communities and should begin in others. A total revamping or modernizing of the criminal codes throughout the United States should also begin. One thought should be foremost when discussing a major overhaul of laws, and that is that no perfect system will ever be devised. But one that lends itself to change and embodies the spirit of justice will have a great advantage.

Student Checklist

1. Can you remember a working definition of overcriminalization?
2. Do you know the three major categories of overcriminalization?
3. Are you able to differentiate between moral statutes and nuisance statutes?
4. Can you identify the two major types of criminal activity that are covered by illness statutes?
5. Can you identify the moral costs of overcriminalization for each of the three categories?
6. Are you able to contrast the consequences of repealing the nuisance and illness statutes?
7. Can you list the consequences of repealing the moral statutes?

Topics for Discussion

1. Discuss the problem of overcriminalization in America.
2. Discuss the disadvantages of repealing the moral statutes.
3. Discuss the advantages of decriminalizing criminal activities that are covered by illness statutes.
4. Discuss the disadvantages of repealing the nuisance statutes.

BIBLIOGRAPHY

LaFave, Wayne R. *Arrest: The Decision To Take a Subject into Custody.* Boston: Little, Brown, 1965.

Parker, Herbert L. *The Limits of the Criminal Sanction.* Stanford, Calif.: Stanford University Press, 1968.

The President's Commission on Law Enforcement and Administration of Justice. *The Challenge of Crime in a Free Society.* Washington, D.C.: U.S. Govt. Printing Office, 1967.

Wilson, O. W. *Police Administration.* New York: McGraw Hill, 1963.

The study of this chapter will enable you to:

1. List five actions that would result in increased professionalization of the police.
2. Identify the three back-up police services that should be provided to local communities by metropolitan counties.
3. Identify the means by which the prosecutor can serve a coordinating role in the justice system.
4. List the advantages of a unified court system.
5. Describe the Merit Plan for selecting judges.
6. Identify the functions of a judicial qualifications commission.
7. List the three means by which corrections can emphasize rehabilitation.
8. Cite some of the recommendations of the National Advisory Commission on Criminal Justice Standards and Goals.

17
Contemporary Issues

Bureaucracies constantly strive to become more efficient and effective. The task in this nation is especially difficult because the federalized nature of government has created a highly fragmented system of justice. The need for improving all segments of the administration of justice is clearly called for and four major governmental reports have been released by study groups. Each of these reports has contained numerous recommendations for reform of the system. This chapter reviews some of the contemporary issues related to reform of the system of criminal justice.

Police Reform

Today's police are the most visible representatives of the criminal justice system—a system that is severely out of balance. They deal most directly with the people at a time when society is under intense pressure; they are in the closest contact with the individual when he is most vulnerable.

The modern police department is called on to demonstrate the skills of lawyer, psychologist, sociologist, physician, and athlete. But the average police department is undermanned and overworked.

In a society where people and crime are highly mobile, the police too often are tied to small, inefficient jurisdictions. The needed recommendations call for intergovernmental efforts to professionalize the police

Primary Source: Advisory Commission on Intergovernmental Relations, *State-Local Relations in the Criminal Justice System* (Washington, D.C.: U.S. Govt. Printing Office, 1971).

function, make it more responsive to modern needs, assure adequate service to all citizens, and improve police-community relations programs.

Professionalizing the Police

Studies of occupational prestige over the past decade showed low rankings for the police—47th and 54th out of 90 listed occupations. Policemen ranked beneath machinists or undertakers in one survey; they tied with railroad conductors in another.[1]

Police work demands intelligence, good judgment, and special training. But police selection standards generally are low, recruitment efforts inadequate, and training programs minimal. Potentially good officers too often seek other fields of employment. High turnover and low public esteem hamper potential police leadership.

The Police Task Force of the President's Commission on Law Enforcement and the Administration of Justice in 1967 summed up the problem of selection: "Existing selection requirements and procedures in the majority of departments . . . do not screen out the unfit. Hence, it is not surprising that far too many of those charged with protecting life and property and rationally enforcing our laws are not respected by their fellow officers and are incompetent, corrupt, or abusive."[2]

Police officers are subject to great emotional stress, and they are placed in positions of trust. For these reasons, they should be carefully screened to preclude the employment of those who are emotionally unstable, brutal, or who suffer any form of emotional illness. A growing number of police agencies have turned to psychological screening to eliminate those who are emotionally or otherwise unfit for the police service.

Charles Saunders, in *Upgrading the American Police*, reported in 1970 that approximately 25 percent of police agencies used such techniques. A 1971 survey by the International Association of Chiefs of Police revealed that 46 percent of city agencies, 40 percent of county agencies, and 26 percent of state agencies polled used such methods.[3]

---

[1] Advisory Commission on Intergovernmental Relations, *Police Reform* (Washington, D.C.: U.S. Govt. Printing Office, 1971), p. 1.
[2] Ibid.
[3] National Advisory Commission on Criminal Justice Standards and Goals, *Police* (Washington, D.C.: U.S. Govt. Printing Office, 1973), p. 338.

The 1967 President's Commission on Law Enforcement and Administration of Justice reported that only 70 percent of the nation's police departments required a high school diploma as a condition of employment. While that situation has improved somewhat—with police departments in at least nine states and 32 police agencies in California alone requiring education beyond high school—the majority of state, county, and municipal law enforcement agencies still require no more than the high school level of education (Police Personnel Selection Survey, 1971).[4]

Even when police departments set selection standards, they sometimes hinder instead of facilitate efficient recruitment. Inflexible physical standards, such as minimum height, maximum weight, or perfect vision, do not necessarily measure the overall physical ability or agility of the applicant, yet they do sometimes keep otherwise qualified men from becoming police officers. The requirement that a police recruit be 21 years old (and not have a college education) sends high school graduates into other careers before they would be eligible to join the force and stops many college graduates from applying. Only 11 percent of police departments had cadet programs for youth interested in a police career. Residence requirements limit the geographical range of recruitment. In addition, some states have rigid veterans preference requirements for local police for both recruitment and promotion.

Closely related to the problem of selection is that of training. Here again, many police departments are deficient. Nearly one-fifth of all municipal police agencies provide no training at all, and about half of the departments that have training programs conduct them with one or two members of regular staff. The President's Commission recommended that a minimum of 400 hours of training be required. The best police departments provide about half of that, and then generally not at the outset of the recruit's career.

The importance of early training was pointed out with a touch of irony in the report of the President's Commission on Crime in the District of Columbia in 1966. It noted that recruits who had not gone through training before their assignments to a stationhouse were not issued ticket books immediately because it was felt they lacked sufficient judgment to

[4] Ibid., p. 369.

write citations. However, they were immediately issued guns and ammunition!

Efforts are under way to remedy the situation. About two-thirds of the states have established councils on police standards to develop and administer minimum standards for local police selection and training. The Advisory Commission on Intergovernmental Relations recommends that all states set up councils composed of state, local, and public members to implement such mandatory local standards. It also urges states to pay the full cost of local training programs that meet the mandatory state standards. It calls on states and localities to encourage higher education programs for the police and provide incentive pay plans to encourage further education among police.

The Commission proposed that states should modify restrictive civil service regulations, such as veterans preference, that hamper local personnel practices. In order to centralize local authority and responsibility, every local chief executive should have the power to appoint his police chief, who would then have the authority to appoint department heads and assistants who report directly to him.

The police exercise wide discretion in the performance of their duties. That is one reason highly qualified policemen are so vital. However, even the most experienced policemen have difficulty determining the extent of legitimate authority, because state criminal codes often define only vaguely the bounds of police powers. State legislatures should clarify their criminal codes to define better the scope of police power, especially in arrest, search, and interrogation procedures. This would provide the police with a legal guide to their powers and citizens with a knowledge of the extent of their rights.

The Commission urges states to provide comprehensive government tort liability insurance for police employees. This would protect the police and at the same time enable the public to collect for damages to person and property that arise from the misuse of police discretionary powers. Furthermore, if the government is paying for insurance, it will see to it that police discretion is kept within legitimate bounds.

Meeting Modern Needs

Emphasis on local control of the police stems from seventeenth-century Britain, when the lords noted oppression by the national police on the continent and decided to keep English police local. The response carried over to the American colonies. Fear and distrust of a national police remains ingrained in most democratic societies. That is one reason why most local jurisdictions in this country have their own police, whether or not a department is big enough to provide adequate service. There are at least 30,000 police forces in the country—90 percent of them with fewer than 10 full-time personnel. Yet, a 10-man force has difficulty providing even full-time patrol and investigative services, in addition to the essential back-up services of communications, laboratory, and records.

Of prime importance in eliminating these deficiencies is the need for minimum police services in all segments of the metropolitan areas. If local government cannot provide such services, the county or the state should step in. In rural areas, a thorough restructuring of police organization through such measures as state resident policemen programs and incentive grants for consolidation of rural police forces is suggested.

Other recommendations focus on developing better back-up police services. Metropolitan counties are to provide records, communications, and crime laboratory services to constituent localities in order to prevent duplication. State police departments should play a similar role in rural areas, as well as instituting mandatory crime reporting systems in which all local police forces in the state participate.

Taking the Police Out of Politics

Politics is another remnant of the ancient past of the American police. Since the turn of this century, efforts have been made to professionalize urban police, but—especially in rural and suburban areas and at the county level—vestiges of the seventeenth century too often remain.

The American colonies adopted the offices of sheriff, constable, and coroner from England. At that time they were important political figures at the shire and local levels. Some of the powers and duties of these officials have changed, but many of the historic functions remain— at least on paper.

The Commission recommends the abolition of two offices—the constable and coroner—and the modernization or abolition of the sheriff's office. Most counties in 47 states still elect their sheriffs. The office is so sacrosanct that it is preserved in the constitution of 33 states. The sheriff retains his traditional authority as countywide coordinator of law enforcement, but in practice he rarely provides police services in urban areas and frequently operates only in unincorporated areas. In addition, the sheriff usually divides his time among other responsibilities, most often court and corrections functions, and sometimes tax collection. In some states he is compensated for these services by fines and fees. Elective sheriffs often are important local party figures, which partly accounts for the survival of the office.

Politically oriented, with little inclination and meager resources to provide modern services, with inadequate means of recruiting and no merit system, it is little wonder that most sheriff's offices lack professionalism.

As a minimum, the office of sheriff should be made statutory instead of constitutional. That would give the state or local legislative bodies the option of abolishing the office. The next step proposes permitting metropolitan counties the option of creating a modern, independent county police force, responsible to the central county executive. Where this is neither feasible nor desirable, the sheriff should be assigned countywide police authority. He should be compensated solely on a salary basis, providing for civil service tenure and adequate benefits for his department's personnel. His outside responsibilities of court and jail functions should be eliminated, to permit him to devote full time to police matters.

In addition, the office of coroner should be abolished; his medical responsibilities should be exercised by an appointed local medical examiner, and his judicial functions by the local prosecuting attorney.

Improving Police-Community Relations

Of the multitude of problems confronting modern law enforcement, probably none is more urgent than police-community relations. Without the active support of the community, no police department can function effectively. But mistrust of the police—even contempt for them—is rampant. Some citizens view the police as tyrants; others as lackeys to be paid off.

The opening of lines of communication between the police and all segments of society has a high priority for all localities, regardless of size. Police-community relations programs are not a luxury item. Yet only five percent of Federal Omnibus Crime Control and Safe Streets Act money was used for community relations programs last year.[5] Such programs, however, should not be merely public relations campaigns for the police. Every community must find the most appropriate way to get the police and the people on the same wavelength, talking the same language, seeing the same needs. Otherwise, all the manpower and all the hardware, even all the reforms, will fail to assure justice under the law in our society.

Prosecution Reform

The American way of justice—the adversary system—assumes that "truth will out." But that outcome requires a "good, clean fight" between competent, well-prepared prosecution and defense counsels.

The reality of our criminal justice system too often presents a different picture. In the cities, a politically beholden prosecutor may be more interested in the next election than the present case. In rural areas, a part-time prosecutor may be more involved in his private practice than in the government's business. Across the room, an indigent defendant may be represented by an overworked, poorly paid public defender who has had no time to learn the details of the case, or by an inexperienced or begrudging lawyer assigned at random to the case by the court.

The upgrading of both sides in the courtroom struggle is essential to improve our adversary system.

The Prosecutor

The prosecutor's role is not only deeply important but broad in scope. His decisions can affect the future freedom and even the lives of many people. He is a major link between the police and courts. The prosecutor has substantial influence on investigations; he frequently determines the disposition of cases brought to him by police, and he influences police arrest practices. He decides whether charges will be brought and what those charges will be. His actions affect the volume of cases in the courts and the number of offenders referred to the correctional system.

And yet more than half the local prosecutors in more than half the

[5] Advisory Commission on Intergovernmental Relations, *Police Reform* (Washington, D.C.: U.S. Govt. Printing Office, 1971), p. 4.

states spend less than half of their time on public business. Part-time prosecutors are open to the suspicion of conflict of interest between their public duties and private practice. And there is the underlying question of whether an official who spends much of his time in private practice is giving the taxpayers their money's worth for the little time spent on the public job.

Although in larger cities the prosecutor has a staff of assistants (more than 200 in Los Angeles and more than 150 in Chicago), the typical district attorney or county attorney has a staff of one or two assistants, frequently part-time employees. For his efforts, an assistant prosecutor is meagerly compensated. A survey of the National District Attorney's Association several years ago indicated that annual salaries of less than $4000 were not uncommon.

Training and preparation to perform this vital function is also very limited. Two important prerequisites for success in prosecuting a case are a thorough knowledge of criminal law and expertise in the courtroom. But most law schools concentrate primarily on civil law—most law students look toward a career in civil law—and most attorneys enter the prosecutor's office with little trial experience.

Once they become prosecutors, the odds are that these attorneys will not make it their lifelong profession. The state attorney general is elected in 42 states and local prosecutors are elected in 45 states. Both offices are traditionally viewed as stepping-stones in a political career. The office of local prosecutor, particularly, seems to be viewed as a temporary job; the terms average two years. A survey in a comprehensive report by the National Association of Attorneys General showed that of 430 prosecutors responding, 184 were in their first term and 122 in their second term. The Maryland State's Attorneys' Association reported that the average seniority in the Baltimore State's Attorney's office is only 13 months and the whole staff turns over every two years.[6] Perhaps the most extreme example of the low estate of the office was given in Oklahoma in 1964: no attorneys sought election as local prosecutor in 55 of the state's 77 counties that year.

Because of his relationships to police, courts, and corrections, the prosecutor would seem to be in a perfect position to serve a coordinating role. Far from that ideal, in most states the prosecution function itself is

[6] Ibid., p. 3.

badly fragmented, which makes it nearly impossible for the state legal code to be used consistently throughout the state and is a major cause for long delays in improving the system.

Most states give the attorney general and local prosecutors overlapping or concurrent responsibilities. A major function of the local prosecutor is his responsibility for criminal investigations. But in many cities, the corporation counsel is responsible for some investigations. Frequently, a case is turned over to the prosecutor after the corporation counsel has had it for several months. The prosecutor must begin the investigation again, after witnesses have disappeared or have forgotten the details.

At the opposite extreme, three states—Alaska, Delaware, and Rhode Island—have a unified statewide prosecution system. However, it does not seem that this approach is generally applicable, since responsiveness to local needs is an important factor in prosecution. What is needed is coordination and basic consistency. The state attorney general can play a major role here, setting minimum prosecutorial standards, providing technical assistance, and establishing statewide councils of prosecutors.

However, state-mandated standards are unfair if the localities must pay the whole tab; equal justice under law cannot be provided where a great disparity exists in financial resources. But the tradition in this country is for local responsibility for financing the prosecutorial function. In 18 states, the counties pay the entire cost of the prosecutor's salary; in 5 states, the state pays the entire bill; the others share.[7]

All states should require that prosecuting attorneys be full-time officials. Where prosecutorial districts are too small to support a full-time prosecutor, it is suggested that the boundaries be redrawn to provide enough work and enough financial resources for a full-time official. In 1965, Oklahoma replaced its county prosecutorial districts with a system corresponding to state judicial districts. Interest in the office as well as efficiency of the office increased.

The local prosecution function should be centralized in a single office responsible for all criminal prosecutions. That would eliminate much of the fragmentation and delay. The states should pay at least half the cost of investigations by local prosecuting attorneys' offices. That

[7] Ibid.

would help equalize the quality of performance throughout the state, raise the level of funding and thus of personnel, and provide a lever for greater state coordination.

It is most important that the states strengthen the authority of the attorney general to oversee the work of local prosecutors: through a state council of prosecutors under his leadership; through the power to consult and advise local prosecutors; to attend local trials and assist in the prosecution; and, where necessary, to intervene. At the initiation of the attorney general, state supreme courts should have the power to remove prosecuting attorneys for cause.

The Grand Jury

The grand jury is the traditional vehicle for investigation and bringing official charges. All states provide for grand juries; 21 of them require that the prosecutor initiate all felony cases by means of a grand jury. However, grand juries have also been accused of delaying justice, causing unnecessary expense, and reducing the powers of the prosecutor.

The subpoena powers of the grand jury and its ability to compel criminal testimony greatly increase the power of the prosecutor in an investigation. Because it is made up of lay citizens, the grand jury assures some public participation, especially in cases of extraordinary public concern, such as the investigation of official corruption. But to avoid unnecessary delay and expense, prosecutors should be given the discretion to use a grand jury or bring indictments through information procedures. Prosecutors should use grand juries primarily in cases of alleged official corruption or extraordinary public concern. Grand juries should be empaneled on a frequent enough basis to prevent unnecessary court delay. However, the traditional investigative powers of grand juries should not be limited.

The Defenders of the Poor

The right of the poor to defense attorneys at all stages of any federal or state criminal proceeding has been established by the Supreme Court. But implementation lags.

Although there is an abundance of lawyers in this country—the American Bar Association estimated 200,000 in private practice a few years ago—there are not enough criminal lawyers available to serve even those who can afford to pay them. One survey estimated that only 2500 to 5000 lawyers accept criminal representation more than occasionally. The National Legal Aid and Defenders Association indicated there were 900 defenders in the United States in 1966 and half of them did not work full time. But the need for defenders of the indigent is placed at 8300 to 12,500 full-time attorneys.

Two procedures predominate in the states to secure counsel for the indigent defendant: the public defender system, under which the state retains salaried attorneys who are appointed or elected; and the assigned counsel system, under which private attorneys in the city are assigned defendants on a case-by-case basis, through a coordinated system or at random. A variation of the public defender system is that of private defenders, generally retained by a nonprofit organization. The assigned counsel system—being cheaper—is used more frequently: only 11 states have public defender systems; assigned counsel systems are used in 30 states.

A principal reason for the lack of good defense for the poor is that states have left it up to local communities to provide the service. The states should set minimum standards, and administer and pay for the system to meet the need. Only seven states now do so: Alaska, Connecticut, Delaware, Massachusetts, New Jersey, North Carolina, and Rhode Island.

Considerable flexibility can be built into a statewide system. Public defenders could be used in urban communities: rural communities could have either a coordinated, assigned counsel system or "circuit rider" public defenders.

State and local criminal justice systems need more system and more justice. Better coordinated prosecution and improved procedures for defending the poor can perfect and preserve the adversary system.

Court Reform

Designed to guarantee the rights of the individual and protect those of society, the courts must strike a balance between fairness and effectiveness. But overwhelming caseloads in one jurisdiction and part-time judges in another; overlapping jurisdictions; widely varying procedures for trying similar types of offenses; wide disparities in the quality of judicial personnel—in short, little "system" in the court system—pose a severe threat to the independence, reputation, and functioning of the judiciary at state and local levels.

Most of the country's judicial business is conducted in the state and local courts. They handle about 3 million cases a year, compared with about 140,000 in the federal courts. About 90 percent of these cases are disposed of in the lower courts—primarily those in urban jurisdictions—where the dockets are heaviest and the most severe problems prevail.

The Advisory Commission on Intergovernmental Relation's recommendations seek improvements in court administration and organization, financial arrangements, judicial qualifications and selection, and federal-state court working relationships.

Administration

One basic problem is the lack of coherent organization and administration of the courts in many states. Eighteen states have substantially unified their court systems. In the remaining 32 states, responsibility and

Figure 17-1. Overwhelming caseloads interfere with the effectiveness of the courts. These court calendars for one day announce where cases are being heard. Each calendar lists 50 to 100 cases!

principles and procedures in the administration of justice

authority—to greater or lesser degrees—are scattered among state, county, and municipal courts, with some of the lower courts having general jurisdiction and others having limited jurisdiction.

Ultimately, the state is responsible for all these courts, whether their authority comes directly from constitutional provision or statute, or indirectly from the power delegated to a municipality. Over the years, all three methods have been used to establish courts to meet varying needs. But some of these needs no longer exist, while others have emerged.

Confusion is worse in many urban areas where state, county, and municipal courts with overlapping jurisdictions frequently may hear similar cases. The following situation might occur in many cities throughout the country.

A man is arrested for petty larceny. Depending on the arbitrary choice of the policeman, he may be taken before the municipal police court, the county court, or the state trial court. If he goes before the police court, he might appear before a judge who is not a lawyer, and the prosecutor will be the policeman. If he goes before the county court, there may be no provision for probation. If he is taken before the state court, he will probably appear before a judge with legal training and a full-time professional prosecutor, but he may have to wait in jail for weeks because the calendar is so backed up.

And the nonurban lower court? In 33 states, that is still the justice-of-the-peace court, a holdover from the colonial period. In all but five of these states, the justice of the peace is compensated at least in part by fees collected when he convicts, earning him the epithet, "justice for the plaintiff."

To cut through this maze and provide one system of justice for everyone in the state, it is recommended that each state establish a simplified and unified court system, consisting of a supreme court; an intermediate court of appeals, if necessary; a general trial court; and special subdivisions of the general trial court performing the duties of courts of limited jurisdiction.

The states should abolish justice-of-the-peace courts, or overhaul them by placing them under state supervision, direction, and administration; by compensating justices in salaries instead of in fees; and by requiring them to be licensed to practice law in the state or pass an appropriate qualifying examination.

All courts should be subject to administrative supervision and direction by the state supreme court or the chief justice; to uniform rules of practice and procedure promulgated by the supreme court subject to change by the legislature; and to the flexible assignment by the supreme court or chief justice of judges from court to court within and between levels. More modern management practices are a basic factor in rendering many judicial systems more effective, and these proposals are geared to filling this gap.

State court systems are large-scale operations, spending hundreds of millions of dollars every year and employing personnel in the tens of thousands. To obtain fair and swift justice and get the most output for the judicial dollar demands modern management. It necessitates new procedures and modern techniques, including computers and microfilm and new systems of statistical recording and reporting. It means up-to-date recruiting, testing, and training of administrative personnel. And above all, it means administrators who understand and can utilize these management devices.

Overall supervisory responsibility for the courts is vested in the supreme court, the chief justice, or the chief judge of an individual court, depending on the degree of unification. However, the qualities of a good judge do not necessarily coincide with the skills of a good administrator. For these reasons, all states should provide an administrative office of the state courts, headed by a professional administrator to assist in the administrative supervision and direction of the state court system.

Finances

As states move to unified and simplified court systems—and the move in that direction is steady if not speedy—they are also moving slowly to a greater sharing of court costs. States should assume full responsibility for financing state and local courts. Where the state has unified the court system and thus assumed the full responsibility for the courts, it obviously should pay for them. But even in a fragmented system, the state government has a fundamental responsibility for seeing to it that all state and local courts administer justice fairly, consistently, and effectively. This is practically impossible if the state relies heavily on local funding. Variations in local levels of financing produce wide disparities in the performance of the courts. If a state is going to mandate salary levels, standards for nonjudicial personnel, and facilities, it should be prepared to pay the bill.

Quality of Judges

The best jurist in the world would be hampered by weak court administration, but despite the most modern administration and most generous funding, the courts will fail if they have incompetent judges. Nothing can make judicial selection and retention foolproof, but over the years various states have adopted approaches to raise standards, improve selection procedures, and ease removal when that becomes necessary.

The most basic requirement for a competent judge is that he know law. Yet 14 states do not require their appellate judges to be learned in the law; and 11 of them do not make this requirement for trial judges, either. Half the states do not stipulate a minimum period of legal training and experience for judges at these levels. And the overwhelming majority of the 33 states with justices of the peace have no formal training requirement for them. All states must require all judges to be licensed to practice law in the state.

A second elementary requirement is that all judges be required to devote full time to their judicial duties. The possibility of conflict of interest in part-time judges is obvious. In addition, it does not enhance their stature or the stature of the court. Yet all of the states with justice-of-the-peace courts permit those officials to engage in outside work, and 14 states (in 1968) permitted judges of other lower courts—mainly municipal and county courts—to render only part-time service.

The problem both of unqualified judges and of part-time judges arises most frequently in sparsely settled areas where there is a shortage of adequately trained individuals and an insufficient caseload to occupy them full time. The answer to both problems would be solved in part by streamlining the court system and enlarging jurisdictions to provide a wide enough base to attract and support judges with high qualifications.

Another significant element in improving the standards of the courts is the manner of selecting judges. In 25 states, judges still must run for election; on partisan ballots in 15, and nonpartisan in 10. The idea of judicial elections grew out of the belief in the last century that this would assure greater sensitivity to public opinion and needs. This has not proved to be the case: the skills necessary for running a successful election campaign have little in common with the needs of the bench. And in partisan elections, the emphasis might be on party loyalty instead of fitness for office. However, the judge should not be insulated totally from popular control. The most widely accepted compromise was

Figure 17-2. This part-time judge is also the mayor. The possibility of a conflict of interest is strong.

reached in Missouri in 1940, when it adopted its prototype Merit Plan, now in effect in whole or in part in 17 states.

The Commission endorses the Merit Plan of selecting judges, whereby commissions consisting of representatives of the bar, the judiciary, and the public screen and nominate qualified candidates for appointment by the chief executive. Judges so appointed should be required to submit themselves to voter approval or disapproval at an election at the end of each term.

Once even the most eminent judge is selected, there is no guarantee that he will remain competent. He will age, may grow tired, and his attitudes may become obsolete. However, compulsory retirement for older judges is controversial. Many will point out that mandatory retirement would have compelled Justices Brandeis, Holmes, and Black to step down when they were still vigorous. Yet the argument for mandatory retirement is persuasive.

Twenty-two states have compulsory retirement; one fixes the age at 71, two at 72, four at 75, and the remainder at 70. Five of these states extend the age limit to the end of the judge's term and often permit extended services in special cases. The Commission recommends that states require mandatory retirement of state and local judges at age 70.

But what about the younger judge who physically, mentally, or ethically turns out to be less than competent? Twenty-two states have no provisions for disciplining judges of general trial courts other than the cumbersome and largely ineffective methods of impeachment, legislative address, or recall. Often, removal is not necessary.

The 31 states that provide a special means of disciplining judges take a variety of different approaches. Thirteen states authorize courts of the judiciary, either the existing high court or specially constituted tribunals, to hear charges and either dismiss them or order removal of the judge. In 18 states, there are judicial qualifications commissions composed of judges, lawyers, and lay persons who receive and investigate complaints, hold formal hearings, and make recommendations for dismissal of the charges, disciplinary action, or retirement.

The Commission prefers that the judicial qualifications commission be established and recommends that such bodies be modeled after the California Commission on Judicial Qualifications. Under it, commissions are set up composed of judges appointed by the supreme court, lawyers appointed by the state bar association, and laymen named by the governor. The commission evaluates complaints: rejects those it considers unfounded; cautions the accused on those not very serious; or orders a formal hearing on serious complaints. Based on the hearing, the commission may dismiss the charges or recommend to the supreme court that it impose involuntary retirement or undertake removal or some lesser disciplinary action. Removal for misconduct is used only as a last resort, and thorough investigation is assured.

State–Federal Working Relationships

There is a growing need for closer working relationships between state and federal court systems. One symptom of the problem is the dramatic increase in postconviction petitions of state prisoners to federal courts (from an annual rate of 89 to 12,000 in 30 years).

Some state courts, federal district courts, and individual judges have developed informal relationships to deal with joint problems. But the Commission feels that much more should be done on a much broader scale, especially as it relates to joint conviction petitions, judicial rules, and criminal codes.

State and federal district judges, judicial officers, and bar associations should initiate and support the development of state–federal judicial councils, composed of chief judges of state and appropriate federal district courts, to cooperatively explore problems of joint concern.

The courts are a vital component of our criminal justice system, but they are only one segment of an interdependent whole. The need for court reform to unify administration and modernize management of the court system, increase state financial responsibility for the courts, improve the quality and standards of the judges, and gain a closer working relationship between state and federal courts must be accomplished. The system must be treated as a whole by recognizing the interdependence of its police, prosecution, courts, and corrections components. Custom and tradition tend to accentuate and perpetuate the separateness and autonomy of these functions. But the time has come for balanced consideration of the relations of each element to all the others, and their collective impact on the public.

Corrections Reform

Corrections is the stepchild of the criminal justice system. Fragmented internally and isolated both physically and administratively from the rest of the system—the police, courts, and prosecution—corrections tends to be forgotten by government and the public alike. Yet prisons, jails, detention facilities, probation and parole agencies, and the other components of corrections are an integral part of the criminal justice system. Their isolation contributes to a particularly vicious spiral of crime, incarceration, worse crime, producing rising crime rates of astronomical proportions.

Eighty-five percent of the crimes in this country are committed by repeaters. Most of the offenders held in the corrections system now are young—between 15 and 30 years old—and 98 percent of all offenders eventually will return to the community. The cycle of crime is one reason jails have been termed "factories of crime" and prisons are called "colleges for advanced criminal education." To break the cycle will require a major reordering of priorities to support a new emphasis on rehabilitation instead of custody, to upgrade personnel and institutions, and consolidate and streamline administration.

Personnel

Almost everybody now in prison will be released, but most of them will return. One of the most critical factors in this process is the personnel involvement in rehabilitation. The Task Force on Corrections of the President's Crime Commission summed it up: "In corrections, the main ingredient for changing people is other people."

About 133,000 people were employed in state and local corrections in 1969; more than two-thirds in institutions, less than one-third in parole and probation. They handled about 1.1 million offenders—about one-quarter in institutions and three-quarters on probation, parole, or in community-based facilities. In custodial institutions there were about seven offenders for each employee; parole and probation officers averaged about 100 cases, which permitted them about 15 minutes per case per month.

States and localities must improve recruitment, compensation, training, and promotion practices to attract sufficient numbers of high-quality personnel to corrections. Yet, these factors alone still would not solve the severe shortage of trained manpower available. To meet the immediate need, the Advisory Commission on Intergovernmental Relations suggests the use of paraprofessionals, including ex-offenders (except those who may be former policemen). It also recommends that states and localities provide training and educational opportunities to help potential workers meet appropriate standards.

The inadequacy of personnel is especially acute in jails and other short-term institutions that generally confine people for more than 48 hours but less than one year. Frequently managed by a sheriff or other law enforcement officials, these facilities have neither the personnel nor the capacity for any rehabilitation; they are merely holding operations. Yet offenders sit in them for months—sometimes years—with no counseling, no job training, nothing to do except fuel their resentment and plan bigger and better crimes.

It is suggested that short-term penal institutions be administered by appropriately trained correctional personnel, and that states establish minimum standards for all correctional personnel. One problem with achieving these minimum standards is that many localities cannot afford to hire correctional personnel or to develop rehabilitation programs. The localities do not have the money, nor do their jails have enough inmates to warrant the expenditure. States should encourage the development of regional institutions that would have both the financial base and enough inmates to make progressive rehabilitation programs economical.

Inmates

Besides those charged with caring for him, fellow prisoners can make the biggest impact on an offender—particularly a juvenile first offender. Yet in jails across the country juveniles and adults are mixed; untried detainees and convicted felons are placed in the same cell; misdemeanants can sit at the feet of hardened criminals and "learn the finer points."

It is generally assumed that persons under 16 years are not held in jail, but only nine states prohibit the placing of children in adult jails; only three of those states assert that jails are not used for children. It is generally assumed that city and county jails are reserved for detention until trial or incarceration of misdemeanants—offenders sentenced to less than one year. A survey of 215 county and city jails showed that half of them held convicted felons as well. And in one state, more than 2000 prisoners were serving sentences exceeding two years in city and county jails.

Furthermore, a 1965 study showed that 93 percent of the juvenile court jurisdictions in the nation lack detention facilities other than city jails or police lockups. It found that more than 100,000 children were being admitted to city and county jails and police lockups. In the case of the juvenile offender or convicted misdemeanant, this commingling with convicted adult felons hinders later attempts at rehabilitation.

In the case of the untried person (who is presumed to be innocent), the situation in the jails and lockups around the country is the baldest form of injustice. Yet, a 1970 survey showed that more than half the inmates in local jails had not been convicted of crime.

States and local governments should work together to provide adequate adult and juvenile detention services and facilities to end the mixing of children and adults and of untried persons with convicted offenders, and to expedite the trial of untried detainees.

Figure 17-3. The Kennedy Youth Center in Morgantown, West Virginia, has been architecturally designed to the special needs of the youthful offender. He is assigned to a cottage and to education, work, and counseling programs based on his specific needs.

Rehabilitation

If the corrections systems is to train a person to live in society, it must provide him with a means of earning a living in the community and help him adjust to community life. But most penal institutions are far removed from the community. Vocational education and training often are irrelevant, prison industries inadequate. Psychological counseling generally is meager, if available at all.

Three recommendations are to refocus corrections on rehabilitation by strengthening community-based treatment, expanding education and vocational training, and increasing programs and facilities for work release. Community-based programs have a variety of advantages. Studies in California, New York, Wisconsin, and elsewhere indicate that participants are less likely to become repeater offenders than those who receive only institutional care.[8] In addition, community-based treatment is cheaper. Probation costs only one-sixth as much as institutional care, and parole only one-fourteenth as much.

[8] Ibid.

Academic and vocational training are inadequate. Studies generally indicate a high relationship between employment success and post-release success. A 1964 study showed that less than one-fifth of the offenders who were successful on parole were making use of training they received in prison. But management of prison industries is poor and many states have severe restrictions on the sale of prison-made goods—largely because of union opposition. A first step would be to upgrade management and repeal the restricting laws. In addition, hospitals, universities, and state agencies could be encouraged to purchase products manufactured in penitentiaries; and the business community might be spurred into cooperating in rehabilitation programs.

Work-release programs generally permit the prisoner to work during the day and live in a small community-based facility—frequently a halfway house—at night. Or they enable the prisoner to take a furlough to look for work. In general, work-release is used for prisoners the last few months before parole to ease the transition back to the community. More and earlier use of this type of program is suggested.

Administration

Very little is "systematic" about the state and local corrections system. Three states—Alaska, Rhode Island, and Vermont—have consolidated all corrections functions into one agency at the state level; Delaware has consolidated eight of nine functions into one agency; Alaska, Connecticut, and Rhode Island pay the entire cost of corrections; and Vermont pays nearly the total expenditure.

But a comprehensive approach generally stops there. In most situations, administrative responsibility is divided among the state, its counties and localities; split at each level between agencies that handle adults and those that deal with juveniles; and sliced up within jurisdictions among various functions. Many functions are not even handled by the corrections system, but are performed by the courts.

Every state, most of the 3050 counties, and all but the smallest cities in the nation have at least one prison or jail. The average state bears two-thirds of the financial burden for corrections; its localities, one-third.

The most widespread split in administration is between adult and juvenile care. This is based on the historical separation in the concept of justice for juveniles and for adults. Useful at one point, bifurcation has led to duplication and overlap in responsibility, difficulties in comprehensive planning, and vagueness in the status of older juveniles and young adults. This separation has outlived its usefulness: one overall agency should have the responsibility for planning and developing programs for all ages of offenders. A separate division for dealing with juvenile problems might be warranted, but only in the largest agencies.

There is a need to keep the operation and partial financing of some institutions at the local level. These primarily are the functions that relate most closely to local court jurisdictions. It is therefore suggested that localities retain the operation and some of the fiscal responsibility for detention facilities, jails, and other short-term adult institutions, and misdemeanant and juvenile probation. States are urged to assume the full financial administrative and operating responsibility for all long-term correctional institutions, adult probation, parole, and juvenile aftercare. In addition, the states should establish and monitor minimum standards of service, furnish planning and technical assistance, and provide a reasonable share of the cost of all corrections programs.

Reordering Priorities

In order to lower crime rates we are going to have to raise the priority of corrections significantly. This means greater public attention, more funds, and a shift of policy focus to bring about fundamental reforms in the system.

Federal, state, and local governments together spent less than one fifth of their criminal justice budgets on corrections in fiscal 1969. They spent more than three-fifths on police. States and localities did a bit better that year, putting about one-quarter of their $6.5 billion criminal expenditures into corrections in fiscal 1965; four-fifths went into the walls and bars of institutions and the custodial personnel to maintain them; only one-fifth into community-based treatment and rehabilitation.

There are indications that the states are earmarking more money for corrections. But just as essential is the shift in approach from punishment to rehabilitation. That will take longer, for it requires a change in attitude on the part of both the government and the public. A 1971 Gallup poll conducted for *Newsweek* found that even though a majority of those polled considered conditions of prisons deplorable and expressed concern, 83 percent opposed putting more money into improving the corrections system. And although 44 percent called for subsidizing bigger and better police forces, only 21 percent "would be willing to finance the construction of additional prisons to handle the additional felons that better police would inexorably produce."

The National Advisory Commission on Criminal Justice Standards and Goals

To combat rising crime rates and to build more justice into the system, states and localities must make far-reaching improvements in courts and corrections, police and prosecution—and must carefully tie together these component elements of criminal justice into a coherent system. Out of these grave and urgent needs and to achieve these stated goals, a new federal commission was formed—The National Advisory Commission on Criminal Justice Standards and Goals.

Much of the material developed through the studies funded by the federal government in the past 10 years has been of great value for further development by the criminal justice participants. But other suggestions and recommendations did not receive the attention that they warranted. As a result of the varieties of the studies and multiplicity of books released, many important recommendations were overlooked. There appeared to be a need to gather a group of experts in the field of criminal justice to discuss the wealth of material available and, in addition, to expand on ideas or develop new ones so that they could make some firm recommendations to improve the process.

The National Advisory Commission on Criminal Justice Standards and Goals' first release of information was made early in 1973. Since that time more work has been done by the Commission, and recommendations are being released as the work continues.

The ultimate goal of the Commission's work is to reduce crime through the combined efforts of all in the criminal justice process, including federal, state, and local governments. The Commission did not undertake new research; instead, it developed standards that took a fresh look at the process, unhampered by traditional practices that no longer apply. It further took the view that wherever policy, program, procedures, and law are in need of improvement or should be eliminated, the legislatures should make the necessary changes, and the agencies in the process should implement the changes.

As with any study where recommendations are made, the recommendations are subject to attack. And those who oppose several recommendations might try to discredit the entire work because of some opposition. The work of this Commission may be subject to this pitfall. There are many ideas put forth that should receive serious attention in order to upgrade the criminal justice process. Some of these recommendations will be enumerated as they relate to police, courts, corrections, and crime prevention.

Recommendations for the Police

Seven objectives were identified by those studying the police. They did not give priorities for their objectives nor those specific items that can be developed as programs, to tackle the objectives. The Commission called for immediate action to: fully develop the offender-apprehension potential of the criminal justice system; stimulate the police and the citizens to work together as a team; motivate those in the criminal justice system to work in unison; clearly determine and act on local crime problems; make the most of human resources; use technological advances to their fullest capacities; and fully develop the police response to special community needs. The Commission made numerous recommendations for implementation of each objective.

Offender-Apprehension Potential. To develop the offender-apprehension potential of the system fully, programs of crime prevention must be implemented by police agencies. Volunteer neighborhood security can be developed where citizens mark personal property with identification numbers or call in suspicious acts taking place in their community, to name just two examples. Crime prevention through physical planning can be undertaken for citizens or businesses by using design ideas calculated to reduce the opportunity to commit crime. Security standards can be enhanced by enactment of necessary laws and ordinances.

Police and Citizen Teamwork. The objective of creating a team attitude could be met by programs that make the citizens aware of the written police policy that deals with authority, law, misconduct of the police, and every aspect where the police and the public must work together.

Criminal Justice System Teamwork. The police and all others in the system must communicate with each other. Diversion programs, for example, involve all in the process; they must cooperate to execute their roles so that adults and juveniles do not become enmeshed in the system. Areas that require a particular team effort are alcohol and drug abuse centers.

Other Recommendations. Some of the approximately 50 program recommendations are: deployment of officers; use of communication equipment; command and control; developing specialists; resources development; combination of services; developing intelligence information; use of civilian personnel; personnel development; and administration of promotions. Some agencies may argue that these recommendations are not new for them, but one must realize that the report addresses the entire police service.

Recommendations for the Courts

The subcommittee considered the major components of the court procedure to include the judiciary, the prosecution, the defense, and the court administration. It viewed each component in terms of changes that could be implemented to reduce crime on a national scale. The subcommittee developed programs for: screening; diversion; negotiated plea; the litigated case; sentencing; review of the trial court proceedings; the judiciary; the lower courts; court administration; the prosecutor; and the defense. Within these major items are 50 programs for the improvement of the total court's efforts.

Screening. Screening is the action taken before formal entry into the process; diversion, the action taken after some of the formal action of the process has started. The subcommittee indicated that an accused should be screened out of the criminal justice process when the benefits gained from prosecution or diversion would be outweighed by the costs of such action. Screening standards should be developed so that prosecution and police have guidelines in as specific terms as possible so that they can identify the cases when a person would not be taken into custody.

Diversion. Diversion programs can be developed that would state the categories to be selected. No program should impair the impact that criminal punishment may have. The person must offer some hope of rehabilitation as protection against the commission of further crimes.

Negotiated Pleas. A strong position was taken against plea bargaining, yet there is a need to develop some form of negotiated plea with uniform policies and practices. These standards or guidelines must take into consideration the impact of the plea on society and on the offender and his rehabilitation.

Sentencing. Sentencing of offenders is an important aspect of the process, crucial both to society and the defendant. The reaction of the defendant to a sentence can materially affect the outcome of a rehabilitation program. The feeling was expressed that juries should be removed from the sentencing procedure and that courts should be required to impose the sentences provided by statute.

Review of Proceedings. The committee sees the need for improvement for: unified proceedings in review; dispositional time in reviewing court; further review at all levels in prior adjudication; and prior factual determination.

Judicial Selection. Judicial selection should be based on merit. Although this may seem obvious, the committee stated that selection procedures must be aggressive in seeking out the best qualified individuals to sit on the bench. In addition, after the selections are made, judges should be subject to discipline or removal from office if reasons are found that might interfere with the performance of their duties.

Other Recommendations. The subcommittee has made recommendations for: unification of state court systems; state court administrators; local and regional trial court administrators; case flow management; professional standards for prosecuting attorneys; public representation of convicted offenders; workload and salaries for public defenders. All of these are worth of study, development, and implementation for the benefit of the courts and society.

Recommendations for Corrections

Sixty-three recommendations covered all aspects of corrections. The emphasis was based on developing standards for: rights of the offender; diversion; pretrial release and detention; sentencing; offender classification; corrections and the community; juvenile intake and detention; local adult institutions; probation; major institutions; parole; manpower; research and development; information and statistics; and statutory framework. Although some of the standards may seem minor, when the corrections procedure is viewed nationally, it becomes apparent that many simple or minor items have not been dealt with in a great many institutions or by correctional personnel.

One standard suggests that each correctional unit develop and implement policies and procedures that fulfill the right of persons under supervision to have free access to the court. Those under supervision have the right of access to the following: challenge the legality of conviction or confinement; seek redress for illegal conditions or treatment while under control; seek remedy in connection with civil problems; seek all remedies against any one individual or group that violates the person's constitutional or statutory rights. The access is also to be extended for the person to receive all legal services.

A number of standards are recommended that relate to the person in custody—for health, welfare, and the protection of his rights. They can be described in a few words and are self-explanatory: healthful surroundings, searches, rules of conduct, discipline, grievance procedures, exercise of religious beliefs, and access to the public.

This subcommittee also had suggestions for standards on the subject of diversion, pretrial release, pretrial detention, and alternatives to arrest. Again, this dramatizes the need for active communication between courts and corrections, each of whom has attitudes based on different perspectives. All recognize the twofold responsibility of the rehabilitation of the offender and the protection of society, with a common interest in sentencing.

Classification teams or committees should be established to provide the offender with meaningful programs: often the program an offender is placed in does more harm than good. There is a need to develop the criteria to be used by classification committees composed of both professionals and the community.

Since the community becomes involved in many areas, a plan for community-based alternatives to confinement could prove helpful. This plan could specify the services to be provided directly by the correctional unit and those provided through community resources. This requires that the correctional process establish a good working relationship with major social institutions and agencies in the community.

Other Areas of Recommendation. The committee also took into consideration the juvenile problems and suggested standards for the police, juvenile intake, and diversion programs. They also suggested the need for legislation in this general area to enable the court to establish organized intake services. Juvenile detention, another field of attention, became involved because of the need to renovate facilities to accommodate intake.

Other standards thought to be helpful were areas such as: total correctional systems planning; state operation and control of local institutions; service of probation; planning new institutions; parole grant hearings; community services for parolees; recruitment of personnel; evaluation of corrections; and corrections legislation.

A subcommittee of the Commission dealt with community crime prevention. The suggestions covered the need to organize, implement, and manage everyone's efforts to reduce crime, delinquency, and recidivism. Even though this same theme ran through the recommendations on police, courts, and corrections, the Commission felt that this area had sufficient impact to merit a special public committee to emphasize its importance.

Prospects for the Future

This book in its entirety sets forth the tone of what needs to be done in the future. Each of the chapters makes suggestions for those in the criminal justice process. One recurrent theme throughout is the need *within each subsection* to turn the process into a real system. This is probably the greatest single challenge.

The process must develop and make use, as fully as possible, of modern scientific and technological advances. Of extreme importance is the need to develop data gathering and manipulation. A criminal justice information system that can provide comprehensive, up-to-date information on which policy, programs, procedures, and management decisions can be made for the entire process is an absolute necessity.

Everyone must realize their responsibility. The process can gear up, reduce delay, and perform hundreds of other activities, but society must reassert its emphasis on the individual's responsibility for his conduct and the conduct of others.

Besides protecting the rights of the accused, we must remember the rights of the rest of society. Each individual has the right to expect to be able to live and work in safety without threat against his person and property.

All of the suggestions stated in this book can be achieved; better law enforcement, efficient corrections, certain justice can all be accomplished. Crime, delinquency, and recidivism can be greatly reduced without the system developing into a "police state."

Effective criminal justice guarantees individual freedom; it will also provide domestic tranquility.

Student Checklist

1. Can you list five actions that would result in increased professionalization of the police?
2. Are you able to identify the three back-up police services that should be provided to local communities by metropolitan counties?
3. Can you identify the means by which the prosecutor can serve a coordinating role in the justice system?
4. Can you list the advantages of a unified court system?
5. Do you know how to describe the Merit Plan for selecting judges?
6. Can you identify the functions of a judicial qualifications commission?
7. Are you able to list the three means by which corrections can emphasize rehabilitation?
8. What are some of the areas of recommendation of the National Advisory Commission on Criminal Justice Standards and Goals?

Topics for Discussion

1. Discuss the trend toward regionalization of law enforcement agencies.
2. Discuss the need for coordination between law enforcement and the courts.
3. Discuss the need for better coordination between law enforcement and corrections.
4. Discuss the concept of a ministry of justice.

ANNOTATED BIBLIOGRAPHY

The National Advisory Commission on Criminal Justice Standards and Goals. Washington, D.C.: U.S. Govt. Printing Office, 1973.

The President's Commission on Law Enforcement and Administration of Justice. *The Challenge of Crime in a Free Society.* Washington, D.C.: U.S. Govt. Printing Office, 1967. This general report embodies all of the major findings of the Commission on Law Enforcement and Administration of Justice. Those findings were drawn from the Commission's examination of every facet of crime and law enforcement in America.

State-Local Relations in the Criminal Justice System. Washington, D.C.: U.S. Govt. Printing Office, 1971. The Advisory Commission on Intergovernmental Relations spent 18 months of intensive study of the criminal justice system. This report includes 44 specific recommendations for state-local action to improve all segments of the system. Also included are action packets on police reform, court reform, correctional reform, and prosecution reform.

Glossary (Administration of Justice Terminology)

Perhaps the fastest way to gain a general knowledge of a particular vocation is to acquire an understanding of the terminology used. The criminal justice system uses many unique words and phrases in carrying out its duties. Many of the most frequently used terms will be defined in this terminology guide. It must be emphasized that the definitions presented here are not intended to be complete interpretations of the words. For a complete explanation, consult a law dictionary or a textbook on criminal justice terminology.

Notations

Abet
To encourage or advise another to commit a
crime. To aid by approval.

Accessory
One who aids or conceals a criminal so that he
may avoid arrest or punishment.

Accusation
A charge of a violation of the law, which may
be in the form of a complaint, a presentment,
an indictment, or an information.

Acquit
To find a person not guilty of the crime charged.

Admission
A statement by a defendant tending to prove
his guilt. Not a complete confession.

Affidavit
A written statement made under oath.

Alias
A false or assumed name.

Alibi
The defense that the accused was in some place other than that where the crime was committed.

Alienist
A person who specializes in the study of mental diseases.

Allegation
The statement or plea of a person setting forth what the party expects to prove.

Amicus Curiae
A friend of the court who volunteers to assist the court.

Appeal
The transfer of a case to a higher court, in which it is asked that the decision of the lower court be altered or reversed.

Appellant
One who makes an appeal or who takes an appeal from one court to another.

Appellate Court
A court that has jurisdiction of review and appeal.

Appellee
The party in a proceeding against whom an appeal is taken.

Arraignment
A court proceeding in which the defendant is
informed of the charge against him, advised of
his constitutional rights, and at which he may
enter a plea or deposit bail.

Arrest
Detaining a person in a manner authorized by
law, so that he may be brought before a court
to answer charges of having committed a crime.
Both peace officers and private persons may
make arrest.

Attest
To bear witness to a fact, or to affirm to be true
or genuine or to certify to verity.

Bail
Security, in the form of cash or bond, deposited
with a court as a guarantee that the defendant,
if released, will return to court at the time
designated to stand trial.

Barratry
The unlawful practice of initiating lawsuits or
police complaints without just cause.

Bond
A written promise or obligation to perform a
duty, to pay money, and the like.

Bondsman
A surety of one person for another.

Booking
The formal registration of the date, time, charge,
name of arrestee, and the name of the arrestor.

Brief
A summary of the law pertaining to a case,
prepared by the attorneys for submission to
the judge. Useful in police work for case
law reference.

Capital Crime
A crime punishable by death.

Caption and Asportation
Generally, to prosecute for theft, it is necessary
that both taking (*caption*) and carrying away
(*asportation*) be proven.

Certiorari *(writ of certiorari)*
An order issued by a higher court
to a lower court directing that a
case be transferred to the higher court
for review or trial.

Change of Venue
A change of the place of trial in a criminal or
civil proceeding.

Circumstantial Evidence
Evidence tending to prove a fact through a
logical association of other facts, but without an
actual witness to the act to be proven.

Citation
An official summons issued by a court or peace officer directing a person to appear before the court for some official action. Frequently referred to as a ticket.

Civil Action
A law suit to recover damages or correct some wrong between two parties. Does not usually involve a crime and is apart from a criminal action. A person may be convicted in a criminal court and also sued in a civil court for the same act. *Example:* A drunk driver may be sentenced to jail in a criminal proceeding and then sued in civil action by the owner of a car damaged by the drunk driver.

Commitment
An official court order directing that a person be taken to a jail, prison, hospital, or other location (usually a place of confinement).

Common Law
The basic, unwritten concepts of English and American law. In many states there are no "common law crimes." For an act to be a crime, there must be a specific, written statute so declaring it.

Complaint
The formal accusation of crime presented to the court that acts as the formal commencement of a criminal prosecution.

Compounding a Crime

The unlawful act of accepting money or other reward for agreeing to refrain from prosecuting a crime—concealing it from the authorities or withholding evidence.

Confession

A voluntary declaration admitting the commission of a crime.

Confidential Communication

Communications between a person and his attorney or clergyman, or between husband and wife, which may be legally concealed in court testimony.

Contempt of Court

Disobedience to the court by acting in opposition to the authority, justice, or dignity thereof. Punishable as a crime.

Conviction

The finding of a person guilty of a criminal charge.

Coroner

A county official whose principle duty is to determine the manner of death of any person.

Corpus Delicti

The complete set of elements necessary to constitute a particular crime.

Crime

An act committed or omitted in violation of a
law forbidding or commanding it, for which
a punishment is provided.

Criminal Action

A court proceeding instituted and prosecuted
by the state for the punishment of crime.
Not to be confused with civil action.

Criminal Procedure

The method prescribed by law for the
apprehension, prosecution, and determination
of punishment of persons who have
committed crimes.

Defendant

The person sued or charged in a court action,
whether criminal or civil.

Demurrer

A plea made to the court that the actions
alleged in the complaint, even if true, do not
constitute a crime.

Deposition

The written testimony of a person, who, for
some reason, cannot be present at the trial.

District Attorney

A county official whose duties require him to
act as attorney for the state in prosecution of
criminal cases.

Double Jeopardy
The act of placing a person on trial a second time for a crime for which he has already been tried once (forbidden by criminal procedure).

Duces Tecum
A subpoena whereby a person is summoned to appear in court as a witness and to bring with him some piece of evidence (usually a written document).

Dying Declaration
A statement made by a dying person regarding the cause of his injuries. Acceptable evidence in a homicide prosecution. Based on the theory that a person about to die will be inclined to be truthful in any statements he makes.

Et Al.
And others. For example: *"People* v. *Jones,* et al."* indicates that Jones and others are the defendants in a criminal case. This form is used to prevent repeating the names of all persons involved every time the case is referred to.

Evidence
Testimony, physical objects, documents, or any other means used to prove the truth of a fact at issue in a court proceeding.

Ex Post Facto
After the facts. Usually refers to a law that attempts to punish acts that were committed before it was passed.

Extortion
Similar to blackmail.

Extradition
The surrender by one state or nation to another,
on its demand, of a person charged with a
crime by the requesting state.

Fine
The financial punishment levied against a law-
breaker that is paid to the government funds.

Former Jeopardy
Same as double jeopardy.

Fugitive
One who has fled from punishment or
prosecution.

Grand Jury
A group of men and women whose duty it is to
make inquiries and return recommendations
regarding the operation of local government.
They also receive and hear complaints in
criminal cases and, if they find them sustained
by evidence, present an indictment against the
person charged. It is called a grand jury because
it is composed of a greater number of jurors
than a regular trial jury.

Habeas Corpus (writ of)
A court order directing that a person who is in
custody be brought before a court in order that

an examination may be conducted to determine
the legality of the confinement.

Habitual Criminal
Many states have statutes providing that a
person convicted a certain number of times may
be declared an habitual criminal and therefore
unsuited for attempts for rehabilitation. A person
so declared may then be sentenced to life
imprisonment for the protection of society.

Hearsay Evidence
Evidence that deals with what another person
has been heard to say. This evidence is usually
excluded in a trial.

Indeterminate Sentence
A court or board-imposed sentence with neither
minimum nor maximum limits.

Indictment
An accusation in writing, presented by the
grand jury, charging a person with a crime.

Information
An accusation in writing, presented by a
prosecuting official, such as a district attorney
or city attorney, charging a person with a crime.

Informant
One who supplies information leading to the
apprehension of a criminal.

Injunction

A court order whereby a person is ordered to do, or restrained from doing, a particular thing. Not enforced by the police without an additional court order to that effect.

Inquest

An inquiry with a jury conducted by the coroner to establish the cause of death.

Intent

In general, there must be a concurrence between a person's acts and his intentions in order to constitute a crime. A person cannot be convicted of a crime if he committed the act involuntarily, without intending injury. If a person acts negligently, however, without regard for the rights of other people, this is sufficient in itself to establish criminal intent. Thus, the drag racer who kills an innocent party may be convicted of manslaughter even though he did not intend the death or injury of anyone.

Interrogation

The art of questioning or interviewing, particularly as applied to obtaining information from someone who is reluctant to cooperate. May apply to the questioning of witnesses, victims, suspects, or others. Requires the use of psychology, salesmanship, good judgment, and a knowledge of human nature. The use of physical force to obtain information has no legitimate place in modern law enforcement.

Jail

A place of confinement maintained by a local authority, usually for persons convicted of misdemeanors. The terms prison or penitentiary apply to such institutions operated by the state or federal government, usually for more serious offenses.

Judiciary

That branch of the government concerned with the administration of civil and criminal law.

Jurisprudence

The science of laws.

Jury

A group of men and women whose duty it is to determine the guilt or innocence of persons charged with a crime.

Limitations, Statute of

The statutory time limit within which a criminal prosecution must be begun. For felonies, this is usually three years from the date the crime was committed. For misdemeanors it is one year. There are some crimes that have a longer time limit and a few, such as murder, that have no time limit.

Magistrate

A judicial officer having authority to conduct trials and hearings in criminal and civil matters and to issue writs, orders, warrants of arrest, and other legal documents.

Mala in Se and Mala Prohibita
A basic grouping of crimes according to the
nature of the act. *Mala in se* means "bad in
itself" and refers to those crimes, such as murder,
robbery, and rape, that are deemed to be wrong
in almost all civilized societies. *Mala prohibita*
means "bad by prohibition" and refers to those
offenses, such as building and safety regulations
and certain traffic violations, established by
statute for the public convenience, that are not
immoral or bad in themselves.

Mandamus (writ of)
An order issued by a court, directed to a government agency or to a lower court, commanding
the performance of a particular act.

Mens Rea
The mind of the thing. One of the essential
elements of a crime.

Misfeasance
A neglect of duty—the failure to do a
lawful act.

Modus Operandi
Literally, method of operation. Refers to the
habit of criminals to continue to pursue a
particular method of committing their crimes.
Through study of a criminal's habits (or *modus
operandi*), it is possible to link several crimes
committed by the same person and even to
determine where he can be expected to commit
his next crime.

No Bill
An indictment is returned No Bill when the
grand jury determines that there is not sufficient
evidence to bring a person to trial.

Nolle Prosequi
A motion by the prosecuting attorney in which
he declares that he will not prosecute a case.
Used when extenuating circumstances in a case
indicate that, although a crime has been
committed, it is in the best interests of justice
to forego prosecution.

Notary Public
A public officer authorized to administer oaths,
witness signatures, and acknowledge the
genuineness of documents.

Oath
Any form of attestation by which a person
signifies that he is bound to perform a certain
act truthfully and honestly. A person making a
false statement while under oath to tell the
truth may be prosecuted for perjury.

Ordinance
Term used to designate any law enacted by
a local governmental legislative body.

Panel
A group of men and women summoned for jury
duty. A panel of approximately 25 prospective
jurors is examined by attorneys for both sides

prior to the start of a case. Through this examination, 12 are selected to hear and decide the case.

Pardon

An act of grace, proceeding from the power entrusted with the execution of the laws, that exempts the individual on whom it is bestowed from the punishment the law inflicts for a crime he has committed.

Parole

The conditional release of a prisoner from jail prior to the completion of his sentence, usually on the condition that he remain under the supervision of a parole officer.

Peace Officer

General term used to designate a member of any of the several agencies engaged in law enforcement.

Penal Code

A collection of statutes relating to crimes, punishment, and criminal procedures. This is the portion of the law most frequently used by police officers.

Perjury

The crime of knowingly giving false testimony in a judicial proceeding while under oath to tell the truth. Subornation of perjury is the crime of procuring or influencing someone else to commit perjury.

Plaintiff

In a civil action, the party initiating the suit.
One who signs a complaint or causes a complaint
to be signed. Other party to the suit is the
defendant.

Plea

The answer that the defendant makes to the
charges brought against him.

Pleadings

Written statements reciting the facts that show
the plaintiff's cause for bringing the action and
the defendant's grounds for defense to the
charges. These are prepared by the attorneys
for each party and presented to the judge.

Posse Comitatus

The authority of the sheriff to assemble all
able-bodied male inhabitants of the county to
assist in capturing a criminal, keeping the peace,
or otherwise defending the county. Refusal to
obey the summons is a criminal offense.

Precedent

A parallel case in the past that may be used as
an example to follow in deciding a present case.

Preliminary Hearing

An examination before a judge of a person
accused of a crime in order to determine if there
is sufficient evidence to warrant holding the
person for trial.

Prima Facie
"On its face" or "at first view." Refers to evidence that, at first appearance, seems to establish a particular fact, but that may be later contradicted by other evidence.

Principal
A person concerned in the commission of a crime, whether he directly commits the offense or aids in its commission. All principals to a crime are equally guilty; therefore, the driver who waits in the getaway car during a robbery is as guilty of murder as the accomplice inside the building who fires the fatal shot.

Private Person's Arrest
The authority granted to a private party to make an arrest under certain conditions. Sometimes referred to as a "citizen's arrest," although it is not limited only to citizens.

Privileged Communication
See **Confidential Communication.**

Probate Court
A court that establishes the legality of wills and administers the distribution of the estate of a deceased.

Probation
Allowing a person convicted of a criminal offense to go at large under the supervision of a probation officer instead of confining him to prison or jail. The probationer must comply

with certain conditions set forth by the court
and must be on good behavior. Failure to
comply with these conditions will cause the
probationer to be placed in jail to serve his
sentence.

Proof
The establishment of a fact by evidence.

Prosecutor or Prosecuting Attorney
A public officer whose primary duty is to
conduct criminal prosecutions as attorney in
behalf of the state or people. The district
attorney and city attorney are examples.

Recognizance
Official recognition of some fact by a court.
In criminal procedure applies to a person
accused of an offense being released on his own
recognizance without being required to post
bail on his promise to appear for trial. Employed
where the accused is well known to be reputable
or is charged with a minor offense.

Remand
To send a case back to a lower court.

Res Gestae
Things done. Facts and circumstances
surrounding a particular act. Refers particularly
to acts or exclamations overheard by a third
party that would be inadmissible in court under
normal rules of evidence but, because they
occurred at the moment of the particular act in

question, are admissible under the rules of
res gestae evidence.

Return
A short account in writing made by an officer
in respect to the manner in which he has
executed a writ or process.

Reversal
The setting aside or annulment of the decision
of a lower court by a higher court. *See* **Appeal.**

Search Warrant
An order to a peace officer, issued by a court,
directing that a certain location be searched and
that certain specifically described property, if
found, be seized and delivered to the judge.
A search warrant can be executed only by a
peace officer and is valid for ten days from issue.

Stare Decisis
To abide by or adhere to decided cases.

Statute Law
A written law enacted and established by the
legislative department of a government.

Stay of Execution
An order of a court postponing the carrying out
of the penalty or other judgment of the court.

Stipulation
An agreement between opposing attorneys

relating to certain portions of a case. Usually refers to minor points in a case that are accepted without demanding proof in order to shorten the time of trial.

Subpoena

An order issued by a court commanding the attendance of witnesses in a case.
See **Duces Tecum.**

Summons

In a civil case, an order directed to the defendant giving notification that an action has been filed against him and giving instructions as to how and when he may answer the charges. Failure to answer the summons will result in the case being awarded to the plaintiff by default.

Suspended Sentence and Judgment

Suspended sentence is where no sentence is pronounced by the court and the offender is released after being found guilty on condition that he abide by certain rules laid down by the court, such as making restitution to the victim. Suspended judgment is where the offender is released as above after sentence has been pronounced. In either case, the offender may be returned to court at any time to be sentenced or, in the case of suspended judgment, have the sentence carried out.

Testimony

Oral evidence given by a witness under oath.

Tort
A civil wrong. An invasion of the civil rights
of an individual.

Transcript
A printed copy of a court record, including
the verbatim testimony of witnesses.

Trial
That step in the course of a judicial proceeding
that determines the facts. A judicial examination
in a court of justice. May be held before a judge
and jury or before judge alone.

Versus
Against. Abbreviated "vs." or "v."

Valid
Having full legal force and authority.

Waive
To surrender or renounce some privilege or right.

Warrant
A written order from a court or other competent
authority, directed to a peace officer or other
official, ordering the performance of a particular
act and affording the civil protection for the
person executing the order. Examples are a
warrant of arrest and a search warrant.

Witness
A person who has factual knowledge of a
matter. One who testifies under oath.

Case Index

Apodaca v. Oregon, 406 U.S. 404, 92 S.Ct. 1628, 32 L.Ed. 2d 184 (1972), 73
Argersinger v. Hamlin, 92 S.Ct. 2006 (1972), 43

Barron v. Baltimore, 7 Ret. 243 (1833), 158
Betts v. Brady, 316 U.S. 455, 86 L.Ed. 1595, 62 S.Ct. 1252 (1942), 42, 158, 159
Blue v. United States, 384 U.S. 251 (1965), 284
Brown v. Mississippi, 297 U.S. 278, 80 L.Ed. 682 (1936), 40

Carroll v. United States, 267 U.S. 132 (1925), 108
Catalano v. United States, 444 F. 2nd 1095 (1971), certiorari denied 404 U.S. 1001 (1971), 161
Chambers v. Moroney, 399 U.S. 42, 26 L.Ed. (2d) 419, 20 S.Ct. 1975 (1970), 38
Chimel v. California, 395 U.S. 752, 23 L.Ed. (2d) 685, 89 S.Ct. 2034 (1969), 38
Coblentz v. State, 264 Md. 558 (1933), 289
Commonwealth v. McCloskey, 443 Pa. 117, 277 A. 2d 764 (1971), certiorari denied 404 U. S. 1000 (1971), 161
Commonwealth v. Woodward, 157 Mass. 516 (1893), 289
Culombe v. Connecticut, 367 U.S. 568, 6 L.Ed. (2d) 1037, 81 S.Ct. 1860 (1961), 40

Douglas v. California, 372 U.S. 353 (1963), 160, 175

Escobedo v. Illinois, 378 U.S. 478, 12 L.Ed. (2d.) 977 84 S.Ct. 1758 (1964), 43, 175
Ex parte Wilson, 114 U.S. 417, 5 S.Ct. 935, 29 L.Ed. 89 (1885), 67

Furman v. Georgia, 92 S.Ct. 2726, 225 Ga. 253, 171 S.E. 2d 501 (1972), 44

Garcia v. United States, 364 F. 2d, 306, 10th Cir (1966); and In re Disbarment Proceedings, 321 Pa. 81, 160
Garske v. United States, 1 F. 2d 620 (8th Cir. 1924), 59
Gideon v. Wainwright, 372 U.S. 335, 83 S.Ct. 792, 9 L.Ed. 2d. 799 (1963), 42, 160, 182
Goldberg v. Kelly, 397 U.S. 254 (1970), 161
Griffin v. Illinois, 351 U.S. 12, 76 S.Ct. 585, 100 L.Ed. 891 (1956), 52
Griswold v. Connecticut, 381 U.S. 479, 85 S.Ct. 1678, 14 L.Ed. 2d. 510 (1965), 38

Hale v. Henkel, 201 U.S. 43 (1906), 285
Hamilton v. Alabama, 368 U.S. 52 (1961), 160
Hessenauer v. People, 256 NE (2d) 791:Ill. (1970), 160
Hurtaldo v. California, 110 U.S. 516 (1884), 190, 287

Johnson v. Avery, 334
Johnson v. Louisiana, 406 U.S. 356, 92 S.Ct. 1620, 32 L.Ed. 2d. 152 (1972), 73
Johnson v. Zerbot, 304 U.S. 458, 58 S.Ct. 1019, 82 L.Ed. 1461 (1938), 42
Johnson v. Zerbst, 304 U.S. 458 (1937), 158

Katz v. U.S., 389 U.S. 347, 88 S.Ct. 507, 16 L.Ed. 2d. 576 (1967), 38
Kent v. United States, 383, U.S. 541 (1966), 159

Subject Index

coordination of prosecutorial functions by, 150, 151

Attorney General of the United States, 133, 134, 135, 136
functions performed by, 134, 135

Bail, 65, 66, 88, 163, 165, 182, 190, 253-268, 333, 409
advantages of being free on, 253, 257
bonds, 259, 260, 409
bondsmen, 66, 168, 259, 260, 265, 409
role of, 259, 260
counsel, influence of on, 163
court-administered, 265
decision, 256, 257
judge, setting of bail, 256
prosecutor and counsel, influence of on, 256, 257
excessive, 65, 255, 256, 258
Eighth Amendment's excessive bail clause, 255, 256, 258
protection against, 255, 256
money, 253
nominal, 257
personal recognizance, 257
and the poor, 253, 257, 258
primary purpose of, 253, 254
recidivism to, 268
right to, 255, 256, 266, 306
and the unpopular, 258, 259

Bail reform, 66, 138, 258, 262-268
citations, 265, 266
court-administered bail, 265
toward nonfinancial alternatives to money bail, 258, 263-268
preventive detention, 266, 267, 268
release on personal recognizance, 264
summonses, 265, 266

Bail Reform Act of 1966, two principles established in, 262, 263, 268

Bail system, 65, 66
alternatives to, 254
bondsman in, role of, 259, 260, 409
cost of, 260, 261
effect on justice, 261, 262
bailed versus unbailed defendants, 261, 262
English, historical antecedents, 254
financial discrimination in, 253, 258
monetary, 254
abuses of, 257, 259, 260

Bill, 285

Bill of Particulars, 286

Bill of Rights, 15, 32-33, 34, 35, 106,

158, 160, 274
due process clause, 35-36
Blackmun, Harry A., 29, 30, 44
Booking, 60, 64, 266, 410
Brennan, William J., Jr., 30, 44, 283
British solicitors, duties of, 132, 133
and barristers, distinction between duties, 132
British system of criminal justice, and American system compared, 132, 133
Attorney General in, 132, 133
Director of Public Prosecutions, 131, 132, 133
disadvantages of, 133
history of, 131, 132
Solicitors Department, 133
Bureau of Narcotics and Dangerous Drugs, 348
Burger, Warren E., Justice, 29, 30, 44, 223
Byrne, William Matthew, Jr., 94

California Commission on Judicial Qualifications, 196, 391
California Juvenile Court Act of 1961, 323, 329
Capital crimes, 45, 65, 67, 158, 159, 274, 275, 410
grand jury indictment, 287
right to bail in, 256
right to counsel in, 158, 159
Capital punishment, 6, 42, 44, 54
declared unconstitutional by Supreme Court, 44, 256
see also Death penalty
Casper, Jonathan, 167, 169, 176, 177, 181
Certification, 193, 194
Certiorari, 41, 161, 193, 194, 410
Change of venue, 70, 164, 301, 302, 410
Citation, 56, 303, 378, 411
as alternative to money bail, 265, 266
versus arrests, 56
Civil commitment, 343, 344-346, 347, 350
alcoholic offenders, 345, 346, 350
criticisms of, 344
legality of, 344, 345, 346, 347, 350
need for, 343, 344
social value of, 344, 345, 346
U. S. Supreme Court's attitude toward, 345
Civil liberties, 35-45
history of, 37
Civil rights, example of social change through law, 45-47
Civil Rights Act, 136
Civil rights laws, history of, 45-47
Title II of the 1964 Civil Rights Act, 47

Common law, 131, 287, 411
  police power, early English history, 106
  principle, 365
Community-based corrections, 219, 220, 221
  concepts of, 220, 221
  nonprofessional volunteers, use of, 219, 220
  paraprofessionals, use of, 220
  private industries, involvement of, 220, 221
Community treatment, 206-218
  concept of, 207, 208
  importance of family ties, 215-218
  programs, 204, 206, 207
    modern community-based alternatives, 207
  values and dangers of, 204
Complaints, 59-60, 62, 84, 86, 87, 231, 275,
        276, 299, 301, 303, 411
Compulsory treatment, 343, 344, 346-350, 351
  alcoholic offenders, 350, 351
  contemporary beliefs, 346
  disadvantages of, 346, 347
  for narcotic addicts, 347-350, 351
Confessions, 42, 164, 233, 289, 290, 412
  coerced, 40, 64, 114
Conjugal visitation, 215-218
  Mississippi State Prison at Parchman, 217
Constitution, the, 15, 32-34, 51, 106, 109, 158,
        193, 255, 297, 304, 305, 308
  see also Eighth; Fifteenth; Fifth; First; Four-
        teenth; Fourth; Sixth; and Thirteenth
        Amendments
Constitutional amendment, process of, 31, 33
Conviction, 11, 15, 42, 53, 55, 56, 68, 105,
        161, 165, 232, 233, 234, 237, 238, 299,
        412
  for capital crime, 45
  defendant's right to appeal, 75, 76
  for felonies, 74
  illegally obtained evidence and, 284
  at jury trial, 73
  for misdemeanors, 43
  post-, remedies for, 76, 77
  resulting from grand jury action, 281
  reversal of defendant's, 76
  without trial, 243
Corpus delicti, 68, 412
Corrections, 11, 13, 20-21, 23, 53, 98, 137,
        203-223
Corrections reform, 392-398
  administration, juvenile and adult, split in,
        396, 397
    overlapping in responsibility, 396, 397
  inmates, 394
  National Advisory Commission for Criminal

  Justice Standards and Goals, recom-
        mendations of, 401, 402, 403
  rehabilitation, 395, 396
    strengthening community-based treatment,
        395
    use of work-release programs, 396
  reordering priorities, from punishment to re-
        habilitation, 397, 398
Corrections system, conflict in, 204-208; *see
        also* Corrections reform
Counsel, 19, 72, 166
  court-appointed, 169, 170, 171-173
  effective, importance of, 162, 164
  need for, 162-164
  right to, *see* Right to counsel
  types of, 157
  waiver of, 162
  ways to obtain, 169-183
Court administrators, duties performed by, 198
Court reform, 385-392
  administration, 386-388
    abolishing justice-of-the-peace courts, 387
    unified court system, importance of, 386,
        387, 388
  closer state–federal working relationships,
        need for, 391, 392
  to unify administration and modernize
        management, 392
  finances, 388
  judges, eliminating part-time, 389
    judicial qualifications commission be estab-
        lished, 391
    legal training, 389
    mandatory retirement, 390, 391
    manner of selecting, 389, 390
    need for, 385, 386
    and reorganization, new direction in, 188
Courts, 11, 13, 19-20, 23, 55, 83, 423
  appellate, 19, 20, 75, 76, 88, 94, 187, 298,
        313, 314, 319, 333, 408
  federal, 188, 193
    of appeal, 194
  functions performed by, appellate jurisdiction,
        187
    general jurisdiction, 187, 189
    limited jurisdiction, 187
  general characteristics of, 187, 188
  inferior, *see* Inferior courts
  lower, 19, 20, 134, 138
  state, *see* State Courts
  supreme, *see* Supreme Court
  trial, 19, 20, 134
Crimes, capital, 45, 65, 67, 158, 159, 274, 275, 413

control of, 399
  Hopkins's war theory of, 116
  social-order role of police and, 118, 125
cycle of, 392, 393
definition of, 4, 55, 56, 84
federal, 68
felony, 106, 107, 108, 109
index, 7, 8, 9
infamous, 67, 287
"major", 7, 10
misdemeanor, 106, 107, 108, 109
police investigation, 56-60
"official," 7
prevention of, 13, 399
property, 7, 8, 9
and society, 7-10
violent, 7, 8, 9
Criminal bar, 166-169, 173
Criminal justice, crisis in, 6, 10, 23, 54
  legal foundations of, 31-34
  nonsystem approach to administration of, 10,
    11, 12
  professionalism in, 22, 23
  see also American system of criminal justice
Criminal Justice Act (1967), 173, 182
Criminal justice personnel, professionalism in,
    22, 23
  recommendations made by President's Com-
    mission on, 13
  selection and training of, 22, 23
Criminal law, basic characteristics of, 4, 5
  definition of, 4, 5
  police role expectations and, 113, 114, 115
  procedural, 113, 114, 115, 117
    policing style and, 117
  substantive, 113, 114, 115, 118
    policing style and, 117
Criminal lawyers, 166-168
Criminal Procedure, Federal Rules of, 64
Criminal procedures, 16, 19, 37, 61, 62, 76, 87,
    160, 164, 166, 168, 175, 277, 302, 306,
    413
  accusatory system of, 297
  adversary system, 297, 381
  codes of, 34, 35
Cruel and unusual punishment, 43-45, 54, 325;
    see also Capital punishment; Death
    penalty

Davis, Kenneth C., 81, 82, 83, 92, 94, 100, 229,
    230, 232
Death penalty, 6, 44, 45, 54, 256, 275, 287
  Supreme Court decision on, 44, 256

Defendants, 15, 42, 70, 108, 157, 183, 413
  indigent, 19, 42, 159-162, 166, 169-183
    and bail system, 66
  legal services, available for, 180, 181
    eligibility for, 166
Defense attorneys, 13
  criminal lawyers, 167, 168
  prestige of, among general public, 168
  pretrial motions available to, 69-70
  role of, in juvenile cases, 328, 329, 330, 331
Defense counsel, 72, 163, 172, 174, 381
Delinquency, 55, 191, 207
  adjudication of, 342
  definition of, 355, 356
  juvenile, 209, 322
Delinquency jurisdiction, 323, 326
Delinquency statutes, 324
Demurrer, 70, 72, 306, 413
De nova, 189
Department of Justice, U. S., 134, 135, 136,
    148
Deposition, 413
Detention, 253-268
  alternatives to, 205-218
  authority, 110, 111
  effect of on conviction and sentencing, 262
  juveniles in, grounds for holding, 333
  and the poor, 257
  pretrial, 255, 258, 266
  preventive, 259, 266-268
    alternatives to, 268
    criticisms of, 268
    juvenile court law, 333
    precluded by presumption of innocence,
      267
  role of bondsmen in, 259, 260
  unlawful, 77
Discretion in justice system, 81-101
  abuse of, 82
  application to administration of justice, 341,
    342
    to other areas of criminal violations, 341,
      342, 354
  civilian, 83-85
    impact of, 84, 85
    importance of, 83, 84
  control of, 95-98
    disadvantages of, 82, 83, 85, 86, 87
    need for, 95
  correctional, four factors that effect, 88, 89
    parole decision, 88, 89
  definition of, 81, 82
  discretion points, major, 89-95

abolition of recommended, 247, 248, 400, 401

American Bar Association standards for, 246-248

controversy over system of, 243

juvenile court, 330

many forms of, 244

nontrial adjudication and, 243, 244

potential abuse of, 245

procedures of, improvement of, 247, 248

prosecutor's discretionary powers and, 87, 93, 98, 137, 230, 231

types of, 308

value of, 245

see also Plea

Police, 11, 13, 14, 23, 55, 83, 88, 97, 98, 175

civilian discretion and, 83, 84, 85

discretion, 6, 81, 85-86, 115, 341, 354, 369, 370

importance of, 85, 86, 378

policing style and, 115, 117

discretionary powers of, 85, 86, 97

misuse of, 378

functions performed by, 14-15

investigation, 56-60, 61

prosecution decision and, 61

ultimate goal of, 56

isolation of from communities, 116, 117, 380, 381

methods used by, apprehension, 122-123

deterrence, 122

educational, 121, 122

mediation, 122

referral/diversion, 122

saturation, 122

negative methods used by, 120, 121, 122, 123

enforcer role, 123

positive methods used by, 120, 121, 122, 123

counselor role, 123

power and authority, 105-111, 378

arrest, in area of, 105, 106, 107, 108, 109, 110

history of, 106

search and seizure, in area of, 105, 106, 107

professionalism in, integrated policing and, 126

managerial efficiency, 118

integrated policing and, 126

professionalization of, *see* Police reform

prosecution decision and, 61

role of, concept of, 112, 113, 375, 376

conflict in, 112-115

adjustments to, 117, 118, 120

counselor role, 123, 124, 125

enforcer role, 123, 124

expectations for, community, 113, 114, 115, 118, 120

conflict in, 113, 114, 115

legal, 113, 114, 118, 120

police organization, 114, 115, 118, 120

style of, *see* Policing style

use of violence, 116

Police reform, 375-381

improving police-community relations, 380, 381

to meet modern needs, 378, 379

deficiencies in police services, 379

develop better back-up police services, 379

National Advisory Commission for Criminal Justice Standards and Goals, recommendations of, 399, 400

need for, 375

professionalizing police, 376, 377, 378

provide with legal guide to powers, 378

provide liability insurance, 378

selection standards, problem of, 376, 377, 378

training, importance of, 377, 378

urban police, 379, 380

removing police from politics, 379, 380

abolition of constable and coroner, 379

modernization of sheriff's office, 379, 380

Policing styles, 115-126

Hopkins's war theory of crime control, 116

integrative concept of, 125-126

balance between enforcer and counselor roles, 125, 126

professionalism in, 126

efficiency versus effectiveness, 126

model, 120, 121, 123

passive concept of, 124-125, 126

passive-punitive cycle, 125

peace-officer role versus law-enforcer role, 117, 118, 120

personalized, 125, 126

development of favoritism, 125

lack of objectivity, 125

police professionalism and, 118

punitive, 125, 126

social-order role, disregard of legal expectations, 118, 120

versus legal-actor role, 117, 118, 120, 126

Wilson's three policing styles, 118, 119, 120, 124, 126

Sheriff, 106, 197, 211, 254, 273, 274, 379, 380, 393
  office of, lack of professionalism, 380
Sixth Amendment to the Constitution, 18, 37, 41, 42, 43, 73, 179, 290, 305, 309, 310
  right of assistance of counsel, 158, 160, 290
Skolnick, Jerome H., 117, 118, 126, 176, 330
Society, changing, and the law, 3, 4, 5, 11, 12
  crime and, 7-10
  and justice, 3
  rights of, versus right of individual, 29
Standard Juvenile Court Act, 321, 323, 325, 326, 333, 334, 335
Stand mute, 306
State council of prosecutors, 151, 152
State courts of general jurisdiction, types of cases handled in, 189, 190, 191
State law, 34-35, 41
Stop-and-frisk, 39, 90, 110, 111
Subpoena power, 289, 290, 426
Summons, 205, 231, 328, 426
  as alternative to money bail, 265, 266
Supreme court, state, 188, 189, 190, 313
Supreme Court, U. S., 6, 15, 19, 134, 193, 194, 277, 313, 333, 334
  appeal procedure, 193
  capital punishment ruling, 6, 54, 256, 325
  attitude toward civil commitment, 345, 348
  composition of, 193
  constitutional provisions governing arrests, 107
  Fourth Amendment, interpretation of, 38, 39
  grand jurors selection, 281
  jurisdiction of, 193
  jury unanimity ruling, 73
  right to appeal to, 194
  on right to assistance to counsel, 42, 159, 160, 161, 320
    interpretation of Sixth Amendment, 158, 159, 290
  ruling on evidence received by grand jury, 285
  self-incrimination clause, 39-42
  stop-and-frisk procedure, 39
  system of prosecution, ruling on, 277, 278
  upheld validity of waiver of jury trial, 287
Suspended sentences, 21, 426

Task Force Reports on Corrections, 76, 207, 208, 209, 223, 393
Testimony, 72, 73, 163, 164, 283, 285, 289, 290, 291, 310, 329, 426
Thirteenth Amendments to the Constitution, 45
Trial, 64, 65, 66, 67, 68, 69, 70-73, 135, 164, 165, 310, 311, 312, 427
  discovery at, 311
  fair, 70, 164, 267
  jury, 68, 70, 71, 165, 306, 310, 311
  without a jury, 310, 311
  proceedings of, 70, 71, 72, 73
  see also Judicial process, court proceedings
True Bill, 285, 286, 299, 300, 309

Uniform Arrest Act, 39
Uniform Crime Reports (UCR), 7
Uniform Fresh Pursuit Act, 109

Venue, see Change of venue
Verdict, 72, 73, 311
Violent crimes, 7, 8, 9
Voir dire, 71

Waive, 43, 66, 287, 288, 302, 303, 306, 427
  jury trial, 70, 287
  right to indictment by grand jury, 287
Warrants, 38, 56, 299, 301, 303, 425, 427
  arraignment on, 64
  arrest, 57, 58, 59, 62, 68, 106, 107, 109, 197, 231
  bench, 58
  content of, 109
  search, 112, 135
Warren Court, 29, 97
White, Byron R., 30, 44, 73
Wickersham Crime Commission, 148, 149, 306
Witnesses, 42, 62, 65, 66, 68, 69, 163, 164, 175, 233, 328, 427
  cross-examination of, 72, 163
  in grand jury proceedings, 283
  importance of in charging decision, 233, 234
  prosecution, 66
  right to call, 306
Work release, 204, 209, 210, 211, 212, 215, 396
Writ of certiorari, 193, 194

Youthful offenders, 326, 327, 330
Youth Service Bureau, 332